Theory After Theory

An Intellectual History of Literary Theory
from 1950 to the Early Twenty-First Century

Nicholas Birns

broadview press

LIBRARY AND ARCHIVES CANADA CATALOGUING IN PUBLICATION

Birns, Nicholas
        Theory after theory : an intellectual history of literary theory
from 1950 to the early twenty-first century / Nicholas Birns.

Includes bibliographical references and index.
ISBN 978-1-55111-933-5

        1. Criticism—History—20th century. 2. Criticism—History—21st century.
3. Literature—History and criticism—Theory, etc. I. Title.

PN94.B57 2010   801'.9509045   C2010-901520-7

BROADVIEW PRESS is an independent, international publishing house, incorporated in 1985. Broadview believes in shared ownership, both with its employees and with the general public; since the year 2000 Broadview shares have traded publicly on the Toronto Venture Exchange under the symbol BDP.

We welcome comments and suggestions regarding any aspect of our publications—please feel free to contact us at the addresses below or at broadview@broadviewpress.com.

NORTH AMERICA
Post Office Box 1243
Peterborough, Ontario
Canada K9J 7H5

2215 Kenmore Ave.
Buffalo, New York, USA 14207
TEL: (705) 743-8990
FAX: (705) 743-8353

customerservice@broadviewpress.com

UK, EUROPE, CENTRAL ASIA, MIDDLE EAST, AFRICA, INDIA, AND SOUTHEAST ASIA
Eurospan Group, 3 Henrietta St., London WC2E 8LU, United Kingdom
TEL: 44 (0) 1767 604972 FAX: 44 (0) 1767 601640
eurospan@turpin-distribution.com

AUSTRALIA AND NEW ZEALAND
NewSouth Books
c/o TL Distribution, 15-23 Helles Ave.,
Moorebank, NSW, Australia 2170
TEL: (02) 8778 9999 FAX: (02) 8778 9944
orders@tldistribution.com.au

www.broadviewpress.com

Edited by Karen Taylor
Cover design and interior by Em Dash Design

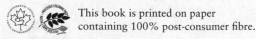 This book is printed on paper
containing 100% post-consumer fibre.

Printed in Canada

Julia Gaunce initiated this project, and I am grateful to her for having confidence in the original idea. Marjorie Mather's responsiveness, professionalism, and percipience with regard to the book have been invaluable. Tara Lowes and Karen Taylor, the production editor and copy editor respectively, were exemplary and most helpful. I am also highly indebted to the two outside readers for Broadview, whose sympathetic concern for the text meant that their suggestions improved it immeasurably.

This book was inspired and sustained by my students at Eugene Lang College and at The New School for General Studies, whose enthusiasm and curiosity about theory made the most compelling case for the project and whose attentiveness as an early audience helped me in unfolding its basic elements. Special thanks to my mother, who was unfailingly encouraging and supportive throughout the project.

For their tremendously valued assistance with respect to the book's composition, I thank especially my colleagues Juan E. De Castro and Inessa Medzhibovskaya, and, for vitally important aid, I thank Paul Allatson, Babette Babich, Carolyn Berman, Sundeep Bisla, Harold Bloom, the late Maddalena Raimondi Capasso, Jules Chametzky, Mia Chen, Donna Coates, George Dickerson, Millicent Dillon, Robert Dixon, Laura Frost, Annette Gilson, Rainer J. Hanshe, Anne Humpherys, Noah Isenberg, Gerhard Joseph, Barrie Karp, Norman Kelvin, Jonathan Kooperstein, Ferentz LaFargue, Irving Malin, Peter Mathews, Anne C. McCarthy, Adrienne Munich, Nikolina Nedeljkov, the late Henry C. Pearson, Michael Pettinger, Jeanne Reed, Rose Réjouis, Elaine Savory, John Scheckter, Henry Shapiro, Carole Silver, Ann Snitow, Rachael Sotos, Herbert Sussman, Val Vinokur, and Judith Walzer. I would like to thank Yunus Tuncel of the Nietzsche Circle and Armand Musey of the Foucault Society for inviting me to give seminars in New York where some of the material was initially explored. And thanks to Samuel Menashe for appreciating the way his superb poetry has been employed in this project.

Part of this book was written when I was Visiting Fellow at the University of Wollongong's Literature, Identity, and Culture project, and I am deeply grateful to Louise d'Arcens, Wenche Ommundsen, Anne Collett, Tony Simões da Silva, and Jenn Phillips for helping to make my time on New South Wales's south coast such a pleasant one. Thanks also to the University of Sydney Arts Faculty, especially Robert Dixon and Helen Hewson, for facilitating my work when I was in Sydney.

I appreciate the helpful comments of the Postcolonial Studies Research Group, University of Calgary, especially those of Donna Coates, Clara Joseph, Victor Ramraj, and Shaobo Xie, comments that were made in response to a draft of a portion of Chapter 5 given as a lecture in Calgary in February 2009.

This book is dedicated to my father, who saw well beyond "the resolved symbolic."

This book is intended both as a handbook for students to learn about theory and an intellectual history of the recent past in literary criticism for those interested in seeing how it fits in with larger patterns of style and culture. It does not emphasize original theorizing itself, but tallies the ideas of various theorists to see why and how people thought they were important in the late twentieth and early twenty-first centuries. The book is inclined towards defending literary theory both as an analytical tool and as of profound significance in the history of literature as a discipline, but it does not necessarily advocate theory as a dogmatic method. The arrangement of the book is chronological; starting with a preface examining the 1950s and then proceeding to seven chapters in which each separate theorist or topic covered begins with the early work of the 1960s and goes forward until the 2000s.

Beyond the "Resolved Symbolic"

The State of Theory

In the late twentieth century, activity in university literature departments was dominated by literary theory.[1] By the first decade of the twenty-first century, this trend had ebbed. The academic world was seen in the early 2000s to be living in an age "after theory" and living with the consequences of an age that was past. This survey of theory is written with the awareness that the era of theory's dominance is over.[2] This book provides a retrospective account of the major figures and schools that defined theory's importance. It also, though, seeks to assess what permanent contributions theory has made. What will come after theory? Does theorizing still have a place in the study of literature? Why have people been—and why in some cases are they still—so emotionally involved, one way or another, in debates about theory?

Students getting their degrees in the twenty-first century may find it hard to understand what "theory" meant to the generations before them. In the late twentieth century, many who would not have been drawn into literary studies entered the field because of the philosophical breadth and intellectual excitement that theory offered. Others, who took literature classes simply because they loved books or cherished the act of reading great books, no doubt left the field because they saw theory as too arid and cerebral.[3] But whatever way one regarded it, theory redefined what a university literary education was. Yet when this sort of redefinition occurs, there are two principal factors. One is the intellectual current responsible for the redefinition. The other is the state of the discipline that is affected by this current. This preface will examine what literary criticism was like before theory. It will try to explain why theory had the massive, seismic impact upon the field that it had.

Theory possessed this impact—then lost it. Today it is impossible to speak of theory as the coming or even the dominant trend in literary studies. However, in the 1970s and 1980s, both theory's advocates and opponents spoke about it this way. Theory became stale as it was monotonously applied in an unenergetic way to texts that emerged from theoretical readings both unchanged and unamplified. Theory criticized earlier attempts at consensus, but brooked few rejoinders to its own conclusions. In addition, as much as theory inspired certain academics, theory alienated others and mystified the sliver of the larger public interested in academia but not strictly a part of it. Theory's insistence that language was often slippery, suspicious, and politically motivated seemed an affront to people who valued words as a way to embody shared ideas and affirm common values.

Still, theory has played such a large role in the recent past that it cannot be dismissed as an aberration. Those who try to dismiss theory in this way are operating as much out of emotion as are those few remaining who will hear no criticism of theory. Much of the emotion concerning the debate about literary theory comes from duelling visions of the 1950s as an academic era.[4] Many of the people who think that literary theory should not matter any more look back with what Svetlana Boym has called a "restorative nostalgia" to the 1950s as a time when a plainer and more comprehensible kind of criticism was practised.[5] Poems and novels were valued for their own sake, as masterpieces of style and form. Others saw the 1950s as, at best, a necessary prelude to future, more expansive developments and, at worst, an era when conservative forces prevailed, when a narrow canon of texts and approaches dominated, and when literary criticism was not yet able to operate as a fully equipped mode of academic study. This book takes the latter position. While respecting both the individual and collective achievements of the 1950s critics, this book will argue that theory, or something like it, had to have arisen in the wake of the limitations of the dominant critical modes of the postwar years. Both theory's appeal and its fading can be seen, in the view of this account, as explicable by the historical course begun by the limitations of 1950s literary dogmas.

The 1950s: The New Critics

There were different critical schools in the 1950s, of course. The three that were the most important in Britain and North America were the New Critics, the New York Intellectuals, and the Leavisites. The New Critics were a set of academics originating in the southern United States, who first began writing in the late 1920s and early 1930s. Most of them ended up, by the 1950s, teaching largely at Ivy League or equivalent institutions in the north. The goal of the New Critics was to not let literature be subordinated to anything external to it, whether that be the author's life, a poem's historical background, what the reader felt about a novel, or the philological quibbles that had often dominated the academic journals of the 1910s and 1920s. They stressed the autonomy of literature and wanted their students to appreciate the importance that literature possessed, on its own, as such. The New Critics stressed reading the text "itself" and tended to privilege short lyric poems that could be read as full of tension and paradox. This stress on the self-sufficient, tightly knit unit discouraged any sort of overt feeling. The New Critics cherished poets such as John Donne and Donne's twentieth-century advocate, T.S. Eliot, for the complexity and tough-minded reasoning that went on in their work.[6] Any excessive display of emotion in poetry was sharply rebuked. Ambiguity, tension, and wordplay were prized. Yet, unlike the deconstructive theorists that arrived in the wake of the work of Jacques Derrida, the New Critics saw this ambiguity, tension, and wordplay as *determinate*. There was a limit to them. They did not endlessly proliferate. As the Australian novelist Elliot Perlman puts it, deconstruction involved taking "the ambiguity of words in poetry, and ... extending its ambit to cover all language."[7] For New Criticism, on the other hand, ambiguity was very much boxed into a certain paradigm, fixed, as Eliot would say, in a formulated phrase.

The New Criticism focused on a small sample of texts and writers. In poetry, these were Renaissance lyrics (by Thomas Wyatt, Shakespeare, the Earl of Surrey, John Donne, Andrew Marvell, and George Herbert, as well as some anonymous ballads); grudgingly, Alexander Pope; less grudgingly, John Keats, Samuel Taylor Coleridge, and a very small slice of William Wordsworth; in the Victorian era, only Gerard Manley Hopkins; and then a significant but still rather sparse scattering of modernists, such as T.S. Eliot and William Butler Yeats. Once New Criticism had arrived at this core set of writers, there were few if any additions. This added to the perception of stasis and incuriosity associated with the school.[8] The impasse in the New Criticism, which led to its eventual undoing, can be seen in a work of literary analysis that explicitly sought to upend its core premises. Paul de Man's famous reading of Yeats's "Among School Children" appeared in his 1973 essay "Semiology and Rhetoric."[9] De Man was born in Belgium (as will be discussed, he was later found to have written pro-Nazi journalism during World War II) and had an extensive background in European philosophy. He was later trained in the New Criticism in the United States and knew intimately what he was critiquing.

In Yeats's poem, "the speaker, a sixty-year-old smiling public man," visits a classroom of five-year-old children. ("The speaker," incidentally, was itself a New Criticism formulation. One was never supposed to think that "the poet" was saying anything, only a "speaker" who was not at all necessarily close to the poet's biographical self.) Yeats himself was more or less a sixty-year-old smiling public man when he wrote the poem. The thoughts and attitudes of the speaker of the poem are fundamentally Yeats's and are known to be so from what we know of Yeats. Yet to make this observation in a New Critical classroom was tantamount to attending a fancy dinner party and spilling beer on your hostess's rug. It would have seemed not only silly but uncouth. The speaker—as we shall, in deference to the milieu, continue to call him—ponders the contrasts between youth and age, potential and fulfilment, the ideal and the material. The poem, according to the view of leading New Critic Cleanth Brooks, which he expressed in his major critical work *The Well-Wrought Urn* (1947), concludes in a privileged moment of fused synthesis:

> O chestnut tree, great-rooted blossomer,
> Are you the leaf, the blossom, or the bole?
> O body swayed to music, O brightening glance,
> How can one know the dancer from the dance?

De Man cites the customary New Critical reading of this line, that the last question was "rhetorical." In other words, there was no intended answer. The dancer could not be known from the dance. The fusion was that complete. And this complete fusion was a metaphor for a state of fulfilled knowledge that could not be analysed into component parts. Any answer that tries to disentangle the fusion would be pointless and reductive. This was the only truth to be drawn from the poem, and anything else would spoil this moment of exquisite rapture. De Man, surprisingly, asked whether the question was not literal. How can we tell the dancer from the dance? How can this distinction be performed? This move seems very puzzling in light of what was mentioned earlier: that deconstruction, with which de Man came to be prominently associated, took the New Criticism much further. The literal reading seems a retrenchment in the other direction. Should not de Man be rendering the poem even *more* metaphorical— not less so? The move that de Man makes reveals the real Achilles heel of the New Criticism. The New Criticism was often criticized for talking only about what was in the text. One of the New Criticism's leading expositors, William K. Wimsatt, co-wrote two essays in which he denounced "The Intentional Fallacy" (1946)—the presumption that an author had anything to do with the work's intrinsic meaning—and "The Affective Fallacy" (1949)—the idea that the reader had anything to do with the work's intrinsic meaning. Many found this textual focus constricting. Inevitably, we know things about an author, and about ourselves, when we read a book. We cannot be wilfully incurious. We may, as the Romantic poet and critic Coleridge put it, willingly suspend disbelief in order to be captured by the magic of imagination. But it is another thing entirely to suspend our cognition.

Eventually, critics recognized the problem stemming from this exclusion of context. Both historical context and what came to be called "reader-response" criticism became prominent parts of the eventual reaction to the New Criticism. Yet many other strands of this reaction, such as deconstruction, heightened the focus on the text, albeit radically pluralizing it. New Criticism was also denounced for being "formalistic." It was scolded for concentrating on literary form. Yet the Russian formalists, who were even earlier than the New Critics, were prized as forerunners of theory. Their foregrounding of formal elements did not make them untheoretical. Nor were the Russian formalists, in the New

Critical sense, suggesting a concentration on poetry and an abstention from bio-graphical or historical study. Viktor Shklovsky wrote an entire book on prose—which, if anything, was *more* the object of Russian formalist investigation than was poetry—and Boris Eikhenbaum wrote two biographical books on Tolstoy, although, admittedly, this was after he stopped being a card-carrying formal-ist. An interest in form did not mean subscribing to New Critical prohibitions. Moreover, in *Marxism and Form* (1971), even a critic as political as Frederic Jameson spent a lot of time on questions of form, if hardly in a New Critical vein. Form, as a term, was used in politically oriented theory coming from a very different orientation about literature's relation to the outside world, an orientation opposite to that of the New Criticism, such as the Marxist work of the Hungarian Georg Lukács or the sociological work of the Brazilian Antonio Candido. Form, for these thinkers, had a genealogy in the nineteenth-century philosophy of Hegel and encompassed the cumulative totality of a society's self-imagining. There is nothing apolitical about form. And, as the work of the Italian theorist Giorgio Agamben (to be discussed in Chapter 7) shows, close analyses of lyric poems can certainly coexist with political awareness.

If the flaw of the New Criticism was not its textual orientation or its for-malism, what was it? De Man elsewhere suggested that the main problem with the New Criticism was that it adhered to a bastardized, diluted version of the Romantic idea of "organic form." But his Yeats essay limns a problem wider than this. De Man's essay suggests that New Criticism's limitations were based in its adherence to what we will call the "resolved symbolic." The mistake of the conventional account of the Yeats poem is to assume that "Among School Children," in de Man's words, "yields a consistent reading that extends from the first line to the last and that can account for all the details in the text."[10] The reading de Man opposes at once raises the poem's meaning above ordinary life, making the text "symbolic" and metaphorical, and insists it has a coherent, indissoluble meaning, making the text determinate and "resolved." The goal of this reading was ultimately to separate Yeats decisively from the Romantics, to make sure he could not be confused with a Wordsworth or a Shelley.

The New Critics derived their approval of the symbol from Coleridge, who, in 1816, had differentiated between the allegory, with its one-to-one correspon-dence between the literary work and external reality, and the symbol, in which the "translucence of the special in the individual or the general in the especial" is seen. In other words, the more particular level is seen in the light of the more general one, yet still retains its individual meaning. There is room here for time and abstraction, figure and ground. The symbol is discernible from the main run of signifiers (to use terminology associated with the linguistics of Ferdinand de Saussure), unlike its allegorical counterpart. Yet the relationship between the symbol and the rest is still traceable, still pertinent. Even when the symbol became more subjective and mysterious in the hands of the French *symboliste* poets and the Latin American *modernistas*, the mystery of the symbol was still a mystery meant to lead us towards a euphoric, if rarefied, artistic revelation.[11] The New Critics stepped away from the mystery and the interactive quality of the various nineteenth-century symbolisms, leaving the symbol clean, taut, and lofty. Just as their interpretation of the Yeats ending was Romantic synthesis trimmed down to a private and reflective context, so was the idea of symbol controlled and neutered when compared to earlier uses of the term. That Coleridge laid out his theory of the symbol in a tract called *The Statesman's Manual*, which read, largely, the Old Testament in order to give instruction to post-Napoleonic political leaders, was a fact that the New Critics would have sought to sidestep, viewing such connections to the political and the religious as messy.[12] Coleridge's idea of the symbol was elevated and tightened by the New Critics.

Despite its manifest enthusiasm for ambiguity, the New Criticism, as part of the "resolved symbolic," ended up packing literature tightly into prefabricated intellectual containers. The New Criticism began to purify literature so much that it would be rid of anything disorderly; and art, as any painter will testify, is inevitably disorderly at least in process. New Criticism, in many ways, made literature safe for the modern American university, in which the postwar economic boom and the cold war panic about America's scientific pre-eminence after the Soviet launch of the Sputnik satellite made possible a formalization of academic procedure such as never had occurred before. New Criticism was a method, and literature had heretofore lacked its own method. To add to this strange affinity, their fear of anything emotional often lent the writing of the New Critics a mechanistic quality. R.P. Blackmur spoke of criticism as "the formal discourse of an amateur." But his New Critical colleagues became more and more professionalized. Many of the New Critics started as "southern Agrarians" who critiqued the ravages modern industrialism had wreaked on traditional ways of living such as the family farm. The southern Agrarians were anti-capitalist, anti-urban, and anti-modernity (although not anti-modernism; they very much favoured modernist aesthetics, in their more formal, restrained avatar). They also started out, in many cases, as explicitly racist. Yet, ironically, the New Critics ended by reaping the benefits of technocratic educational complexes funded by scientific grants and beginning to pioneer racial integration.

Despite this ease with the bureaucratization of the modern academy, there was also an anti-intellectual element in the New Criticism. Indeed, one of the problems of the "resolved symbolic" was that, by elevating intellectual problems to a lofty artistic sphere and yet implying that they had been settled for once and for all, it discouraged intellectual curiosity. The New Critics dismissed poets who felt too much and thought too little. But the New Critics, who emulated their own prescriptions by tamping down any feeling in responses to literature, did not follow through in elevating thought in their own practice. The poets were allowed to think. But the critics were not. This is one of the several ways the New Critics differed from T.S. Eliot, who was conspicuously erudite and cerebral in his criticism and who indeed was as much an intellectual historian as he was a literary critic. Eliot, when he ribbed Henry James about having "a mind so fine no idea could violate it," was being mildly puckish about James. But his words could have applied more cuttingly to those critics who were among Eliot's most fervent admirers.

There were some more probing and intellectually challenging commentators numbered among the New Critics. Among these were the British poet and critic William Empson; the British semanticist and "practical critic" I.A. Richards, who would give poems to his students at Cambridge without telling them their authorship or temporal provenance and dare them to give an analysis, and the American essayist R.P. Blackmur, whose rich, often murky prose showed a streak of "creative criticism" rare for the period. Blackmur, for instance, was one of the few critics of Henry James to attempt anything like the idiosyncrasy of a Jamesian style. Yvor Winters, so strait-laced that some of his favourite writers were austere poets such as Elizabeth Daryush or Frederick Goddard Tuckerman, of whom people had barely heard, could not be accused of being humdrum. Winters knew his mind, had firm convictions, and did not care if the consensus thought otherwise. Despite his adamant conservatism, Winters gave a valuable lesson in the importance of personal taste in an era when the same writers—Donne, the Jacobean dramatists, Keats, Yeats, James, Faulkner, T.S. Eliot—seemed to be everybody's favourites. Yet Winters, Blackmur, and Empson were seen as admirable but idiosyncratic thinkers. The beginning student was certainly not encouraged to emulate them.

Empson's interest in the ambiguity and "plurisignation" of words, the way a word could hold several meanings at once or hold diverse meanings in different contexts, came very close to how language was discussed in the theoretical era. So did the "logology" of the independent American critic Kenneth Burke, whose work ranged from sociology to rhetoric and who was fascinated by the strategic deployment of language to achieve these purposes. In both these thinkers, though, there was a tension between exploring the richness and unpredictability of language and trying to burrow down to the fundamentals, to find out just what was going on in language. In this way, their work was as close to the logical positivism of the British analytical philosophers, such as Bertrand Russell or A.J. Ayer, as it was to later theory. Also relevant here is the general semantics of the Polish scholar Count Alfred Korzybski, systematized in the United States by future Senator S.I. Hayakawa. General semantics sought to determine what people were really saying when they used language. It placed language in a situational perspective, but, in its belief in an isolable meaning and in a generally measurable linguistic universe, it was much more pragmatic in its assessment of communication. General semantics was also very cautionary. Korzybski and Hayakawa recognized the misleading and propagandistic abuse to which the Nazis and other totalitarians had put language and sought to free language from distortion and bias. In this light, Richards's interest in Basic English, a rudimentary set of words that could express all major relevant concepts, can be seen as complementary to Korzybski's aspirations. In a sense, these thinkers—Burke, Empson, Hayakawa, Richards, and Korzybski—did not believe that language was as arbitrary as later thinkers. But, if anything, they were *more* concerned about the use to which bad or manipulative language could be put. Semantics had potential to break beyond the formalist confines of the era. But this breakthrough never happened to an appreciable or influential extent.

The 1950s: The New York Intellectuals

The utility of the "resolved symbolic" as an umbrella term is that it explains why people became dissatisfied with the entire literary-critical scene of the 1950s, and not just with the New Critics. Other influential critics on this scene, critics who eventually became the object of dissatisfaction, were the New York Intellectuals. The primary focus of the New York Intellectuals was the relationship of literature, especially the novel, to society. They sought to establish a public arena of conversation about literature that would touch on politics and social questions but not be contaminated by or held hostage to them.

The New York Intellectuals, a coterie of largely male and largely Jewish thinkers, included, most famously, Lionel Trilling, Alfred Kazin, and Irving Howe. They had grown up in New York, suffered both attraction to and disillusionment with communism, as history instructed them, and yet consistently maintained a privileged place for literature in their worldview.[13] The Jewishness of these thinkers must be stressed as it explains their key role in functioning as a bridge between an American intellectual scene that, until the forced emigration of so many intellectuals from Europe in the 1930s and 1940s, was still parochial and isolationist, and a Europe whose ideas were produced amid the cauldron of modernity and seemed daring and innovative to American eyes. But it is important to realize that this group did not include every intellectual in New York, or every Jewish intellectual in the United States. Saul Bellow, the great novelist from Chicago, knew this group socially but distanced himself from it, as, in a different way, did his younger contemporary Philip Roth. Perhaps the two most inventive critics coming from a Jewish background in twentieth-century America, Leslie Fiedler and Harold Bloom, were independent of the group. So were many other thinkers of note, especially religiously inclined Jews such as Arthur Cohen, who would not have been at home in the determinedly secular milieu of the New York Intellectuals, and those like the playwright Lillian Hellman, who remained *undisillusioned* with communism.

The New York Intellectuals were identified by a particular set of attitudes toward literature and politics. Yet often they saw literature and politics as separate. This separation is how they participated, along with the New Critics, in the discourse of the "resolved symbolic." In truth, the separation of literature and politics is hard to sustain in practice, as literature and politics (or history) have many things in common. An interest in narrative, an interaction between ideas and human character, and the interplay between precedent and occurrence inform both. A society can have poetic qualities just as a poem can have social aspects. As Percy Bysshe Shelley, the notable Romantic poet (perhaps not accidentally, particularly belittled by the New Critics) said of ancient Rome in his *Defense of Poetry* (1821),

> The life of Camillus, the death of Regulus; the expectation of the senators, in their godlike state, of the victorious Gauls; the refusal of the republic to make peace with Hannibal after the battle of Cannæ, were not the consequences of a refined calculation of the probable personal advantage to result from such a rhythm and order in the shows of life, to those who were at once the poets and the actors of these immortal dramas.... These things are not the less poetry, *quia carent vate sacro*. They are the episodes of that cyclic poem written by Time upon the memories of men.[14]

Ancient Rome's poetry, in a formal sense, did not, in Shelley's view, equal the poetry of its Greek predecessors. But Rome, in creating, as it were, a social imaginary in its lived history that had some of the qualities of poetry, showed it understood poetry's structural principles. One would definitely not want to push Shelley's analogy too far, as states that have been deliberately poetic have often been the most tyrannous. It is this suspicion of the state aspiring to a kind of false perfection by linking itself with aesthetic absolutes that has haunted those who have tried to assure literature of a democratic environment in the wake of the twentieth century's calamities. The New York Intellectuals, wary of Stalinist reductivism, rightly wanted to separate literature from a political line. Yet they tended to end up with vague generalizations, such as great works of literature being about the individual versus society, with both the individual and society being conceived as unalterably opposed yet eternally interdependent. This formula led directly to a blanched and uninspiring view of how literature can be read against political horizons without losing its formal and textual independence.

One of the problems with the New York Intellectuals is that their disillusionment with communism, which they rightly saw as totalitarian and brutal, made them suspicious of any sort of disruption of the status quo, political or imaginative. Like the disillusioned onlookers in the Irish poet Seamus Heaney's "The Mud Vision," they often "figure in ... [their] own eyes for the eyes of the world."[15] In other words, they thought that since the hope they had strived for had failed, everybody's hope must necessarily fail. The link between the New York Intellectuals and the later neoconservatives has at times been exaggerated. The major figures of this group (named in ascending order of political leftwardness) were Lionel Trilling (1905–75), Alfred Kazin (1915–98), and Irving Howe (1920–93), and all voted for liberal, Democratic candidates until they died. Yet the neoconservatives, such as Gertrude Himmelfarb and Norman Podhoretz, who claim descent from these men (and who largely wrote about politics rather than literature) can point to a common strand of being, at best, flummoxed and, at worst, outraged by the 1960s. Few would now argue that the protest movements of that decade were not without severe flaws. In fact, even theorists such as Michel Foucault and Jacques Derrida, who rose to prominence in this era, were practically as corrective with respect to sixties enthusiasms as they were participatory in them.[16]

Many of the opponents of theory proclaim a stance tacitly or openly opposed to what they see as radical leftist academia. These antagonists of academic orthodoxy included some maverick academics, such as the spirited Ecuadorian critic Wilfrido Corral, co-editor of the influential *Theory's Empire* (2005), and a set of writers for general-interest journals, such as the non-academic Roger Kimball and the academic Frederick Crews, who basically made their name attacking trends in academia they disliked as excessively wayward and experimental. Yet one cannot square theory and anti-theory with the Left and the Right. Some explicitly link the opposition to theory to a left-wing humanist agenda, or an unreconstructed Marxism. Moreover, theorists such as Derrida and Foucault were certainly anti-communists, who hoped and worked for the downfall of the Soviet Union, and, in that way, they were more in line with neoconservatives on the issue around which they first made their name. And it cannot be pointed out too often that the original New York Intellectuals saw themselves on the left, sometimes even the "Far Left," despite their disillusionment with communism. But the New York Intellectuals, as contrasted to the next generation, often seemed determined to hold on to their disillusionment. They saw the lesson of caution and constraint that the exposure of the communist nightmare had taught them as valid for all time and every circumstance, not just for the late 1940s in the wake of Stalin's tyranny and Soviet expansionism.

Although some New York Intellectuals, such as Trilling, had successful, conventional academic careers of teaching and publishing critical books, most did not. Kazin and Howe accepted professorships at the City University of New York. But their lifeblood was as much outside academia as in it. Between them, they produced only one full-length critical book mounting a unified argument, and this one, the wonderful survey of modern American literature entitled *On Native Grounds* (1942), was Kazin's first and was written before his time became so taken up by writing reviews, journalism, and, eventually, memoir. Both Kazin and Howe wrote many book reviews and articles for general-interest journals such as *The New Republic*, *Commentary*, and *Dissent* (which Howe for a long time edited), journals that contained far more political than literary commentary and did not come out of the self-deliberation of an academic community the way the learned journals that the New Critics published in did. There is only so much thinking one can do in a book review. One has to tell the reader what is going on in the book and whether it should be purchased.[17]

It is hard to formulate new paradigms while doing that. One can apply a paradigm relentlessly in reviewing books, as Marxist critics such as Granville Hicks, Maxwell Geismar, or Arnold Kettle did routinely, but the original enunciation of Marxist views on literature was done in longer, more theoretical treatises. (Indeed, despite the political and aesthetic missteps of many Marxist critics, the very idea of highbrow literary interpretation mattering, being thought socially important, would not exist in quite the same way without Marxism.) It is true that many of the nineteenth century's finest pieces of literary criticism were book reviews. And some critics of the late twentieth century, such as Irving Malin and Harriet Zinnes, excelled in the small book review for the special interest literary or little magazine, making it into an art form. But the rise of academic criticism in the late nineteenth and early twentieth centuries gave literary thinking an outlet that it did not have before. To forsake this for the book review was a step back.

Yet this turn to the book review in the 1990s held great appeal in the aftermath of the hegemony of literary theory. Just as many entered the academy in the 1970s and 1980s because of theory, in the 1990s, many left it for the same reason. Theory seemed to have stalled, and the idea of a rebirth of the "public intellectual" became appealing. This exodus from the academy, amusingly satirized in the first section of Jonathan Franzen's novel *The Corrections* (2001), led to a lot of young people writing book reviews and literary journalism rather than scholarly articles. This led to an elevation of past figures that had done the same. Indeed, the New York Intellectuals are not really valued today for any work they actually did. Whenever overall examinations of their careers are made (or of cognate figures such as the slightly older and far more patrician Edmund Wilson), their flaws are readily admitted. It is the aura they present that resonates, an aura that reflects what Noah Isenberg has termed a worry that "the notoriously jargon-filled, obscurantist prose associated with theory has served as an impediment to effecting change and reaching an audience beyond academic elites."[18]

As members of a marginalized immigrant group, as scrappy, street-wise savants making their way in the big city, the New York Intellectuals present a very attractive image of an embodied intellectual life. Similarly, when people thought nostalgically about the New Critics in the aftermath of theory, they often pictured kindly old southern gentlemen in smoking jackets, scholars who loved great poetry and who did not need to arm themselves with the intimidating jargon of their deconstructionist successors.[19] This is partially because people often confuse the close reading of a text with New Criticism. New Criticism helped popularize the practice. But it performed this practice itself only in a highly specific, historically situated way, which should not be extrapolated out of its particular context. There were many texts—well-known works by famous, acclaimed writers—that were not and *could not* be explicated by the New Critical method of close reading. This non-inclusion was because these texts did not fall into the New Critical ideological framework, which led these critics to spurn most British literature of the eighteenth and nineteenth centuries because it was too liberal and optimistic. There were some exceptions to this exclusion—Samuel Johnson and John Keats were highly valued by the New Critics—but the sense of a constricted canon was vexatious. Had the New Critics read more broadly even within the *mainstream English* canon while using the same methods, they would have been what their latter-day admirers wish they were.[20]

That somewhat rosy retrospective images of the 1950s prevailed can be laid at the feet of the imperviousness and elitism of deconstruction in America. This imperviousness and elitism did much to almost ruin the momentous changes in reading and interpretation that deconstruction genuinely brought about. As opposed to deconstruction, the idea of a more approachable mode of writing about literature gained credibility. The 1950s critics seemed, in retrospect, like real people, not soulless products of a smug academic system. Yet often this approachability was overplayed.[21] There was a fantasy that Kazin, Howe, and Trilling were widely read in the 1950s, that every middle-class suburban household reverently discussed their essays in the Sunday newspaper or the newsweekly.[22] In fact, these households were likelier to subscribe only to the far more accessible *Reader's Digest*, if indeed to anything at all.[23] Realistically, the audience of the New York Intellectuals was broader than that of the more academic critics, but only slightly so. Any intellectual work, even that which eschews jargon and tries to speak in accessible language, will inevitably reach only a small fraction of even the literate and educated population. The audience of the New York Intellectuals was often people who were academics, but in fields other than literature, such as the social sciences. Or they were general readers who read the magazines in which the New York Intellectuals appeared not for the literature but *for the politics*. The New York Intellectuals exerted a narrower influence than their admirers realize, or perhaps even than they themselves realized.

There was a definite cultural pessimism in both the New Critics and the New York Intellectuals, a corollary of a sense of caution stemming from World War II and the spectre of totalitarian ideologies.[24] Not only was any sort of utopian social vision seen with great suspicion, but there was a concomitant reservation about the possibility of groundbreaking intellectual work. This pessimism was bound to dissipate as time went on. In an era when society was booming economically and when the 1959 election slogan of British Prime Minister Harold Macmillan—"You've never had it so good"—could well have been echoed across the Atlantic, this muted, self-limiting mood was bound to wane. The criticism of the 1950s had a historical context that makes it more difficult for that era's responses to literature to be as simply revived "after theory" as some of its more romantic latter-day advocates seem to desire. The New York Intellectuals, in particular, emerged from such a precisely defined time and place that re-imagining their milieu in the early twenty-first century would be a very elusive task.

The 1950s: The General Climate

Yet the New York Intellectuals also opened out to a wider arena. Unlike the New Critics, they wrote largely about fiction and were, in general, more inclusive. The New York Intellectuals could discuss the New Critics in their writing. It was hard, given their self-restriction, to see how the New Critics could ever have discussed the New York Intellectuals. The connection with the public world the New York Intellectuals so avidly sought entailed a sense of gusto that made the intellectual atmosphere they inhabited admirable. They paid attention to film (see the writings of Robert Warshow, and note the interest of second-generation New York Intellectual Susan Sontag in film). They included three prominent women, the novelist Mary McCarthy (1912–89), the philosopher Hannah Arendt (1906–75), and, in the next generation, Susan Sontag (1933–2004). These women were also the three members of the group with the most sustained intellectual production. European exiles, such as the philological critics Erich Auerbach and Leo Spitzer, who had no affiliation with the New York Intellectuals, nonetheless fit into their more cosmopolitan view of literature more so than would have suited a New Critical world.

The same was true of figures such as Walter Kaufmann, whose translations of Friedrich Nietzsche renegotiated Nietzsche in the English-speaking world (in the wake of people's association of his thought with German aggression in the two world wars) and paved the way for the later "new Nietzscheans" such as Jacques Derrida to be appreciated. The connection with modern European history that the New York Intellectuals maintained provided a base for later more erudite critics such as George Steiner, who managed to review books, to write original academic works, and, despite appearances, to prepare the way for the reception of European theorists who, albeit in very different ways, shared the New York Intellectuals' interest in Freud, Marx, and the fate of modernity. Steiner also deliberately guyed the New Critics by provocatively subtitling his first book *An Essay in the Old Criticism*.

It must be realized that many European intellectuals who were alive and active in the 1950s, such as Georges Bataille, Maurice Blanchot, Walter Benjamin, Mikhail Bakhtin, and Theodor Adorno, were either not known in the English-speaking world or not seen as relevant to literature. (Now these intellectuals are considered proto-theorists.) As Thomas Gray put it in his great eighteenth-century elegy, "Full many a gem of purest ray serene / The dark unfathomed caves of ocean bear." It took 1970s literary theory to bring Bataille, Blanchot, Bakhtin, Benjamin, and even Adorno (who was certainly known by sociologists and political thinkers) to light. When Paul de Man spoke on the limitations of New Criticism to the History of Ideas Club at

Johns Hopkins University in the mid-1960s, he spoke of the "German essayist Walter Benjamin," implying that Benjamin's was not a household name among advanced undergraduate and graduate students in one of the nation's most rigorous universities. A strictly chronological look in anthologies of theory will give the illusion that these thinkers were contemporaries of Lionel Trilling and Cleanth Brooks. They were in that they were on the planet at the same time. *But they were not part of the same climate of opinion.*

This contemporaneousness of existence but not of popularity was also true of the Russian and Czech formalists, who are often compared with the New Critics. Roman Jakobson was well known among linguists and Slavicists in the United States, where he lived in the last decades before his death in 1982. Jakobson also wrote about poetry—his sense of himself as a writer about poetry gave birth to his legendary quip. When his colleagues at Harvard were thinking of hiring Vladimir Nabokov, at the height of his fame, to teach literature, Jakobson asked, "Gentlemen, even if one allows that he is an important writer, are we next to invite an elephant to be Professor of Zoology?"[25] But much of Jakobson's research was not only linguistics but dealt with cognitive issues and the mechanics of how the brain structured language, and this range of work was not one the 1950s would easily understand. In that era, Slavic thought was screened through more formalistically and historically inclined critics such as René Wellek and Victor Erlich. Jakobson only became a figure in the general academic-literary world once theory had given literary readers access to his linguistic work. The salient aspect of the "resolved symbolic" of the 1950s and 1960s is that many strands of thought, such as the work of thinkers as different as Adorno and Jakobson, were excluded at the time but later deemed applicable to literature.[26] Had the Russian formalists and Adorno been translated, read, and generally ventilated in intellectual terms in the 1950s and 1960s, theory probably would not have been needed, and it certainly would have proclaimed its arrival less melodramatically. But it is important to recognize that, although these earlier European critics had written before theory, they were not at all understood in North America in the terms that theory later occasioned. It was not until the next era, the era of high theory in the 1970s and 1980s, that the Europeans mentioned previously became household names.[27] In the 1950s and 1960s, what connections between literary theory and Europe did exist were embodied, in many ways, by the New York Intellectuals, and they should receive credit for that.

The 1950s: The Leavisites

The third major contribution to the 1950s consensus was the criticism of F.R. Leavis (1895–1978).[28] Born in Cambridge, England, of middle-class background, Leavis became the leading literary intellectual at that city's famous university, challenging the dominance of the genteel aristocracy that had long prevailed there. Like the New York Intellectuals, who as Jews had felt prejudice and discrimination, and the New Critics, who as southerners felt the burden of humiliation and defeat, Leavis and his school at first represented a new wave of empowerment on the part of the previously marginalized. Leavisites represented a recently empowered non-elite class, and their advocacy of D.H. Lawrence, a writer from the north of England and of working-class origins, was an important badge of their social agenda. Very quickly, though, Leavisism became static, just as the work of the New Critics and the New York Intellectuals did.

One of the major differences between Leavis's school and the two others is that Leavis's critical work embraced both fiction and poetry, enabling him, for one thing, to celebrate two people born with or having assumed the name "Eliot." In poetry, he had some of the same favourites as the New Critics, for instance T.S. Eliot and Gerard Manley Hopkins, though he liked both for different reasons than the New Critics did, valuing their erudition and reserve less than their unsentimentality and sense of gravity. Seriousness, indeed, was a major goal of Leavisite criticism, and his preferences in fiction similarly emphasized seriousness. George Eliot (born Mary Ann Evans) was for Leavis the ultimate English novelist. Very typically, though, he did not embrace all Eliot's work. Indeed, he largely favoured *Middlemarch* (1871–72), as a kind of social novel that criticized a fossilized order without subverting it too much, as well as, memorably, half of *Daniel Deronda* (1876)—meaning not half of the physical book but one plot strand that alternated with another throughout the novel. Leavis liked the narrative involving Gwendolyn Harleth, a young woman who makes a loveless marriage to the loathsome Henleigh Grandcourt. He disliked the other strand, the story of the title character, a young aristocrat who finds out he is of Jewish ancestry. Leavis's preference for the first strand was so adamant and even obsessive that he, in his mind, restyled the novel *Gwendolyn Harleth*.[29] This preference was neither unreasonable nor unprecedented. As Leavis pointed out, Henry James had come to similar conclusions when first reading the novel. What was notable, though, was the utter, brazen confidence with which Leavis handed down a judgement. He was unafraid not only to criticize novelists he disliked but also to, in essence, rewrite works by novelists he liked. Leavis may have been clearer in his writing style than later theorists. But he exemplified the potential power of the critic over the text later associated with theory.

This Leavisite selection of only some of the works of a preferred novelist was often explained as focusing on the writer's "mature" work. Part of this discrimination was chronological. Early work did not count because it was immature; later work did not count because it was decadent and cut off from the wellspring of the writer's inspiration.[30] Maturity was the fulfilment of early promise; maturity was also the peak of fortitude before age ebbed strength. But part of the emphasis on maturity came from the tacit sense that both early and late were developmentally, or even sexually, abnormal. Freudian theory came in here, with its sense of passing through the Oedipal or phallic stage into the genital stage, the only state of fulfilled sexuality, and its dismissal of the "pre-Oedipal" as inchoate, anarchic, and perverse. Oedipus, who unknowingly killed his father and then married his mother, and D.H. Lawrence, the modern writer most emphasized by Leavis, who wrote explicitly about passionate sexual relationships, had a lot in common. They were sexually transgressive yet avowedly heterosexual and patriarchal. They were both rulers of their roost during the time and in the spheres in which they prevailed. This kind of insurgent centrality was what "maturity" meant in Leavis's era. Edward Said's idea of "late style," cannot be explained, in its intellectual background and in its ramifications without reference to this idea of mid-career maturity by dint of which both early and later styles were inadequate. Concomitantly, the note of defensiveness in this era's discussion of not only Shakespeare's early plays, such as the bloody *Titus Andronicus*, but also some of his now-revered later romances, such as *The Winter's Tale*, comes from the sense that these plays were outside the spectrum of Shakespeare's maturity, as defined by Leavisite paradigms. For some writers, the window of "maturity" was even briefer. Leavis, for instance, at first maintained that *Hard Times* (1854), Dickens's shortest and most "social" completed novel, was the only Dickens one truly had to read. (Dickens was too great for Leavis to have ignored him entirely.) This circumscription of the Dickens canon to *Hard Times* spared the student from a non-traditional background the need to read Dickens's other, longer novels, deemed eccentric, decadent, or immature.

The whole emphasis on "maturity" ran parallel to the 1950s being an era in which reproductive heterosexuality was the only publicly acknowledged mode of human sexual conduct. "Maturity" was heteronormative. In other words, it affirmed heterosexuality as a universal norm. The Leavisite dismissal of Woolf and E.M. Forster was at least partially based on a fear of their gay or bisexual personal lives. This also explains the key role played by D.H. Lawrence for Leavis. Indeed, the twentieth-century equivalent of George Eliot for Leavis was D.H. Lawrence. This was so although Lawrence's robust libido could not have been further from the inferentially quiescent erotic affects of most Leavisites. But Lawrence's unbridled sexuality was read as being macho (despite the repeated instances of queer affect in Lawrence's work), and macho meant normative and therefore safe. The authority of the patriarchy, especially the outwardly insurgent but still domestically suzerain rogue male, was not challenged.

The above sketch is more conceptual than Leavis would have wished. Leavis scorned ideas, even to the extent of basically dismissing Plato and Aristotle.[31] But this extreme swerving away from abstraction brought with it a benefit. Leavis's work had a welcome pugnacity. Literature was important to him, and he was prepared to fight for it. Relevant here is the *bolekaja* criticism later epitomized by the Nigerian critic Chinweizu—*bolekaja* connoting the idea of "come on down and fight" or, as translated into New Yorkese, which Howe and Kazin would have well understood, "ya wanna make something of it?"[32] Leavis was ready to do this at least rhetorically. But the downside of this was a perceptiveness that started being rigid as soon as it came remotely near to attaining power. With both Leavis and the New Critics, one sensed a discomfort with power, an inability to display the flexibility that those in power need in order to stay in power. Once these critics were in harness in the academy (which the New York Intellectuals never were), an unchanging monotony set in. The New York Intellectuals, incidentally, in many ways, turned to Leavis as the default mode when they needed any sort of framework. Kazin's *Bright Book of Life* (1973), with its title from D.H. Lawrence and its inclusion of "life" in the title, could not have been more Leavisite—Kazin gives a nod not only to Leavis's key author but also to the Leavisite idea that the socially realistic novel captured "life" more than, say, a Virginia Woolf story about flowers in the snow.[33]

Leavis's canon revision, ultimately inspired by class resentment against an upper-class establishment he scorned as both genteel and frivolous, lost its sense of upsurge once Leavis achieved more power, at least in his own world, than the upper crust he despised. Leavis only wanted fiction that was about "life." Yet, for him, the term "life" clearly had a restricted not a general definition. According to Leavis, life was not about private, intimate, and socially unimportant experiences, such as those described in Virginia Woolf's novel *Mrs. Dalloway*, for example. Mrs. Dalloway's memory of once having lost a shilling in the Serpentine (a small river in London) was clearly not "life"—as Leavis saw it. Indeed, one doubts if Leavis saw anything Virginia Woolf ever wrote, or even ever did, as being about life. Life meant F.R. Leavis's life—earnest, striving, combative, morally serious. But there is too much more to life for this definition of life to suffice. By endorsing only a few of the many aspects of existence and then defining even those narrowly, Leavisism was as much a part of the "resolved symbolic" as were the New Critics and the New York Intellectuals. It elevated a few texts to a privileged position and, that having been done, tended to discourage further change.

Leavis's criticism was surprisingly exportable. Even Leavis himself, despite his parochially English aspects, wrote well about American and Russian as well as British literature. Thus Leavisism, despite its very English roots, dovetailed well with a North American postwar psychology that stressed the men coming back from the war, getting married, and having 2.5 children. Better middle-class stolidity, in this respect, than the hedonistic abandon practised by the "Bright Young Things," the socialites of high-society background or aspiration associated with writers such as Evelyn Waugh. Even though the class circumstances of Leavisism were uniquely British, this sense of standardized social conformity mirrored postwar conditions across the Atlantic. Indeed, of the three ideologies discussed here, Leavisism lasted the longest—partially because so many Leavisites got positions in Commonwealth countries (former British colonies) from Sierra Leone to Sri Lanka to Australia—and had the greatest influence. This was because it was the most socially optimistic. (On those few occasions when Leavis wrote about race, such as his analysis of Mark Twain's *Pudd'nhead* well, some people

Wilson, he did so with insight and a sense of what a truly civil society could potentially be.) Leavisism bolstered people's own self-esteem instead of reminding them of their inherent flaws in a climate of cultural pessimism. Thus, it could be adapted to a variety of social circumstances.

The social prevalence of the stolid, cautious, doggedly persistent go-getter, epitomized by the character of Lewis Eliot, the protagonist of C.P. Snow's *Strangers and Brothers* novel sequence (1940–74), helps explain the all-pervasive pre-eminence of Leavisite views of fiction in the 1950s. This was so despite the fact that Leavis and Snow (1905–80) were famously antagonistic. The antagonism was manifest in "The Two Cultures" dispute, named for a lecture in which Snow, although, like Leavis, a literary figure, scolded humanists for knowing nothing about science. Leavis replied that they did not need to do so.[34] Notwithstanding this difference, Snow's earnestness was Leavisite in its lack of imagination as well as its distinct comfort with this lack being so evident. This inability to re-imagine circumstances made impossible a long-term tradition of Leavisite critics. There were imitators by the score. But there was nobody to re-engineer Leavis for the next generation. By then the sclerotic effects of conformity had set in.

Indeed, there was a succession problem in all three schools of criticism discussed here. They were not really overthrown but simply ran out of steam after a point, producing no new original statements. The path was clear for a new school—which turned out to be French-influenced theory—a school that was, inevitably, affected by the social changes of the 1960s. Also clearing the way for new ideas was the fact that the three schools predominating in the 1950s did not colour the thought of many of the prominent critics of the time. However, the aura of these three schools nonetheless dominated the era. True, the New Criticism, or a complementary approach, did not reign equally in all fields. Victorian studies and American studies, which pioneered interdisciplinary methods from the 1950s onward, developed, early on, the ties to sociology and cultural history that other fields had to develop later and under the explicit aegis of theory.[35] There were also individual critics of European origin who taught in the United States, such as the Spanish cultural historian Américo Castro, who were far more wide-ranging and interdisciplinary than the North American norm. However, the marginality of their fields often prevented them having any notable influence.[36] Had all fields been as pluralistic, theory would have had far less to do in transforming literature departments. However, Victorian studies in this era had little impact on other fields. American studies, for all its interdisciplinarity, was dominated by myth-and-symbol criticism. This work tended to elevate certain images of the American experience as characteristic and immutable, in a way characteristic of the "resolved symbolic." (In its elevation of Herman Melville and Nathaniel Hawthorne over Ralph Waldo Emerson, myth-and-symbol Americanism also privileged cultural pessimism.) It was not easy to write criticism that was more thematic than stylistic in the 1950s. Apologies had to be made and a textual warrant had to be sought before thematic questions were even tentatively assayed.

The Quandary of the "Resolved Symbolic"

In the discourse of the "resolved symbolic," even when theme was permitted or necessitated, literary criticism had a limited, hemmed-in quality. Medieval studies were dominated by D.W. Robertson, Jr., who read medieval texts in an exegetical fashion that reaffirmed Christian morality in a prescriptive way.[37] Similarly, although with more suppleness and literary skill, Rosemond Tuve, a powerful figure in Renaissance criticism, saw even the writing of Shakespeare's time as informed by traditional patterns and symbols that were ultimately Christian, although other Renaissance scholars viewed this writing as far more modern than that of the Middle Ages.[38] Tuve and Robertson differed from the New Critics in some ways. They had a sense of history and admitted the idea of the author's cultural background into the analysis of the text, even if they read that background as conservatively Christian. Robertson and Tuve undeniably, in their own terms, knew what they were talking about. (This was also true of comparable critics such as the Shakespearean scholar Roy Battenhouse, who saw the theology of St. Augustine as the key to Shakespeare.) Despite the monotony of their projects, which often consisted of cataloguing images or motifs in texts according to their preconceived notion, they were representative of the strong strain of solid, historically grounded scholarship, which was at its best on the medieval and Renaissance periods but also manifest in studies of other eras. This scholarship continued throughout the period of the New Critical and Leavisite hegemony and was unaffected by the dogmas of the ideologies that, in their day, were more trendy and flashy. Robertson's disciples could productively plough his narrow vein the way that Brooks's or Wimsatt's could not. (Some went further and became theoretically inflected new historicists.) Much of the unravelling of New Criticism occurred because its productive energy was so quickly used up. In other words, there were no second-generation New Critics.

Necessarily, external influences contributed to the waning of New Criticism as well. The civil rights movement, the feminist movement, and the protest movement against the Vietnam War radicalized academic life and attitudes and, as will be explored in Chapters 3 and 4, led to advocacy of a wider canon— one that included women, African Americans, and Latino writers—and of less formalistic viewpoints. But, even without these external pressures, the resolved symbolic would not have lasted eternally—or even for a couple of more decades. In its time, though, it exerted a stranglehold.

Nevertheless, other books, avowedly historical or sociological in framework, adhered to, or were read as adhering to, the resolved symbolic formula. Almost like Foucault's idea of an episteme, explored in the following chapter, the dominant critical paradigm of the resolved symbolic tended to govern even methods and approaches not largely compliant with it. M.H. Abrams's *The Mirror and the Lamp* (1953) postulated a categorical difference between classicist and romantic ways of thinking about imagination. Ian Watt's *The Rise Of The Novel* (1957) insisted that the novel rose at a determinate time and that many other texts that could be called novels distinctly were not. Both books are troves of learning and make effective arguments still sensible fifty years after, and both would not have seemed so limiting were they not received within the resolved symbolic paradigm. As it was, these books, for all their wisdom and trenchancy, tended to exclude as many aspects of literary criticism as they included within that discipline. The period covered by these two books—the eighteenth and early nineteenth century—is a testing ground for many major theoretical assumptions, especially those of Foucault. The 1950s consensus tended to want to sample this period minimally, wishing, ideally, to conceive of a giant arch stretching between Eliot himself and the seventeenth century, the first half of which was valued by T.S. Eliot as the time anterior to the "dissociation of sensibility" in which thought became detached from feeling. (Such critics as F.O. Matthiessen, Leslie Fiedler, and Jules Chametzky, all of whom later became important figures in the study of American literature, started out as Renaissance scholars, so all-pervasive was this Eliotic preference for the years before 1650.) The esteem given to this period explains, in part, the currency in the 1950s of dissertations on Donne and Marvell and (Eliot's "specialty") Jacobean drama. Sometimes, it was best for a period the less attention was paid to it in the dominant paradigm. Leavis's claims on the Victorian period were so limited, despite his love of one and a half of George Eliot's novels and one of Dickens's, that criticism on Victorian literature was basically unimpeded by Leavisism. This freedom enabled Victorian studies to be an incubator for dissident ideologies such as feminism.

What many who fought against theory in the culture wars of the 1980s and 1990s did not realize is that the modes of criticism that seemed comfortable because they grew up with them were themselves reforms, and highly polemical ones, of what had existed previously. The budding New Critics and Leavisites expected the world of their teachers to endure forever. They were traumatized when it did not. Peers of theirs strayed from their mentors' suggestions and developed more dynamic models of reading and of writing about reading that excited more students and provoked more discussion. It is very understandable how displaced followers of the older ways of reading must have felt. But this sense of disinheritance was often fallaciously reconfigured as a sense that theory itself was illegitimate and an objectionable newfangled intervention in a field that had been otherwise going well for decades. Neither idea was true.

Part of the instability that led to the rise of theory had to do with the small canon of both the Leavisites and the New Critics. So few books were admitted into the canon that, eventually, most of the arguments that could be made had been made. To admit new texts into the canon, rather than simply chastise them

for not being mature or tightly knit enough, would possibly have required interrogating the original assumptions. The prevailing methods preferred the known
texts on which they had operated so brilliantly. In both the United Kingdom
and the United States, the small canon was very useful for training students new
to the academy, students whose parents had not instilled in them any sense of
culture as a meaningful entity. The resolved symbolic *was* easily learned and easily emulated. It had something in common with a general mid-century taste for
simplified ideologies, and, in that way, it had a strange commonality with both
American and Soviet versions of standardized modernization. But soon what
Ulrich Beck describes as the phenomenon of "reflexive modernization" set in.[39]

By making the very changes they had sought, the New Critics and Leavisites
put themselves out of business. These methods succeeded in democratizing the
academy to the extent that the newly expanded ranks of academics wanted
newer and more complex theories than those in which they had been trained.
New Criticism and Leavisism, according to this reading, did not fail. They
worked so well that they brought about their necessary replacement. In the
early twenty-first century, bewildered by so many works now able to be studied in the academy, adrift in a world where no one person, however well read,
can know everything that is taught, we may well be captivated by the tidiness
of the 1950s' canon. But, structurally, there is no going back to it. Some of its
originators seem to have agreed. Even Cleanth Brooks, who spent his later years
writing insightful thematic books about fellow southerner William Faulkner,
changed as a critic after his heyday in the 1950s. And when Leavis made his late
recantation and admitted a far more popular Dickens novel, *Great Expectations*
(1861), to the "great tradition," he was himself responding to an evident thin-
ness in his canon that necessitated amendment.

Literalizing Reading

A writer admired by both the Leavisites and the New York Intellectuals was
Joseph Conrad. Conrad was valued for his combination of morality and complexity. Conrad critiqued bourgeois society, so he was acceptable to the Left.
But he opposed terrorism and revolution, so he was acceptable to the moderate
Right. In effect, he was, after his death, resurrected so as to be the Anglophone
equivalent of Albert Camus, in the era when critics positioned Camus as
opposed to the less moderate Jean-Paul Sartre. *Nostromo* (1904), the Conrad
novel particularly favoured by this period, was like *Hard Times* in that it was
read as depicting social injustice, but, ultimately, according to the critics of that
era, the reader found most sympathetic the figure who defied the ideological fervour of those who protested against the original injustice. Conrad was serious,
earnest, and heteronormative yet also abstruse, modern, and existential. There
was not a lot of humour or play to him. And he was international. As a Pole
born under tsarist Russian occupation, Conrad learned English as an adult and

sailed around the world. He was thus not merely provincial or local. (Precisely because the three major schools discussed previously were all local or provincial in origin, they had a particular horror of the writer who was only regional.) Conrad was the furthest thing from Oscar Wilde—who, in many respects, ended up playing the role in the postmodern canon that Conrad did in the modern.

"International" in the modernist use of the term was very different from what later became "post-colonial" or "global" literature. Thus Conrad's cosmopolitanism was read in a different way by Chinua Achebe (1930–). The well-known Nigerian novelist found himself teaching Conrad at the University of Massachusetts in fall 1974.[40] Conrad's novella *Heart of Darkness* (1902) is about a man who had disappeared in the Belgian-occupied Congo and the attempts to find out what had happened to him. The book is often seen as a searing revelation of existential horror, since the end of the searched-for character, Kurtz, was grisly or, conversely, as a daring experiment in narrative technique, as Marlow, the searcher, tells the story from his own, semi-detached point of view. Even though it is a story about Africa, few critics mentioned the importance of the locale, other than pointing to Africa as a metaphor for emotional darkness and despair. Achebe, himself African, found not only the book's depiction of Africa shocking in its negativity but the praise heaped on it for its compelling portrait of Africa to be fuel upon the already existing fire of cultural imperialism. While respecting Conrad's talent as a writer, Achebe wholly dismissed Conrad's vision of Africa. He did this even though, if Conrad had any political intent at all, it was anti-imperialist. Writing in the wake of the imperial fervour of the 1890s, Conrad's tale warned that imperial expansion might come back to haunt Europeans. That this entailed being negative about Africa as a locale was not seen as anti-African but as "realistic" in its acknowledgement of the vast cultural differences between Africans and Europeans. Conrad's anti-imperialism, in other words, involved racism. Other races were too different for the European to be in contact with them.

But Achebe was objecting less to Conrad's empirical politics than to the metaphysical anti-politics of those who had raised the novella to its place in the canon, scholars such as Albert J. Guerard. Guerard was a gifted critic but one more or less in the grip of then-dominant paradigms. In 1950, Guerard had called Conrad's *Heart of Darkness* one of the six greatest novellas in the English language. How can a book so filled, in Achebe's view, with hatred and contempt for Africans be worthy of this merit? How can the critics who raised Conrad to such a level have ignored so wilfully this hatred of Africans?

Achebe's analysis will not let the reader explain away Conrad's anti-African phraseology as the by-product of a search for a metaphysical ground for despair. Like de Man, who insists that Yeats could actually wonder where exactly dance and dancer (or poem and poet) leave off, Achebe insists that there is a real Africa that cannot be subsumed into a symbolic one.[41] Achebe is writing politically and asking that Eurocentric notions be dispelled in favour of ideas that acknowledge an African contribution to world civilization. (As some do; Achebe notes that modern cubist artists were crucially influenced by the sculpture of the Fang, one of the Congo River peoples Conrad demonizes, even though he does not stoop to name them.) But Achebe is also insisting that the literal Africa matters. This insistence was important in a West still coming to grips with decolonization. But note that decolonization had occurred by the 1970s. Both Nigeria and the former Belgian Congo had been independent for over a decade when Achebe wrote. Even those political commentators sceptical of the future potential of Africa acknowledged that African countries existed, in literal terms. But literary analysts of Africa in Western texts were more uneasy about literal African independence—partially because they were uneasy about the literal, as such.

The "resolved symbolic" was horrified at the idea of the literal. It wanted everything to be metaphorical. It desired that not the referent but what the writer was doing with the referent imaginatively should matter. This general perspective, admittedly, is not a bad one for reading literature. Often, to take a referent too literally is to under read. But when the tendency relentlessly goes the other way, not taking account of the real Africa, then stasis and sclerosis has set in. Like de Man, Achebe seeks to literalize strategically in order to puncture the realm of closed metaphor. Just as de Man introduced the linguistic instability of using the literal to undermine the complacency of the metaphorical, Achebe let the reality of Africa puncture the psychological abstractions imposed on Conrad's text by standardized modernist readings. For all his castigation of Conrad's text, Achebe's treatment of it frees Conrad up in ways that the more figurative models of Leavisism and the New York Intellectuals never could have. Even though Achebe is attacking previous critical paradigms from a political vantage point, and de Man from a textual one, the parallel nature of their arguments is notable. Achebe, like de Man, showed that to literalize is neither to reduce nor to erase the play of language. It is to introduce another tool in our reckoning with literature, a process in which we should never either overly use one tool or rule out too many of the tools at our disposal.

Both de Man and Achebe wrote their essays out of particular pedagogical contexts. However sweeping their theoretical reverberations, the readings were teachers' readings that aimed to find a new angle on professing these texts in the classroom. The "resolved symbolic" could not have collapsed out of mere expiration of its energy and novelty. Only when new readings, which were practical and came out of in-classroom experience, became current and applicable did theory fully become prevalent. De Man and Achebe also both wrote their articles in the 1970s. By this time, the "resolved symbolic" was beginning to collapse. This was because of the new popularity of figures such as Jacques Derrida (1930–2004) and Michel Foucault (1926–84). It was also because, as discussed above, the "resolved symbolic" did not produce any innovative thinkers or new thoughts. And of course the political upheaval of the 1960s also played a role (even though the sixties aesthetic was as close to New Criticism as to deconstruction), showing the generation of the New York Intellectuals that a diagnosis of permanent political paralysis was too pessimistic. But individuals were also important. This preface will conclude by looking at three very individual critics whose individuality helped set the tone for the stimulating development literary study was to undergo in the decades after 1960. They are Roland Barthes, Harold Bloom, and Wayne C. Booth.

Many have seen Northrop Frye's *Anatomy of Criticism* as heralding the first break with New Criticism. Frank Lentricchia's eloquent positioning of Frye (1912–91) as "the father of us all" in his *After the New Criticism* (1980), a book that introduced many to theory in the 1980s, has been very influential in establishing this idea. Frye well could have been this figure. His criticism is massively erudite, flexible, and capacious. But the way he was immediately read and imitated was formulaic and pat, and played straight into the priorities of the "resolved symbolic." (As de Man pointed out, Frye affirmed the New Critical idea of the intentional fallacy, even though what he saw as "the text" was far wider and, in a sense, the author's exclusion from it far less of a deprivation.) Archetypes, myths, stock figures were discerned in many texts in a monolithic way that did violence to the brilliance of Frye's vision. Frye was conflated with mythic and anthropological critics of an earlier era such as Maud Bodkin and Jane Harrison in a way that was unfair to all parties concerned. More supple concepts ventilated by Frye such as the idea of "Menippean satire," which broke down the boundaries between prose and verse and art and ideas that the New Critics so strongly tried to maintain, had to wait for later decades to have their full impact felt. If Frye had published his book later, he would have been more in time to break this stranglehold. Even without this credit, though, Frye may well stand as one of the most significant critics of the twentieth century. Arguably, *The Bush Garden* (1971), which collects the criticism on Canadian literature he wrote in the 1950s, is, at least in potential, the most revolutionary. The consensus at the time wanted no literature from countries previously unheralded as producing writers. Such an arrival of new literature would disrupt New Criticism's finely honed stasis. This is why the rise of post-colonial literature, as discussed in Chapter 5, was such a formal as well as a thematic challenge.

Harold Bloom: A New Kind of Reading

That we are today able to see Frye as more of a brilliant commentator and less of an overambitious classifier is probably due to the effect of a younger scholar crucially informed by Frye, Harold Bloom (1930–). Bloom's work of the late 1950s and 1960s was important for two reasons. It decisively refuted the canonical preferences of the New Critics. Bloom rejoiced in everyone the New Critics disliked—Shelley, William Blake, Walt Whitman. He made it safe to champion the Romantic and Victorian poets once again. Bloom excused himself from the customary deference towards Eliot (who in an odd way was also his great rival) and the by-then perfunctory acclamation of Donne. Bloom also, though, brought a style into criticism that admitted that critical interpretation was, in fact, an act of creation. Indeed, Bloom not only admitted it. He gloried in it. Criticism became a risky, exciting metapoetry. Bloom's subsequent emphasis on *misreading* and *the anxiety of influence* used relations between poets and other poets who came before them—*precursors*—to develop the idea of literary history as a place where passionate individuality mattered. Poets inevitably misread those who came before them, both out of built-in misunderstanding and from a psychic desire to carve out their own distinct identities. But this misreading was creative. It generated subjectivity, as the ground of a series of often dark textual-emotional "revisionary ratios" conducted on turbid but fiercely exhilarating psychic terrain. No method could smooth out this subjectivity, and thus there was no need to confine or corral it in order to make it resolved.

Also, Bloom was simply able to read a broader range of writers than the New Critics, to extend his sympathies across period, genre, and national origin and to interact meaningfully with both psychology and religion. Bloom, an unorthodox Jew, aligned the study of literature and that of religion far closer than had the New Critics, some of whom, such as Brooks, were committed Christians but expressed their religion only guardedly and tacitly in their critical work. Bloom's unabashed display of his Jewishness and his keen interest in Kabbalistic Jewish mysticism represented a challenge to the established consensus not only in orientation but also in mode. It was less an assertion of identity than of subjectivity. Bloom was the most gifted critic of his generation worldwide *because* he was able to be subjective without being merely personal. He showed how an intense individuality could also be a responsible mode of apprehending literary meaning.

Bloom's mode of treating a poem resembled that of the New Critics in that he would generously quote major portions of it or perhaps an entire poem within the body of the critical essay and then give a close, detailed analysis of it. Yet Bloom's reading practice differed from that of the New Critics. Whereas the New Critics would focus on verbal elements of the poem, its texture of language and why particular words had to be used to express thoughts in ways that could not be otherwise expressed—thereby avoiding the "heresy of paraphrase"—Bloom, above all, looked to what the poem was *saying*, how it made its argument. In his middle-period work, when questions of "influence" came in explicitly, he would often pause as if to hear what other voices of past poets within the tradition could be heard in the poem. For instance, in his analysis of "The Poems of Our Climate" by Wallace Stevens—a poem that gave Bloom's 1977 book on Stevens its title—he notes the phrase "cold porcelain" in the poem. Then, through first having the reader look at the entire poem itself on the page, Bloom elucidates how Stevens's wording, consciously or unconsciously, alludes to "cold pastoral" in John Keats's "Ode on a Grecian Urn," a poem written over a century before.[42] Bloom cherished the text. But he also thought poets had subjectivities and that a poetic subjectivity, both the author's and those of predecessor poets, could meaningfully inhabit the verbal contours of a text.

The New Critics feared that too much critical subjectivity would infringe upon the autonomy of the text. But Bloom, who emerged as the best-known advocate of a view of literature that rejected the sociological or political as a constitutive determinant, positioned *subjectivity* as a vehicle, if not a guarantor, of autonomy. Even Bloom's later emphasis on Shakespeare, at first glance a determined return to pre-theoretical modes, is work that could never have been done in the New Critical era. At mid-century, Shakespeare's abundance and multifariousness, too central to literature to displace, were seen as somewhat of an embarrassment, and therefore strangely undervalued. (In a way, this was Leavis on Dickens writ large.) Bloom, in many respects, returned to a nineteenth-century delight in Shakespeare that was chained by a twentieth-century caution and deliberate self-limitation.[43] The "Shakespearean fish" of the New Critics' beloved Yeats "swam the sea, far away from land," sundered from any sort of cathartic dancer-and-dance fusion. This abstention from bombast was a strong argument in favour of New Criticism, which certainly had the virtue of decorum. But decorum that becomes a constant ends up being wearisome and wan. Like the New York Intellectuals' abstention from political optimism, this New Critical reserve was meant to be prudent and measured in the wake of an era swept away by too many ideological fantasies. But, by the time Bloom began writing, intellectual ambition had learned to coexist with an egalitarian social atmosphere. Bloom, above all, represented this very American coalescence of cognitive daring and democratic instincts.

Roland Barthes: A New Kind of Writing

Like Bloom, Roland Barthes wrote a major book on the central playwright of his language's tradition—in Barthes's case, Jean Racine. Although Bloom's *Shakespeare: The Invention of the Human* came in 1998, late in his career, and Barthes's *On Racine* came early (1963), the two books have similar agendas. Both the erudite Bloom and the incisive Barthes strove to deliver "their" playwright from the mouldy clutches of the specialists and to reanimate his work as a locus of literary plenitude and eventfulness. In both cases, this process entailed opening up accumulated conventional wisdom and reading the plays as at once more self-conscious modes of representation and more urgent in their embodiment of flesh-and-blood individuals than previous criticism, more codifying than insightful, had managed. Barthes is associated with such phrases as "the pleasure of the text." He is often pictured as an irresponsible aesthete, with all the non-referential abandon of the New Critics but none of their cautious sobriety. Barthes, in fact, strongly historicizes Racine, seeing him as possessing a past mentality that we, as readers, must try to understand. Given that Racine himself was trying to come to terms with both classical and biblical pasts, as well as facing the contradiction, often pointed out by Bloom, that the West has drawn its intellectual sources from two such disparate bodies of thought, Barthes, as critic, is only doing with Racine what the playwright has already done with the subjects of his plays. This book was less shocking in substance than in manner. Barthes avowedly did not practise the genteel, decorous mode of biographical superficiality associated with the early twentieth-century critic Gustave Lanson. His insights into Racine showed a greater subjectivity and creative insight.

Barthes, in his 1971 essay "From Work To Text," detailed how a shift away from a narrow construction of the literary work can open up the field of analysis that literature crucially mediates. Traditionally, there was a literary work, and there was a set of forces outside it. The duty of the critic was to mark off the boundaries between the two and to guard the integrity of the art-object, whether in order to create a privileged sanctuary to protect the art-object from menacing outside forces or to make sure its subversiveness did not percolate out and create a more disorderly world. Barthes, by seeing the art-object not as a self-sufficient work but as an interactive text, elucidated the possibility of literature to ramify and extend outside of a narrow conception of "work" into a more plural and ample idea of "text." Though the New Critics had spoken of "the text" and had made that term an established one in literature classrooms, Barthes's usage of "text" was far broader. For Barthes, everything that could be read in a literary way could be a text.

His broader view of the "text" is one of the reasons that Barthes, the most pleasure-seeking of late twentieth-century theorists (even if he often sought after difficult, less conventional pleasures) could also be considered, in many ways, the father of modern cultural studies. One of the factors that disconcerts more traditionally educated people about recent literary theory is its interdisciplinary nature. Recent theory draws from many disciplines and applies itself to as many. It does not start or end in the literature department but fosters creative dialogues with fields and practices from architecture to sociology. In his early work *Mythologies* (1957), Barthes gives readings of various cultural and media images.[44] While exposing the way that the media and advertising seek to put across messages, he does not automatically dismiss these commercially or ideologically generated products. Rather, by reading them insightfully, he confers on them the same status, that of "text," that he, less controversially, accorded Racine's plays. The capacity of today's literary scholar to shift effortlessly from reading a reality TV show to reading a lyric poem, from analysing a NASCAR auto race to analysing Dickens, stems from the probing and path-breaking work of Barthes in the late 1950s. It is because of his concomitant elevation of various creations to the status of "text" and his insightful analysis of these texts as sites of resistance to stable signification that Barthes could be seen in France as diverting intellectual energy away from politics and yet, in the United States, as bringing a more politically committed cast to aesthetic response. Barthes epitomizes the way criticism after the 1950s became more interested in highlighting the self-referential and metafictive nature of texts. Witness Barthes's dissent from the more sociological Lanson. But Barthes also understood that literature and the outside world could not be antiseptically cordoned off from each other. This is how his "textuality" was very different from that of the New Critics.

Barthes had many different phases to his career. Moreover, in his essay "The Death of the Author," he sees the text not as a determinate unit of meaning but as a "multi-dimensional space" in which the reader has as much authority over what the text means as does the author. (This seems, on the face of it, similar to Wimsatt's intentional fallacy; the difference is that Barthes's conception of the text is multiple and not discrete.) Barthes cannot be pinned down to just one position. But, importantly, the critic who insists that the text cannot be pinned down to one position was himself an individual who wrote in a distinct, unmistakable style. His critical perspective was not just a dictum from above mandated by an impersonal machine of theory, as is so often alleged. And unlike Derrida and Foucault, Barthes *was* taken up by individuals with more belletristic connections, such as the poet and translator Richard Howard, who translated Barthes, and Susan Sontag, who wrote discerning and appreciative commentary on Barthes.[45]

Wayne C. Booth: A New Formal Perspective

Wayne C. Booth (1921–2005) is, at first glance, a less exciting critic than Bloom or Barthes. His immediate background was in the Chicago neo-Aristotelian school. The Chicago neo-Aristotelians, as represented by Richard McKeon, R.S. Crane, and Elder Olson, were often posited as the alternative to the New Critics and sometimes even (despite their unflashy writing style) as the "broader" alternative because of their advocacy of critical pluralism. As such, they even attracted the attention of no less than the young novelist Thomas Pynchon.[46] However—despite individual achievements such as Crane's essay on Henry Fielding's *Tom Jones*, which kept the eighteenth-century novel in view when Leavisism tended to sideline it—their major effect on literary criticism was through the work of Booth.[47] In *The Rhetoric of Fiction* (1961), Booth does more than provide the systematic reading of fiction that the New Critics, for all their desire to prevail in that genre the way they had in poetry, never did.[48] (Mark Schorer's 1948 essay "Technique as Discovery," much heralded at the time, now seems a non-starter.[49]) Booth decisively solved one of the most immediate problems of New Criticism: the insistence, mentioned in the context of Yeats's "Among School Children" on differentiating "the poet" and "the speaker" or, in fiction, "the author" and "the narrator." Booth introduced the concept of the "implied author." This author was not the same as the biographical individual who literally wrote the book. It was the author that the reader, while reading the book, sensed as the guiding presence behind the narrative. The concept provided a way to talk about intentionality in a book, or at least the

reader's experience of intentionality, without falling into biographical reductivism. Booth retained the undeniable insight of New Criticism—that a work of
art, once produced, is independent of its creator, that to publish something is
to make it public and no longer solely part of the author's private imagination.
The idea was similar to those assumed by critics of myths, who saw literature
as the instancing of archetypes not at the individual author's command, and to
those of Russian Formalist Vladimir Propp, who suggested that all basic narratives have the same succession of elements irrespective of author, setting, or
ideological purpose. (Although Propp's *Morphology of the Folktale* was first
published in 1928, it was not translated into English until 1958 and did not
reach the literary world until the 1970s.) But Booth, in a sense, went further. He
took the independence of the text and added the possibility of authorial direction without making that direction dependent on determinate personal identity.

Others among Booth's concepts have become part of common parlance, such
as the concept of "the unreliable narrator," the narrator who is not necessarily
telling the full truth or whose biases are seen by the implied author as flawed.
Many use the phrase without knowing Booth invented it. The "unreliable narrator," which seems a very deconstructive idea, actually is not, because it implies
there *is* such a thing as a reliable narrator, whereas deconstruction casts doubt
on finding a coherent meaning in language or a definitive reading of any text,
let alone a consistent and dependable narrator or author. (Also, Booth's terminology, in terms of theories of narrative, was later superseded by narratologists
such as Seymour Chatman, Gérard Genette, and Mieke Bal.) However, by decisively separating discourse and message, the idea of the "unreliable narrator"
goes well beyond a "resolved symbolic" paradigm.

Booth also opposed a popular maxim of the "resolved symbolic" era: "show,
not tell." Writers were supposed to be non-discursive, to concentrate all their
efforts into making an image that would evoke attitudes rather than explicitly
state them. Frank Kermode, in his *Romantic Image* (1957), traced this view
back to Romanticism and its rejection of rhetorical discourse.[50] Yet the New
Critics, as part of their general truncation of the Coleridgean symbol, had made
the image so autonomous as to be almost meaningless—"palpable and mute/As
a globed fruit," as Archibald MacLeish put it in his poem "Ars Poetica." Booth,
by insisting on a place for rhetoric in fiction, reintroduced discourse into narrative. Echoing Bloom's poetic preference for Shelley and Robert Browning over
Keats and Hopkins, Booth's revaluation of rhetoric meant that the palpable and
tangible was no longer necessarily privileged over the rambling and capacious.[51]
The need of the "resolved symbolic" for image to prevail over discourse was
no longer so urgent. Indeed, the word "discourse" itself, once indicative of all
that had to be cropped away from literature for the text to be salient, began
to re-emerge. "Discourse" became the all-purpose term for any sort of literary
communication, both inside and outside texts. This emphasis on "discourse"
represented a return to the genuinely Coleridgean vision of the imagination as

"one life," threading together many different constituents without flattening them into unanimity.

Theory's Idiosyncratic Companions

Response to the "resolved symbolic" was idiosyncratic, plural, and widespread in the late 1950s and early 1960s. Critics were, to use Denis Donoghue's felicitous terms, both epireaders, such as Booth and Bloom, and graphireaders, such as Barthes. According to Donoghue, an epireader believed that texts embodied the moral ideas of an imagined human voice and could communicate them, and a graphireader privileged language above this voice.[52] Critics with diametrically opposed views of how writing related to experience were united nonetheless in their desire to go beyond the "resolved symbolic." Even more independent critics such as Christopher Ricks, Helen Vendler, and William H. Pritchard, all ingenious close readers who were sharply opposed to or indifferent towards theory, flourished in theory's era, arguably more so than they would have in that of New Criticism. These three critics were much more adept and interesting close readers than any of the New Critics except Blackmur and, if you count him, Empson. And, although they dissented strongly from most theoretical assumptions, they prospered in an age that permitted greater idiosyncrasy than the previous climate. What became literary theory for the three decades after the 1950s was simply the extension, systematization, and logical consequence of this idiosyncrasy. Theory was not suddenly interjected into the cultural system by aliens from outer space. It came out of a diagnosable set of historical processes and because of the existence of a few notable individuals. Bloom, Barthes, and Booth were not systematizers. Though they formulated ideas and terms that became household words in literary academia, they were never fitted into a prefabricated mould, and they never had disciples in the way that Derrida or Foucault did. The presence in the post-1950s intellectual constellation of all five of these thinkers—Barthes, Bloom, Booth, Foucault, and Derrida—all very different, presents a common thread. All five defied the potential arrest the "resolved symbolic" threatened to put on literary study. All five brought new, fresh viewpoints into literary criticism that made it one of the most intellectually eventful disciplines in the latter half of the century. All five were, whether they acknowledged it or not, part of a new, postmodern moment in letters.

The systematizers outside the world of letters—Derrida and Foucault—had a more concentrated impact than the freer spirits who had trained within literary studies and drastically innovated the field. Yet the world of literary criticism needed both types. Derrida's dismantling of the certainties of linguistic meaning and Foucault's reconception of the relations of power and organization in the culture of the modern West, to be explored in the following two chapters, may appear less opaque and more human when seen in the light of other critics whose influence was equally liberating. Theory may, in its heyday, have become jargon-filled and intolerant. However, this book will argue that theory's ultimate effect on intellectual history has been emancipatory.

Theories either have the power to revise themselves, to respond to new situations, or to fail entirely. That we have seen so many theories come into view in literature departments in the past fifty years does not mean the ones that faded from view are inherently flawed. It means they lacked an academic constituency, lost the one they had, or succeeded so well as to become beside the point. The third option is one of the most frequent. Often, indeed, the series of theories that successively dominated the academic landscape seemed like corporate products pre-programmed for planned obsolescence. This was not so. Yet the parade of theory after theory can be bewildering unless understood in its historical and intellectual context. That is what this book seeks to do.

NOTES

1   See Valentine Cunningham, *Reading After Theory* (London: Blackwell, 2002).

2   See Wilfrido Corral and Daphne Patai, *Theory's Empire* (New York: Columbia University Press, 2004) for a trenchant example of such an assessment.

3   Much was made, for instance, of the *New York Times* television critic Virginia Heffernan, who attained a PhD in English from Harvard, foregoing an academic career in order to write general-interest journalism (http://www.mediabistro.com/articles/cache/a57.asp). The standard post-1990 media reference to deconstruction saw it as a foolish, sesquipedalian game that tried to entrap its audience in a maze, from which only the ingenious could emerge. As Janet Maslin said in her review of Walter Kirn's memoir *Lost in the Meritocracy*, "He learned to enjoy tossing the vocabulary of deconstructionism back at his teachers. He brought his SAT whiz's skill to the deployment of 'liminal,' 'valuational,' 'heuristic' and 'praxis.' He felt empowered to attack a Western canon that he had never really read, skipping 'straight from ignorance to revisionism'" (see "Whiz Kid in College, Hold That Attitude!" *New York Times*, 18 May 2009: C1). Deconstruction here seems a phase society has outgrown rather than a still-resonant episode in contemporary intellectual history, and this is generally how the journalistic media has tended to cover the "story" of late twentieth-century theory.

4   It is unfortunate that, like most surveys of recent theory, this book cannot go back further and look at the criticism of the 1920s and 1930s, if only to point out that scholars such as Vernon Louis Parrington and Van Wyck Brooks had, as intellectual historians, many of the virtues ascribed to the public critics of the 1950s; that New Humanists such as Irving Babbitt and Paul Elmer More, though attitudinally stodgier than the New Critics, exceeded them in breadth of reading; and that, in formal or rhetorical terms, the work of Percy Lubbock and the early criticism of Kenneth Burke did far more than the 1950s New Critics to extend formal analysis out of the narrow range of lyric poetry.

5   Svetlana Boym, *The Future of Nostalgia* (New York: Basic Books, 2001) xviii.

6   For the general background of US English department history, see Gerald Graff, *Professing Literature* (Chicago: University of Chicago Press, 1989). For a particularly discerning social critique of the New Critics, see John Fekete, *The Critical Twilight: Explorations in the Ideology of Anglo-American Literary Theory from Eliot to McLuhan* (London: Routledge, 1977). For a sympathetic biography of the greatest of the New Critics, which gives a full and generous assessment of his critical vision, see Mark Royden Winchell, *Cleanth Brooks and the Rise of Modern Criticism* (Charlottesville: University of Virginia Press, 1996). It is interesting that, although the New Critics identified themselves as Democrats, the figures in the next generation who are interested in them in a positive way tend to be those who seem more in the conservative camp like Winchell. Of course, transitions in the nature of the Democratic Party and the politics of the south lie behind this shift, although Winchell makes sure to remind the reader that Brooks, until his dying day, considered the Republican Party far too capitalist.

7   Elliot Perlman, *Seven Types of Ambiguity* (New York: Riverhead, 2004) 202. Perlman's title is a deliberate play on William Empson's critical book of the same name.

8   It is striking that the New Critics really did not have an international audience at the time and were not translated into other languages. In this era, American fiction and poetry were sweeping the world!

This discrepancy between the fame of American literature and the relative obscurity of New Criticism is worth noting.

9   Paul de Man, "Semiology and Rhetoric," *Diacritics* 3.3 (1973): 27–33.

10 De Man, "Semiology" 30.

11 See Rosemary C. LoDato, *Beyond the Glitter: The Language of Gems in Modernista Writers Rubén Darío, Ramón Del Valle-Inclán, and José Asunción Silva* (Lewisburg: Bucknell UP, 1999).

12 Samuel Taylor Coleridge, *The Statesman's Manual* (London: Gale and Fenner, 1816).

13 The Holocaust and Nazism were not mentioned as much by these thinkers, although clearly World War II was a major part of the horizon of their life experience.

14 Percy Bysshe Shelley, *The Defense of Poetry*, ed. Albert Cook (Boston: Ginn, 1904) 24.

15 Seamus Heaney, "The Mud Vision," *The Haw Lantern* (New York: Farrar, Straus, and Giroux, 1987) 48.

16 Donald Barthelme's short story, "City Life," contains the line "The System Cannot Withstand Close Scrutiny" that suggests New Critical techniques of close reading are potentially revolutionary. See Donald Barthelme, *Sixty Stories* (New York: Penguin Books, 2003) 147. Moreover, Homer Hogan's *The Poetry of Relevance* (New York: Methuen, 1970) applied New Critical standards as it compared rock lyrics and political protest songs to traditional, tightly knit poems.

17 Gail Pool, *Faint Praise: The Plight of Book Reviewing in America* (Columbia: University of Missouri Press, 2007) goes thoroughly into the strengths and limitations of the book review as a genre. As Pool's title implies, the reviewing culture in the United Kingdom and Australia is very different: it is less genteel and more combative there than in America, and, interestingly, with a more dynamic relationship to the academy, though not necessarily a closer one.

18 Noah Isenberg, "Theory Out Of Bounds," *Raritan* 21.1 (2007): 82–103.

19 David Lee Rubin, for instance, speaks of New Criticism's "dense, resonant, and potentially unifying relationship' of part to whole" (*Virginia Quarterly Review* 84.3 [2008]: 287) and Eric Bennett, on page 288 of the same issue of this journal, which was largely written by and oriented towards younger, belletristic scholars, says the New Critics and New York Intellectuals "loved the same authors." The first comment flattens the New Critics' complicated relationship to Romanticism and particularly to Coleridge; the second observation ignores the fact that the New York Intellectuals did not particularly read John Donne, and the New Critics did not particularly read the tracts about Stalinism and Trotskyism that often preoccupied the New York Intellectuals.

20 See, for instance, William Logan, "Forward into the Past: Reading the New Critics," *Virginia Quarterly Review* 84.2 (2008): 252–59.

21 One wonders if theory had a bit of a branding problem—perhaps a superior press agent presenting the human side of theorists would have staved off the revived cult of the 1950s critics.

22 See the (London) *Times* obituary of Kazin, 23 June 1998.

23 Alan Filreis, in *Counterrevolution of the Word: The Conservative Attack on Modern Poetry, 1945–1960* (Chapel Hill: University of North Carolina Press, 2007), points out that many intellectual figures far more "traditional" than the New Critics were often ignored in conventional accounts of the period.

24 See Alan Wald, *The New York Intellectuals: The Rise and Decline of the Anti-Stalinist Left from the 1930s to the 1980s* (Chapel Hill: University of North Carolina Press, 1987).

25 Brian Boyd, *Vladimir Nabokov: The American Years* (Princeton, NJ: Princeton University Press, 1991) 303.

26 Even philosophers such as Martin Heidegger, who were hugely influential in the general culture in the 1950s, only entered literary criticism in the mid-1960s, and here eventual "deconstructionists" such as de Man, Miller, and Geoffrey Hartman were important. Other thinkers associated with or taken up by existentialism, such as Jean-Paul Sartre, Søren Kierkegaard, or Friedrich Nietzsche, were far less influential in 1950s literary criticism than their general cultural currency at the time would suggest.

27 The same was true of Maurice Blanchot, who was advocated by Jacques Derrida, and of the American rhetorical and sociological critic Kenneth Burke, underappreciated until taken up by figures such as Harold Bloom, Fredric Jameson, and the historically inclined Americanist Frank Lentricchia.

28 Francis Mulhern, *The Moment of "Scrutiny"* (London: Verso, 1981) is still the best critical survey of Leavis's ideas, though it is complemented by Gary Day's more sympathetic *Re-Reading Leavis: Culture and Literary Criticism* (London: Macmillan, 1996). Day points out that Leavis's perspective is now

"easy to caricature" (233) but that his achievement was complex and exacting. It is a mark of how far Leavis's star had fallen by the beginning of the twenty-first century that he was not included in the first edition of *The Norton Anthology of Theory and Criticism*, ed. Vincent Leitch (New York: Norton, 2001).

29 See F.R. Leavis, *The Great Tradition* (London: Chatto and Windus, 1948).

30 See Ian McKillop and Richard Storer, eds., *F.R. Leavis: Essays and Documents* (New York: Continuum, 2005) 188.

31 F.R. Leavis, *The Critic as Anti-Philosopher: Essays and Papers*, G. Singh, ed. (Chicago: Ivan R. Dee, 1998).

32 Onsucheka Jemie Chinweizu and Ihechukwu Madubuike, *Toward the Decolonization of African Literature* (Washington, DC: Howard University Press, 1983).

33 See Alfred Kazin, *Bright Book Of Life* (Boston: Little, Brown. 1973).

34 F.R. Leavis and Michael Yudkin, *Two Cultures* (New York: Pantheon, 1963).

35 It is notable that the most systematic "deconstructionist" in the United States, J. Hillis Miller, started out as, and to some extent remained, a Victorianist in his core professional identification.

36 Américo Castro, *The Spaniards* (Berkeley, CA: University of California Press, 1971).

37 See D.W. Robertson, Jr., *A Preface to Chaucer: Studies in Medieval Perspectives* (Princeton, NJ: Princeton University Press, 1962). For an analysis of Robertson in his own milieu, see Lee Patterson, *Negotiating the Past: The Historical Understanding of Medieval Literature* (Madison: University of Wisconsin Press, 1987).

38 See Rosemond Tuve, *Elizabethan and Metaphysical Imagery* (Chicago: University of Chicago Press, 1947). For a sharply critical assessment of Tuve, which points out many of her limitations, see Richard Strier, *Resistant Structures: Particularity, Radicalism, and Renaissance Texts* (Berkeley: University of California Press, 1995).

39 Ulrich Beck, *Risk Society: Towards a New Modernity* (New York: Sage, 1992) 155.

40 Chinua Achebe, "An Image Of Africa: Racism in Conrad's Heart of Darkness," *The Norton Anthology of Literary Theory and Criticism*, ed. Vincent Leitch (New York: Norton, 2001) 1781–93. Originally, Achebe's article was published in *The Massachusetts Review*, 1975. That the latter is a leading belletristic journal, which has historically included literary as well as scholarly writing and has mixed creative writing and essays with cultural commentary, shows how Achebe's essay was a sharp radicalization, not a total repudiation, of the characteristic practices of the "pre-theory" generation of humanities intellectuals.

41 Intriguingly, both Achebe and de Man were associated with Bard College in upstate New York at different points in their careers. Another link is that the title of Achebe's most famous book, *Things Fall Apart*, comes from another famous poem by Yeats. Still another connection (not to Achebe, but to Conrad) is that de Man came from Belgium, colonizer of the Congo about which Conrad wrote.

42 Harold Bloom, *Wallace Stevens and the Poems of Our Climate* (Ithaca: Cornell University Press, 1977) 141.

43 Harold Bloom, *Shakespeare: The Invention of the Human* (New York: Riverhead, 1998). Bloom's pivotal work on influence was largely unfolded in a tetralogy of books published in the 1970s, *The Anxiety of Influence* (New York: Oxford University Press, 1973), *A Map of Misreading* (New York: Oxford University Press, 1975), *Kabbalah and Criticism* (New York: Seabury, 1976), and *Poetry and Repression* (New Haven: Yale University Press, 1976). These were augmented by his essays in *The Ringers in the Tower* (Chicago: University of Chicago Press 1971) and in the *Figures of Capable Imagination* (New York: Seabury, 1974), by his Wellek Library lectures published as *The Breaking of the Vessels* (Chicago: University of Chicago Press, 1982), and by the single-author books on Yeats (New York: Oxford University Press, 1970) and Stevens (Ithaca: Cornell University Press, 1977). The capstone was the 1982 essay collection *Agon* (New York: Oxford University Press, 1982). For an overview of Bloom's work both early and late, see Roy Sellars and Graham Allen, eds., *The Salt Companion to Harold Bloom* (Cambridge: Salt, 2007).

44 Roland Barthes, *Mythologies*, trans. Annette Lavers (New York: Hill and Wang, 1972).

45 See, for instance, Jonathan Gottschall, "Measure for Measure," *The Boston Globe* 11 May 2008, who speaks, incongruously, of Barthes's "swaggering authority."

46 See Thomas Pynchon's introduction to *Slow Learner* (Boston: Little, Brown, 1984), in which he states that people at Cornell University in upstate New York in the late 1950s looked towards Chicago, even for its neo-Aristotelians, as a comparative hotbed of cultural stimulation.

47 R.S. Crane, "The Plot of Tom Jones," *Journal of General Education* 4 (1950): 112–30.

48 Wayne C. Booth, *The Rhetoric of Fiction* (Chicago: University of Chicago Press, 1961). Booth's unapologetic foregrounding of rhetoric anticipated a large-scale revival of ancient rhetoric and its emulation in the medieval and Renaissance worlds, as seen in the work of Richard Lanham; his *Style: An Anti-Textbook* (New Haven: Yale University Press, 1974) was in many ways a rebuttal to the standard New Critical idea of style. Lanham's perspective was instrumental in and indicative of the return to prominence of rhetoric, which manifested itself both in high theory and in the very different but equally broadening expansion of rhetoric and composition programs in universities, whose openness to greater political contingency as a result of their augmented rhetorical flexibility in many ways told the story of theory in a nutshell. Gerald Graff's *Poetic Statement and Critical Dogma* (Evanston, IL: Northwestern University Press, 1970) was another book that attempted to reintroduce argument aid discourse to criticism. Lee T. Lemon's *The Partial Critics* (Oxford: Oxford University Press, 1965) was an interesting attempt to group the New Critics with others holding manifestly different views but all being spiritedly contentious; had it included a few more European, linguistically influenced figures, it may well have burst the bounds of "the resolved symbolic."

49 Mark Schorer, "Technique as Discovery," *The Hudson Review* 1.1 (Spring 1948): 67–87. Schorer's essay was, however, valuable for calling attention to Emily Brontë's *Wuthering Heights*, a text belittled by the Leavisite consensus, but (more than *Jane Eyre*) beloved of the New Critical era. As Booth points out, the New Critical power couple of Allen Tate and Caroline Gordon also wrote many essays enunciating, though less subtly, Schorer's position on how fiction operated artistically.

50 Frank Kermode, *Romantic Image* (London: Routledge, 1957).

51 The word "revaluation" is, ironically, associated with Leavisism.

52 See Denis Donoghue, *Ferocious Alphabets* (New York: Columbia University Press, 1984).

CHAPTER ONE

Foucault
DECONSTRUCTING CATEGORIES

The Basics of Theory

Theory, as such, is any kind of abstract knowledge or any kind of general principles that are applied to particular circumstances. In disciplines from music to physics, there has long been a theoretical element and a place for theory in the field, even if it was recognized that practice would generally carry the day. Literary study only really started in the late nineteenth century. Before that, what language had been studied in the universities were the classical and sacred languages—Greek, Latin, Hebrew. The modern languages, including English, were a new academic phenomenon and, as such, had no theory. Whereas even history departments in the 1940s and 1950s had courses on historiography and the theory of history (I say "even" because history, as practised, is usually so empirical a discipline), literature departments may have had a seminar on critical techniques but no "theory" courses.

For reasons discussed in the preface, for example, the impasse of "the resolved symbolic," literary study in the late 1960s needed theory. That literary studies found theory in the work of certain French thinkers was neither inevitable nor necessary. Intellectual history, like history generally, is full of such odd turns. As we have seen, there were other sets of thinkers—the Russian formalists, the Frankfurt theorists, Kenneth Burke—who could have played the role French theorists did. But French theorists ended up influencing English literary studies because, among other reasons, the Anglo-American disciplines that would have most obviously accepted them, such as philosophy or sociology, were already dominated by other theories—logical positivism and functionalism—with very different emphases than the new French thinkers had. Perhaps even smaller contingencies were at work. Had Jacques Derrida not attended the 1966 conference at Johns Hopkins University, where he encountered Paul de

Man, literary theory might well have taken a different course. As it happened, *these particular French theorists* (Foucault and Derrida) came to dominate literary theory in the English-speaking world for the remainder of the twentieth century.

French theory embodied the extension of the practice of literary criticism to include the application of philosophical frameworks to textual circumstances. In a way cognate with Bloom's and Booth's emphasis on argumentation, theory widened criticism's reach to include more abstract or philosophical ideas, often calling upon philosophers from Plato to Nietzsche as well as modern movements such as Marxism or psychoanalysis. But theory was less interested in abstract ideas than in threading these ideas through the practice of reading literature. This is why "theory," despite the word's abstract implication, can be so close to "literary criticism." Consequently, theory presented less intellectual novelty than *methodological* revolution. Many of the basic principles and sets of intellectual propositions sued by French theorists descended from critiques of longstanding assumptions made from the mid-nineteenth to early twentieth centuries by Karl Marx, Friedrich Nietzsche, and Sigmund Freud. Marx's sense of bourgeois society as a historical formation whose continuance was not inevitable, Nietzsche's sense of absolute truths as a projection out of a larger world of perspectives and affectivities, Freud's vision of the conventional self being constituted by a welter of inward biological and psychic drives, all were vital to the French theorists' critiques of inherited notions. All of these thinkers sought to subvert appearances and not take for granted what was on the surface—thus rubbing against the instinctual approaches of "the resolved symbolic." They felt free to bring ideas and issues not patently in a book to bear on how they read it. So the general stance espoused by theorists, one critical of and resistant to the obvious, had its basis in the work of these earlier thinkers. What the theorists brought instead of new ideas, though, were new methodologies, and especially a new predilection for bringing different disciplinary languages into touch with each other. Importantly, although literary theory was applied *to* literature, it was not strictly, or even primarily, *of* literature. It did not draw all of its examples or its nodal figures from a strictly literary milieu as, for instance, New Criticism did. Literary theory was *interdisciplinary*, soliciting insights from philosophy, the social sciences, and psychology. In turn, once theory became popular in literature departments, it was exported to many other humanistic and social science disciplines, from art history to criminology.

Nietzsche, Marx, and Freud were "for" something—Nietzsche for his own idiosyncratic sense of subjectivity, Freud for the clinical method of psychoanalysis, Marx for socialism and the empowerment of the proletariat. Their critique of existing institutions promoted positive principles, although far more visibly in Freud and Marx's than in Nietzsche's case, which is why Nietzsche, of the three, was the greatest influence on both Michel Foucault and Jacques Derrida.

Foucault and Derrida took all the critique of the earlier thinkers and sharpened it, all the while not advocating any positive alternative. This lack of a determinate ideological framework led them to be accused of cynicism, but it also left them untethered to any sort of master set of beliefs. Furthermore, Marx, Freud, and Nietzsche operated as or were perceived as being social prophets. Derrida and Foucault, on the other hand, were not gurus for the general public. Their effect was within, not outside, academia.

Foucault and Derrida were the two "big names" of the theoretical era. They were the two thinkers whose names evoked the most cheers or shudders in the corridors of academic departments. Yet, in the 1980s, Foucault and Derrida had very different images and constituencies in the English-speaking world. Foucault was perceived as more socially probing and politically relevant, whereas Derrida was seen as preoccupied exclusively with language.[1] In other words, Foucault's name was used as shorthand for socially oriented perspectives, and Derrida's name was used as shorthand for perspectives that favoured questions of form and figuration. This formula underrated the complexity of both thinkers.[2] It also overstated their opposition. Though each thinker has his very distinct emphasis, the effect of both on the course of intellectual inquiry was strikingly parallel.

The work of both Derrida and Foucault far exceeded the limits established by "the resolved symbolic" and decisively outsoared its limits. Both thinkers sought to tear down the basic structures of intellectual work, as they then existed. But both were not narrowly partisan. Their target was not the immediate academic establishment or the practices of the generation before them. They took aim at the entire way intellectual inquiry had been conducted in the West, certainly since the beginning of modernity and perhaps since the beginnings of European civilization. They did not wish to do intellectual business as usual. As Foucault says in a brilliant quotation from *The Archaeology of Knowledge*, "We must ask ourselves what purpose is ultimately served by this suspension of all the accepted unities, if, in the end, we return to the unities that we pretended to question at the outset."[3] Deconstruction is different from immediate, polemical critique. Derrida and Foucault were not out to change the system directly; indeed, they often pointed out that direct attempts to change the system or to redefine human nature, such as Rousseau's philosophy or that of nineteenth-century prison reformers, ended up reinforcing or reaffirming the status quo. Derrida and Foucault sought instead to reframe the terms by which systems are set up and understood. In this way, they were very different from other French contemporaries such as Henri Lefebvre and Gilles Deleuze who more directly protested against the shackles of bourgeois modernity and proposed radical, if hardly simple, solutions to the plight these shackles signified. Foucault and Derrida, conversely, tried to rethink the entire notion of categories. In a sense, their acknowledgement that this reconception could never be done is, in its daring redefinition of the effects of language, the most emancipatory thing about them.

Introducing Michel Foucault

Michel Foucault, the son of a prominent physician, was born in 1926 in the French provincial city of Poitiers.[4] Much of Foucault's work is preoccupied with medicine and with issues of sex, soul, and body that traditionally have been understood as under the aegis of medicine.[5] But Foucault's work undermined the ability of medicine to see itself as neutral, technical, and disinterested. Psychiatry, for instance, could not provide a greater insight into the human soul as such than did ancient or medieval psychologies. Yes, the methods were different. But those different methods described a different set of battleground assumptions, not a reality that was being apprehended with greater keenness of knowledge. And psychiatry, for Foucault, should not be used as a punitive doctrine to discipline those who did not agree with the world's current dominant paradigm.[6]

Foucault was trained as a philosopher, oriented intellectually toward sociology, and gained early practical experience in psychology.[7] Although his concepts strayed far from the usual routines of modern sociological thought, certain traits of the sociological imagination remained with Foucault throughout his career. Although he did massive and diligent work in archives, Foucault was never confined to specifics, nor is his writing immersed in documentary citations. He is prone to generalizations in a sociological mode. In addition, he writes in a French tradition that often assumes allusions or tacitly hints at a previous reading rather than explicitly footnoting and citing sources as English-language scholarship is prone to do. The generalizations Foucault makes can always be nullified by pointing to certain examples. Yet, as in sociology in general, the assertions Foucault makes cannot be invalidated by one contrary fact. Indeed, Foucault's generalities are not intended to govern specifics the way previous generalities, such as those associated with the ritualizing systems of Hegel or even Marx, were intended to do. They are intended to provoke the reader to further thought and to lead to self-awareness about the ways and means by which generalizations are made in the first place.

Yet Foucault was not *just* a sociologist. In fact, no recent thinker has ranged across so many disciplines (albeit, he was sceptical of the very idea of disciplinary boundaries). At different times, Foucault wrote on history, literature, ethics, pedagogy, art history, medicine, sexuality, criminology, psychiatry, politics, philosophy, religion, economics, and the history and philosophy of science. Foucault's influences were diverse ones also, for example, such avant-garde, twentieth-century French literary figures as André Breton, Georges Bataille, and Maurice Blanchot.[8] Gaston Bachelard was a particularly important precursor, as he combined thinking about science with poetic and literary imaginings in a way that foreshadowed the breadth of Foucault's work.[9] Foucault was also influenced by French Hegelians such as Alexandre Kojève, Jean Wahl, and Jean Hippolyte, whose thought had important reverberations in later transatlantic writing: Kojève's reading of Hegel influenced the political writer Francis Fukuyama's idea of the "end of history" in the post-Soviet world; Hippolyte and Wahl are scrutinized in the first book of Judith Butler, whose theories of gender performativity will be examined in Chapter 6.[10]

Thus, Foucault did not spring out of nowhere, a ferocious monster condemning all previous modes of thought and language to obsolescence. Foucault's own writing, though far more academic in tone, has a quality of experimental exuberance paralleling the work of these earlier French writers and scholars. Foucault saw modern experimental poetry as a new reshuffling of the ways that language and thought had been talked about in previous eras, and he viewed its inventiveness as culturally significant. Foucault, indeed, was part of the French literary world. When apprised in 1984 that Foucault was dying, René Char, the dean of French poetry, famed for his sparse, elliptical verse, asked that a poem of his be read in Foucault's honour.[11] In France, theory and poetry could be comrades in arms not inveterate enemies. Foucault's repudiation of the language of traditional humanistic inquiry did not mean he jettisoned the ideals of intellectual practice exemplified by those in the senior generation whom he admired. Foucault, perhaps surprisingly, helped bridge the gap between "The Two Cultures" (to use the terms of the Snow-Leavis debate), the breach between science and the humanities, technocracy and creative passion that many discerned in European culture in the 1950s and 1960s.

Foucault's first two books, *Madness and Civilization* (1961) and *The Birth of the Clinic* (1963) concerned medicine and psychiatry. *Madness and Civilization* started out by wondering why so many more people were classified as insane in the modern era than in the Middle Ages. His research uncovered that, whereas the segmentation of the sick from the well in the Middle Ages was performed according to physical health, as demonstrated by leper houses and other refuges for the sick, in the 1600s, the leper houses waned, and the insane, not the physically ill, became the principal subjects of physical confinement. The insane, argued Foucault, were among the abject of society; they were despised outcasts. There was no residue from the medieval Christian idea of the holy fool. The insane were the new lepers, thought to be unclean and, in at least a moral sense, contagious.

In the nineteenth century, though, a new wrinkle emerges in the treatment of the insane: the beginnings of an ethic of compassionate care. The insane were no longer reviled by the sane but treated by doctors. The goal became not to exclude them but to rehabilitate them. Earlier medical historians had hailed this development as an unequivocal advance. Foucault asks, though, that we not take these social developments so innocently. The treatment and rehabilitation of the insane may have been less cruel than the former regime. But the insane were still being told who and what they were by other people. They were being certified as insane by certain medical and governmental authorities that had the power to impose these categories on people. Foucault is, in effect, asking a series of questions. Just what are these means of classification? Who practises them? Who gains by them? Why does society, in different ways, seem to define and ostracize certain populations, thereby purging them from the mainstream of those who are permitted to be self-governing?

Though Foucault gives a history of madness in this book, he is not just saying that the way madness was understood changed from age to age, as certain styles in painting, music, or literature change from century to century, period to period. Rather, he was saying that these changes in, for example, how the insane are classified call us to understand the power of those who are responsible for classification. How and why do they classify? If different eras do things differently, who makes sure things are done differently?

Foucault continued researching the history of psychiatry in *The Birth of the Clinic*. In this book, Foucault asserts that modern medicine began around 1800, in the wake of the French Revolution and against the background of rising capitalism. It also was enabled by a change in perspective towards the body.[12] ("The body" as a critical term of art in postmodern theory largely came out of Foucault's thought.) Before modern medicine, body mutilation after death was disapproved of, as it infringed upon a bodily integrity connected with the Christian doctrine of bodily resurrection.[13] Because God could raise bodies whole, it was not man's prerogative to take them apart. This view changed after 1800 or so, when doctors in training began to use cadavers in order to gain knowledge of human anatomy. God had been ousted from authority over the body, and medicine had taken His place. This shift either caused or coincided with a quantum growth in the prestige of the medical profession. Doctors now possessed the aura of doing good works that had formerly attached to priests.

Again, Foucault is not merely making the historical observation that science "replaced" religion or that doctors assumed the role of priests. Many books preceding *The Birth of the Clinic* had made these sorts of observations. Foucault makes two innovations. First, as always, he asks that the reader not automatically see this development as a sign of progress, even though to some temperaments it may at first seem to be. Foucault asked that we look at the transition from religion to science from a particular vantage point: that of the body. In passing from the sphere of divine control to that of human supervision, bodies became able to be practised upon, to be subject, either when living or dead, to the incisions and operations of medical authorities. Medical professionals gained control of the body. By being under their care, the body came under their sphere of expert influence.

Foucault is not out to demonize doctors. Nor does he see the medical profession as simply an instrument of capitalist control. This point was missed by many Foucauldians in the 1980s and 1990s, who rifled through literature and denominated every medical character as an instance of a controlling, instrumental approach to life. This tactic was suitable enough for a doctor such as Sir William Bradshaw in Virginia Woolf's *Mrs. Dalloway*, but it was less apt for more ambiguous figures, such as Tertius Lydgate in George Eliot's *Middlemarch*. Foucault agreed that, after the advent of modernity, individuals were better cared for in illness. But Foucault did demand that we see medical authority as neither natural nor neutral. Institutions such as hospitals or prisons are capable of sustaining self-interest and do not operate neutrally for the greater good, as their rhetoric may allege or as even the people confined to them may believe.

One sees how this approach was different from that of the "resolved symbolic." Yet, in fact, there was considerable continuity, and it is not for nothing that Foucault matured in the decade of the 1950s. Foucault's writings generated two seemingly contradictory, but in fact mutually informative, procedural approaches to intellectual history. On the one hand, Foucault understands that certain things are only sayable at certain times. In this way, he is very close to historically minded anglophone political scientists such as Sheldon Wolin or Quentin Skinner. Foucault affirms that practices of a certain period tally within the terms of that period in a way that just seeing the past from the vantage point of the contemporary inevitably gets wrong. On the other hand, Foucault was always insisting on stubborn continuities between periods. He was particularly adamant that humans cannot categorically disclaim pasts they would like to jettison: paganism always subtends Christianity; the medieval is always a palpable vestige in the modern. In this way, Foucault was very much on the same page as the New Critics, who opposed romanticism and optimistic liberalism partially because those movements disdained any sense of the past. But Foucault differed from them, and from many previous European conservatives and anti-modernists, by not sentimentalizing the past either. If Marxists, in an odd way, were nostalgic about the future, and existentialists, in an even odder way, were nostalgic about the present, then conservatives, in seeing every moment as open to clarifying personal authenticity, were not alone in manifesting nostalgia. Foucault was pessimistic about past, future—and present. But, within the grain of his work, there is a stubborn secondary optimism that diligent research and a capacious reckoning with what is afoot in the world can generate at least temporary insight.

This reserve of optimism, in other words, was made possible by Foucault's multidisciplinarity. Foucault, as read in the English-speaking academy, compensated for the New Critics' unwillingness to look beyond the text and that of the New York Intellectuals and Leavisites to do so only in empirical or moralistic ways. Foucault's systematic tendencies brought all of contemporary thought into the orbit of literature and sanctioned the use of nearly anything as a spur and background to produce a stimulating literary reading, one that, furthermore, was no longer bound strictly to textual explication.

It is in the subtitle of *The Birth of the Clinic*, "The Archaeology of Medical Perception," that Foucault uses for the first time a word often associated with him, *archaeology*. Foucault is being metaphorical here. He is not using "archaeology" in the literal sense of digging for cultural artefacts of the past. He is talking about probing beneath layers of cultural meaning, or, as he would say, discourse. Rather than just understanding the history of medical perception in a straightforward, sequential way, Foucault wants us to dig beneath the surface, to excavate the meanings and contradictions available at any point in the past archives of medical knowledge. Yet Foucault does not want to let us forget the ordinary-language meaning of the word "archaeology" entirely. Archaeology is often associated with anthropology, the study of culture itself and not just of a culture's material remains. In his next book, *The Order of Things* (1966), Foucault will call for a freeing of cultural study from its "anthropological sleep," from an excessive concentration on man as maker of meaning. Emphasizing the more material practice of archaeology, which seeks for mineral substance rather than affirming humanistic absolutes, is a gesture to the new kind of inquiry into the past that Foucault wishes to undertake.

The Order of Things and Foucault's New Cultural History

The Order of Things was Foucault's breakthrough book. With it, he became a celebrity and was reviled by no less than Jean-Paul Sartre, world-famous as the great sage of existentialism, who may have felt some jealousy at the spotlight being assumed by a man a generation younger than himself. Sartre called Foucault "the last bourgeois man." But despite this castigation, the book was a public sensation in France. (Its original French title was *Les mots et les choses*, which translated to "words and things," but Foucault came to prefer the title under which it was translated into English.) *The Order of Things* both attracted notice and ruffled feathers in the United States. George Steiner, a similarly ambitious and brilliant but more traditional thinker, admitted Foucault's accomplishment but withheld full praise in his examination of the book for *The New York Times Book Review*.[14] The controversy and acclaim the book generated was a result of the daring way in which Foucault retraces intellectual history in this book. Notably, the book's Library of Congress classification number is AZ101 pertaining to the "history of scholarship and learning." Most of the other books in this classification are second-order compendia, archives of scholarship that are more bibliographical and encyclopaedic than interpretive. (The A classification as a whole is dominated by encyclopaedias.) One might imagine the book more conventionally in the CB (History of Civilization) classification or in the Q (General Science) classification. This latter rubric is occupied by Thomas Kuhn's *The Structure of Scientific Revolutions*, with which Foucault's book is often compared.[15] Not only is Foucault's book hard to pin down, not only does it vault between typically hardened categories, but it also turns the process of classifying knowledge inside out. Foucault does not stress what is classified and sees the process of classification as a handmaiden. He focuses our attention, above all, on the *process of classification itself*. He tries to get behind the structure of this intellectual discipline as routinely practised, thus the importance of the book's subtitle—"An Archaeology of the Human Sciences."

The key concept of *The Order of Things* is the *episteme*. *Episteme* comes from the Greek word for "knowledge," and is seen in words like "epistemology," the philosophy of knowledge. An *episteme* is analogous to a "period" in traditional intellectual history. More specifically, an *episteme* refers to any given period's set of organizational practices and ways of classifying knowledge. Foucault argues that each succeeding period in modern European history has its own *episteme*. On the surface, this approach would seem to resemble a traditional history of ideas, which imagines succeeding eras, each having its own characteristic style or cultural predisposition. But Foucault is up to something different. First, the successive *epistemes* do not derive from one another. They are not arranged in an ascending order of progress. The next is not premised upon the last. This proposition resembles one outlined in Thomas Kuhn's theory of scientific paradigms, elaborated independently of Foucault but at roughly the same time. Kuhn did not see the history of science as progress towards reason and enlightenment. He saw it as a series of discontinuous paradigms, in which one paradigm, or way of thinking, followed upon the other but was less an improvement of the same underlying project than something totally new. (Kuhn, however, especially as time went on, did see paradigms as having some relationship to reality, whereas, for Foucault, *epistemes* are divorced from "reality.") Second, *epistemes* are far more all pervasive than styles. Even the most independent or idiosyncratic of thinkers cannot step outside them. They posit norms of knowledge so ingrained, and that attempt to "control" reality so seamlessly, that most people are not even aware they have them. Thus, for instance, Foucault's famous quip that even Marxism swims in the nineteenth century like a fish in the sea.

Foucault calls the first *episteme* he discusses the mode of similitude. He describes this mode as envisioning "the prose of the world." This phrase denotes a "Book of Nature" in which both words and things had significance. Thus, in Velázquez's painting, "Las Meninas," the fact that the artist himself is part of the picture, shown painting the very canvas the viewer sees, is not the self-conscious aestheticism it would have been in the twentieth century. It is, rather, the expression of a certitude that everything could potentially signify; everything could be both reality and the symbol that represented reality.

The usual names the reader expects in an intellectual history of modernity—Descartes, Pascal, Vico, and Rousseau—are nearly absent in *The Order of Things*. What replaces them are, often, anonymous archives or obscure treatises Foucault unearthed during his long researches. But *The Order of Things* focuses on the individual when one would least expect it. This happens twice in its early portions. Two individuals are highlighted. One is real; one is fictional. The botanist, doctor, and natural historian Ulisse Aldrovandi (1522–1605) is famous among historians of science and has a handsome museum dedicated to him in the Italian university city of Bologna where he worked.[16] But he is hardly a household name in the humanities. Aldrovandi is well known among botanists and natural historians. He invented, more or less, the very idea of the botanic garden—a way of arranging things that now seems natural but, in its own day, was an innovation that presupposed a certain kind of approach to knowledge. How Aldrovandi arranges things, how he operates through *taxis* but not taxonomy, was Foucault's emphasis. Aldrovandi mixes the fantastic with the real, the insignificant with the inconsequential, the whimsical with the urgent. Aldrovandi is both a doctor and a dreamer, both a specimen collector and a sage. He does not seem to be able to tell the difference, to rank, to prioritize. In this, he resembled the Argentine fabulist Jorge Luis Borges's vision of an encyclopaedia that does not abide customary hierarchies of knowledge. Foucault said a passage from Borges is what gave him the idea for the entire book:

> This book first arose out of a passage in Borges, out of the laughter that shattered, as I read the passage, all the familiar landmarks of my thought—*our* thought, the thought that bears the stamp of our age and our geography—breaking up all the ordered surfaces and all the planes with which we are accustomed to tame the wild profusion of existing things, and continuing long afterwards to disturb and threaten with collapse our age-old distinction between the Same and the Other. This passage quotes a "certain Chinese encyclopaedia" in which it is written that "animals are divided into: (a) belonging to the Emperor, (b) embalmed, (c) tame, (d) suckling pigs, (e) sirens, (f) fabulous, (g) stray dogs, (h) included in the present classification, (i) frenzied, (j) innumerable, (k) drawn with a very fine camelhair brush, (l) *et cetera*, (m) having just broken the water pitcher, (n) that from a long way off look like flies.[17]

The vogue of Borges (1899–1986) in both France and America in the 1960s was an instance of what Pascale Casanova later discussed as the canonizing power of the "world republic of letters." Foucault was most likely introduced to the work of Borges by the great theorist of play and games Roger Caillois, who was principally responsible for Borges's French popularity.[18] In any event, Borges's deep historical knowledge and insight, combined with the Argentine author's repudiation of any discourse of historical depth for any ultimate horizon of meaning, was tailor-made for the younger Frenchman. Borges's text makes us see that there is an arbitrary element in all classifications. Furthermore, classification can be fanciful and factual. In this, it resembles arrangement in Aldrovandi's era. Aldrovandi's arrangement is based as much on an aesthetic order of preferences as on scientific or mathematical rankings, as seen in his overt mention of scripts and languages.[19] It is not a pragmatic method or hierarchy but an interdependent arrangement of God's creation that Renaissance orderings were designed to indicate. In Aldrovandi's classification, art and science meet but do not converge. Consequently, Aldrovandi's methods are not simply quaint or outdated but can be seen as a precedent for the reconception of ordering that Foucault envisions. Notably, Foucault does not treat the botanical method of Aldrovandi as a "forerunner" of modern scientific inquiry; nor does he stress those aspects of Aldrovandi's career, such as his trial for heresy, which were well known to Foucault and which a "sentimental modernizer" would emphasize. Aldrovandi's virtues do not lie solely in his being judged "ahead of his time."

In many ways, Foucault's critique of teleological intellectual history, of seeing the Enlightenment and modernity as a progressive, continuous, benign development out of a murky past, is related not only to the radical critique of the Enlightenment offered by Theodor Adorno and Max Horkheimer but also to books of the 1930s through 1950s that sought, in one way or another, to disturb purposive or normative accounts of history or of systems. Alexandre Koyré's *From the Closed World to the Infinite Universe* and his later *Astronomical Revolution* were well known to Foucault, and these books were forerunners of *The Order of Things* in seeing the succession of views of the physical universe from the Middle Ages to the twentieth century as radically discontinuous from one another. Koyré also, though, saw traces of medieval cosmology even in modern astrophysics. There are analogous books in English, which Foucault did not necessarily know but which equally represent a precursor model for *The Order of Things*: Carl L. Becker's *The Heavenly City of the Eighteenth-Century Philosophers* (1932), E.A. Burtt's *Metaphysical Foundations of Modern Physical Science* (1924), and Hiram Haydn's *The Counter-Renaissance* (1950).[20] (Haydn, who taught at the New School in New York and was an ally of and mentor to Southern American writers, is just the sort of figure who links Foucault's thought, for all its methodological differences, to the anti-technocracy of the New Critics.) All these books cast doubt on modern science's ability to emancipate itself completely from the past or to surpass it. Unlike Foucault, though, most of these thinkers had an axe to grind.

They were either conservatives who wanted to go back to the past or people trying to deflate the arrogance of those who thought modernity could constitute itself fully without any anterior dependence on the past. For all his radical critique of orthodox academic arrangements, however, Foucault is not partisan in the narrow sense and is, in a way, exposing the Enlightenment's claims to self-sufficiency only because these claims constitute the most flagrant example of a general tendency toward intellectual periodization.

Foucault implies that every era arranges things in its own way, that these arrangements are discontinuous, that none is preferable to the other, that each has its own perceptions and illusions, its own modes of, as de Man might put it, "blindness and insight." This orientation was important for literary theory because it suggested that, though theory could not, as the New Criticism sometimes seemed to wish, avoid history, it could not presume that history was ordered in a steady and discernible story of progress or decline (or even of cause and effect), a presumption that would lead to overly convenient or reductive readings. Foucault's reading of Aldrovandi is paradigmatic here. Aldrovandi is not, for Foucault, a quirk of history, nor is he a mere predecessor to be superseded and elegized patronizingly by later scientific masters. His thought articulated the sense of words and things as signifiers in one uninterrupted, interdependent order of being, a syntax of the world that prevailed until it was itself interrupted by a new order. Whereas conventional thinkers would see transitions between eras, Foucault discerns cracks, fault lines, and precipices. One of these is visible in one of the world's greatest literary works. In four brilliant pages, Foucault gives a reading of Miguel de Cervantes's early seventeenth-century novel *Don Quixote*, a reading that shows the potential both for Foucault's methods to illuminate literary texts and for literature to register profound shifts in cultural meaning. Foucault's reading of *Don Quixote* is important because, for a theorist so often cited in literary contexts, he gives very few close readings of literary texts. That he gives a dense, if relatively brief, overall reading of a classic Western text early on in his first intellectually definitional book is worthy of notice and extended treatment.

Foucault's Way of Reading: *Don Quixote*

As happens often in his work, Foucault is writing from France, as a Frenchman—and one of his fundamental acts of honesty is that he does not seek to avoid this context. Foucault is fascinated by Spanish-language writers and artists; in *The Order of Things* alone, he discusses Velázquez, Borges, and Cervantes. There is even in Foucault, who was not immune to particularities of taste and sentiment, a vestige of the *espagnòlerie* that motivated nineteenth-century French composers to create a fantasy Spain of their own making.[21] Certainly, Foucault looked to Spain for an alternative to the linear thrust of progressive Europe. Spain was a place where varied temporal discourses could exist side by side—which is just the aspect of Spain lamented by cultural historians such as Américo Castro in the time of Francisco Franco's right-wing dictatorship and quickly jettisoned by the intellectuals of post-Franco Spain. Yet, whatever Foucault's motivation, his deft, economical reading of *Don Quixote* is one of the touchstones of his entire oeuvre, and shows conclusively that interdisciplinary approaches *can* yield pivotal readings of indispensable master works.

Perhaps, however, one should not classify Foucault's interaction with Cervantes's text strictly in national terms. *Don Quixote* quickly became a French book (popularly adapted by Jean Lesage). This act of national appropriation was one of the points of Borges's short story "Pierre Menard, Author of the *Quixote*," a parable showing that the same text could mean different things if it were produced in different ages. Indeed, *Don Quixote* had a tremendous and early influence on the rise of the English novel, and, especially in Tobias Smollett's translation, the book became an English one.[22] After US writer Hugh Henry Brackenridge imitated Smollett's version, *Don Quixote* became part of American literature. Cervantes's great work is incomprehensible without knowledge of an anterior literary genre—the romance. If Don Quixote is the first modern man, how, Foucault's treatment suggests, does this dependence on an already existing genre affect modernity's almost inherent claim to unhindered self-assertion, to independence from the past?

Don Quixote, the book, deconstructs the romance but is dependent on the romance as a genre for this deconstruction. As Roger Chartier has shown, this sense of the difference between the romantic genre and the text and context of *Don Quixote* would be impossible without the printing press and the rise of print culture. The romances—chivalrous tales of knightly derring-do such as those of Amadis de Gaul, which were often impossibly fantastic and nonhistorical and which Cervantes's account of the fatuity of his ineffectual protagonist skewers—existed and indeed flourished before print culture. Print gave them better distribution but did nothing really to change their form.[23] The novel, though, is, in its Cervantine form, *totally* a product of print culture. The ability of the printing press to quickly reproduce many copies gave the novel much more of an immediate reading public than the romance ever had, and this reading public, in turn, influenced the manifestation of the form. This technologically induced change, rather than any greater proximity to any construct of "reality," enables *Don Quixote*'s generic perspective on the works it satirizes.

The only problem of Don Quixote, the person, according to Foucault, is not that he is out of touch but that he is out of time. He still acts as if the medieval, chivalric, preprint cultural world were firmly in place, but the other characters—the ones who determine what is "real" and "normal" in the world of the book—do not. Just a few centuries before, Don Quixote's behaviour would have been totally appropriate, even routine and banal. (Don Quixote is only interesting in a time when he is perceived as crazy.) Dante, for instance, whether speaking in his own voice in the *Vita Nuova* or portraying himself as a character in *The Divine Comedy*, makes a metaphysical ordering principle out of a woman he barely knows in real life, Beatrice Portinari. Don Quixote does the same thing, making the lady Dulcinea out of the quite this-worldly Dolores del Toboso. The only real difference between our perceptions of the writers' two protagonists, then, occurs because they live in two different symbolic orders or systems of representation. Dante the pilgrim has no more metaphysical ground than Don Quixote. Dante, though, lived in a time that granted his proposition more metaphysical ground. Dante in Don Quixote's world would have been rather like Don Quixote, whereas the hapless Don, had he lived in Florence circa 1300, might have had the chance to write one of the great works of world literature rather than to just *be* in one. This point, though not originally made by Foucault, would have been impossible to make without him.

Don Quixote, the character, thinks he is in a representational groove with the signifiers around him, but the other characters, the reader, and the author know he is not. Don Quixote is "Different insofar as he is unaware of Difference." This is his "madness," and, in this way, madness is reinterpreted as a semantic disconnect between hermeneutics and semiology. In *Don Quixote*, language "breaks off its old kinship with things" and enters into "lonely sovereignty." Foucault reframes the traditional link between "the lunatic and the poet"; instead of having a passionate yet tortured imagination in common, their affinity is expressed in terms of operating via similarly dislocated sign systems. Quixote is "homosemantic," awaiting "the great, unbroken plain of words and things" of the previous era. He runs on a one-track groove. This would be fine if it were the same track the other characters in the novel, including his steadfast if irreverent servant Sancho Panza, ran on. Unfortunately, it is not. Yet this divergence is what animates not only the comedy but also the conceptual backbone of *Don Quixote*. In a weird way, madness is just being born out of one's time; insanity is anachronism that is so visible as to be noticed. Or, to put it in a more Foucauldian way, sanity is, in fact, a particular consensus of meaning that also expresses itself in the self-description of historical periods.

Foucault and the Enlightenment

No period had more of this coherent sense of itself than the Enlightenment. Foucault is not sophomorically anti-Enlightenment, though he writes in the wake of thinkers such as Adorno and Horkheimer, who saw very "dark" aspects in the Enlightenment mentality, for example, coordination and social control, which were far from the confident, benign rationality usually associated with the era. Foucault's generation, born during and after World War II, could not unequivocally confirm or deny the Enlightenment, as seen in

the poem "Enlightenment" written by Foucault's near-contemporary Samuel
Menashe (born 1925), who studied in the late 1940s at the Sorbonne with
Foucault's mentor and sometime interlocutor Jean Wahl:

> He walked in awe
> In awe of light
> At nightfall, not at dawn
> Whatever he saw
> Receding from light
> In the sky's afterglow
> Was what he wanted
> To see, to know[24]

Foucault shares this apposition of scepticism of Enlightenment clarity and
resolute, dogged pursuit of knowledge for its own sake. Foucault does not attack
the Enlightenment directly, nor does he wish to go back to a pre-Enlightenment
past. Indeed, his own personal conduct and his sense of himself as a thinker are
reminiscent of Enlightenment figures such as Voltaire and Diderot. But Foucault
wanted to let the air out of the balloon of the Enlightenment's sense of its own
uniqueness and forward-looking qualities. For Foucault, the Enlightenment was
a period as organized around a conceptual language as any other. Foucault calls
the Enlightenment's particular ordering of things "general grammar."

This emphasis is perplexing at first to the contemporary reader. Why, when
the past two generations of scholars from Peter Gay onward have shown the
complexity and multiplicity of Enlightenment thought, is Foucault so seemingly
monologic and monochromatic? Foucault is faced with a dilemma common
to intellectual historians of modernity: how to differentiate the Renaissance
and the Enlightenment when both seem premised as transcending medieval ignorance? Is the Baroque, which lies between the Renaissance and the
Enlightenment in most periodizations, simply a bubble, a stillborn revival of
medieval modes doomed to sterility? The Baroque as an era fascinated certain
modern thinkers, such as T.S. Eliot and Walter Benjamin, precisely because
baroque styles of thought and modes of emotion were articulated in the presence of modernizing discourses but did not simply merge into the modern rhetoric of "moving on" and "getting over it." The Renaissance and Enlightenment,
in other words, both connoted a certain sloganeering bourgeois self-improve-
ment of which Eliot, Benjamin, and Foucault were equally sceptical. (Note that
Benjamin, a near-contemporary of Eliot's, was seen as postmodern, for very
Foucauldian reasons of dissemination and reception, while Eliot was seen as
modern, despite many similarities in the thought of both men.) Foucault has
the option of either equating the Renaissance with modernity (a step taken by
certain would-be disciples of his such as Stephen Greenblatt) or of deliberately

differentiating it from the Enlightenment periods. By seeing the Renaissance as the place where the prose of the world wobbled into inconsistency and the Enlightenment as where this prose was repackaged and systematized as general grammar, he secures a definitive distance between the two. Consequently, even though Foucault's general sense of the eighteenth century was not even controversial in the 1960s, he is still considered an originator. His idea of "general grammar" as the era's unifying feature marks an innovation. When Foucault writes that the "grid of comprehension is at once both authoritative and arbitrary" and that imagination is "the suture of body and soul," he is drawing connections between habits of mind and conduct in a far more thoroughgoing way than a less interdisciplinary thinker would have.[25]

Foucault refers frequently, and elliptically, to the Port-Royal grammarians. These were Calvinist-leaning Catholic scholars of the seventeenth century in France who, in their own right, had considerable historical importance. Here, Foucault is not referring just to their historical identity but also to the study of their relationship to the writing of Pascal and Racine, which was first explored by Charles Augustin Sainte-Beuve in the nineteenth century and which Marxist critic Lucien Goldmann presented in his 1955 book *Le dieu cache* (translated in 1964 under the title *The Hidden God*). Whereas Goldmann studied imaginative writers and philosophers, Foucault is not interested in such merely humanistic distractions. For Goldmann, there is but a hair's breadth between the wholly other God of Port-Royal and the buoyant confidence of the Enlightenment; without a visible God, all is staked on the coherence of the system. As Goldmann says, "In the infinite space of rational science God falls silent." The tragic mind, according to Goldmann, had to decide "whether there still was some means and some hope of reintegrating supra-individual values into this rational concept of space."[26] In the eighteenth century, interpretation did not stand out against scientific experimentation. The arrangement of knowledge into the observational and interpretative, so foundational for the way our universities are divided and organized, did not exist. People nostalgic for the Middle Ages often ascribe to that era a "unity of being." In the Enlightenment, being may not have been unified, but the way in which being was studied and categorized *was* unified. This meant the Enlightenment could not totally "know" itself.

Foucault and Modern Humanism

In the nineteenth century, according to Foucault, the grid of geometric generality yields to images of organic, evolutionary continuity. In many ways, Foucault is epitomizing the classic-Romantic distinction that is virtually a cliché among intellectual historians and that comes with tremendous complications, such as the French Revolution at once surrounding itself with classicizing rhetoric yet having its rhetoric of political transformation reverberate in many Romantic discourses, which yet also reacted to the Revolution on nationalistic grounds. The new point he is making does not have to do with the content of the two eras' mentalities. What he stresses is how the ordering of these two very disparate intellectual orientations—the classical and the Romantic—was patterned according to analogous principles. Foucault shows that romanticism is not really characterized by the embrace of the irregular and idiosyncratic that it promises. Its use of the language of individuality and biological specificity is applied in an overall, highly general, and standardizing way. Moreover, its identity is contingent on the idea of "man," which it elevates as a metaphysical principle. Foucault is not the only thinker to contend that the uniquely "human" emerged at a date later than the biological evolution of *homo sapiens* (a term that is itself a concept of the Enlightenment grid, naming man as but one of the hierarchy of animals). Indeed, both Harold Bloom and Stephen Greenblatt, in different ways, argue that either the human or the individual, as the West has come to understand this designation, emerged at the time of and in the works of Shakespeare. But Foucault gives particular emphasis to the idea of man not as the culmination of all human history but as a blip on the screen, a hiatus between two flanking *epistemes* of non-humanity. The nineteenth century was the century of anthropology for Foucault. Again, he does not use "anthropology" in a conventional dictionary way. Foucault does not mean the study of other cultures but the direction of academic study towards the knowledge of man, towards what German thinkers such as Wilhelm Dilthey later termed "the human sciences." Nineteenth-century anthropology is a complex phenomenon. It posits man as an absolute in the same moment as the replacement of the Enlightenment grid by nineteenth-century biological continuity shows that neither human rationality nor human dominion is endless, that all species and lives can come to an absolute end. Nineteenth-century anthropology thus faces an "analytic of finitude" that comes out of man's awareness of death. Foucault's ideas here seem particularly influenced by the thought of Martin Heidegger with respect to "being-towards-death." But the idea of man tries to transcend this analytic by positing itself as an "empirico-transcendental doublet."[27] "Man" as concept tries to be both particular and transcendent. Man is both the initiator of a course of study and the object of such a course.

For Foucault, this concept of man fails because it is trying to do two things at once, juggle two balls in the air in a fundamentally contradictory way. This concept of man both tries to place man at the centre of the process of inquiry and have man be what the inquiry is about. The analytic of finitude boxes all cultural expression within the closed notion of "humanity." At first, it seems far more capacious and stimulating than the endless grid of rationality. But it is just as exemplary of a certain humanistic mentality that, in Foucault's view, extended from the Renaissance to the nineteenth century and then prevailed no more.

And so Foucault, deliberately echoing Immanuel Kant's famous claim that the scepticism of David Hume wakened him out of his "dogmatic slumber," wishes to awaken modern culture out of its "anthropological sleep."[28] He wishes to make man less central. In this, he was following the Marxist Louis Althusser (1918–90), who suffered from insanity, which eventually led him to murder his wife. Althusser posited an "epistemological break," which was influential and separated conclusively the humanistic from the scientific Marx. This displacement of man ranges from, in literature, no longer taking account of the genius of the individual author to, in history, no longer looking for the figure of singular achievement. As Goldmann suggests, perhaps the person who expresses the group mentality and not the idiosyncratic individual is more finally significant.[29] On the other hand, Althusser gave this idea a darker cast by pointing out that ideology is, in fact, "interpellated," although it often thinks of itself as individualistic, the spontaneous expression of a solitary will. In other words, ideology addresses the individual from society; the individual is called out by or constructed by ideology. Thus the elimination of man, even for French Marxists, is not entirely benign. Althusser was particularly influential on film theorists, especially those largely British figures associated with the journal *Screen* such as Stephen Heath and Laura Mulvey, whose essay on "the male gaze" was perhaps the most cited piece of the theoretical age. For writers on film, Althusser's work was helpful because its avoidance of humanistic clichés let the visual and structural operations of film exist unencumbered by any metaphysical assumptions about "man."

Does getting rid of the idea of man mean that Foucault is against humanity? It surely does not mean that he dislikes humans, as a species. He is far from the misanthropic or man-hating attitude exemplified in the final book of Jonathan Swift's *Gulliver's Travels* (which, despite its negative attitude toward humankind, was celebrated by the traditional humanistic mentality). It reflects an inclination against man *as subject*. For Foucault, inflated concepts of humanity delude us into thinking that individual agents are far more in control of their own fate than is actually the case. A key text of this period is "What is an Author?"[30] In this text, Foucault is at his closest to Derrida. Indeed, he tacitly cites Derrida as favouring a notion of writing that, in Foucault's view abolishes the author only to reinscribe it as a higher level of pristine anonymity. Foucault himself admits that he has taken authorship too naively. When, in *The Order of Things*, he mentions the names of individuals who have authored texts, figures such as Buffon or Marx, he refers to these individuals as indices of their thought, using a kind of shorthand. But he realizes that this shorthand entails the metaphysical presupposition that the author represents an internally unified field of thought, that this concept of the author decisively separates authorship from the text and its context.

Foucault, Authorship, Periodization

In "What is an Author?" Foucault revises his practice, stating that the author is "a function of discourse" and that this "author-function" has less to do with personhood than it does with the gathering together of a multiplicity of social and linguistic energies. Much like Barthes, Foucault does not mean by this that authors do not exist or that, say, Nietzsche and Marx are indiscernible from each other. Foucault, again like Barthes, was, as an author, very idiosyncratic, and he would not wish to efface the idiosyncrasy or personality of his own or others' authorship. He is not saying authors do not exist. When Foucault and Barthes's revisions of the idea of authorship first became widely broadcast, it was common in readings staged by creative writing programs to introduce the author featured in the particular event and announce triumphantly that his or her presence was a living rebuke to the author-slaying claims of "the deconstructionists." As we shall see in Chapter 2 with our discussion of Robert Hass's "Meditation at Lagunitas," this criticism set up a straw man, which is but a foil. Foucault believes in authors and authorship. He just thinks that the idea of an author is not necessarily bound to a discrete, individual psyche and that the effects of what an author does cannot be limited to his or her immediate acts of writing. Foucault, in other words, asks us to be sceptical about just the sort of discussion we are conducting about "Foucault." And that is a scepticism that simply was not there in the criticism of the 1950s and 1960s.

Why did Foucault excite people so much? Why was he seen as an improvement on the "resolved symbolic"? We can get a hint from the convulsive force of the revision of authorship described above. Foucault pointed out the naïveté of the traditional ways in which things were discussed, just as Derrida did on a more abstract level. This made people who had been trained in the old methods feel delegitimized, so they sought to delegitimize theory in turn. Many people sought to undermine French theory by pointing out that people in America and other parts of the English-speaking world were more excited about it than were people in France. Much as the French unaccountably thought that the out-of-date work of comedian Jerry Lewis was funny, they argued, anglophone academics revered as gurus intellectual figures who, within the French "hexagon" itself, were seen as period pieces from the 1960s. As François Cusset has pointed out, "French theory" was invented in America.[31] It is a measure of what a powerful force theory was in the late twentieth century that its opponents held it in such fear and contempt that they would resort to such delegitimizing tactics.

What if the permanence of the French theorists revered in the United States were only a phantom of the American imagination? What if their fame faded in France itself once their initial vogue had petered out? Even if these accusations were true and Derrida and Foucault's work of the 1960s deserved period-piece status—and French-authored books published within France such as François Dosse's *Histoire de structuralisme* (1991–92) suggest otherwise—the people making these accusations simply did not understand how intellectual history works.[32] There is often a lag, a gap, what the French might call a *coupure* between a text's articulation and its reception across a different national context. An idea that means one thing in one country can mean a very different thing in another. Scholars who are minor figures in their home countries might become major when their ideas are received in a new context, one in which, by happenstance or just because of greater applicability to circumstance, these ideas flourish. Here are some examples. Much of the universalist zeal of the French Enlightenment, so neatly structured by Foucault as "general grammar," was, in many ways, abducted or at least gleaned from English liberal thinkers such as the third Earl of Shaftesbury, by whom dissident French intellectuals such as Voltaire were inspired, although they employed "English" ideas for their own purposes. Lord Shaftesbury was not necessarily *de rigueur* within London when Voltaire cited him.[33] Nor was the Baron de Montesquieu outstandingly *au fait* in Paris when Thomas Jefferson and the framers of the US Constitution were crucially influenced by him in articulating the democratic liberties and norms of the new nation.[34] In the nineteenth century, many South American thinkers were influenced by Romantic idealism. But this influence was mediated through the earlier work of the German philosopher Karl Christian Friedrich Krause.

Krause was a figure of apparently little importance within Germany. But within the nineteenth-century Spanish-speaking world, he stood, benignly, for a progressive but not too radical approach to law and liberalism.[35] The example of Krause shows that even the work of thinkers who are less original or insightful than Derrida and Foucault, or whose reputation has waned or was never established in their own countries, can have significant and lasting import. The accusation that "Derrida and Foucault are no longer trendy in France" was an attempt to delegitimize their scholarship. This tactic seems a variant of the procedure Hans Blumenberg eviscerated in *The Legitimacy of the Modern Age* (1966): the "refutation" of modernity by casting doubt upon its pedigree or its empirical validity.[36]

Foucault himself, in his analysis of *Don Quixote*, eviscerates those who castigate a phenomenon by claiming that it is out of style, that it is yesterday's news. The attempt to see Derrida and Foucault as back numbers risibly seized upon by befuddled anglophones is an attempt to solve a polemical difference through the manipulation of time. We are reminded that periodization can delude or deceive as well as explain. Periodization can constitute what the Israeli-French historian Daniel Milo calls "betraying time" by bundling it in ways that render normative the elements within the frame.[37] Furthermore, periodization can enable what the anthropologist Johannes Fabian has called the European colonizers' "denial of coevality" to the people they have conquered—in other words, casting the colonized peoples as inferior, by alleging that they are "backwards," that they do not share the same current "time."[38] There is a comic aspect about the way Don Quixote is made fun of because he is a knight trying to operate in unknightly times. But, as Foucault shows, society's treatment of him also has a punitive aspect, one that is seen whenever people are put down on the basis of their being "out of date" (e.g., the fan of late 1970s ballad rock arriving at college in the early 1980s amid a host of new wave aficionados or heavy metal fans scourged by hip-hop enthusiasts). Perhaps the people who are making the phenomenon out of date are the wilful ones, not those who continue to practice a mode of behaviour that seems meaningful for them. Even if the French long ago bid *adieu* to the currency of Foucault and Derrida, who is to say the French are always right? Besides, what Ulrich Beck calls "zombie categories"—categories no longer understood in the way originally meant—may end up generating a provocative plurality of forms that straight temporal supersession would bar.

Foucault himself, in *The Archaeology of Knowledge*, suggests that tracing knowledge to a single source, such as an author or historical period, simplifies and diminishes it to the point of making it meaningless. The full panoply of intellectual argument can, for Foucault, only be unfolded across many different tracks and lines of thought. This idea is enough to outflank any discourse that would claim time for its own or that would deign to argue what ineffable qualities and meanings lie behind the name of even a single author—a Foucault or a Derrida.

Foucault and the Prison

It is paradoxical to try to give a sequential account of such a non-sequential thinker as Foucault. Foucault would likely have spurned talk of "the next phase" of his career. This wording would imply a scenario of relatable succession, a Horatio Alger-esque rising up the ladder of life that may well have elicited from him a sneer as to the guileless optimism it implied. As has been noted, however, he attained his greatest celebrity in the land of self-help and human potential and, indeed, according to his biographers, felt more at home in the United States than in the country of his birth. Thus we will speak reluctantly of "the next phase of Foucault's career." *Discipline and Punish* (1975) dominates this phase.[39] Foucault gives a comprehensive history of the prison system from the Renaissance onward. But, more important, he overhauls our ideas not just of prisons but also of how society in general is kept under containment. Foucault relates how public executions, conducted in full view of the populace, were once the norm. Although, historically, we might associate this phenomenon with absolute monarchy, it reached its apogee in the days of the French Revolution, when the guillotine was used to execute those who had taken actions felt to be politically inappropriate. Then, in the "humanistic" nineteenth century, punishment was privatized and taken inside. The audience no longer was aware of the outcome. If citizens heard news of this punishment, it was only in reported whispers, not direct seeing. Conventional ways of relating the history of prisons would contend that incarceration and the attempt to rehabilitate each prisoner was more humane than public execution.[40] For Foucault, though, both are means of control.

Foucault does not frequently discuss prison colonies, such as Australia's Nauru or France's Devil's Island in French Guiana off the coast of South America. (Although, intriguingly, Foucault did once compare these prison colonies, and the process of relegation over which they presided, to the Soviet Gulag.[41]) Indeed, in general, his work is silent about European colonialism, even though imperialism and colonialism are central aspects of the discourses of cultural modernity. Part of this omission involved a shying away from traditional political history. But colonialism, as Edward Said argued, does seem to be a blind spot in Foucault's oeuvre.[42]

Foucault, though, exposes the delusions of the modern European intellectual project, especially proponents' claims that this project represents a quantum social advance. He is sceptical of proclamations of reform, improvement, and humanitarianism, for all that he deeply desires the values for which these words purport to stand to be lived realities. Foucault is especially sceptical of the beneficent effects of science and technology. This scepticism is evident in his analysis of Jeremy Bentham's proposal for a panopticon. A panopticon, in Bentham's vision, was a modern and efficient type of prison that consisted of cells ranged around a central point from which wardens could observe prisoners without being observed themselves.

Foucault's discussion of Jeremy Bentham's panopticon and of the mode of passive surveillance it can give society over those it wishes to control is at the core of *Discipline and Punish*. Despite his frequent ability to cross the gap between the sciences and the humanities, Foucault, in many ways, takes the traditional literary attitude towards Bentham, an attitude evident in the work of Leavis. Leavis famously denounced "technologico-Benthamism," meaning by this a view that saw science as an instrumental technique that would render creative expression meaningless, neutralize it.[43] Bentham was thought more highly of in social science and philosophy, where he was seen as a reformer, somebody who usefully and pragmatically desired the greatest good for the greatest number of people. But the Panopticon is revealed by Foucault to embody the deepest structures of modern authority. By watching everyone but not allowing any of those being watched to watch anyone else, it leaves each individual subject vulnerable. Indeed, to be an individual is to be vulnerable. Power is no longer exercised by or in the name of individuals. Power becomes systemic. Whereas Leavis thought that humanists, with a clear-sighted morality, could wrench themselves free of technologico-Benthamism, Foucault is not so sure there is any escape from it. Foucault says, "It does not matter who exercises power."[44] It is no longer the image of a malevolent tyrant or a self-entitled elite that denotes the powerful; the system exercises its own power, a power greater than that of the particular individuals who happen to implement it and greater even than their interests.

Discipline is continuous between prisons, schools, and hospitals. The Panopticon lets the authorities see the prisoners without the prisoners knowing that they are being seen; but they know there is the possibility of being seen, so they internalize a sense of being under observation even when this observation is not explicit. Foucault refers to the prison system as the "carceral archipelago," which is an allusion to Aleksandr Solzhenitsyn's great exposé of the Soviet prison camps, *The Gulag Archipelago, 1918–1956* (1958–68).[45] Foucault does two things here. He lends his support to Solzhenitsyn at a time when the Russian writer's description of the immensity of the Soviet torture system was often received with scepticism by Western leftists predisposed to be sympathetic to a communist regime.[46] But he also asserts that Western disciplinary institutions can operate by the same totalitarian logic as their far more obviously menacing Soviet counterparts. (It is an example of Foucault's breadth that he is one of the few writers to be seriously influenced by both Borges and Solzhenitsyn.)

Foucault's sense of psychiatry as a discipline that often operates by labelling social dissidents as insane also had a real-world analogue in the psychiatric facilities maintained by the Soviet regime for the purposes of locking up those people who did not agree with the mentality of the then-dominant state order. Because they did not agree with the power structure, these people were deemed mad. This equation of dissidence and insanity had occurred in previous authoritarian societies. For instance, American southern whites in the 1850s diagnosed fugitive slaves as falling victim to the syndrome of drapetomania for thinking that life was better away from the plantations.[47] That life clearly was better away from the plantations had little discursive efficacy against a syndrome that classified this thought as delusive. Drapetomania needed Sherman's march through Georgia to refute it conclusively. In this case, although the institution of slavery was the object that should have been diagnosed as insane and abnormal, its *victims* were classified as mad and delusional instead. The asylum was the place society could put dissidents and not be embarrassed, as a society, by this confinement.

Some commentators assumed that Foucault was saying prisons and insane asylums should be simply shut down, that their inmates should be let out. If this were so, then, every crime or incident perpetrated by a discharged inmate could be laid at Foucault's door! Indeed, this is what Foucault's detractors often did, even when such releases were conducted for budgetary reasons, because the state no longer felt like spending its money on caring for or "rehabilitating" inmates, for example. Foucault did not think that society could do without institutions. It is of note that Foucault's final illness and death occurred in the Hôpital de la Salpetrière, whose asylums and women's prisons frequently figured in Foucault's histories of confinement.[48] One might have thought that Foucault, even on the verge of death, would avoid such a place, would want to be outside its grasp. That he died within its confines illustrates an important point. We may notice the existence of prisons, both literal and conceptual, but we can never entirely evade them. The ironic location of Foucault's death demonstrates that institutions often play cruel jokes upon those who traffic with them.

Foucault was a revolutionary in terms of his impact on the fields he affected, but he did not believe in direct, political revolution. He was not against such a thing; he just did not believe that revolution was possible. Some have seen this view as a capitulation to the powers that be, a pusillanimous retreat into paralysis, or a reluctant exultation of the way dominant discourses combine knowledge and power. Foucault, by his own lights, was working as a theorist of resistance, not domination. Yet he understood that the existing order could not be upended totally and instantly, that this project needed work, and that a close study of institutions was the way to achieve it. Foucault's study of hospitals and prisons is reminiscent of the vision portrayed in George Orwell's novels of the late 1940s, both in its nightmarish depiction of societal institutions and in its sense of the fragile and foredoomed nature of any resistance to them. But, most important to remember is that Foucault's zeal in analysing these institutions and the problems of resisting them does not mean Foucault was on their side.

Discipline and Punish exemplifies Foucault's championship of the outsider, the prisoner, the asylum inmate, the medical patient, without romanticizing them. Foucault does not, in a modernist way, merely champion the exception or, in a Romantic way, champion the individual against society. He sees the institution of the prison as itself an actor, not just as a frame for human action. In this way, he takes ideas of form beyond the resolution that modernist formalism had propagated. Texts can have forms—so can prisons. (We will see in Chapter 7 how Caroline Levine's early twenty-first century criticism explained these resemblances as a cardinal principle of a rearticulated formalism.) And texts about prisons, or about any other seemingly non-literary subject, are not merely substantive just because they may be non-fictional.

Genealogy

Foucault was not universally popular. Some objected to his apparent romanticization of the outsider. What for Foucault was the person who managed to slip between systems, to evade the norms of classification, seemed to others to be a hyperbolically valued rogue figure who was romanticized even as the institution was demonized. Moreover, many area specialists saw Foucault's research method as sloppy. Nearly every generalization Foucault made could be and was refuted by specific data concerning the area in question. Finally, although Foucault was valued by many on the left for his exposure of the self-interest of so many ostensibly neutral and benevolent institutions, many saw his work as leading to excessive scepticism and even political paralysis. Foucault was clearly very pessimistic about the possibility that human society could undergo wholesale change, could reinvent itself. Foucault was a radical thinker. But he was an anti-utopian one.

Despite these oft-made criticisms, Foucault, like Derrida, was taken up by academic interpreters in the English-speaking world, and was made the centre of a network of elaborate and often arcane theorizing.[49] Unlike Derrida, though, Foucault was also part of the intellectual mainstream, albeit on the fringes of it and unsusceptible to its sustaining pieties. His books were respectfully, if not always positively, reviewed by mainstream media outlets such as *The New Yorker*, the *New York Times Book Review*, the *TLS* (*Times Literary Supplement*), the *New York Review of Books*, and National Public Radio.[50] He generally did not inspire the paranoia and revulsion that Derrida and what was termed "the deconstructionists" did. A New York intellectual in, say, 1975 was far likelier to have heard of Foucault than of Derrida, and that fact both reflected and helped construct a difference in the North American profiles of the two thinkers.

Foucault's later work turns from *archaeology* to *genealogy*. As in the case of "archaeology," Foucault does not use "genealogy" in its usual dictionary sense. He is not conducting researches into family history! However, this time, Foucault's specific use of the word has a precedent—in the way Friedrich Nietzsche used "genealogy" in his book *On the Genealogy of Morals* (1887). "Genealogy" in the Nietzschean sense does not refer to ancestry. It indicates the power struggles by which conventional morality came to be. A genealogy is the account both of the origin of an idea, how it is worked out in human terms before it ever becomes a cold heading in an encyclopaedia, and of what moral energy, or even moral cost, has been expended on behalf of its formulation. Far from being a natural outcome of inherent laws, morality is the product of a ferocious contest for domination. Nietzsche, with his perspective-based approach that used whatever disciplines or resources were available to articulate ideas, was an important influence on Foucault and, indeed, on all theory. Nietzsche was the eccentric grandfather of deconstruction, which took his wild, questioning maxims and made them institutional and academic. Theory, though, also provided the comprehensive and philosophically rigorous reading of Nietzsche that earlier readings, with their reductive emphasis on phrases such as "will to power" or their literalistic rendering of complicated Nietzschean concepts such as "eternal recurrence" had not. It is crucial to realize, though, that this view of Nietzschean philosophy is itself the product of a deconstructive *reading* of Nietzsche, done by Derrida and Foucault as well as by figures such as Philippe Lacoue-Labarthe, and that Nietzsche himself was a late nineteenth-century figure who cannot simply be abducted into the ranks of "the theorists."[51] Nietzsche has his own theoretical identity, and he is not just a forebear of Foucault or Derrida.

It is also important to realize that "genealogy of morals" means, for Nietzsche, the ways in which states of preference, such as good or bad, were converted into states of value. As Rainer J. Hanshe has pointed out, "the genealogy of morals" is not something that Nietzsche's text seeks to propound as either methodology or desired object; in fact, Nietzsche, by revealing the process by which this genealogy came about, seeks to repeal it or at least expose how it was constituted.[52]

Nietzsche's genealogy, or his genealogizing, was an attempt to explode origins, to act, as de Man once put it, as a "de-bunker of the arche (or origin), an archie Debunker," a demolisher of ancient truths.[53] Foucault shares Nietzsche's scepticism, but he has a far more palpable sense of his own methodology. Thus, Foucault's genealogy is against origins generally, but it does allow for origins within the framework of his own methods, which aim to explain the genesis of cultural formation as much as to debunk existing ones. Foucault converts Nietzsche's use of "genealogy" into something that is much more positive and, in truth, something that resembles much more the search for enabling origins in German historiographic practice from romanticism to the early twentieth century. But even Foucault does not advocate either genealogy or archaeology as a method that will give a superior and more political reading of texts and circumstances than is promised by other methodologies. The historicism of the late 1980s and 1990s, with its affirmation of "what was there," often turned genealogy and archaeology into empirical history stripped of its obligation to fact and the record but retaining the aura of correspondence to lived reality. Foucault, on the other hand saw these methodological tools as aids to reflection and testimony, not as touchstones of deliverance.

Many critics have assumed that the shift from archaeology to genealogy is also a shift from the synchronic, or structural, to the diachronic, or historical.[54] There is some basis for this appraisal. But it is not that simple. Foucault does take a more chronological approach and does place more focus on the willing, deciding human subject. However, in the 1980s, those who were hostile to post-structuralist thinkers such as Paul de Man, Jacques Derrida, Luce Irigaray, and Hélène Cixous misleadingly used Foucault as a figure for "the historical." Foucault was also said to allow for greater "agency," which usually meant giving scope for the old-fashioned prerogatives of the active, willing self. Even in *The History of Sexuality* books, though, Foucault does not make simple assumptions about what history is or what it can be used to illuminate. The reason Foucault became so important for the historical analysis of literature is precisely that he did *not provide* simple historical solutions to compelling literary problems. Foucault's history is always a history filled with contesting powers that will never let a tendency that is the direct expression of human will reign unhindered.

Beyond Consensus

Since the mid-1800s, "neopagans" had exalted the pre-Christian Greco-Roman era as a time of less inhibition and more unfettered sexuality.[55] As should be apparent by now, Foucault would never endorse such a conception. For him, sexuality will always be differently fettered, and freedom consists of being as aware of as many of these fettered states as possible. But, in the second and third volumes of *The History of Sexuality,* Foucault does prize the classical era for its articulation of practice over identity. For the ancient Greeks, Foucault asserts, it is not what one is sexually but what one does sexually that provides a person's sexual definition. With this stress on conduct comes a notion of the self that is aligned with the self's actions rather than with an essential definition or its social function.[56] *Epimeleia heautou*, care of the self, is not self-knowledge, epitomized by the more famous Greek phrase, *gnothi seautou*, "know thyself."[57] There is a limit to individualism here. Foucault redirects our attention to the practices surrounding the self, away from any core sense of personal identity. Unlike orthodox followers of Freud, Foucault did not believe in a true self that could be unearthed. Unlike orthodox existentialists, he did not believe in the possibility of coming to terms with what it meant to be human. Unlike orthodox followers of Marx, he did not believe that the self's full articulation is only as part of a collective social whole. But, unlike the New Critics (though like figures such as Barthes and Sontag), he thought that the self mattered to culture. Textual objects were meaningless without some sort of articulated philosophy of the self, however rigorous and sceptical. Foucault outlines a multiplicity of individuated practices of sexual conduct. But he is not a prophet of sexual freedom. In the 1970s, when "the sexual revolution" was understood as a quantum feat of liberation that had brought humanity into a praised land of unfettered sexuality, Foucault warned that there was no such thing as true sexual freedom, that every form of sexual expression was a regime, which possessed socially mandatory aspects. Foucault refused to accept that sexuality had been repressed only in the past and was liberated through modernity.[58]

But if advocates of freer sexual expression were disappointed in Foucault's belief that sexual expression was never really free, they were heartened by his refusal to accept a standard or normative model of sexual morality. The care of the self, though, is not simply cultivating a public image or showing a certain face to the world. Sexuality or any kind of human affection is less a revelation of an interior self than an imprint of an action, a stance, and an attitude. Foucault's mode of the care of the self also leaves room for actions expressing the self to be more premeditated. As opposed to unrestrained spontaneity, the care of the self stresses strenuous diligence, a thoughtful design that is, however, never final or frozen. What Foucault opposes is a *libidinal economy*, in which individual sexualities are corralled together under an overarching and controlling definition. This libidinal economy could be mandatory sexual puritanism. Equally, it could be mandatory sexual liberation. Foucault criticizes the tacitly mandatory as well as the officially mandatory aspects of sexuality. In a way, his entire history of sexuality is an expansion of the baleful effects of that colloquial maxim, "If it is not forbidden, it is compulsory." Foucault is suspicious of broad rhetorical structures, which compel a certain mode of action, whether that action is the suppression of any sign of sexuality, such as the anti-masturbation campaigns of the nineteenth century, or the mass orgies of the 1970s. Both the repressive bleakness of Victorian sexual puritanism, as seen in the early portions of Samuel Butler's *The Way of All Flesh* (1903), and the dreary desolation of compulsory sexual liberation, as seen in Michel Houellebecq's *The Possibility of an Island* (2005), were stifling of the full range of creativity and reflection. Each stifling consensus was an overly "resolved" rhetorical structure that compelled the individual to put aside personal truth. Foucault insisted that the individual must be the occasion of truth, even if, by definition, truth did not emanate from organic roots in a deep subjectivity. For this act of truth speaking, he used the Greek word *parrhesia*, which had its greatest currency among rhetoricians just before Christianity assumed cultural power in the Mediterranean world.

Parrhesia is speech as such, speech for its own sake. It is not speech that strives to achieve rhetorical effect. In an ancient world where rhetoric was defined as eloquent words meant to persuade an audience, *parrhesia* had boldness and immediacy. Foucault admired *parrhesia* not so much for any deep authenticity it contained as for its abruptness and its resistance to larger conformist structures. It was radically contingent: particular, only itself, not part of a larger framework. The apostles of Christ availed themselves *of parrhesia* in defying Roman authority.[59] Yet *parrhesia* is equally at odds with the eventually dominant Christian practice of confession and of reciting dogma. Foucault not only notes the church's prescribed liturgy, which the community of all believers must recite aloud, but also descries the formulaic structure in seemingly spontaneous acts of speech, such as the private confession. However individual the specific points visited on its course, the confession followed a prearranged trajectory. It constituted a rhetorical structure, which would subsume *parrhesia* in an overall conglomerate.

The transition from classical culture to Christianity is the earliest (in chronological time) and last (in terms of where Foucault came to it in his career) of the three major cultural transitions that intrigued Foucault: from classical culture to Christianity, from the Middle Ages to the Renaissance and from the Enlightenment to the nineteenth century. This interest in cultural transition, in the eddies between one *episteme* and another, is an aspect of Foucault that is as liminal as it is political, as interested in borders as it is in defining centralities. This rogue and interstitial sense of temporality is as crucial to Foucault's later works as what they have to say in denotative terms about sex or sexuality. Despite his enormous influence on queer theory, Foucault was less interested in sex or gender in themselves than he was fascinated by the range of classifications that sought to coordinate and control both.[60] Thus, though queer theory is inspired in many ways by Foucault, it does not directly found itself upon his work. Foucault's conception of *parrhesia* has some connectors with the idea of truth as at once radically contingent and adamantly affirmed by personal witness, an idea articulated by the Czech dissident-turned-president Václav Havel. This idea is now known by the clichéd phrase "speaking truth to power."[61] But Foucault was also aware, as indeed is Havel, of how truth can also be a form of power.[62] In his last works, Foucault presents a challenging vision of truth speaking both against and through power. He also embodies a heartening vision of the intellectual unafraid to experiment, and of a deeply sceptical temperament yet unabashed by hope.

The Legacy of Foucault: Biopower and Governmentality

Foucault died of an AIDS-related illness in June 1984 (just as French and American scientists were identifying HIV as the virus that causes AIDS).[63] His sexuality project remains unfinished and covers in depth only the chronologically earlier era (ancient Greece and Rome). In the second half, he would have reconnoitred ground that he had covered in his earlier books, and this might have produced new perspectives. Foucault died at the beginning of a new moment in history, and how he would have conducted himself politically or intellectually can only be a matter for speculation. As Todd May puts it, since Foucault's death "we have seen the rise of the Internet, DVDs, cell phones, gated communities, Tivo, sport-utility vehicles, e-mail and instant messaging.... Neoliberalism has come to replace welfare liberalism in many quarters as the reigning economic philosophy of the state."[64] Foucault, as Lauren Goodlad points out, never paid that much attention even to nineteenth-century English discourses of exercising power through proclaimed reformist liberalism.[65] This lack of a precedent for responding to doctrines of free markets and democracy, principles promulgated with increasing fervour in the 1980s and 1990s, might well have hindered Foucault in maintaining an original stance through the last two decades of the twentieth century.

It is appropriate, given that Foucault did so much to decentre "man" as the fulcrum of thought and culture, that Foucault's thought should continue to affect theory even after his death. Part of this continuing influence is due to far more prosaic factors than the above statements would indicate: Foucault's lectures at the Collège de France and his other uncollected essays were steadily shepherded into print in the two decades after his death. Even more important, though, was the way that two particular concepts of Foucault's, not enunciated in any of his well-known books, came to the fore after his passing. These are biopower and governmentality. Foucault first introduced the term "biopower" in his 1975–76 lectures at the Collège de France, lectures that were later translated and published as *Society Must Be Defended*. Biopower indicates the use of massive literal and tacit social force by a consensus in control of society, Biopower often operates through biopolitics. Biopolitics refers to the control of institutions over individuals' bodies—through public health, immigration, education, sanitary facilities, population control, military conscription, housing, and any other medium through which people's bodies are controlled and massed. Biopower can also function as a channel of resistance when it is deployed against the reigning forces of the day. The concept of biopower was later explored further by Giorgio Agamben, Michael Hardt, and Antonio Negri (see Chapters 5 and 7).

Governmentality is not a fancier-sounding synonym for "government." It refers to those processes beyond nominal government that yet still govern. Any mode of the administration or classification of people, even if it is done through private agencies or interests, is a mode of governmentality. Anywhere there is bureaucracy, there is governmentality. Indeed, Foucault sees these administrative processes as embodying actual power more than the nominal sovereignty of the state and the law, which he discounts. No major thinker about politics has seen less significance, one way or the other, in the state and in law and legal authority than Foucault. This focus outside the state makes Foucault refreshingly unpolemical in immediate terms. Foucault's scepticism toward political neutrality should not blind us to how nonpartisan he was in his work. His critiques of society did not aid a short- or medium-term political platform.

Nor should one look to Foucault's immediate politics to provide an overall ideology or platform. Foucault was fascinated by the Iranian Revolution of 1979 led by fundamentalist Shiite Muslims, and he did not agree with the consensus in the mainstream Western media concerning the right thing to do politically.[66] In fact, few can doubt that, had Foucault lived, he would have come to regret his misdiagnosis of the Iranian Revolution profoundly, that he would have seen its brutal repressiveness. (Foucault's attention to the Middle East did show, however, an increasing interest in the non-European; Foucault's only extended sojourn in a non-European country was in the Muslim North African nation of Tunisia.[67]) On the other hand, his advocacy of the Solidarity movement in Poland in the wake of its suppression by the Soviet Union is much more admirable in the eyes of most observers, and is seen as more justified by the historical events that have occurred since.[68] For Foucault, both Iranian and Polish circumstances were radical contingencies into which he made particular interventions. They were acts of *parrhesia*, not foundations of a politico-religious creed. Foucault was certainly, at this point in his career, highly anti-communist. But, unlike many American anti-communists, he did not make a positive belief system out of his opposition to the communist positive belief system. Whether Foucault would have become a French version of a US-style neoconservative, been an avuncular adoptee of the group of *nouveaux philosophes* that included Bernard-Henri Lévy and André Glucksmann and that was largely rightist in content if still leftist in tone, or remained a stalwart, if ragingly original, leftist in the manner of Derrida will never be known.[69] Nor perhaps does it matter crucially to Foucault's thought.

Foucault was very political. But he was not *conventionally* political. He was not the kind of public intellectual who operates as a higher-than-average weathervane, telling others which way to gravitate in order to echo the coming trends. And Foucault's unique political stance has often led to his being misread and misunderstood by people who want him to be more conventionally political than he is. Foucault severely downplays the role of the state in governing. Traditional political theory had seen sovereignty, the exercise of rule by individuals or bodies constituted formally as exercisers of power, to be the centre of public authority. Although he certainly did not deny that sovereignty exists in the formal sense—Foucault's own political activism indicated that he knew it mattered who was president of what country at any given time—Foucault places the stress elsewhere. Rather than concentrating on the sovereignty of one person, whether as monarch or democratically elected leader, or of one political system, he is interested in the rule of many people by the disciplinary mechanisms only partially in synch with state power.[70]

Ideas of biopower and governmentality seem, on the face of it, to have much more to do with social than with literary thought. But the application of Foucault's body of work to the process of literary criticism—by literary critics and by Foucault himself, as in the reading of *Don Quixote*—problematizes the difference between the two. Moreover, processes of governmentality and biopower are seen not only within literary works, in the fictional representation of societies in imaginative literature, but also in the control of the literary sphere. These processes affect what is published, what books receive notice, and how books are taught, promulgated, and handled. In turn, the concepts of biopower and governmentality illuminate social practices as having forms, shapes, and configurations. Many before Foucault saw a universal rationality as paradigmatic of the Enlightenment. But Foucault came up with the idea of a grid of rationality as a visual form. This capacity for giving shape to ideas is one in which literature has persistently participated. The key phrase "prose of the world" from *The Order of Things* demonstrates this. In his zeal to "transform and reverse the systems which quietly order us about," Foucault is as much a practitioner of literary forms as he is of any other discipline.[71]

Too often, Foucault was invoked in the 1980s as a kind of gentrified Marxist, as someone who provided a social panacea for literature that constituted a reassuring alternative to the more playful, vertigo-inducing, and non-conformist tendencies of Derrida's deconstruction. But Foucault, when read attentively, is no less deconstructive than Derrida in the way he makes impossible glib generalizations about historical periods and temporal causation that previously reigned rampant in academia. By confronting the totality of what went on (and goes on) at any given time, by not sentimentally noting the most politically or morally congenial aspects while sealing off the rest, Foucault at once has his eyes open to all possible sources of context while, at the same time, through this permeability, he establishes a framework for making context articulable in a literary context that simpler formulations have to either fake or bypass altogether. Foucault acknowledges social forces, but he disappoints Marxists by remaining within what Fredric Jameson famously termed "the prison house of language." By acknowledging this imprisonment, though, Foucault is able to glimpse more plausible possibilities for liberation than were provided by the conformist and goal-directed philosophies of Marxism, the Enlightenment, and existentialism against which he swerved.

Foucault practised both the interpretation of literature in the light of social developments and the potential for social developments to be seen as literature. Whereas the "resolved symbolic" had tried to keep literature in a high castle, moated off from ambient social discourses, Foucault broke down this barrier and imaginatively engaged the two in a way that was not reductive, unilateral, or hegemonic. This consummately quixotic feat was, despite all of Foucault's difficulties and indirections, amply appreciated within his own time. What was not so appreciated is how complementary his work was to that of the thinker with whom he was most often contrasted—Jacques Derrida. It is to Derrida's convulsive effect on literary theory we must now turn.

NOTES

1   For an example of the way this distinction is usually made, see Andrew Vincent, *The Nature of Political Theory* (New York: Oxford) 247. Also the Peruvian novelist Mario Vargas Llosa makes the point both in the article "Postmodernism and Frivolity" from *The Language of Passion* (New York: Farrar, Straus and Giroux, 2003) and in *The Bad Girl* (New York: Farrar, Straus and Giroux, 2007).

2   Roy Boyne, *Foucault and Derrida: The Other Side of Reason* (London and New York: Routledge, 1990) is one of the few studies to see the complementarity of Foucault and Derrida's work.

3   Michel Foucault, "The Archaeology of Knowledge," *Literary Theory: An Anthology*, ed. Julie Rivkin and Michael Ryan (New York: Blackwell, 2002) 93.

4   Because of his early death and his iconic status in the gay community, Foucault has attracted an unusual amount of biographical attention for a theorist. For Foucault's medical forebears, see Didier Eribon, *Michel Foucault*, trans. Betsy Wing (Cambridge, MA: Harvard University Press, 1991) 3. Eribon's book, Jim Miller's *The Passion of Michel Foucault* (New York: Simon and Schuster 1993) and David Macey's *The Lives of Michel Foucault* (London: Hutchinson, 1993) are the standard

biographies of Foucault, all of them published in the early 1990s. Eribon is the most attentive to the French intellectual scene and to Foucault's sexuality, Macey the most adept at putting Foucault's life into a theoretical content, and Miller the most accessible and the most directed toward Foucault's public role. David Halperin, *Saint Foucault* (New York: Oxford University Press, 1995) takes on Foucault's role as gay icon and the uncanny emotional appeal of this most cerebral of thinkers. For such an innovative thinker, Foucault owed a great deal to certain intellectuals of the previous generation, of whom he was a devoted and attentive student. Foucault, by example, shows how much a student can learn from teachers while qualitatively innovating upon their work. From the Indo-Europeanist Georges Dumézil, Foucault learned about the way historical manifestation can possess inherent structures. From the philosopher of science Georges Canguilhem, Foucault learned that the difference between the normal and the pathological, both in health and in society, is not as wide as most supposed. From the philosopher Jean Hippolyte, Foucault learned how speculation could be applied analytically and still be speculative. From the Russian-Jewish immigrant Alexandre Koyré, Foucault learned that the history of both culture and science can have an interdependent, yet often unpredictable, relationship to the modes in which we think about those histories

5   Alan Peterson and Robin Bunton, *Foucault, Health and Medicine* (London and New York, Routledge, 1997). Foucault was apparently no direct relation of Léon Foucault, the prominent nineteenth-century scientist of pendulum fame.

6   Alexandre Kojève, *Introduction to the Reading of Hegel: Lectures on the* Phenomenology of Spirit, trans. James H. Nichols, Jr., ed. Allan Bloom (Ithaca: Cornell University Press, 1980); Koyré, *From The Closed World to the Infinite Universe* (New York: Harper, 1958).

7   Gary Gutting, *Foucault: A Very Short Introduction* (New York: Oxford University Press, 2005) is a valuable, concise overview of Foucault by a leading Foucault scholar.

8   Simon During, *Foucault and Literature: Towards a Genealogy of Writing* (New York: Routledge, 1992) is sensitive toward Foucault's links with the French avant-garde.

9   For Bachelard's influence on Foucault, see During, *Foucault and Literature*, 23.

10   Francis Fukuyama, *The End of History and the Last Man* (New York: Harper, 1992) and Judith Butler, *Subjects of Desire: Hegelian Reflections in Twentieth-Century France* (New York: Columbia University Press, 1988).

11   Macey, *The Lives*, 473.

12   In the way "body" is used here, there are echoes of Ernst Kantorowicz, *The King's Two Bodies: A Study in Medieval Political Theology* (Princeton: Princeton University Press, 1997).

13   Michel Foucault, *The Order of Things: An Archaeology of the Human Sciences*, trans. Alan Sheridan (New York: Pantheon, 1970).

14   George Steiner, "The Mandarin of the Hour," rev. of *The Order of Things*, by Michel Foucault, *New York Times Book Review* 28 February 1971: 28–31.

15   Thomas Kuhn, *The Structure of Scientific Revolutions* (Chicago: University of Chicago Press, 1962).

16   Nicholas Jardine, James A. Secord, and Emma C. Spary, *Cultures of Natural History* (New York: Cambridge University Press, 1996) 61.

17   Foucault, *The Order of Things*, xv.

18   According to Jason Wilson, *Jorge Luis Borges* (London: Reaktion, 2006), Borges told his fellow Argentinean Alberto Manguel, "I'm an invention of Caillois."

19   Foucault, *The Order of Things*, 37.

20   E.A. Burtt, *The Metaphysical Foundations of Modern Physical Science: A Historical and Critical Essay* (London: Routledge, 2001); Carl Lotus Becker, *The Heavenly City of the Eighteenth-Century Philosophers* (New Haven: Yale University Press, 2003); Hiram Collins Haydn, *The Counter-Renaissance* (New York: Grove, 1960). It is intriguing that Haydn was published by the "counter-cultural" Grove Press. Foucault would delight in this proximity of an essentially conservative book with some of the early beatnik poets. It is also fascinating that the books by Becker and Burtt are still in print in the early twenty-first century; if the same professors who assign them also assign Foucault, theory may have a more fruitful interchange with more conventional modes of intellectual history than it has so far had.

21   Robin Holloway, "Festive Delight," *The Spectator* 30 December 2006, explicitly links *espagnolerie* with Edward Said's term, "Orientalism."

22   Thomas Shelton, working in 1607, hurriedly translated the first part of *Don Quixote* into English. This translation was first printed in 1612.

23   Roger Chartier, *Inscription and Erasure: Literature and Written Culture from the Eleventh to the Eighteenth Century*, trans. Arthur Goldhammer (Philadelphia: University of Pennsylvania Press, 2007) 18.

24   Samuel Menashe, *New and Selected Poems* (New York: Library of America, 2003) 57.

25   Michel Foucault, *The Order of Things*, 62, 70.

26   Lucien Goldmann, *The Hidden God: A Study of Tragic Vision in the Pensées of Pascal and the Tragedies of Racine* (London: Routledge, 1964) 35.

27   Foucault, *Order of Things*, 318.

28   Foucault, *Order of Things*, 371.

29   Goldmann, *Hidden God*, 35.

30   Michel Foucault, "What is an Author?" *The Foucault Reader*, ed. Paul Rabinow (New York: Pantheon, 1984).

31   François Cusset, *French Theory: How Foucault, Derrida, Deleuze, & Co. Transformed the Intellectual Life of the United States*, trans. Jeff Fort (Minneapolis: University of Minnesota Press, 2008). For further discussion of deconstruction in America, see Chapter 2. In a sense, the "theory is now out of style in France" motif is a variation on the "we don't need French theory in solid, empirical Anglo-America" motif, which is explored by David Simpson in *Romanticism, Nationalism, and the Revolt Against Theory* (Chicago: University of Chicago Press, 1993).

32   François Dosse, *History of Structuralism: The Rising Sign, 1945–1966*, trans. Deborah Glassman (Minneapolis: University of Minnesota Press, 1998).

33   Ian Buruma, *Anglomania: A European Love Affair* (New York: Random House, 1999) 198.

34   See Strobe Talbott, *The Great Experiment: The Story of Ancient Empires, Modern States, and the Quest for a Global Nation* (New York: Simon and Schuster, 2008) 129.

35   See F.S.C, Northrop. *Philosophical Anthropology and Practical Politics* (New York: Macmillan, 1960) 128.

36   Hans Blumenberg, *The Legitimacy of the Modern Age*, trans. Robert Wallace (Cambridge, MA: MIT Press, 1983).

37   Daniel Milo, *Trahir le temps* (Paris: Les Belles Lettres, 1991).

38   Johannes Fabian. *Time and the Other: How Anthropology Makes its Object* (New York: Columbia University Press, 1983).

39   The translation into English was published in 1977. Michel Foucault, *Discipline and Punish: The Birth of the Prison*, trans. Alan Sheridan (New York: Pantheon Books, 1977) 103.

40   Norval Morris and David J. Rothman, *The Oxford History of the Prison* (New York: Oxford University Press, 1998).

41   Jan Plamper incisively explores the corollaries between Foucault's meditations on the prison and the Soviet Gulag in "Foucault's Gulag," *Kritika: Explorations in Russian and Eurasian History* 3.2 (2002): 255–80.

42   Edward Said, *The World, the Text, and the Critic* (Cambridge, MA: Harvard University Press, 1983) 246.

43   F.R. Leavis, *Nor Shall My Sword: Discourses on Pluralism, Compassion, and Social Hope* (London: Chatto and Windus, 1972) 174.

44   Foucault, *Discipline and Punish*, 202.

45   The phrase "carceral archipelago" is found in Foucault, *Discipline and Punish*, 297. Aleksandr Solzhenitsyn, *The Gulag Archipelago, 1918–1956*, trans. Thomas P. Whitney, vol. 1 (Boulder: Westview, 1997).

46   Michael Scammell, *Solzhenitsyn: A Biography* (London: Hutchinson, 1985) 910.

47   See Junius P. Rodriguez, *Encyclopedia of Slave Resistance and Rebellion*, vol. 1 (Westport: Greenwood, 2006).

48   See Miller, *The Passion*, 34.

49   See Mark Poster, *Foucault, Marxism, and History: Mode of Production Versus Mode of Information* (London: Polity Press, 1984) and Frank Lentricchia, *Ariel and the Police: Michel Foucault, William James, Wallace Stevens* (Madison: University of Wisconsin Press, 1989).

50   For a survey of Foucault's coverage in the mainstream press of this era, see John Wakeman, *World Authors, 1970–1975: A Biographical Dictionary* (New York: Wilson, 1980) 261.

51 On Lacoue-Labarthe, see John Martis, *Philippe Lacoue-Labarthe: Representation and the Loss of the Subject* (New York: Fordham University Press, 2005). See David Allison, *The New Nietzsche, Contemporary Styles of Interpretation* (Cambridge: MIT Press, 1985) for an overview of how a redefinition of Nietzsche was a corollary of French theory. Alexander Nehemas, *Nietzsche: Life as Literature* (Cambridge, MA: Harvard University Press, 1985) undertakes a literary approach to Nietzsche that, though not deconstructive, is analogous to Derrida and Foucault's post-existentialist view of Nietzsche. And see Babette Babich, *Words in Blood, Like Flowers: Philosophy and Poetry, Music and Eros in Hölderlin, Nietzsche, and Heidegger* (New York: Fordham University Press, 2006) for an independent viewpoint on the postmodernist Nietzsche that is yet enabled by deconstruction.

52 I am grateful to Rainer J. Hanshe for sharing with me his work on this question.

53 Paul de Man, "Semiology and Rhetoric," *Diacritics* 3.3 (1973): 29.

54 Synchronic and diachronic are terms from linguistics popularized by latter-day readings of the early twentieth-century work of Swiss linguist Ferdinand de Saussure. For Saussure, synchronic linguistics is the study of language at a particular point in history while diachronic linguistics is the study of the history or evolution of language over time. See Robert M. Strozier, *Saussure, Derrida, and the Metaphysics of Subjectivity* (Berkeley: University of California Press, 1988) 244.

55 Paul Delany, *The Neo-Pagans: Rupert Brooke and the Ordeal of Youth* (New York: Free Press, 1987) provides a good sense of the term "neo-pagan," as well as discussing a poet underrated for not fitting in with the modernist *episteme*.

56 Wolfgang Detel, *Foucault and Classical Antiquity: Power, Ethics, and Knowledge*, trans. David Wigg-Wolf (Cambridge: Cambridge University Press, 2005).

57 See Edward McGushin, *Foucault's Askesis: An Introduction to the Philosophical Life* (Chicago: Northwestern University Press, 2007).

58 Jana Sawicki, *Disciplining Foucault: Feminism, Power, and the Body* (London and New York: Routledge, 1991) 34.

59 For more on Foucault's use of *parrhesia*, see Arpad Szalockai, *The Genesis of Modernity* (London: Routledge, 2003) 211.

60 There was a small body of Foucauldian feminist work during the 1980s, which has gathered momentum during the 2000s. See Sawicki, *The Genesis*, as well as the work of Ladelle McWhorter, *Bodies and Pleasures: Foucault and the Politics of Sexual Normalization* (Bloomington: Indiana University Press, 1999).

61 Jonathan Arac started work on the Foucault-Havel connection; see his "Foucault and Central Europe: A Polemical Speculation," *Boundary* 2 21.3 (1994): 197–210.

62 For an early statement of Foucauldian approaches to "truth," see Alan Sheridan, *Michel Foucault: The Will to Truth* (London and New York: Methuen, 1980).

63 Michelle Cochrane, *When AIDS Began: San Francisco and the Making of an Epidemic* (London: Routledge, 2004) 11.

64 Todd May, *The Philosophy of Foucault* (Montreal: McGill-Queen's University Press, 2006) 132. May is exemplary in rethinking Foucault's applicability to the cultural and intellectual circumstances of the twenty-first century; he probes beyond Foucault's initial reception in the English-speaking world. A very different, if complementary, project, with pertinence to our discussion of the "religious turn" in Chapter 7, is Jeremy Carrette and James William Bernauer, eds., *Foucault and Theology* (London: Ashgate, 2004). See also on Foucault in the twenty-first century, Jeffrey Nealon, *Foucault Beyond Foucault: Power and its Intensifications Since 1984* (Palo Alto: Stanford University Press, 2008); the book presents an argument roughly parallel to May's.

65 Lauren M.E. Goodlad, *The Victorian Novel and the Victorian State* (Baltimore: Johns Hopkins University Press, 2003) 5.

66 For a detailed and in many ways damning portrait of Foucault's involvement with Iran, see Janet Afary and Kevin Anderson, *Foucault and the Iranian Revolution: Gender and the Seductions of Islamism* (Chicago: University of Chicago Press, 2005). The authors write from a post-9/11 "Western-feminist" vantage point much like that discussed at the end of Chapter 3. This illustrates, as if we needed another lesson, that theoretical intellectuals should not automatically be expected to be reliable pundits on current events. The authors err, though, when they see Foucault's interest in Iranian Shiism as stemming from a simple anti-modernity rather than from a desire to *question* modernity, which is something different.

67 Robert Young has seen Foucault's Tunisian sojourn as making him tacitly postcolonial in perspective. See Robert Young, *Postcolonialism: A Historical Introduction* (London: Blackwell, 2001).

68   Macey, *The Lives*, 440. As Macey demonstrates, Foucault shied away from the extremes of left and right. In the late 1970s, when the Left was still in international vogue, he refused to support the Baader-Meinhof terrorist gang when urged to by certain acquaintances of his. In 1983, after the world had turned to the Right, he also refused to urge the French government to supply troops to the government of the African nation of Chad, which would have meant supporting the policy of the US administration of Ronald Reagan. He took this stand against the urging of certain other acquaintances.

69   Bernard-Henri Lévy's *La barbarie à la visage humain* (Paris: Grasset, 1977) and André Glucksmann's *Les maîtres penseurs* (Paris: Grasset, 1977) were the spearheads of the *nouveaux philosophes* movement; both were translated into English shortly thereafter, but failed to find the constituency that Foucault's and Derrida's publications did—they were too critical of Marxism for the Left, and did not have points of reference sufficiently recognizable to the anglophone Right. Lévy only became widely known in the United States in the early 2000s, and even then mainly as a high-cultural journalist and as someone famous for being famous in France—the exact obverse of Cusset's point about Derrida and Foucault

70   Michel Foucault, *Society Must Be Defended: Lectures at the Collège de France, 1975–1976*, trans. David Macey (London: Macmillan, 2003).

71   Plamper, "Foucault's Gulag," 258.

CHAPTER TWO

Derrida
DECONSTRUCTING HIERARCHIES

Derrida's (Anti-)Tradition

The duo of Foucault and Derrida again beckons—a binary composed of two thinkers who loathed binaries. Though many French intellectuals contributed to the age of theory, Derrida and Foucault were always the "big two" as far as theory's North American reception was concerned. Yet these two major influences on literary theory were very different, although often discussed in the same breath. One was Jewish. One was Gentile. One was born in the colonies. One was born in the provinces of France. One was heterosexual. One was homosexual. One was inexorably preoccupied with language. The other was cognizant before anything else of power relations.

Derrida and Foucault also possessed a good deal in common, however. Both sought to disestablish normative fashions of describing intellectual experience. Both had a sense of play and did not view themselves with excessive serious-ness, despite reaching a level of fame and professional eminence that many far more self-satisfied figures would envy. Both did not have a clear set of ideas for which they were known. If one had to settle on an overarching description of their ideas, one would say Foucault's had to do with "the discourse of what can be said and done socially" and Derrida's with "the instability of meaning as manifested in language" or, as Ian Balfour puts it, "our inability to know certain things with certainty."[1] But Derrida and Foucault expressed these ideas through myriad engagements with different texts and contexts, making their work not only complex but a diffuse braid of references from which it is often difficult to extract a formulated "idea."

Both men were radical critics of the existing social order without sopho-morically believing it could be immediately overhauled in a cathartic reversal. Indeed, though both men were associated with the atmosphere of "May 1968" (the French general strike and student revolt of that era), their mentality was very different than that commonly associated with those protests. Far from endorsing unmediated expression or direct action, both Foucault and Derrida, for all the genuine challenges they posed to intellectual routine, had a sense of tradition (both were deeply versed in the history of the West that they so fundamentally interrogated) and a sense of irony. This ironic sense did not sanction an easy defiance of constituted authority to no good use. Derrida and Foucault were "rebels" in the same ways Socrates, in Plato's portrait of him, was. Society may not have liked what Socrates said. But Socrates did not deliberately set out to offend society. Derrida and Foucault, for all their transgressions, were not far from this model. Indeed, for all their skewering of inflated platitudes about truth, they were as much in search of truth as any other thinker famous for doing so. In his celebrated late work *The Gift of Death*, Derrida quotes the Czech dissident and political philosopher Jan Patočka on civic truth and responsibility. If Derrida's roots are in the events of 1968, they can just as easily be traced to the Prague Spring of that year (the short-lived Czechoslovak dissent against Soviet-line socialism) as to the protests in Paris.[2]

For all that Derrida was portrayed as a remote and intimidating figure, even by his admirers, his life touched and was touched by the major events of twentieth-century European history. Derrida grew up in Algiers as a Jew, during an era in which being Jewish was supremely perilous. The policy of the collaborationist Vichy administrators of North Africa, which was anti-Semitic yet not genocidal, and the distance imposed by the Mediterranean Sea between Algerian society and the Nazi gendarmes meant that his family, though severely discriminated against, came to no material harm. Only after the US Army arrived in Algiers in November 1942 was Derrida out of danger.[3] Yet Derrida would not have expected to be considered a Jewish thinker or philosopher or to be seen as particularly insightful on Jewish questions. Unlike the New York Intellectuals or, in a far different way, the French philosopher Emmanuel Lévinas, Derrida did not write "as a Jew," although Derrida's Judaism has been a source of fascination to his readers. See, for example, Susan Handelman's *The Slayers of Moses* (1982) and Hélène Cixous's lyrical *For Jacques Derrida, Portrait of a Young Jewish Saint* (2004).[4] On the other hand, Derrida avowed his own Jewishness as inescapable. As Handelman points out, Derrida's technique of taking a previous text by a well-known writer or philosopher and explicating and eviscerating it, paying tribute to it and subverting it, can be seen as an emulation of the medieval Talmudic commentators on the Hebrew Bible. This sense of critical and philosophical writing as commentary was also shared by Harold Bloom, and Derrida and Bloom—born four days apart in 1930—had, for all their different views of humanity and of language, a shared sense of playfulness as well as complicated idiosyncratic intellectual personalities in which vulnerability was intimately meshed with intellectual daring.

Derrida moved to France in the late 1940s and gained admission to the prestigious École Normale Supérieure (where Foucault also studied, as did many French intellectuals of previous generations), where he specialized in philosophy.[5] Derrida's early work was on the philosopher Edmund Husserl, who worked in the early twentieth century. Husserl was a complex, rigorous thinker, vitally interested in subjectivity but pursuing that interest through logical and mathematical means. Yet his restructuring of the idea of phenomenology—the sense of how we experience things, irrespective of their basic "reality"—was foundational for more (in an odd way) "accessible" thinkers such as Martin Heidegger and Jean-Paul Sartre. Derrida's basic argument about Husserl was that the sense of a transparent, unhindered knowledge of his system's own postulates, which Husserl's method assumed, was, in fact, impossible: there could be no going back to an ultimate origin; meaning was already displaced. These ideas were to become important hallmarks of Derrida's way of reading other thinkers, not just Husserl. But it matters what thinkers Derrida chose to read, and his choice of Husserl here is significant. Had he made this critique of an earlier figure, such as Kant or Descartes, it would not have caused too much controversy. Established French philosophers such as Sartre or, earlier, Henri Bergson had made similar observations about Kant and Descartes, and, although these excited controversy, they did not appear to be beyond the intellectual pale. By questioning the basis of Husserl's primal point of reflection, though, Derrida was questioning the subjectivity that was at the base of existentialism. Just as Foucault's early work marked a turn away from concentrating on the subject in historical methodology, Derrida's early work problematized the philosophical enunciation of subjectivity, of a naive idea of "the self."

In this respect, Derrida was both reacting against and continuing the work of Heidegger (1889–1976). Heidegger, whose initial support of the Nazi regime is well known (and was tacitly turned against deconstruction in the work of the anti-theory Chilean historian Victor Farías), seemed to call in his early work for a "philosophical anthropology" that would disclose the essential nature of man.[6] This humanistic Heidegger was the one popular in the heyday of existentialism. But Derrida was inspired by the philosopher's more gnomic and demanding work, which was published after the *Kehre* (turn) in Heidegger's thought. In this later work, Heidegger focused on "being as such," being as a self-sufficient entity, and he disposed of the redemptive, humanistic language he had previously used. In doing so, though, he called for a "*Destruktion*" or "*Abbau*" (unbuilding) of all previous rational, Western philosophies, a project based on a concept that very much resembled the critique of logocentrism that Derrida was later to mount.[7] Derrida himself speaks of the idea of deconstruction as "adapting" the Heideggerian concept to his own ends.[8]

The two thinkers, who could not be more different in personal style— Derrida impish and subversive, Heidegger grave and melancholy—shared a sense of the exhaustion of conventional philosophy and of the need to dislodge it from being overly centred in a humanistic definition of "man." Foucault similarly tried to decentre a priori concepts of the human subject. Compared to Derrida, however, Heidegger was far more historically nostalgic. Heidegger viewed, for instance, the pre-Socratic thinkers in ancient Greece as representing

a more adequate (because puzzled and puzzling) account of being. Derrida
would never have looked to the past for this sort of redemption. Heidegger also
professed a lofty (and genuine) disdain for many of the trappings of the modern
world while Derrida was far more invested in the provisional than Heidegger
was. Note, however, that Derrida was by no means about to capitulate to popular culture. One of the most endearing aspects of his participation in the Amy
Ziering Kofman film *Derrida* (2002) was his refusal to accept a methodological equivalency between deconstruction and contemporary television comedy.
Heidegger lived for better or for worse, under the implied aegis of a fundamental judgement around which Derrida danced far more nimbly. Heidegger
was deeper and more thoughtful, Derrida keener and more curious. But both
Derrida and Heidegger originated fundamental critiques of what they saw as the
entrenched assumptions of Western philosophy.

What is "Post-Structuralism"?

In their aim of critiquing the centrality of the human subject as the West's core
philosophical assumption, both Derrida and Foucault were allied with the dominant intellectual movement of the 1960s in France—structuralism. Structuralism
came largely out of anthropology, as practised by Claude Lévi-Strauss; out of
the influence of Russian and Czech formalism; and out of the heirs of the Swiss
linguist Ferdinand de Saussure. Saussure, unlike Lévi-Strauss, did not really
know he was working as what later scholars called a "theorist"; he was a comparative linguist, the last and greatest of the tradition that ran through the
nineteenth and early twentieth centuries and, more or less, saw linguistics grow
from a discipline riddled with bogus nationalistic and ethnic claims to a quasi-
scientific discipline that stood on its own intellectual strengths. Scholars such as
Boris Gasparov and Tuska Benes have recently argued that there is a deep connection between the linguistic turn epitomized by Saussure and, by extension,
that evinced by Derrida with respect to German Romantic speculations about
language.[9] But, in immediate terms, the important things are that Saussure's
thought belonged to the twentieth century and was part of its general interest
in linguistic analysis and scepticism (a characteristic as true of British analytic
philosophy as of deconstruction).

Saussure's *Course in General Linguistics* was published after his death in
1914 from notes compiled by his two leading students, Charles Bally and Albert
Sechehaye.[10] Saussurean linguistics saw language as a closed system in which the
state of language as it existed at any given time (synchronic) and as it developed
through time (diachronic) had to be seen as existing under disparate criteria.
Saussure also made a parallel distinction between *langue* and *parole* (language
as it was or is actually spoken). Most crucially for theory, Saussure pointed out
the arbitrary nature of the sign, that the linguistic marker had no inherent relation to the idea or thing it stood for and was merely a convenient, agreed-upon

designation. Derrida was to take this idea further. Not only was the relation between the signifier and signified arbitrary, it was almost an impossibility; the signifier, its foregrounding as writing, confronted the perceiver with questions even without reference to the signified. Generations after Saussure's death, his mode of linguistics had become "structural linguistics" and was complemented by Lévi-Strauss's "structural anthropology."[11] Frank Kermode said that Lévi-Strauss had shown "that Saussure's idea of language as but the preeminent instance of structured sign-systems, and of a possible general science of signs, could be applied to anthropology."[12]

But Derrida reacted against Lévi-Strauss in important ways. Lévi-Strauss tended to see societies as constituted by binary oppositions. To affirm a certain kind of social principle was to deny another, inversely complementary one. Thus, to uphold neatness was also to negate disorder, to say one part of the tribal lands was holy was to say the other parts were non-holy. Derrida did not divide referentiality into sharply cleaved and perpetually opposite segments. Deconstruction, instead, put binary oppositions into endlessly deferred play, within which no one term is victorious over another one in a conclusive manner. Derrida was arguing *against* certain formulations, but he rigorously refused to slide into arguing *for* certain others. This method overturned structuralist assumptions yet was premised upon structuralist conjectures. As de Man pointed out in his essay "Criticism and Crisis," structuralism's suppression of the self led to questions of literariness that structuralism itself bypassed. The sequence of structuralism and post-structuralism moots both a formal metalanguage and the possibility of breaking down and problematizing that metalanguage in many disparate textual circumstances.

But, with respect to structuralism, the work of Derrida and Foucault presents a potential pitfall. Because Derrida and Foucault have been termed post-structuralists and because their cumulative impact within literary criticism has been far greater than that of anyone associated with structuralism, there arises a problem in terms of intellectual history. We have a very influential term. But it is a term that is expressed as "post-x," when x is a body of thought not nearly as influential. This is an unusual circumstance. Postmodernism, as its great French expositor Jean-François Lyotard made sure to underscore, refers back to modernism, and both were very important movements in contemporary history, of roughly equal impact. A term such as "late antiquity" (a period, as we have seen, whose renewed relevance was crucially connected to Foucault) refers to early antiquity as well as to itself, and that earlier antiquity is very important in order for us to understand the later period. Yet Derrida, although he criticized Lévi-Strauss for assuming an ahistorical, ideal situation, and also for tacitly sentimentalizing non-Western cultures, did not see the anthropologist as his main intellectual target. If one is to construct lines of dissent from a previous ideology, both Derrida and Foucault are better described as post-existentialists than post-structuralists.

The term "structuralism" is a stumbling block in histories of theory. Many never succeed in differentiating between structuralism and post-structuralism at all. *The New York Times* obituary of Michel Foucault called him, astonishingly, a structuralist. Furthermore, the great British novelist and philosopher Iris Murdoch (1919–99), who was highly opposed to theory, always referred to what this book is calling "theory" under the umbrella term "structuralism." The use of the term "post-structuralism" easily slipped into and fortified this habit. (The proposed term "superstructuralism," which mixed an awareness of the surpassing of structuralism with the Marxist idea of the superstructure—that which is not motivated by immediate functional needs—was richer but never caught on.[13]) Moreover, there really was little structuralist literary criticism. The early work of Barthes perhaps verged on it, but he quickly moved towards a post-structuralist position. Tzvetan Todorov also did structuralist work before becoming a far more "humanistic" critic. The early work of feminist theorists such as Julia Kristeva could be said to be structuralist. Michael Riffaterre's analysis of poetry strung together structuralist and formalist methods in a way that, in practice, became very nearly post-structuralist. The work of Slavic formalists such as Roman Jakobson, some of which was influenced by structuralism, was more concentrated in linguistics than literature. Furthermore, Jakobson's pivotal distinction between metaphor (as designating a relation of similitude) and metonymy (as designating a relation of disjuncture) had literary influence only in the intellectual atmosphere bequeathed by *post*-structuralism.[14] This paucity of structuralist literary criticism was even more evident in the Anglo-American world, where post-structuralism succeeded not structuralism but the "resolved symbolic." In North American literary theory, post-structuralism might be better termed "post-formalism." This term would be especially apt for the work of de Man, Derrida's chief North American disciple/interlocutor, and even for Bloom's.

Just as "America" is not the ideal name for the Western hemisphere, but will have to stay, so will "post-structuralism." Yet, largely because of this terminological question, historians of theory have felt compelled to construct a genealogy of post-structuralism by giving undue weight to structuralism. Structuralism was indeed important at the time. But the force of Derrida's and Foucault's critiques registered on a far wider plane. The structures they interrogated were those of Western signification and political order. In this very extended way, the term "post-structuralism" applies. But this book will prefer the term "deconstruction," as inevitably inapt and awkward as it sometimes is, because it emphasizes what Derrida's and Foucault's effect was. They did not destroy what came before them; nor did they maintain it. They deconstructed it, exposed it, laid bare its devices (as the Russian formalists might say). Derrida and Foucault did not rebut structuralist premises specifically or primarily as a central thrust of their thought, which use of the term "post-structuralism" implies. Indeed, structuralism's suspicion of old-fashioned humanism and subjectivity was very much shared by both thinkers.[15]

Thus "deconstruction" is a preferable term to "post-structuralism" and, finally, a far more clarifying one. Derrida himself echoes this, saying, in his lucid and invaluable "Letter to a Japanese Friend" that post-structuralism "was a word unknown in France until its 'return' from the United States."[16] Derrida prefers "deconstruction," although he is at pains to point out the limitations of that term as well. In "Letter to a Japanese Friend," Derrida disabuses his readers of several misapprehensions about deconstruction. It is "neither an *analysis* nor a *critique*," as these words would imply that deconstruction has a positive agenda towards what it deconstructs, that it is trying to hone it down to a core or judge it in the light of ultimate standards.[17] It is not a method because it cannot simply be turned into a cookie-cutter mode that can be arbitrarily performed. What Derrida is saying, basically, is that no one can truly do deconstruction unless one is Derrida or is willing and able to conduct deconstruction in a Derridean style. He admits, and tacitly laments, that, in the United States, deconstruction did become a kind of assembly-line method. But Derrida claims that delineating this method was not his intent. Incidentally, Derrida takes exception less to the "mass" quality of this method or to the appropriation of his ideas by others than he does to the assumption inherent in the idea of a method that one uses it to get somewhere, to achieve a determinate result, is on a trajectory to meaning. Deconstruction takes little stock of outcomes. It is not goal oriented, either on the level of theory or that of practice. In fact, Derrida points out that any definition of deconstruction can also be deconstructed, that there is an indefiniteness that is part of the word's endemic verbal articulation. Deconstruction takes a term that is hierarchically privileged, in a binary—as Derrida claims that the West has valued "presence" over "absence" or "speech" over "writing." It then reverses that hierarchy, at least temporarily, examining what it would be like, rhetorically, if the de-privileged word is privileged. Stable hierarchies are overturned. They are replaced by a more indefinite relation. This sense of indefiniteness is perhaps the most salient aspect of Derrida's thought, important both because of the terms in which the indefiniteness is expressed and because of the ways in which indefiniteness manifests itself.

For good or ill, Derrida seemed to have lost literature in a maze of bewildering signifiers or in a hall of mirrors with no way out—a cul-de-sac or what the Greeks called an *aporia*. Or he was thought to make literature into a series of infinite regresses with no bottom, an abyss without the satisfaction of a final touchdown. In French, this technique is called "*mise en abîme*" (meaning, "putting into a bottomless abyss" or "placing into infinity"), a phrase that commonly describes a sense of infinite regress, as when boxes are nested within boxes within boxes, and so on. Derrida was often seen as opposed to humanism—and he *was* opposed to humanism insofar as it elevated certain socially constructed attributes of "the human" to an unearned position of prominence.

But no twentieth-century thinker was more deeply humane in his attention to individual circumstances of language and meaning, and he refused to have his thought absorbed into clichés and truisms, which only serve to reassure and buttress existing authoritarian systems. Derrida's thought was thoroughly anti-totalitarian in doctrine, but even more in enunciation. Difference is in the grain of his thought, which utterly opposes homogeneity or conformity and even discourages the attempt, inevitably made by "cultists" of deconstruction, to turn deconstruction itself into a conformist system.

Derrida's Terminology

Deconstruction does not endow any word with inherent meaning. It is profoundly opposed to such a practice. Deconstruction works by letting words unfold their plurality and the fields of difference in which they operate. By exposing contradictions in normative language, it demonstrates how the slipperiness of language is its most salient attribute. But it does operate with a set of privileged words. Not every word can be used deconstructively, given a deconstructive valence. Those that can be used operate in multiple and unusual ways. Derrida admits that "deconstruction" as a word, although "good French" in a lexical sense, is not a *bon mot*, is not a "good word" in stylistic terms.[18] In terms of the French language, with its tradition of Cartesian clarity and crystalline, cerebral formality, words such as deconstruction, *différance*, supplementarity, and *écriture*; Foucauldian terms such as *episteme*; Kristevan terms (to be discussed in Chapter 3) such as *chora* are baulky and ill formed. Derrida says that deconstruction is not a *bon mot* with, perhaps, a slightly detectable shade of regret, implying that he wished he could have written lucidly, but, given the problems he was dealing with, a thicket of new words was the only way to grapple with them. Part of the issue here is the belated reception of German philosophy in France; in many ways, "French theory" marked the assimilation of Heidegger, Nietzsche, and Freud into the main currents of French intellectual life, an assimilation made even more difficult than normal national disaffinity would indicate by the two nations having fought three bitter wars over the course of eighty years. (Even Immanuel Kant, whose cool and methodical approach should have appealed to the French, was, as Jean-Luc Nancy has shown, regarded as almost creepily hyper-cerebral by the French intellectual tradition.[19]) The elusiveness of "deconstruction" as a verbal item is a partial by-product of the interaction of German conceptual ambition and lexical murkiness with French idealism and order. Deconstruction did not just come between these encrusted national generalities but upended and exploded them.

Yet it could be argued that "*différance*" not "deconstruction" is the most important term in Derrida. Unlike deconstruction, *différance* is a neologism, a totally new word. It did not exist anywhere in the French language before Derrida first used it. "*Différance*" means, basically, "*différence*." Not only the

general meaning but also the pronunciation is the same; the short, nasal "a"
and "e" sound identical in French. The only obvious difference (as it were) is
that there is a *graphic* change rather than a change in pronunciation, which
shows that writing can alter meaning on its own, without a change in speech.
What Derrida styles *écriture*—not just writing but writing as and for itself, not
just writing yoked to speech—can rove unchecked. *Différance*, though, does
not mean only a difference between two states or qualities. Its meaning is also
informed by the French word for "deferral"—*différer* or to defer or postpone.
Différance means we do not, cannot, should not have everything all at once,
experience full consummation or definition of meaning.

His Judaism profoundly informs Derrida's stance here. Judaism is a religion
defined by fulfilment of the promises made to the "chosen people" being postponed. Furthermore, Jewish identity was inextricable from a sacred text, the
Bible, and was epitomized by it as much as in any more palpable quality—land,
language, or culture. Jews not only were denied territorial location (and the
founding of modern Israel neither changed this for many Jews nor negated a
lengthy historical experience) but also were told that the promise given in their
religion had been "fulfilled" in Christianity.[20] Derrida's insistence on deferral
rather than fulfilment, on a hope that is always just around the corner rather
than declaratively manifest, is only fully comprehensible within the framework
of his Jewish background. As Samuel Menashe, an American Jew whose work
Derrida grew to admire, put it in "Promised Land":

> I know Exile
> Is always
> Green with hope—
> The river
> We cannot cross
> Flows forever[21]

As *long* as there are divisions and barriers, we have aspirations to see beyond
them. Thus *différance* expresses not just a lateral instability of meaning but a
temporal lag in it, a sense of separation from source that can never entirely
be repaired. Meaning is not just fractured between writing and speech but
belated in its arrival from past to present. And this inadequacy of meaning is
not something lamented or, as the existentialists would have done, privileged
as an extreme situation. Rather, it is seen as the characteristic state of linguistic
expression. This is why the Derridean concept of the "supplement" is so important and why only that of *différance* eclipses the concept of supplementarity in
its indispensability to understanding Derrida.[22]

"Supplement" for Derrida means that which cannot be eliminated in a purportedly neat definition or that which seems to be unnecessary, supernumerary, or excluded but which then comes back to haunt the formulation that had

sought to set it aside. Supplementarity is always extra, breaking any tightly knit or "resolved" order, bursting the bounds of the self-sufficient. What Derrida terms the "logocentric" tradition in Western philosophy—basically, the tradition that privileged verbal order, coherence, and hierarchy—insisted on its own centrality. Anything that did not agree with it was dismissed as marginal. Even if that which was outside this tradition could not be proven to be untrue, it could be denigrated as unimportant. By privileging the supplement, Derrida deflects the claims of centrality to articulate its own rationale by denigrating that of the alleged margins. Derrida evoked the positive aspect of, as Wallace Stevens put it,

> Desiring the exhilarations of changes:
> The motive for metaphor, shrinking from
> The weight of primary noon,
> The A B C of being.[23]

Supplementarity not only called attention to what lay outside the "weight of primary noon" but stipulated that primary noon, for example, could not be self-sufficient even on its own terms, that there was always something more, something that could not be integrated cohesively into the idea of primary centrality.

It is important to note that Derrida's foregrounding of an intermediate state, his invoking of a linguistic nexus where what Stevens called "the half-colors of quarter-things" were also worthy of notice and were not denigrated, did not mean that he elevated this in-between condition as a kind of vital centre. A Derridean reading of the Stevens poem would not sentimentalize "the half-colors of quarter-things" as a melodramatic opponent of authoritative certainty. But it would celebrate the possibility of many different vectors and strands of meaning; it would posit deferral and play as guarantors against the congealing of any central definition into an immutable essence. *Différance* was thus not just an infolded version of a Hegelian synthesis, a merger of thesis and antithesis strategically held below the level of climax. It attempted to explode and upend the terms that would make such a crypto-synthesis possible, to suspend them perpetually. Derrida thus avoided the overemphasis that caused later, more applied variants of supplementarity, such as *mestizaje* (to be discussed in Chapter 4), hybridity (to be discussed in Chapter 5), and queerness (to be discussed in Chapter 6), to insist slightly too much on their own urgency. One of the reasons Derrida's idea is more slippery than these more directly politicized or referential notions is that he continually emphasized writing, *écriture*. The sign, the mark, the graphic indicator cannot simply be subsumed into sound or meaning. It is itself a supplement, what Derrida would call a "trace," something that cannot be sifted out or distilled as the represented idea seemingly "beneath" it, which would turn it into a more utilitarian and ready-at-hand concept in worldly terms.

Derrida's career cannot be graphed in the relatively conventional way Foucault's was in Chapter 1. But a short conspectus of his major early work is in order. After the Husserl book, Derrida produced his longest and most influential book, *Of Grammatology*. *Of Grammatology* is Derrida's longest and most authoritative book, and it contains the ideas that became most widely disseminated as indicative of his thought.[24] But it was also, in form, the most atypical. *Of Grammatology* is a long, philosophical treatise. In *Of Grammatology*, Derrida, in his own labyrinthine way, argues for a position and even pioneers a new positive methodology. As Foucault did with "archaeology" and "genealogy," Derrida took a fairly innocuous methodological term and adapted it into a subversive science. "Grammatology" (a word whose Derridean valence quickly took over from its more conventional uses) was the comparative study of writing systems. The term asserts that the Western alphabetic system was not the only nor the first system of writing; before the first major phonemic script was developed by the Phoenicians and adapted by the Hebrews and Greeks, there was the cuneiform system of ancient Mesopotamia, the hieroglyphics of Egypt, the logographic scripts of China and of various other East Asian cultures, and the analogous pictographs of the Maya in the Western hemisphere.[25] Derrida seized upon this distinction to argue that the Western alphabetic system was *not* uniquely privileged as a transparent form of representing sound and meaning. There was an anti-Eurocentric point here, and, notably, the translator of the English edition of Derrida's *Of Grammatology*, Gayatri Chakravorty Spivak, was later to become one of the leading post-colonial theorists. In purely linguistic terms, Derrida privileged the externality of writing against the internal plenitude to which writing had, in Derrida's view, traditionally been subjugated as a handmaiden. He also redefined the nature of writing itself. In Shakespeare's sonnets, for instance, writing is seen as the emblem of permanence, as that which outlasts the merely living, transcends the ravages of the merely here and now:

> Not marble nor the gilded monuments
> Of princes shall outlive this powerful rhyme,
> But you shall shine more bright in these contents
> Than unswept stone besmeared with sluttish time.[26]

Derrida, though, emphasizes not writing's permanence but its evanescence—not its solidity but its slipperiness. "Textuality," for Derrida, became a kind of writing that was not only non-correspondent in its relation to what it signified but also protean, hard to nail down. Textuality twisted and turned beyond any isolable meaning. Writing also decentres the human, speaking subject. Note that the quotation from Shakespeare privileges the individual soul of both one honoured and, inferentially, the one who honours. For Derrida, these considerations would all be part of an anterior linguistic structure. "The human being is the place or zone where the particular problem has its play."[27] This structure, displayed in writing, in *écriture*, can subvert established Western, logocentric hierarchies.

In *Of Grammatology*, Derrida's half-playful sense of positive contention just might have led some of his readers to think that he was proposing a new science, just as many Nietzscheans have continued to take Nietzsche's theory of the "eternal recurrence of the same" seriously or literally and not as a figurative metaphor. In his subsequent work (which followed *On Grammatology* quickly), Derrida let the texts he analysed subvert themselves rather than specifically arguing to rebut them. In these works, Derrida laid out the playful, punning, often-opaque style that was to became his hallmark. The major essay here is "Plato's Pharmacy" (1972).[28] In this brilliant exegesis of Plato's *Phaedrus*, Derrida reverses the priorities of the Greek philosopher. Plato mistrusted writing because it is secondary to and can be detached from its source. A piece of writing can function even if its writer withdraws, is no longer alive, or even has a change of mind, whereas speech has the full and immediate authority of its speaker behind it. Derrida goes under Plato's distinction in order to go beyond it. First of all, he notes that Plato's text is itself writing, is read far outside its original context, and is read by many people not in its intended audience who inevitably grasp only a fragment of its meaning—one of the biggest fears articulated by Plato's surrogate, Socrates, in the dialogue. (Ironically, when interviewed, Derrida would often object to the fact that people listening to him would be situated in very different contexts, which was essentially Plato's point.) Nevertheless, Derrida's assertion is that Plato availed himself of the techniques he denounced. Writing is described by Plato as a *pharmakon*, a poison—something external, dangerous, ideally to be eliminated. But *pharmakon* also means remedy as well as poison. *The cure for the problem of writing is also offered by writing*; poison and remedy are two faces of the same coin, according to Derrida.

To add to the complication, *pharmakon* is closely akin verbally to *pharmakos*, the idea of the scapegoat (seen in the Bible in Leviticus 16), the figure who is somewhat arbitrarily cast out of society and who bears its sins into the wilderness in order to secure the health and safety of those who remain within.[29] Yet the scapegoat of the *Phaedrus* is writing—without which we could not read it! The means of representation can also be the rogue outcast; the poison may be just what is needed to cure the poison. Furthermore, writing is described in the myth adduced by Socrates in the dialogue as being invented in Egypt, and the Greeks, although culturally chauvinistic in many ways, always conceded that writing came to them from the ancient Near East. Moreover, Egyptian writing was hieroglyphic, conveying meaning through pictures whose accidental relation to words was all too manifest. Once more, Eurocentrism is critiqued, and Derrida is making a point analogous to those made by Martin Bernal in his analysis of Greek debts to the non-European. Egypt provides the source of its own casting-out by Plato's writing, just as the *pharmakon* is both cure and remedy. Derrida's point here is akin to the quip made by Viennese satirist Karl Kraus about Freudian analysis—that it is the disease for which it purports to be the cure. Writing is both cure and disease. If it is to be cast out, it will also be the operating agency through which the casting out is performed.

One would almost expect Derrida, as a "1960s radical," to oppose Plato, who is so emblematic of the Western tradition. But it is surprising that Derrida would be so critical of the thought of Jean-Jacques Rousseau (1712–78), who, as a philosopher, has a very different image from that of Plato. Far from being associated with the weight of academic tradition, Rousseau is seen as the great advocate of nature and spontaneity, the coiner of the phrase "the noble savage," the apostle of humankind's natural goodness.[30] With an intimate relationship both to the Enlightenment and romanticism, Rousseau embodied many of the aspirations of the modern Left to a more socially harmonious and spiritually wholesome life. This trait made him particularly popular in the 1960s, although, despite being so radical in his views, Rousseau had always been in the canon of Western thought after his death. Indeed, like Socrates, Rousseau was a rebel whose rebellion became normative after the fact. Derrida, though, lets us know not only that he does not share the Rousseauian cult of the natural and spontaneous but also that he sees Rousseau's thought and, in many ways, Rousseau himself as worthy of jest and abuse. He critiques absolutism of feeling as much as of thought—revolutionary upsurge as much as normative constraint. Rousseau's search for a hedonistic breakthrough beyond language is inexorably constrained within language. Rousseau tries to make the medium transparent, but the resistant internal friction of the medium obtrudes and will not be smoothed out.

From the mid-1970s onward, Derrida concentrated less on deconstructing the Western tradition than on showing how deconstruction operated as a practice of the critique of philosophy. In the monumental *Glas* (1974), Derrida divided his text into two columns of commentary, one on Hegel and one on Jean Génet, thinkers with very different reputations. Hegel was the German philosopher of absolute idealism, and all subsequent continental philosophy, including Derrida's, both virulently rejected yet, in a discernible way, referenced his thought. By contrast, Génet, an overt homosexual and convicted criminal, was for many years the iconoclast and wild court fool of French letters. Hegel believed in absolute good, which saw its culmination in his philosophical categories; Génet shocked many by proclaiming the virtues of evil, and himself their personification. And, as important, Hegel was German, and Génet French. Each of these two embodied aspects of their respective countries that were incomprehensible to the other; each seemed to personify national intellectual traditions. Hegel and Génet were the totalizer and the particularistic, but also the philosopher and the literary practitioner. Where does Derrida stand? Trained as a philosopher, he received his greatest intellectual fame as an influence upon literary criticism, though not as a literary critic himself (unlike Paul de Man, his best-known associate, who was trained and always operated as a literary critic).

Hegel certainly overshadows Génet in *Glas*; there is an inherent imbalance; they are not equal contenders. For all his maverick reputation and status and for all his devil-may-care explosion of Hegelian pretensions to absolutism, Derrida was, when compared to someone like Génet, something of an establishmentarian. Indeed, part of Derrida's radicalism is that he *did not* fit into the stereotype of either the upholder of civilization or its innovative destroyer. He presented a contradiction, an enigma that was itself destabilizing. But he did not make the destabilizing his calling card.

The metaphor of messages and delivery animated Derrida's 1980 book *The Post Card*. As in Thomas Pynchon's novel *The Crying of Lot 49* (1966), postal communication is used to model the inherent miscommunication in all messages: even a correspondence between two ardent and reciprocating lovers is always full of mixed messages, betrayed intentions, and codes that do not match. Derrida's idea of *destinerrance*—a fateful deviation or roving—provides the half-vexatious, half-melancholy underbeat of *The Post Card*. The term *destinerrance* indicates this wandering or, in French, *errance* (a wandering knight like Don Quixote was called a knight errant). That this wandering is fated and underlies any sense of destiny or *destin* is also signalled, as is the wayward turn that any desire for resolution will take. *The Post Card* takes place in real time, as it were, across a couple of years in the late 1970s. In fact, the framework is something like a diary, although the text is clearly written as a commentary. But it is also set on at least two other temporal levels. The postcard Derrida buys in Oxford (part of the subtheme of the book is the *destinerrance* between French theory and British doubt about French theory) is a medieval postcard. The love-letter framework reminds us of courtly love (of the sort Don Quixote so vainly pursued) and of its privileging of unrealizable heterosexual yearning. Furthermore, Derrida brings in the relationship of Plato and Socrates in the philosophical dialogues of the former: Socrates as that which is written by Plato, Plato as that which exists in order to write Socrates, and Plato as the hidden genius retrojecting Socrates as his forebear. Ancient rather than medieval, anchored around male-male desire and not male-female desire, written across time rather than across space (Socrates is already dead when Plato writes about him, but even a futile courtship presumes a living interlocutor), Plato's Socrates references provide Derrida with a third temporal level. There is ancient, medieval, and contemporary. This temporal multitracking happens often in Derrida; in *Glas*, for example, there is Hegel, Génet, and ... Derrida.

Derrida did not just stay on one level or even on two (the present seen in light of the past, or vice versa). He pirouetted around, often in a dense thicket of highly specific references and quotations, leaving the reader no firm temporal base. This kind of instability, the sort that Derrida prefers, is, in effect, textuality, and textuality is not substantive, cannot predicate or be predicated. For Derrida, if anything were to "take the place" of logocentrism, it would be textuality. The text exists, but it is not a pure existence or an existence that possesses any authenticity other than in its status as written expression, which, as signifier of that which is traditionally and culturally assigned, has the blatant inauthenticity of the derived and the secondary. Derrida asked what it would be like if we were to invert our established binaries and see writing as anterior to, as underlying, speech. Marshall McLuhan and Walter J. Ong, SJ, saw film, television, and other forms of twentieth-century mass media as "secondary orality" and thought, optimistically, that the media was reaching out to a public no longer seized by print culture and communication. Derrida, on the other hand, inspired a group of media theorists—figures as different as Friedrich Kittler, Avital Ronell, Hans Ulrich Gumbrecht, and McKenzie Wark—to focus on what we might call sec- ondary textuality, what Gumbrecht influentially called "materialities of communication."[31] Of these, only Wark wrote explicitly about the Internet—Gumbrecht and Kittler wrote about the history of media systems, whereas Ronell pioneered explorations into the textuality of daily life. But how the Internet was seen as affecting communication bore more than a few traces of Derridean textuality. Even before the Internet became popular, Stuart Moulthrop was writing about hypertext as expanding the possibilities of print media, possibilities that the digital culture of the 1990s and 2000s fulfilled in a spectacular way.[32] Derridean textuality, once arcane and recondite, seemed to have become part of the world as it was taken. But e-mail and Web surfing relied on a protocol of messages reaching destinations. Derridean textuality always factors in the errant letter. After all, "text" is simply the Latin word for "web"—and the Web was a digitized, endlessly unfolding mega-text.

Derrida's thought on media and technology transpires against the background of a series of French thinkers, from Jacques Ellul to Bernhard Stiegler, who, influenced by Heidegger, are concerned about the inroads of technology upon human life in modernity and look to new ways—often circumventing any nostalgia for individual, autonomous subjectivity—to foil technology's reductive grasp upon us. Derrida's view of technology is not that negative. He sees it as a form of writing, of figuration, in danger of operating in bad faith when its existence is seen as natural or necessary but, when recognized as arbitrary or constructed, of no more inherent menace than any other form of discourse. Derrida does not seek any plenitude of consciousness, nor is he particularly out to redress the ravages of modernity. His conception of language is neither holistic nor redemptive; indeed, he is primed to deconstruct any aspiration towards those conditions. This does not mean that his viewpoint on technology should be confused with that of Jean Baudrillard, who, in an almost futuristic way, tended to hail the simulacra produced by technology as close to inherently laudable in light of their secondariness and reproduction, to see technology as being as liberating as it was potentially stultifying. Derrida's emphasis is on writing and technology as forms of communication. Any ideological interpretation of that communication is, for him, just that—ideology.

Yet, even outside of ideological interpretations of it, communication is not easy and seamless. There is always *destinerrance*. Intriguingly, Foucault's letter to the French government on the Polish crisis of 1981 was called "missed appointments." Both Derrida and Foucault, then, used similar analogies of deferral and botched crossings. Yet Foucault and Derrida often seemed to spar indirectly in the 1970s. Derrida's reference in *Limited Inc* to "the repertoire of a psychology of language" seems to take John Searle to task for confusing him with Foucault.[33] In the same book, one can see a difference between Derrida's and Foucault's ways of reading by looking at their respective treatments of the eighteenth-century philosopher Étienne Bonnot de Condillac. In *The Order of Things*, Foucault sees Condillac as an example of the mindset of general grammar—of a reduplicating, serene Enlightenment whose only limitation is that it defines itself by the same taxonomy that it uses to define external objects. For Derrida, Condillac is not at all lodged within an *episteme*. Condillac is half-wittingly displaying a notion of linguistic absence that, say, Plato and Husserl would equally disclose.[34] For Foucault, meaning was defined by historical difference, for Derrida, by textual gaps. Many people who saw themselves as advocates of Foucault criticized Derrida for what they saw as Derrida's irresponsibility, his verbal opacity, his playfulness, his reluctance to make discursive arguments, and his seeming rejection of history. Foucault, notwithstanding his pessimism, seemed a more constructive figure, somebody who could help provide solutions. Derrida seemed trivial by comparison, and his ideas struck those who did not gravitate to their style and flair as not only unappealing but trivial. There were many similarities between the thinkers. But these similarities were not noticed by immediate factional differences in academia. The reception of each man's ideas in the 1980s, especially in North America, highlighted the differences.

Deconstruction in America: Paul de Man and the Yale School

Reading Deconstructively

Derrida's reception in America was further affected by the presence of Paul de Man, who, though a very different sort of thinker, became Derrida's close American confidant, friend, and mediator. As we have seen in the preface, Paul de Man was able to revolutionize close reading in America precisely because he was trained in New Critical methods as well as familiar with the traditions of European poetry and philosophy. De Man is often seen as the American "leg" of the deconstructive stool. But, from his initial appearance at Johns Hopkins in 1966 at the historic conference on structuralism to his long-time stint as a visiting professor (first at Yale and later at New York University and the University of California, Irvine), Derrida was, in physical terms, a force as constantly present in America as Foucault. As we have discussed with reference to the work of François Cusset, deconstruction, when it was not being accused of being a radical European import at odds with Anglo-American ideas of individual freedom, was often accused of being a transient fad, an academic version of the hula hoop, the pet rock, or the Macarena. Anselm Haverkamp, who taught with de Man at Yale in the latter's last years there, sought to combine these two critiques by seeing deconstruction as a phenomenon perhaps not primarily American but nonetheless palpably present in America.[35] Its presence in America was not, however, equally distributed; it was overwhelmingly associated with a few universities, primarily with Yale. De Man, who had struggled to gain a foothold in US academia after his arrival as an adult from Belgium in the 1940s, came to broad notice while he was teaching at Johns Hopkins in the 1960s. During that time, de Man published book reviews in the newly started *New York Review of Books*. These reviews helped introduce American readers to existentialism and the European avant-garde while also establishing de Man's ability to write strategically and insightfully about a select European canon for an American audience. For all that de Man came to represent "high theory" cloistered in academe, he performed the role of public critic with great acumen, for instance, writing one of the first reviews of Borges to appear in English.[36] In fact, his career was not dissimilar to that of many of the New York Intellectuals: he never produced a large authoritative summa, instead writing essays that became collected into books after appearing in journals. De Man, though, was at home in academia, enjoyed teaching and training students, and was able to turn his very individual literary stance into a perspective that could be the fount of a dedicated protocol of interpretation.

In the early 1970s, de Man was hired at Yale. Here, he joined Bloom, the itinerant Derrida, and two other figures to comprise the "Yale school" of critics. De Man first takes account of Derrida's work explicitly in "The Rhetoric of Temporality."[37] Here, de Man, who profoundly understood the spirit of Derrida's revisionary reading of Rousseau, disagrees with Derrida's conclusion about Rousseau's foolish naïveté, as Derrida delineates this conclusion in *Of Grammatology*. Whereas Derrida sees literary language as corroding Rousseau's faith in the authenticity of his own feelings, de Man sees these feelings as always already laced with what de Man calls "the linguistics of literariness." In other words, according to de Man, Rousseau already anticipates any possible critique that can be made of him, although this anticipation does not mean that a critique should not be made but only that, at the end of its quest, it will meet a self-knowing text. In the same essay, de Man overhauled the way the distinction between symbol and allegory had stood since Coleridge—symbol standing for the image itself, allegory for its connection to the world and to reference. Allegory became revalued in the aftermath of the deconstructive turn because, by reaching back towards reference, it acknowledges its own failure, whereas the symbol remained self-contended in its illusion of aesthetic idealism.

In "Literary History and Literary Modernity," de Man made two moves that outraged much of the academic consensus at the time. He ended with highly polemical concluding sentences, stating that what we construct as history is made up of "not empirical facts but written down texts even if these texts masquerade in the guise of wars or revolutions."[38] This stance placed him on the opposite end of traditional assumptions about the causality between the literary and the non-literary, assumptions commonly favoured by both literary critics and social scientists.

De Man undermined the belief, always somehow guaranteed by the restrictions of 1950s formalism, that external events outside of literature were uncompromisingly real, that they were not somehow "textual." De Man's view upset Marxists particularly. But his scepticism equally questioned *every* doctrine, formal or social, that sought to see text and history as irreducibly separated. (This, paradoxically, included historicists who wanted to connect texts to history; to be so connected, history and the text must first be separated, which de Man's dictum did not permit.) De Man's conclusion accords with Derrida's playful dictum that "*Il n'y a pas de hors-texte*"—there is no outside-text. Perhaps even more convulsive is de Man's model of modernity as something that is continually striven for rather than determinatively achieved. Whereas "the resolved symbolic," for all the interpretive stasis it fostered, had dwelled in curious cohabitation with goal-oriented ideas of modern literature as the newest and most sophisticated wave of writing, de Man's corrosive pessimism about the ability of texts to represent anything straightforwardly extended to the ability of a given period to wrest itself free from its predecessor. In this way, his thought very much resembled Bloom's influence theory, although de Man's focus was on textuality not individual agency. In practice, what this view involves is seeing modernism as but another form of romanticism. Whereas the 1950s had seen Romanticism precisely as that which the twentieth century could and should reject, and the seventeenth century as the ideal towards which contemporary work should helix backward, de Man oriented his practice as a critic around the Romantic lyric.

De Man sharply opposed what he termed "the aesthetic ideology," traceable back to Romantic-era figures such as Friedrich Schiller. This ideology argued that art could be both beautiful and constructive, that it could embody what Wallace Stevens calls "the exhilarations of changes" and also have immediate, cohesive integrity.[39] In other words, de Man did not take romanticism at face value. He was not romantic about romanticism. Like Bloom, de Man was intrigued by romanticism; equally like Bloom, who saw romanticism as a dark crossroads of contending forces, de Man contended that a Romantic reading was precisely not one of innocence or naïveté. For both Bloom and de Man, romanticism, far more than modernism, was where the hard questions were and could be asked.

Aside from Bloom and de Man, the two other major Yale school critics were Geoffrey Hartman and J. Hillis Miller. In 1963, Hartman had written his generation's pivotal book on Wordsworth, *Wordsworth's Poetry*, which had done much to reverse the New Critics' denunciation of Romantic and discursive poetry. J. Hillis Miller was a specialist in narrative and the Victorian novel. All these critics were vastly different. Derrida was neither an American nor, at this point in his career, a literary critic especially, even though his work became more text centred as his career went on. Bloom, although sharing his counterparts' fascination with obscure jargon and with the discontinuities and continuities of tradition, protested that his belief in individual agency made him not one of their number. (Despite Bloom never feeling comfortable within the Yale school, his perceived membership added greatly to its panache.) In Bloom's later work, he dramatically distanced himself from the Yale critics and turned towards a new valuation of the aesthetic and of an emotional and spiritual meaning in literature. Hartman shared Bloom's belief in dividable agency, in the priority of the self no matter how de-romanticized, but he deliberately adopted Derrida's playful métier. Hartman's *Saving the Text* (1976) was, in many ways, Derrida's style Americanized.[40] Miller was very much a textualist, seeing the individual self as constituted by language, discourse, and, to employ one of the favourite words of the Yale school, "trope." "Trope" means "turn," and Yale critics used the term to express the idea of metaphor or other figuration as an irreversible linguistic turn, which made it literary and self-conscious. Miller spent some time as a disciple of Georges Poulet and the "Geneva school," which prastised a "criticism of consciousness" that valued unhindered access to the primal self, or *cogito*, of an author. He then turned in a radically different direction, being interested only in the traces and effects of such a *cogito*, though he still retained the palpable though highly intellectualized affect he exerted as a follower of Poulet.

As thorough and systematic as Miller could be, he yet insisted on particularities of reading, on localities of figured experience, that rebuffed any attempts to mobilize them into a sloganeering generality. Miller propagated these thickly strewn tropes of discourse in such key essays as "Stevens' Rock and Criticism as Cure," which saw criticism as layering over an empty gap or wound of being with the reversible and entrancingly inauthentic constructs of language. Language was valuable precisely because it was all we had to cure this gap. Again, as with Derrida in "Plato's Pharmacy," we have the coincidence of exposure and healing. Reading Stevens attentively resulted in or uncovered a sense of *aporia*, of being at a loss, finding no way out, no road to determinate meaning. Thus, Miller was deconstructive in the doctrinal sense but not in the methodical sense, whereas Hartman's lyricism and (anti-)method was the obverse.[41] Indeed, not only did the Yale School never foster one set approach, but its emphasis was far less on formal method than on the waywardness of reading, what Paul Fry, a second-generation Yale critic and a superb close reader of Romantic poetry, called its "distraction," its straying away from fixed meaning in wandering quest of an asymptotic goal never fully converged upon.

De Man's relatively early death fractured the Yale school. For all the resentment that his perceived position atop the American literary academy occasioned, resentment that was sometimes little more than fear of the foreign, de Man was a late bloomer. He was fifty before he published his first book or became famous. De Man had all too few years in which to enjoy his fame; he died at the height of his influence when he was sixty-four. Quickly thereafter, Hillis Miller decamped for the University of California, Irvine; Bloom declared his distance from deconstruction and, indeed, from theory in general; and Hartman, who had escaped Hitler's Europe as a child, became more preoccupied with writing about the Holocaust and trauma than with practising literary criticism per se.

The Yale school, during the years of its flourishing (roughly 1974 to 1985) constituted the most powerful and influential academic base for literary criticism ever seen. Only Cambridge in the Leavis years remotely rivalled it. Always one of the leaders in literary studies, Yale became the acknowledged site for all that was cutting edge in the profession. The Yale school was often reviled as radical, intent on demolishing ideals of the sweetness of light, the good, the beautiful, and the true. But this depiction was greatly exaggerated. Miller, the most institutionally minded of the Yale critics, expressed this thought, generally true of the school as a whole: "I believe in the established canon of English and American literature and the validity of privileged texts."[42] Like Derrida himself, who, as we have seen, performed his most crucial readings on Plato, Husserl, and Rousseau, the Yale school was revolutionary in *how* it read, not *who* it read. Miller, a Victorianist, wrote about more or less the same set of Victorian novelists that F.R. Leavis or Walter Houghton or Jerome Buckley (prominent Victorianists who persevered through the "resolved symbolic" eras) might have deemed important. Although in *The Ethics of Reading* (1987), half in subversion of the normative and half as a poke at feminism, Miller styled George Eliot "He."[43] Nor did practitioners of deconstruction necessarily prefer the most avant-garde or way-out texts. One of Miller's students, Perry Meisel, downplayed overtly self-referential books in favour of novels that practised "reflexive realism," that, in a sense, were so sophisticated in their self-knowledge that they did not need to ostentatiously parade it.[44] Overtly self-reflexive writers actually fared better with non-theorists, or with more socially minded theorists, than with the Yale school.

Scholars less in tune with theoretical and literary constructs than were the Yale critics had a more difficult time appreciating the nuances of deconstruction. Consequently, those who attempted to adopt deconstruction, or French theory, as a trapping of cultural chic in the 1980s were always somewhat futile in their attempt to affix themselves to the ideas of Derrida and company. They tended not to appreciate the academic and canonical side of deconstruction, which complemented its genuine subversion and far-reaching interrogation of the given. Whereas existentialism was almost totally a movement outside the academy and New Criticism totally inside it, deconstruction, which, as practised by de Man, appropriated and ironized both existentialism and New Criticism, had considerable appeal outside the academy *but remained fundamentally lodged within it*. As such, deconstruction remained far more invested in traditional texts than might be assumed and evinced a corresponding lack of emphasis on primary texts that were themselves self-reflexive or experimental in ways that resembled deconstructive practice. Though Derrida spoke admiringly of Borges, as did de Man, it was Foucault, not Derrida, for whom Borges was crucial. In turn, modernist fabulists such as Vladimir Nabokov and Alain Robbe-Grillet were analysed more frequently, and more insightfully, by traditionalist critics than by the newly emergent deconstructive "Mafia" (as the brilliant traditionalist critic William H. Pritchard of Amherst termed them).[45]

De Man's methods were often accused of being ahistorical. So were Derrida's. We have already seen how Derrida emerged out of the crucible of World War II; indeed, it can be argued that, eventually, much of deconstruction will be seen as a delayed or extended intellectual response to the war and the Holocaust, as a questioning of philosophical absolutes generated by the trauma in their wake. It may not have been May 1968 so much as May 1945—the month when the concentration camps were liberated and the full extent of the Nazi atrocities was discovered—that marked the inception of the crisis in European thought and the prerequisite for the dissemination of deconstructive and, for that, matter anti-racist and post-colonial thought.

The de Man Scandal

In late 1987, several years after his death, it emerged that de Man had been involved in the war's historical crucible—and in a way that did him no credit. A Belgian academic, Ortwin de Graef, who later became de Man's biographer, found collaborationist articles that de Man had written during the early 1940s. The articles were published in the Belgian newspaper *Le Soir*, which had been forced to espouse a pro-Nazi editorial policy and which had become known by the nickname "*Le Soir volé*," the "*volé*" meaning "stolen." De Man's uncle Henri de Man was one of the many figures of that era who started out on the militant left and then shifted to a quasi-Fascist posture. The younger de Man's articles generally shared that position, his Flemish (Dutch-speaking) nationalism making him see Belgium as a bridge between France and Germany that could conceivably contribute to a new European order based on German predominance. (Ironically, the years after the revelation of de Man's articles saw the Flemish population in Belgium assume the lead in terms of economic and, increasingly, political power, spurring a political crisis in the early twenty-first century that the whole brouhaha over de Man's wartime journalism slightly foreshadowed.) The entire issue, like the issue of the influence of Heidegger's thought on Derrida, had at its core the problem of the unresolved relations between "French" and

"German" cultural formations, a problem that haunted Europe throughout much of the nineteenth and twentieth centuries.[46] The Nazi turn of de Man's early work indicated that much of the "German" side of this debate tended towards, consciously or even unconsciously, taking an authoritarian and even racist path. Justifications of German nationalism and selfhood, always obnoxious, became deadly under Hitler's maniacal tyranny. As James J. Paxson has situated the matter, in one of the most sensitive historical studies of de Man's early writing, his early texts call to be read in the context of "the erasure or absorption of competing or personified bodies/states" in "an imaginary allegorical narrative."[47] De Man made a grave mistake in his early years by succumbing to overly categorical accounts of these narratives of territorial absorption.

De Graef's revelation stunned first the small circle of de Man's disciples to whom it was communicated and then the larger academic and even public universe. Much of 1988 was dominated by discussion of the scandal, and many who had never heard of de Man or even of deconstruction encountered both for the first time in this very public and, obviously, negative way. The de Man controversy, waged fiercely at the time but leaving little trace decades later, quickly broke down into various camps. There was a group of people who not only saw de Man as guilty of pro-Nazi sympathies but also decided that these infected his thought with relativism and dishonesty. Among people who defended de Man, there were those who, like Geoffrey Hartman, asserted that de Man, in his later critiques of the organicism of the "aesthetic ideology," atoned for his pro-Nazi wartime journalism. Some others believed that de Man was never seriously pro-Nazi at all, that he was merely uttering implausible absurdities, such as claiming that European literature would be left totally undisturbed by the loss of all Jewish writers, and that these incredible statements were meant to satisfy foolish censors but be read in an ironic way by later initiates.

Whatever "the truth"—to use a phrase that de Man believed in with a fervour that might surprise those who see him as a moral relativist—the basic situation is no different than in the case of many mid-century European intellectuals, a good deal of whom were attracted by unconscionable totalitarian ideologies such as Nazism, Fascism, or Soviet communism. Do we restrict our idea of an acceptable intellectual to those who support impeccably democratic and middle-of-the-road political parties? Does this political litmus test not discriminate in much the same way as do more extremist ones? Do we want our literary theorists to have *exactly* the same values as those whom we vote into office? These questions, present since the time of Plato, cannot be answered merely by reference to the mid-twentieth century, though that era may be their toughest proving ground. But what cannot be contested is that the scandal cost de Man and his adherents serious ground in the critical arena. Part of this was unavoidable, especially as, in an odd way, the personal aura of de Man—his image as rigorous, challenging, and uncompromising—was part of the source of his intellectual appeal, whether one had literally been a student of his or not. De

Man made noting textual unreliability an act of responsibility, not one of way-wardness, and that brought people into a deconstructive orbit who otherwise would not have entered it. His authority depended as much on his personality as did that of someone more obviously "personal" in his preferences among writers and attitudes, such as Leavis. But part of de Man's posthumous loss of ground had to do with more contingent factors.

De Man's thought already had many enemies, and among those to eagerly pounce on the scandal were not only historicists, who loathed de Man for seem-ing to discourage politically purposive and historically referential readings, but also poets, who resented deconstructionist criticism's usurpation of the right to creativity with respect to literature. This latter group played an important part in the antagonistic response to deconstruction in the 1980s. For instance, it was David Lehman, a talented poet, an editor of poetry anthologies, and, at the time, a critic at *Newsweek*, who did the most prominent journalistic work in explor-ing the de Man scandal. For the community of practising poets, the challenge that deconstruction—or, as was often said, "the deconstructionists" or even "the deconstructionalists"—posed was summed up in a poem by Robert Hass. Hass was a student of Yvor Winters in the 1960s, though he was considerably less metrically strict than his mentor. In the 1990s, Hass became poet laureate of the United States, but an early poem, his "Meditation at Lagunitas" (1979), clearly addresses deconstruction when it begins "All the new thinking is about loss. / In this it resembles all the old thinking." Hass concludes by implying that sheer love of language can overcome the lack of necessary correlation between word and referent, abstraction and particular, a lack that the poem had earlier, in line with Derrida and with de Man, generally conceded:

> Such tenderness, those afternoons and evenings,
> saying *blackberry, blackberry, blackberry*.[48]

The suggestion is that saying "blackberry" in a poem will compensate for the absence of a demonstrable correlation between the word and the thing. (Hass seems to read Derrida as if he were Saussure, as if Derrida actively lamented this gap.) In this way, poetry can, for Hass, after a momentary ruffling, move on serenely unencumbered by the deconstructive challenge. But perhaps refutation is not enough. Another American poet, Richard Wilbur, who was hardly ever accused of being a deconstructionist, shows that even the senses do not refute this challenge; he does this with reference to the eighteenth-century anecdote about Samuel Johnson attempting to refute Bishop Berkeley's ethereal philoso-phy by kicking a stone and thus proving the stone was real:

> Kick at the rock, Sam Johnson, break your bones:
> But cloudy, cloudy is the stuff of stones.[49]

"Meditation at Lagunitas" is a fine poem and deserves its fame. Furthermore, if many poets did not read enough Derrida, it is equally true that not enough Derrideans read Hass's poem. But, too often, the poetic mainstream and the critics associated with it, such as Helen Vendler, either finessed their way out of the entire dilemma in the mode of Hass or, following the lead of the "Language Poets" and critical associates of theirs such as Marjorie Perloff, mounted arguments that ostensibly attacked Derrida and de Man from a more experimental and political perspective, invoking Marx and Foucault. But these reactions only heightened the sense that it was deconstruction that was exciting and provoking people.

What deconstruction offers to literature and literary study in general, an offering that tended to be missed by these circumventions, is a salutary openness, a breaking out of the confinement imposed by the "resolved symbolic." To verbalize this sense of freedom and release, deconstruction in America often turned to a vocabulary that might have been thought not ideal for it, that of "the sublime." In Western criticism, the idea of the sublime had stretched back to the ancient critic 'Longinus,' whose treatise *On the Sublime* was translated into French in 1674 by Nicolas Boileau. The re-established idea of the sublime was crucially reiterated by Edmund Burke and far more systematically given new expression in the early Romantic period by Immanuel Kant. But the tradition of the sublime had never been in the major channel of criticism. This is partially because the idea of the sublime itself—something so grand, so majestic as to be beyond immediate comprehension or representation, something that overwhelmed the perceiver, knocked them out—was difficult to situate within an ongoing tradition that tended to tug phenomena down to size. On a totally different level, though, the sublime was seen as too irrational, too threatening to a philosophical tradition that, as Derrida had pointed out, sought above all to keep things in order. Aristotle was privileged over Longinus, and Aristotle prized method and gave literature an imitative role that at once privileged its power and kept it in a box of "production" rather than original thought.

Romantic thinkers such as Kant and Burke were admired in other areas of philosophy. But the "resolved symbolic" put its adherents on notice that the unbridled reach of the Romantic sublime was to be rejected in favour of more austere, disciplined outlooks that did not represent, in T.E. Hulme's phrase, "split religion." As often happened, though, even during the hegemony of the New Critics, people continued to be interested in the sublime. Samuel Holt Monk published an influential work on the subject in 1935, which he continued to revise until the 1960s. When critics became once again interested in the sublime via deconstruction, Monk's thoroughgoing explication of what the concept had meant in the eighteenth century was there, waiting for them.[50] Thomas Weiskel, in *The Romantic Sublime*, explored the sublime as a place replete with fullness yet haunted by emptiness, at once a plenum and a vacuum. Weiskel, who died tragically young in an accident in 1975, was, along with Angus Fletcher and Justus George Lawler, the potential spearhead of a vision of the sublime that was affective, in the mode of Bloom, more than textual, in the mode of Derrida.[51] But Weiskel's passing meant that the major American expositor of the sublime would be Neil Hertz, a follower of de Man who wrote in a Derridean mode, although Hertz's own critical style displayed an independent tone. (In France, Jean-François Lyotard provided a more strictly deconstructive version of the sublime.) In seeing the sublime as "the end of the line," the limit situation in which perception was flummoxed and the ordinary function of perceptions vanished, Hertz designated the sublime less as a knockout punch of aesthetic ecstasy than as an ever-receding horizon of mystification that, nevertheless, tantalized the perceiver to persist in trying to construct meaning.

The deconstructive sublime promised no redemptive overall meaning. But there was an exhilaration to it, an exuberance, a sense of openness and daring, of risk and adventure, of ecstasy—albeit fragmented ecstasy. This was an aesthetic feeling, though a fragmented one. It is notable that, before he became interested in Derrida, Miller's chief allegiance was to critics such as Georges Poulet who tried to get inside the mentality of the work of single authors. Hartman's work, too, always had a sense of existential and phenomenological authenticity to it, even if this sense was laced with a linguistic edge. As compared to a slightly earlier set of structuralist-oriented figures at Yale, such as Jacques Ehrmann, who were interested in a more playful, game like idea of literary experimentation, the Yale school of the de Man era was very involved with emotion, although at a heightened and rigorous distance. This involvement informed their valuation of art and the idea of "the aesthetic." Indeed, the Yale critics paid much more attention to thinkers of the past who had been labelled "aesthetes," for example, Walter Pater and Oscar Wilde, than had the New Critics, for whom these late nineteenth-century thinkers were too Romantic, too close to Shelley. Deconstruction's embrace of Pater and Wilde paved the way for their later appropriation by queer theory.

Yet there was an elitist air around deconstruction in America. A sense predominated that it trafficked in obscure jargon. Admittedly, this was true of nearly every other school of theory too. Even more, most jobs, such as working in a bank or even in an auto repair shop, require at least some specialized terminology. What fuelled these claims about deconstruction's language being snobbishly jargonistic was that, in the early 1980s, deconstruction was taught primarily at elite institutions such as Yale, Stanford, and Cornell. Later, departments at the University of Southern California and especially the University of California, Irvine, where Miller moved in 1985, became "deconstructive," but, by then, deconstruction, as a method, had lost the fight for influence to historicism. The forbidding allure of deconstruction, or even its invocation of the awe and indiscernible might of "the sublime," could be seen troping the difficulty many citizens found in accessing those institutions. There were some efforts, such as Gregory Ulmer's, to make deconstruction more practical and accessible without simply coarsening it or watering it down to pragmatism.[52] In a far more indirect way, Cathy Caruth, a student of de Man's, adapted deconstruction to her study of the aftermath of suffering; the ideas of the temporal lag and the linguistic gap were especially useful in her influential theories of trauma.[53]

Though Gérard Genette's narratological theories were not actually associated with deconstruction, his complex and unfamiliar terminology sounded like that of deconstruction. Genette's theories were descriptive, not diagnostic, and they were useful to critics otherwise theoretically uninflected because, as with the theoretical approaches in Wayne Booth's work, they could specifically describe what was actually going on in narrative terms in a book.[54] Indeed, Genette's paradigmatic novelist, Marcel Proust, was also a great favourite of de Man. If deconstruction and narratology had managed to combine their methods and present the result in a simple and appealing way, such a mélange might have become the dominant mode. (What Michael Riffaterre was able to do with poetry gave a foretaste of what this mélange could have been, although Riffaterre would have been more influential in the United States if he had written about something other than French poetry.) As it was, the rivals of deconstruction—reader-response theory and new historicism—proved much more successful at reaching undergraduates. This was not because deconstruction is really any more difficult to teach—de Man, after all, had honed his pedagogical skills under the mentorship of Reuben A. Brower (1908–75), whose teaching-oriented classes at Harvard stressed close reading above all. It was because reader-response and historicist critics were more able and willing to teach at the so-called second-tier institutions, where they could reach and instruct far larger numbers of students. And, in turn, these sorts of institutions, alienated by the jargon of deconstruction, were more willing to hire historicists and reader-response critics than emulators of de Man's linguistic rigour and irony.

Alternatives to Deconstruction: Reader-Response Theory, Hermeneutics, Dialogism, Historicism

Enter the Reader

Reader-response theory and historicism were two alternatives to deconstruction. They both undid credos of the New Criticism. Reader-response theory repealed the affective fallacy, which New Critics defined as confusing a literary work's objective qualities with its subjective results. Instead, said reader-response theorists, the reader's response meant something. Historicism, with its sense that social background mattered, repealed the intentional fallacy, the New Critical argument that a literary work, once published, had an existence distinct from the original creator's intention. There had been some attention to the role of the reader as early as the 1950s, but most of it, such as the work of Louise Rosenblatt of New York University, was bottled up in composition programs unfairly slighted by their more pretentious literary counterparts. In the next generation, reader-oriented criticism became far more prominent. A distinction is often made between reader-response theory, which is most often concerned with the private responses of individual readers, and reception theory, which is more interested in the historical changes affecting the reading public than in the individual reader. Critics such as Norman Holland focused on the preferences of individual readers and profited from the insights of Freudian psychology. Scholars such as Peter Rabinowitz and David Bleich had a more communitarian emphasis, exploring how a class or group reading a text achieved a collective experience that at once provides a range of perspectives yet exhaustively solicits the potentialities of a given text. European critics such as Wolfgang Iser retained the emphasis on the private rather than the public reader but saw the reader as orchestrated by the text. As we will recall from the preface, Wayne Booth spoke of the "implied author" as a way of getting over the New Critical fixation on the separation between the author and the narrator of a text. Iser turned this concept around and spoke of "the implied reader," the reader a text posited as part of its inherent matrix. In other words, for Iser, the reader of a text was the particular sort of reader *that* text made—*had* to be that sort of reader. Neither personal subjectivity nor external social forces had any effect. Hans Robert Jauss took a more social position; his theory of "*Rezeptionsästhetik*" sought to analyse how a text was received publicly, what its social significance was at the time it was written, and, going beyond these strictly definable categories, what the "horizon of expectations" was at the time it was produced; what climate was *expecting* a text? In the 1980s, Jauss and Foucault were often paired as antagonists of Iser and Derrida, the socially minded versus the text-centred thinkers. But this "mixed doubles" match between teams of linguistic and reader-response theorists gainsaid Jauss's fundamentally more empirical bent and his far less philosophical orientation.[55] Indeed, in the twenty-first century, Jauss's impact can be seen in the slew of treatments of book history and print culture as much as in the more avowedly political historicist methodologies of what de Man described (sceptically) as reception theory's "far-reaching synthesis between the private and public dimensions of the literary work."[56] But both Iser and Jauss represented the practicality and accessibility of reader-response theories, which could be introduced, overtly or tacitly, into the beginning literature classroom in a way that Derridean deconstruction could not. Like deconstruction, though, reader-response theory was not automatically or naively radical or subversive; Stanley Fish's *Surprised by Sin* (1967) reread Milton's *Paradise Lost* and argued that the exaltation of Satan in the poem prized by so many Romantic critics was a snare into which the text preprogrammed the reader, or at least the unprepared reader, to fall. In *Self-Consuming Artifacts* (1972), Fish replaced the New Critical totem of the tightly knit unit with the book that corrected, and thereby annulled, itself mid-course; as is typical of Fish's criticism, there was both a radically subjective and a fundamentally instructive or even didactic aspect to this idea.

Mikhail Bakhtin

Reader response's greater immediate accessibility than deconstruction was apparent. That the thought of Mikhail Bakhtin (1895–1975) also appeared more accessible might have seemed surprising, however. The tradition that Bakhtin was centred in was exceedingly remote to most Anglo-American readers. Derrida and Foucault were deeply immersed in continental thought, and reading them required anglophone readers to adapt themselves to the style and assumptions of a more philosophical, European mode than had been their wont. Still, the intellectual milieus of France and Germany were, in large measure, familiar to such readers, but that of Russia and of Slavic languages in general were less familiar. When theory is spoken of as broadening reading climates, what is largely meant as the agent enabling this broadening is the literature by various peoples overtly subordinated by the European tradition. But theory importantly also broadened the English-speaking tradition out to the European continent.

Yet Russia, known in literary terms mainly for its novelists, became latterly known for its theorists, the exotic becoming familiar. Not only Bakhtin but also the Russian formalist predecessors such as Viktor Shklovsky (who actually outlived Bakhtin), Nikolay Trubetskoy, and Boris Eikhenbaum became part of anglophone critical parlance. Part of the lag in these critics' repute was the tumultuous and oppressive political circumstances under which they lived. Bakhtin lived for most of his life under government suspicion and had to eke out a living in marginal positions. At one point, according to some, he even had to publish his work under the names of several of his students. Bakhtin's thought was first introduced to the West by émigrés from Eastern Europe such as Todorov and Julia Kristeva (see Chapter 3), but his writings were translated quickly and popularized by American Slavists.[57] Bakhtin's major emphasis was on the idea of dialogue, which, for him, meant not just conversation but also a deep double-sidedness or multi-sidedness, an ability to take on different vantage points and views and hold them all at once in suspension and in a kind of creative competition. Bakhtin saw the medieval idea of carnival, in which the usual assumptions of society were overturned and an anarchic spirit of play prevailed, as representing an irruption of the grotesque, the uncontrolled, "the body." Bakhtin's emphasis on the social body paralleled that of Foucault, although Bakhtin, by intellectual temperament at least, was far more optimistic than Foucault. As opposed to the Hegelian "dialectic," which saw thesis and antithesis as moving together in a lugubrious and complicated embrace as a synthesis, the dialogic did not resolve in finality. It was unfinished, in perpetual creative discord, an unresolved fertility. The elements in dialogue were radically other in mutual terms; they were not reducible to a formula of resolution. Bakhtin spoke of "unfinalizability" (*nezavershennost* in Russian) and also of "polyphony." Though we tend to think of polyphony as a musical mode in which contending elements counterpoint one another but no single element dominates, for Bakhtin polyphony was strictly verbal, indeed reached a range of contrariety and flux in words that could not be achieved in a more static or one-dimensional mode. Bakhtin particularly appreciated texts in which different languages entirely, but also different levels of speech and modes of discourse, interacted and proliferated. Importantly, even though Bakhtin's celebration of social dissidence inspired much work in what came to be called cultural studies, and was even read in a Marxist way by some critics, Bakhtin did little work that could be called cultural or sociological. For him, the literary was always supreme, and it was social dissidence *in the literary* that he valued. The cultural studies movements that proliferated after the 1980s made productive use of Bakhtin, but this use was largely outside the original purview of his work.

Bakhtin's dialogism was, at least, relatable to Derridean ideas of supplementary and *différance*. Both Derrida and Bakhtin reject a predetermined or prescribed method and encourage multiplicity even if it threatens to undermine coherence. But Bakhtin seemed more humanistic than Derrida or Foucault. Derrida and Foucault came to be known as living, breathing individuals by the end of their lives. Bakhtin, even though dead by the time his work became widely read in the West, seemed to be alive as soon as he was translated. Bakhtin was a believing Orthodox Christian, and his ideas were adopted with enthusiasm by some Christian thinkers, who saw the incarnation of Christ as the ultimate dialogic event. Whereas analyses of Christianity and literature had, since the 1950s, generally remained in the vein of T.S. Eliot, Bakhtinian influence enabled critics of faith and of a largely traditionalist standpoint to relate to at least one of the trendy new theorists their colleagues were talking about, and that was important for intellectual continuity and commonality. Conservative intellectuals had to respect Bakhtin's perseverance under Stalinist oppression, and his thought implied a critique of the monologic nature of Marxist philosophy. Moreover, discourse about Bakhtin took full advantage of the greater comfort with interdisciplinary thought and the social sciences in Slavic studies, which had always been there, even before Soviet dogma perverted these tendencies into the calcified dictates of socialist realism and other government-compelled modes of thought. (Nonetheless, these very traits made Bakhtin's theories surprisingly palatable to Marxists.) Linguistics, psychology, science, as well as history were familiar notions in Slavic studies, whereas in both French and Anglo-American literary circles, these had to be introduced with much more fanfare. Bakhtin also seemed a large-minded figure. In his scope and ambition, as well as in his humanistic motivation, Bakhtin had traits in common with Northrop Frye, who shared his interest in the genre of "Menippean satire" (a prose-verse hybrid that allowed ideas to be animated using literary images and devices).

Yet Bakhtin's popularity in North America, though at one point broader than Foucault's or Derrida's, was not as enduring. Part of this transience was due to notions such as dialogism and carnival having a wide but shallow currency, which soon faded. Another aspect proceeded from Bakhtin's own limitations and biases. Bakhtin had disdain for the literature of the ancient world, which he considered "monologic," allowing no possibility for human freedom. This stance would not have been shared by Foucault and Derrida, who were, in their own ways, both avid classicists. In this attitude, Bakhtin was no doubt influenced by Marxist theories of history that saw medieval feudalism as an advance over ancient economic production, and modern capitalism even more so. Bakhtin's literary likes and dislikes permeated his work—for him, not only nearly any literature before 1500 but all epic poetry, lyric poetry, or, indeed, poetry of any sort was "monologic."

Even though, until Stalinist literary doctrines began to be imposed in the early 1930s, Bakhtin would have had some access to modern novelists such as Joyce, Woolf, and Proust, he showed no interest in them. He also rejected the paramount modern mode of stream of consciousness (arguably first used by Tolstoy in *Sevastopol Sketches*) as not dialogic, not truly involving different voices but presenting only one inner voice. The modern novel is thus not included in Bakhtin's account of fictional polyphony.[58] His canon is even more conservative than Erich Auerbach's! To make things worse, Bakhtin was sometimes oversimplified and made more palatable and convenient than he actually was. His celebration of the subversive, carnivalesque spirit of François Rabelais's work was often seen as an unqualified celebration of the bawdy that ignored those moments when, in Michael André Bernstein's phrase, "the carnival turns bitter."[59] Moreover, Bakhtin's championship of the polyphony of Dostoevsky perhaps overstated the case when it came to the Russian writer's actual work, and certainly Bakhtin very much took one side in the seemingly eternal question, so brilliantly raised by George Steiner at the beginning of his career— "Tolstoy or Dostoevsky?" The key to the success of Derrida and Foucault was their applicability to texts and contexts that they could not have foreseen and on which they had not written. Bakhtinian readings were even more mechanical than Derridean or Foucauldian ones when Bakhtin's thought was applied outside the texts and milieus for which he had his unique brand of unsurpassable empathy.

Hans-Georg Gadamer

Another important figure from somewhat further west than Bakhtin was the German hermeneutician (scholar of interpretation) Hans-Georg Gadamer (1900–2002) who, though quite elderly, survived well into the age of theory and, in fact, predeceased Derrida by only a couple of years. Gadamer, like Derrida, got much of his intellectual bearings from Heidegger, although Gadamer's Heidegger was more concerned with the radical conservation of tradition than the interrogative destruction of it. (This likely has something to do with the fact that Gadamer actually *knew* Heidegger.) In his theory of *wirkungsgeschichtliche Bewusstsein*, or the consciousness of the working of effects, Gadamer asserted that, though we are not bound to the past in a monolithic way, we are affected by our understanding of it in an inescapable way. As so often with "theory," what seemed radical in an Anglo-American context was in fact the assertion that tradition was subtly omnipresent and could not be evaded.[60] Like Bakhtin, Gadamer was interested in dialogue, although, unlike Bakhtin, Gadamer, who began as a classicist, derived his idea of the dialogic largely from the dialogues of Plato. Though Gadamer's stress on tradition seemed conservative, his sense that the past, though always exerting a tug on the present, could only reverberate in front of a prism that the consciousness could never penetrate, meant that tradition was not unitary and could not be apprehended in a way that would set up a seamless continuity.

In this way, Gadamer was very different from Romantic thinkers such as Schiller and Schleiermacher whom he both emulated and inverted. Gadamer's idea of the consciousness of the working of effects, in fact, was similar to Derrida's idea of "citationality," worked out in his investigation of the tradition of the British linguistic philosopher J.L. Austin. In *Signature Event Context*, Derrida uses "citational graft" or "citationality" to say that linguistic utterance can never happen decisively in the "illocutionary" way described by Austin.[61] For Austin, language has an "illocutionary force" that nudges an event in the direction of happening, though it does not directly cause an event to happen—that would be "perlocutionary." Derrida talks of citationality as causing meaning to migrate, via something very close to illocutionary force, from word to word, so it cannot be pinned down. Similarly, for Gadamer, we are barred by temporal distance from direct insight into the past. But Derrida's idea of citationality then does a kind of backward turn. Having disrupted unitary meaning, it then insists that all the dispersed fragments of meaning are somehow connected in an indirect, but not broken, chain of reference. Citationality, however destructive of linear, progressive temporality or even of a sense of purpose and achievement it may seem to be, does actually attest to some vestige of meaning. Gadamer's idea of the consciousness of efforts similarly bans both full meaning and a meaningless, isolated irrelevance. Yet Gadamer strives for a fuller ideal of knowledge than does Derrida, as was clear on the occasion of the two thinkers' "debate" in 1981. Gadamer believes in the possibility of interpretation, in the quest for understanding, although, for him, this quest was conducted across many roadblocks. Derrida believes language always gets in the way of understanding, that even a process of trying to understand becomes tinged by difference before it can even attempt to know the whole. Gadamer, like Derrida, articulated tradition insofar as it is dispersed in the "always already." What Gadamer's theory subverts is the transparent moment that thinks it can simply stand on its own.

Fredric Jameson and the Rise of Historicism

The most influential counterpart to Derridean and de Manian deconstruction in the 1980s, though, was not Bakhtinian dialogism or Gadamerian hermeneutics but new historicism. Its major practical figure, Stephen Greenblatt, will be discussed in Chapter 7. But this section will deal with new historicism's major theoretical inspiration, Frederic Jameson. Jameson trained as a scholar of French; his major influences were Auerbach's philology and existentialism. And, before gaining fame, he wrote two important books: *Marxism and Form*, which helped introduce the critical theory of Adorno and Benjamin into an anglophone context, and *The Prison-House of Language*, which did the same for Saussurean linguistics (which Jameson saw as insufficiently political). But Jameson's career-making work was *The Political Unconscious* (1981), which began with the pithiest and most famous sentence in all of literary theory: "Always historicize!"[62] (Its only rival is Stephen Greenblatt's equally historical but far more past-directed sentence "I began with the desire to speak with the dead."[63]) Jameson was a committed Marxist and wrote in explicitly Marxist terms that were rare in the American academic community, which, despite the Right's accusation that theory was a form of Marxism, actually, in many ways, used deconstruction as a means to disaffiliate itself with Marxism.

Jameson's political inclinations did not at all preclude his being an agile close reader of literary texts. He wrote with equal poise about Joseph Conrad and Gustave Flaubert, about postmodern architecture and the social progress of the European bourgeoisie. Of the US-based critics who actually spent a good deal of their time working on texts, he was the least parochial. As with Bakhtin, Jameson's sense of totality and the generosity of his intellectual reach were reminiscent of Frye. Like Frye, Jameson found useful the medieval fourfold notion of  typology—literal, allegorical, moral, and anagogic (comprehending the entirety of the horizon)—although he politicized this notion, unlike Fry. Indeed, Jameson was very interested in allegory, and he joined with de Man in wresting away symbol's post-Coleridgean hegemony within the symbol-allegory distinction. In his under-noticed book on the right-leaning British novelist and artist Percy Wyndham Lewis, Jameson coined the term "national allegory," which encapsulated the abilities of fiction to sum up and, often, to congeal national identities artificially. In some ways, Jameson's "national allegory" concept is similar to the approach used in Benedict Anderson's book *Imagined Communities*.[64] Jameson, after Lyotard, was the figure most central in defining what postmodernism was in literary terms: for Jameson, postmodernism was tantamount to late capitalism, to a phase of capitalism that assumed it had withstood all potential threats of revolution and could celebrate itself in ostentatious irony. If anything, Jameson, who was a fierce critic of late capitalism or, as it came to be called, "neoliberalism," esteemed his enemy too much in tactical terms. For Jameson, capitalism became very like Derridean textuality: inescapable. Thus Jameson's criticism, for all its political willpower, offered no more of an escape from "the prison-house of language" than did Derrida's. Or, at best, it saw language itself as being subject to capitalist fiat, which was even less liberating than Derrida's vision of an infinitely regressive textual universe. It was left to a new generation of more empirically sensitive historicists to lead historical critique out of theory altogether. But, in the last decades of the twentieth century, Jamesonian political allegories, not de Manian linguistic ones, carried the day in the academy.

Derrida Alone: The 1990s and 2000s

After all this, Derrida remained. Indeed, Derrida outlived many of his significant intellectual peers—Barthes, de Man, Foucault. Derrida might even be said to have outlived deconstruction. In the 1980s, there were scores of deconstructionists. In the early 2000s, the last years of Derrida's life, he may have been the only one still doing deconstruction in the same sense. He was more famous than ever, more lionized, with more demands on his time. Yet his thought remained constant, concerned above all with language and textuality. As the great nineteenth-century Russian poet Fyodor Tyutchev put it (in Vladimir Nabokov's translation), "A thought once uttered is untrue."[65] Derrida was intent on eliciting and living out the truth of that inherently untrue utterance. His writing became more idiosyncratic and more text-centred; there were few expositions after 1975 or so and many dense commentaries on anterior texts. In the later Derrida, vocabulary becomes more text-specific, anchored in the texts Derrida is immediately writing and writing about. And he is less concerned to rebut or refute these texts than to find the tangled skein of linguistic meaning in them. Derrida is not a nihilist. He is perhaps closer to nihilism than to ultimate affirmation, but only a very little bit closer. Even that small edge is laden with play and ambiguity.

Derrida also came to analyse fewer philosophical and more literary texts. Today, people have become used to deconstructive readings of certain writers, to what might be called applied deconstruction, and de Man certainly was a major node of this sort of reading (though it can hardly be said that de Man merely "applied" Derrida's approach). Applied deconstruction came to be seen as largely a procedure of some other critic taking Derrida's thought and using it to read literary works, but Derrida himself gave lengthy readings of literary texts early on. *Ulysse gramophone*, his reading of Joyce's *Ulysses* was published in 1985 and was second only to Hélène Cixous's book on Joyce as a poststructuralist reading of this author. *Ulysse gramophone* pioneered the comparison of modernist texts to new technologies, which Friedrich Kittler and many historicists furthered. Even earlier, *Signéponge*, Derrida's meditation on the poetry of Francis Ponge, and *Spurs*, his meditations on the style of Nietzsche, had established his view of literary style as multiple. This view ran against the grain in the era of the "resolved symbolic" with its view of literary style as unitary and somehow suggestive of a text's inner state of being. This tacit connection between a text and an internal correlate was maintained, for instance, by Auerbach's philology and was the target of critique by Stanley Fish in his 1970s refutations of "affective stylistics"—or the view that one could conjure a isolable state of feeling from an apprehension of a given writer's style.[66]

ethics

Derrida's work is often spoken of as taking an "ethical turn" in the 1990s in that his writings become more preoccupied with issues of ethics and religion. This shift was partially a deliberate reaction to those critics of deconstruction that castigated it as unethical or abstaining from discussions of ethics. Hillis Miller's *The Ethics of Reading* (1987) was a similar riposte in which Miller argued that the undecideabilty of deconstructive methods made reading, as such, a situation that demanded an ethical perspective. Work by philosophers such as Richard Rorty, Stanley Cavell, and Martha C. Nussbaum is also apt here. Rorty's pragmatic yet visionary optimism, Cavell's hope for overcoming scepticism in the miracle of the restoration of the given in the wake of the abyss, and Nussbaum's sense of literature's potential for healing, thoughtfulness, and mutual understanding were all valuable manifestations of the need for a renewed sense of ethical awareness, for an ethical sensitivity that had lain dormant in all the emphasis on playfulness and subversion during the high years of deconstruction. But often people spoke of Derrida's ethical turn, linking it to the work of these other thinkers, as if this turn meant a correction or repudiation of his previous thought. Indeed, the word "turn," which is taken from Kant and Heidegger, connotes a major philosophical shift. In Kant, it signifies the reorientation by empiricism of his thought *with respect to previous rationalist philosophers*, a matter discussed before in this book with reference to Foucault and "anthropological sleep." In Heidegger, it references his mid-career *Kehre* from philosophical anthropology to concentrating on being as such, a "turn" discussed previously in this chapter. For both Kant and Heidegger, turning represented a change of heart. This conversion is not so apparent in Derrida. Nor, as it is thought, did Derrida's concern with ethics only begin to show itself in the 1990s. In *Mémoires for Paul de Man* (1986), Derrida's eulogy of his friend and colleague (published before the de Man scandal came out), Derrida ruminated on the nature of friendship in ways that inherently evoked ethical reverberations. After the news of de Man's early journalism became public, Derrida wrote once more on de Man, in *Like the Sound of the Sea Deep Within a Shell: Paul de Man's War*, published in 1988. Derrida was writing not just in defence of de Man but in defence of himself. He knew that the attacks on de Man were also attacks on him and on his thought and that, even though Derrida was himself exempt from his friend's fate of being characterized as a Nazi (because Derrida was a Jew who had been in some danger during the war), Derrida's own work as well as de Man's was the object of attempted delegitimizing. But the two memorial pieces for de Man do more than just attempt a defence (though not an apologia). They revealed Derrida to be capable of speaking in a more personal voice and searching for how to define a set of values and ideals that could operate within a self-conscious, reflexive matrix.

Derrida's writings after 1990 became shorter and more occasional. This was no doubt a practical response to the demands on his time and to the constant invitations to give lectures and colloquia. (Foucault's later work is largely written for lectures and seminars as well.) But it is important to realize that another thinker in this position would have been content to provide what the French call *vulgarisations* of his previous thought, boiling them down into platitudes for a larger audience. Though Derrida did not change in his later work to the extent that Foucault did, he continued to develop new turns in his thought until the end. When published, Derrida's lectures have an intriguing feel: the great denouncer of the priority of speech over writing in Western metaphysics has his later texts haunted by orality, although Derrida would most likely say that this orality was an orality already written. They are, as Ian Balfour puts it, "sketchier and more improvisatory."[67] They have a poetry to them, an imaginative independence that often evades the classifications of the academic world in which Derrida was so highly laurelled. Derrida became the master of the seventy-page riff, a genre perfected if not invented by him. In this short, but not overly brief, compass—longer than an article, but shorter than a book— he would grab hold of a text, a thinker, or a problem; ambulate around it, sometimes sedately, sometimes frenetically, always with original calculations, gyrations, and spasms of language; and dazzle, amuse, and provoke the reader. Derrida's pieces are performative and self-ramifying with respect to their own arguments—spinning them out, dancing on them. Derrida writes the opposite of a Kantian treatise. But his texts are also far more lyrical and robust and copious than the bite-size aphorisms in the later works of Nietzsche or Wittgenstein.

Shibboleth (1986) was Derrida's meditation on the gnomic, dense, yet morally clear poetry of Holocaust survivor Paul Celan, whose work Derrida considered in apposition to Judges 12 in the Bible, in which a certain tribe of Israelites was marked out for their mispronunciation of the word "shibboleth." Derrida, who knew well the importance of the difference between the spelling and pronunciation of words, provides his usual multitracking approach, responding to more than one text while overlaying commentary on his responses to the texts. Derrida overtly refers here to his Jewish aspects, much as in *Circonfession* (his meditation on the thought of St. Augustine of Hippo) he alludes to the fact that Augustine was born in North Africa, as Derrida was, and that Derrida and Augustine were, at that point, the two "Africans" to be acclaimed as major Western philosophers.[68] Both texts, in other words, are elusively, opaquely autobiographical.

In *Circonfession* Derrida indicates his increased interest in the rhetoric of Christianity. (As we will recall, Foucault also grew interested not only in the idea of Christianity but in the practice of confession, as seen in his contrasting of confession and *parrhesia* discussed in Chapter 1.) This stretching of deconstruction to include religious discourses was often taken to mean that Derrida had "gotten religion." He had not. His deconstruction of religious discourse was what one might call a "Tetragrammatology," playing on the idea of the "Tetragrammaton"—the four letters that, in Hebrew tradition, represented the unsounded name of God. Derrida did not become a follower of Judaism,

Christianity, or any other creed. Indeed, though in his later phase, he wrote mostly about the monotheistic religions descended from Judaism, early work of his, such as his critique of alphabetic reason in *Of Grammatology*, led scholars interested in Buddhism, Hinduism, and Taoism to examine the discourses of those religions in apposition to Derrida's thought, and there has been a long tradition of productive work being done along those lines. Unlike Emmanuel Lévinas, in terms of Judaism, or Christian thinkers such as Jean-Luc Marion and John Milbank, who were allied to or influenced by deconstructive thought and did affirm positive religious belief, Derrida never did. This urge to baptize Derrida is another instance of the absorption of a dissident thinker into a more conformist ideology; it is another form of delegitimizing. But there is nonetheless an important point here. Derrida was not "the village atheist." He acknowledged some sort of spiritual level, even if, as in the mystical tradition of "negative theology" (a connection Derrida disavowed, but which his readers kept raising), God is absent from the universe and only accessible by evocation or by just registering the absence of the divine.[69]

Derrida: The Faithful Sceptic

Derrida did not believe in the narrative of secularization that would hail the modern world as free of religious dogma. (Neither did Foucault, who, after all, was not unspiritual, for instance practising Zen Buddhist meditation on his visits to San Francisco; who saw religion as a mode of "caring for the self"; and who, in general, opposed any sense that the modern world could be independent of states of mind that had come before it.) Derrida acknowledged tradition even as he sought to interrogate it, and the tradition of Europe was unarguably a Judeo-Christian one, primarily. Though Derrida denounced this tradition as "onto-theological," he knew that it could not be dislodged by fiat. In fact, Derrida, in stressing the inescapability of a Christian heritage for Europe, raised questions similar to those of Pope John Paul II and Benedict XVI (who may have been the only two European intellectuals of their time as influential as Derrida and Foucault). But Derrida had very different answers. Derrida, although he entertains the possibility of theism, as he entertained the possibility of everything he interrogated, adamantly does not turn to Christianity in a positive way. In this fashion, albeit very opaquely, he is the heir of the best of the French Enlightenment, the heir of those elements of the Enlightenment that did not inflate an opposition to dogma into what Carl Becker termed its own secular "heavenly city."

As Gil Anidjar says of "the Abrahamic" (meaning Islam, Judaism, and Christianity taken together as figurative descendants of the biblical Abraham), "it inserts itself enigmatically and persistently in an unwritten and unreadable history.[70] Any affirmation there is cannot be predicated, made palpable or tangible. This was a stumbling block for readers who wanted to make Derrida morally convenient. A particular locus of this tendency was Derrida's work on the question of forgiveness. Derrida's work on forgiveness is grounded in history, in particular the two historical legacies the postmodern West has found the most troubling to overcome: the Holocaust and racism. Derrida drew upon the influential work of Vladimir Jankélévitch (1903–85).[71] Also resonant was the process set up by the Truth and Reconciliation Commission in post-apartheid South Africa, which sought harmony between that nation's different races not by suppressing what had happened in the name of an artificial concord but by publicly ventilating all the crimes and violent acts that had been committed in order to clear the air and enable a new beginning that would be premised precisely on the acknowledgement, rather than the suppression to transcendence, of a painful and bloody past.[72] Confession, in this respect, precisely because it does not seek a definitive pardon or resolution in Christian terms, becomes very close to Foucauldian *parrhesia*, bold speech.

Derrida is often seen as advocating or preaching forgiveness. Perhaps on the highest, most remote level, he is doing this, but not on the middle- or lower-range level, as certain of his readers seem to think. Derrida does indeed ask us to forgive the unforgivable. Forgiving the forgivable would make us merely what Wallace Stevens termed "happy people in a happy world"; there would be little point to it.[73] It is the colossal crimes that call for forgiveness not the passing misdemeanours. But this does not mean that he thinks any crime should be forgiven. Some, for instance, have tried to create daylight between Derrida and Jankélévitch by stating that the latter sees the Nazis as unforgivable and that Derrida defines forgiveness as forgiving the unforgivable. But there is not so much of a difference. Jankélévitch notes that the Nazis did not ask for forgiveness, that forgiveness can only be given to those who ask for it. Derrida agrees, but, unlike Jankélévitch, Derrida would not foreclose the horizon of the forgivable because of the nature of an act, not because he wishes to dispense forgiveness easily (and the entire idea of just who is eligible to dispense forgiveness comes in here) but because to make of forgiveness a restricted economy, to make it potentially unavailable to anyone, would simply make it a tool of whim and ideological convenience. So Derrida would join in Jankélévitch's gesture of not forgiving the Nazis, of banning any forgiveness of Nazism, but that is because they did not ask for it. Derrida does not believe in what discourse about the American Left would call a "Kumbaya" mentality (after the let's-all-be-friends gospel folk song). He does not see forgiveness as a kind of cheap grace.[74]

And this point is important in terms of Derrida's own career and reputation. Many who disliked Derrida's thought when he was seen as the leader of deconstruction seem more positive towards it after his "ethical turn." Much of this acceptance came from a sense that Derrida had somehow been brought to heel, been circumscribed, truncated, forced, perhaps by the de Man affair, to acknowledged ethical imperatives that his earlier "bad boy" persona had defied. In this scenario, "forgiveness" could easily operate as a panacea in terms of the fissures of meaning that Derrida had unearthed. Derrida and those who were suspicious of him could "forgive" each other, and Derrida could rejoin the consensus that had made him the scapegoat, the *pharmakos*. But many of these commentators acted as if this coming together would mean that Derrida would come around to their point of view. They wanted a unilateral winner of the culture wars and the criticism wars, and they wanted Derridean forgiveness to somehow enable *his opponents* to be this winner. But Derrida did not come near to doing this; he held his ground; he argued his points; he maintained his integrity.

Another text often read too simply is *The Gift of Death* (1996).[75] In acknowledging mortality as one of the features that give meaning to life, in seeing death and the limitations it imposes as a deliverance, not a punishment, Derrida is echoing not only Heidegger, who was famously associated with "being towards death" but also the Christian belief that mortality lends value to existence and sets up the drama of redemption whose hero is Jesus Christ. Yet Derrida rejects the terms on which the Christian image of an afterlife has been customarily premised. He signals this rejection by considering the wager associated with the thought of the seventeenth-century philosopher Blaise Pascal (written of with great insight by Lucien Goldmann). We do not know whether there is an afterlife or not, argues Pascal, but, if we bet on the possibility that there is, we cannot go wrong: if we are right, then God will welcome us; if we are wrong and there is no God, then the cosmological absence that is in place of God will not mind, and, although we might not die happy, at least we will not be in danger of punishment from the non-transcendent. Derrida sees this wager as in bad faith because it is calculating and self-interested. It presumes too much and asks for conditions in advance, which pure acquiescence in death will not demand. Religion requires an exchange, an economy. (One of the proposed original words for what came to be called economics was "catallactics" or the science of exchange.) This exchange, which will always demand something in advance, is not the pure gift, which must be freely given without any expectation of reward.

Derrida, in other words, does not find the formulas for theism sufficient, although he takes a highly theistic path to reach that conclusion. The reader expects this path to take an overtly Christian turn, which it never quite does, and this is Derrida's way of toying with, in the words of Wolfgang Iser, the "implied reader" that the text itself projects. *The Gift of Death*, though, is not just about Christianity; it is also about Europe. Like the two popes mentioned earlier, Derrida was aware that the end of the cold war after 1989 and the potential reunification of European culture it entailed raised the question of what course European identity would take. Derrida wants a basis for Europe that is not simply a return to the past underlain by an undemocratic or para-religious "state of exception" (see Chapter 7). Nor, however, does he want a bureaucratized European Union, which elevates a quasi-corporate consortium over a historic past that is heavily and undeniably Christian. Furthermore,

Derrida fears a Europe that is racially exclusive and refuses to accommodate "the other" at a time when population flows from the east and south; the re-emergence of Islam among Europeans in Bosnia, Albania, and Kosovo; and the recognition of Muslims in Turkey were making Europe into the multiracial, multicultural space it had not been since Greco-Roman times. Derrida himself, as we have seen, was in many ways fundamentally an outsider to Europe, an "other." Robert Young, who has linked post-structuralism and post-colonialism more than any other thinker except Spivak, puts this aptly when he describes Derrida's theory as "actively concerned with the task of undoing the ideological heritage of French colonialism and with rethinking the premises, assumptions, and protocols of its centrist imperial culture."[76] In this way, Derrida's perspective on European modernity and its fate is performed as both a spectator of and participant in European modernity, and Derrida is both an inheritor of it and a dissident force within it.

Derrida wants to acknowledge modernity without purging it of spirit. In an odd sense, Derrida, in his later writings, is the true successor of the work on the public sphere and communicative rationality begun by Jürgen Habermas in the 1960s.[77] In 1980, Habermas criticized Derridean deconstruction as an instrument of "young conservatism."[78] But, by the 1990s, Derrida shares some of the most commendable features of Habermas: a willingness to scrutinize every constituted position, to be unafraid of the overtly cerebral, and to make the highest ethical demands on thought. By the early twenty-first century, Habermas was, at the very least, not entirely opposed to the US invasion of Iraq, whereas Derrida resisted all attempts to budge him from his long-held place on the sceptical left.[79] Because, as W.J.T. Mitchell points out, the socio-economic changes of the late twentieth century were accompanied by "momentous transformations in the conceptual frameworks for understanding these things," Derrida could be said to represent a sort of liberal pluralism whose chief virtue was to radically resist an easy assimilation of itself into comfortably pluralistic discourses; to assert a tear in its own fabric kept it from being absorbed or assimilated into conformism.[80]

This pluralism kept Derrida from affirming any uniform idea of "the sacred." Derrida, at the beginning of *The Gift of Death*, notes the phenomenon of *laïcité*, of a lay (non-religious) public sphere in France that protects French institutions from religious dogma and authority and promotes certain secular and republican ideals. And, although he shows his great interest in religious discourse, Derrida does nothing in the book to suggest that he is not an advocate of *laïcité*. (Ironically, in the decade after *The Gift of Death* was published, those who advocated Christianization or re-Christianization and those who advocated *laïcité* found common cause in being anti-Muslim, but Derrida showed no signs of going in that direction either.) In many ways, Derrida's social thought was not far from that of the leftward version of the intellectual consensus of the French Third Republic (1871–1940). Indeed, Derrida's thoughts about what a

polity should be are not far from those of Mustapha Kemal Atatürk, the first
president of modern Turkey, who strongly advocated a lay polity.

Derrida, though, is difficult to pin down. So much is going on in his texts
that any definition of him seems inadequate. This is evident in *Demeure*, his
long commentary on a short narrative by Maurice Blanchot, "*L'instant de ma
mort*" ("The Instant of My Death").[81] Blanchot's story recalls an episode during World War II when a rural villa in which he was staying was occupied by
"Vlasov's army"—anti-Soviet Russians fighting on the German side and training in occupied France—and he was threatened with being shot. (There is a
fascinating parallel between the uprooted nature of "Vlasov's army" and the
permanent out-of-body experience that Blanchot has as a result of the incident.)
Even though this "instant of my death" did not actually happen, Blanchot lived
the rest of his life as if it had. What does it mean to be physically alive and yet
to feel continually that death has already happened, that physical life—"bare
life" as the Italian theorist Giorgio Agamben might call it—is always haunted
by the sense of being an aftermath or a prolonged setting in of the death already
administered in a conceptual sense. Derrida, a great admirer of Blanchot from
the next generation (though their deaths occurred less than two years apart,
as Blanchot died in the late winter of 2003), looks backward to discover what
death might be for him in the future.

Derrida's commentary is a meditation on the possibility of commentary, as
are all his commentaries. Both Derrida and de Man were often accused of putting the commentary above the text, of privileging the critic above the author.
Yet the long commentary on the short Blanchot text shows both a sense of
the ambition of the commentator—the length of Derrida's contribution to the
published volume dwarfs Blanchot's—and also of the commentator's humility,
as everything in the long commentary ultimately goes to elucidate, to perform,
the text of the elder writer. Moreover, the Blanchot text clearly hovers between
fiction and nonfiction—no one doubts that this happened to Blanchot, but it
is told in a deliberately abstract and depersonalized way. Is commentary more
true or false than the text? Derrida seems to be asking. As always, Derrida mul-
titracks his commentary by completing what Saussure might call the synchronic
level—the instant of facing death, the here and now that never fades—with a
diachronic dimension supplied by a meditation on Latinity and Europe's Latin
(Roman) heritage. In doing so, Derrida consults the work of the philologist
Ernst Robert Curtius. As opposed to Erich Auerbach, to whom he was often
likened, Curtius was at once more learned and more sceptical, far more steeped
in the minutiae of textual transmission but far less confident of discerning an
overall direction for European literary history. Derrida's use of Curtius seems to
endorse Curtius's mixture of sheer learning leavened by being unencumbered by
a coordinating doctrine. To acknowledge tradition without being yoked by the
past, to upend hierarchies without substituting a new authority in their place
is a goal both Derrida and Curtius have in common. For Derrida, this sense of

tradition and of its inevitable complications is, in a way, a means of dealing with the awareness of death mooted by Blanchot. As Philip Auslander points out (in the context of media studies), Derrida suggests that "the recording of an event in memory is already a means of reproduction."[82] Blanchot's memory of his near-death experience is also a way of staving it off, rendering it just an instant and not an eternity. Similarly, Derrida does seem to trust in a cultural memory that, though inauthentic and perhaps itself a ghost, a spectral haunting of the dead, may well survive.

Of the two great theorists, Foucault had the warmer public reception, even during his shorter lifetime, his image humanized, no doubt, by the wide knowledge of his open homosexuality. Derrida, on the other hand, was a more opaque figure.[83] Yet towards the end, his writing became more personal and autobiographical, and he performed a writerly self not only through an exhibition of style but also through the manifestation of a persona, although, of course, Derrida presented his self ironically, consciously, and cautiously. In *The Animal That Therefore I Am* (2008; based on lectures given in 1997), Derrida describes how his cat follows him into the bathroom, sees him naked, and instantly realizes that she has no business being there, not because of any consciousness of her owner's nakedness but because nothing is happening of interest to her, yet, the following day, the cat pursues exactly the same routine. In separating seeing from consciousness, Derrida not only underscores and problematizes the traditional separation between human and animal—the book is, in many ways, a meditation on Genesis 2, which establishes man's stewardship over the earth and the animals—but also playfully points at his own relationship to the reader.

In telling the story of the cat in the bathroom, Derrida shows us an intimate part of his life. But this intimacy is also highly generic, part of any cat person's life (and Derrida is not above appealing to fellow feeling). So we learn absolutely nothing specific about Derrida's life. He is naked, yet we do not really know anything about his nakedness.[84] Derrida is toying with the reader's insistence that the critic disclose self in a fundamental sense, that the critic let us in on the secret, spill the beans.[85] If Derrida does this, he suggests, it is in some labyrinthine reading of a text, some commentary where the personal "I" is absent. As Oscar Wilde said, "Criticism is the most civilized form of autobiography"; it is certainly the only form in which Derrida chose to speak about "himself."[86] Our readings of texts can never be totally personal or impersonal; there is a debatable space in between where commentary dwells. Derrida took his own secrets to his grave, but he revealed all in reading others. This is why the shockingly irreverent tone of his obituaries in American newspapers—Jonathan Kandell's in the *New York Times* set the tone—were so surprising: they suggested that, in dying, Derrida had experienced a Derridean joke turned against the joker—that Derrida, in his attempt to deconstruct binary oppositions, had failed to deconstruct that between life and death.[87] Death can make sport of all sorts of doctrines. Is it any less fatuous when an optimist dies than when a sceptic does?

Moreover, not only Derrida's thought but also much of literature demonstrates that the line between life and death is indeed porous. Memories of the dead linger on, and the living often, as Heidegger suggested, live towards death when they live most intensely. The descents to the underworld in ancient epic would not be so haunting if there were an impermeable boundary between living and dead states. Even beyond these quasi-mystical considerations, though, the fact was that Derrida, by dint of his prominence alone, deserved a respectful obituary. Foucault received one in 1984 in *The New York Times*, as did Heidegger in the same newspaper in 1976.[88] The philosophies of both thinkers were as subversive and as obscure as Derrida's. But it is Derrida who was lampooned, mocked, made sport of—designated, perhaps not inappropriately, the *pharmakos*, the scapegoat, the representation of the journalistic sphere's thoughtless dismissal of theory.

Derrida may not have been the most popular or the most comprehensible thinker of the late twentieth century, but he was its most influential, at least within the humanities academy. A hundred years after his death, he may epitomize that era's wrestling with the ghost of tradition and the paradoxes of novelty, with the boundaries of expression and the urgency of redressing injustice. That his major impact in North America was achieved via literary criticism, as a genre, is a tribute to literary academia and marked its increasing prominence as a site of vigorous intellectual activity, of *thinking*. Even if—which the present account is not inclined to do—one dismisses Derrida's thought as a passing craze that, a century after his death, will be only archival, one has to admire Derrida's personal integrity and the way he never lent his fame or authority to an ignoble cause or an ideological simplification of his thought. Sartre aside, the last French intellectual to have so thoroughgoing an influence outside France may well have been Auguste Comte, the great formulator of positivism. At the beginning of his fame, Comte was associated with rigorous, analytical thought without metaphysical pretensions. Towards the end of his life, Comte had become a meaningless guru, subscribing to all sorts of inflated, platitudinous versions of his own former ideals. He succumbed not only to the temptations of personal glory but also to a cultural need for convenience and simplification. It was left to Comte's disciple, Émile Littré, to uphold the integrity of positivism "as it was."[89] Derrida, with the celebrity of a Comte, had the integrity of a Littré. He became interested in politics later on, but he did not espouse a political credo. He became interested in spirit, but he did not convert to or practise a religion. His writing became more and more literary, but he did not imagine himself a creative writer and kept in mind the crucial difference between texts and commentary. Derrida respected and cherished the contingent aspects of critical activity, the way it depended *on another text*. It is indicatively coincidental that Derrida used the dictionary originally published by Littré when, in "Letter to a Japanese Friend," he looks for a dictionary definition of deconstruction, the word his own work had injected into the common intelligent dialect, and sees deconstruction already there, in the dictionary, "good French."[90] Although far more original than Littré, Derrida, for all his verbal wildness, was like his forebear principled and unswerving to the end. Derrida's sceptical faith was not a conventional affirmation. Nor was it the hopeless nihilism with which so many confused it. It was Derrida's rigorous sense of what he could and could not believe that combined with his sense of play and subversion to make his thought so applicable to so many different circumstances. It is to the applicability of deconstruction in criticism arising from specific social identities that this book will now turn.

NOTES

1 Ian Balfour, *Late Derrida* (Durham: Duke University Press, 2007) 206.

2 Indeed, Derrida's one official brush with the law came in the early 1980s, when he was arrested—on trumped-up charges of marijuana possession at the Prague airport—in retaliation for the assistance he was providing to Czech dissidents. See Barbara Day, *The Velvet Philosophers* (London: Claridge Press, 1999).

3 See Jason Powell, *Jacques Derrida: A Biography* (New York: Continuum 2006) 15.

4 See Susan Handelman, *The Slayers of Moses: The Emergence of Rabbinic Interpretation in Modern Literary Theory* (Albany: SUNY Press, 1982) and Hélène Cixous, *Jacques Derrida: Portrait of a Young Jewish Saint*, trans. Beverly Bie Brehac (New York: Columbia University Press, 2005).

5 One of the differences between French and Anglo-American intellectual life is that the role played by Oxbridge and Ivy League universities in the United Kingdom and the United States respectively is, in France, played by state-supported institutions that were *founded* as meritocratic, not just *latterly redefined* as such. This is one of the background reasons for the fundamental difference in French intellectual life, and one of the reasons that French thought after World War II—both existentialism and deconstruction—seemed so novel to North Americans.

6 Farías's finding that Heidegger was far more immersed in Nazi ideology and activity than had been thought came out nearly contemporaneously with the de Man scandal, and both discoveries were often jointly used to delegitimize theory. See Victor Farías, *Heidegger and Nazism*, ed. Joseph Margolis and Tom Rockmore, trans. Paul Burrell and Gabriel R. Ricci (Philadelphia: Temple University Press, 1989). Farías, who later discovered youthful eugenic and quasi-Fascist writings of the martyred Marxist Chilean president Salvador Allende, seems to specialize in unearthing the unsavoury pasts of thinkers he does not like. This tendency is both informative and troubling, as if the ideas of a thinker can be proved or disproved simply by considering their author; if they come from a flawed source, they must inherently be flawed. Especially in the humanities, where interpretation and contextualization matter so much, the usefulness of ideas is eminently detachable from their genesis or (as the New Critics saw) even their intended meanings. So these kinds of "gotcha!" discoveries while, again, not to be discounted—the southern origins of the New Critics, for example, tell us a lot about the genesis of their ideas—do not invalidate the extant body of work to the extent often claimed.

7 Manfred Stassen, ed., *Martin Heidegger: Philosophical and Political Writings* (New York: Continuum, 2003).

8 Jacques Derrida, "Letter to a Japanese Friend," *Psyche: Inventions of the Other*, ed. Peggy Kamuf and Elizabeth Rottenberg, vol. 2 (Palo Alto: Stanford University Press, 2008) 2.

9 Boris Gasparov, "The Early Romantic Roots of Theoretical Linguistics: Friedrich Schlegel, Novalis, and Ferdinand de Saussure on Sign and Meaning," Leonard Hastings Schoff Memorial Lectures, Columbia University, November 2006; Tuska Benes, *In Babel's Shadow: Language, Philology, and Nation in Nineteenth-Century Germany* (Detroit: Wayne State University Press, 2008).

10 Ferdinand de Saussure, *Course in General Linguistics*, trans. Roy Harris (London: Open Court, 1986).

11 Claude Lévi-Strauss, *Tristes tropiques*, trans. John and Dorren Weightman (New York: Atheneum, 1974).

12 Frank Kermode, *Not Entitled* (New York: Farrar, Straus and Giroux, 1995) 314.

13 Richard Harland, *Superstructuralism: The Philosophy of Structuralism and Post-Structuralism* (London: Routledge, 1987).

14 Roman Jakobson, "Two Aspects of Language and Two Types of Aphasic Disturbances," *Fundamentals of Language*, ed. Roman Jakobson and Morris Halle (The Hague: Mouton de Gruyter, 1956) 69–76. Jakobson's work was practical, diagnostic, and scientific in intent; like Saussure, he did not mean to do literary theory. See Stephen Rudy, *Roman Jakobson, 1896–1982: A Complete Bibliography of His Writings* (Berlin: Mouton de Gruyter, 1990).

15 Ironically, Lévi-Strauss, who was over 100 when he died in 2009, survived both Derrida and Foucault, whose work was hailed as "post–Lévi-Straussian."

16 See Derrida, "Letter to a Japanese Friend," 3.

17 Derrida, "Letter to a Japanese Friend," 4.

18 Derrida, "Letter to a Japanese Friend," 6.

19 See Jean-Luc Nancy, *Discourse of the Syncope: Logodaedalus*, trans. Saul Anton (Palo Alto: Stanford University Press, 2007).

20 See Handelman, *The Slayers of Moses*, 84.

21 Samuel Menashe, *New and Selected Poems*, ed. Christopher Ricks, expanded edition (New York: Library of America, 2008) 72.

22 G. Douglas Atkins, *Reading Deconstruction/Deconstructive Reading* (Lexington: University Press of Kentucky, 1985) 23.

23 Wallace Stevens, "The Motive for Metaphor," *American Poetry: The Twentieth Century (Henry Adams to Dorothy Parker)*, ed. Robert Hass et al. (New York: Library of America, 2000) 345. Stevens was a poet who, well after his death, was seen as seminal by both Bloom and many disciples of Derrida.

24 Jacques Derrida, *Of Grammatology*, trans. Gayatri Chakravorty Spivak (Baltimore: Johns Hopkins University Press, 1974).

25 Geoffrey Sampson, *Writing Systems: A Linguistic Introduction* (Palo Alto: Stanford University Press, 1990).

26 William Shakespeare, "Sonnet 55," *The Oxford Shakespeare: The Complete Works*, ed. Stanley Wells and Gary Taylor (New York: Oxford University Press, 2005) 785.

27 Gayatri Chakravorty Spivak, Introduction, *Of Grammatology*, by Jacques Derrida (Baltimore: Johns Hopkins University Press, 1974) xiv.

28 Jacques Derrida, "Plato's Pharmacy," *Dissemination*, trans. Barbara Johnson (Chicago: University of Chicago Press, 1981).

29 René Girard is the thinker of Derrida's era who has written most profoundly on the scapegoat phenomenon. See Girard, *Violence and the Sacred* (Baltimore: Johns Hopkins University Press, 1977).

30 Herman Rapoport, *The Theory Mess* (New York: Columbia University Press, 2000) 23.

31 Friedrich Kittler, *Discourse Networks, 1800–1900*, trans. Michael Metteer and Chris Cullens (Palo Alto: Stanford University Press, 1992); Avital Ronell, *The Telephone Book: Technology, Schizophrenia, Electric Speech* (Lincoln: University of Nebraska Press, 1981); Hans Ulrich Gumbrecht and Karl Ludwig Pfeiffer, eds., *Materialities of Communication* (Palo Alto: Stanford University Press, 1994); and McKenzie Wark, *Gamer Theory* (Cambridge, MA: Harvard University Press, 2007). See also Lydia Liu's work in translation theory, new media, and "post-phonocetrism."

32 Stuart Moulthrop "Reading from the Map: Metaphor and Metonymy in the Fiction of Forking Paths," *Hypermedia and Literary Studies*, ed. Paul Delany and George Landow (Cambridge, MA: MIT Press, 1994) 119–32.

33 Jacques Derrida, *Limited Inc*, trans. Samuel Weber (Chicago: Northwestern University Press, 1988) 66.

34 Derrida, *Limited Inc*, 5.

35 Anselm Haverkamp, ed., *Deconstruction is/in America* (New York: New York University Press, 1985).

36 Michael Sprinker, "Determinations: Paul de Man's Wartime Journalism," *Responses: On Paul de Man's Wartime Journalism*, ed. Thomas Keenan, Neil Hertz, and Werner Hamacher (Lincoln: University of Nebraska Press, 1989) 374.

37 Paul de Man, *Blindness and Insight: Essays in the Rhetoric of Contemporary Criticism*, ed. Wlad Godzich (Minneapolis: University of Minnesota Press, 1983) 187–228.

38 Paul de Man, *Blindness and Insight*, 165.

39 Paul de Man, *Aesthetic Ideology*, ed. Andrzej Warminski (Minneapolis: University of Minnesota Press, 1996).

40 Geoffrey H. Hartman, *Saving the Text: Literature/Derrida/Philosophy* (Baltimore: Johns Hopkins University Press, 1982).

41 J. Hillis Miller, "Stevens' Rock and Criticism as Cure (Part I)," *Georgia Review* 3.1 (1976): 5–31; J. Hillis Miller, "Stevens' Rock and Criticism as Cure (Part II)," *Georgia Review* 30.2 (1976): 330–48. For the critics of consciousness who initially influenced Miller's work of the 1960s, see Sarah N. Lawall, *Critics of Consciousness: The Existential Structures of Literature* (Cambridge, MA: Harvard University Press, 1968). For the latent aestheticism in deconstructions' anti-aesthetic demonstrations, see Elizabeth Bruss, *Beautiful Theories: The Spectacle of Discourse in Contemporary Criticism* (Baltimore: Johns Hopkins University Press, 1982).

42 J. Hillis Miller, *Fiction and Repetition: Seven English Novels* (Cambridge, MA: Harvard University Press, 1982) 20.

43 J. Hillis Miller, *The Ethics of Reading: Kant, de Man, Eliot, Trollope, James, and Benjamin* (New York: Columbia University Press, 1987).

44 Perry Meisel, *The Myth of the Modern* (New Haven: Yale University Press, 1987).

45 William H. Pritchard used "hermeneutical mafia," but because he was referring to the Yale Critics, he really meant "deconstructive." See Pritchard, "The Hermeneutical Mafia" *Playing it by Ear: Literary Essays and Reviews* (Amherst: University of Massachusetts Press, 1994) 215.

46 David Lehman, *Signs of the Times: Deconstruction and the Fall of Paul de Man* (New York: Simon and Schuster, 1991); Ortwin de Graef, *Serenity in Crisis: A Preface to Paul de Man, 1939–1960* (Lincoln: University of Nebraska Press, 1993). See also the two volumes published by the University of Nebraska Press in 1989, one containing the wartime journalism itself (*Wartime Journalism, 1939–1943*) and the other containing responses by various hands with various ideological viewpoints (*Responses: On Paul de Man's Wartime Journalism*); both texts are edited by Neil Hertz, Thomas Keenan, and Werner Hamacher. Evelyn Barish is working on a full biography of de Man, forthcoming in 2011.

47 See James J. Paxson, "Historicizing Paul de Man's Master Trope Prosopopeia: Belgium's Trauma of 1940, the Nazi *Volkskörper*, and Versions of the Allegorical Body Politic," *Historicizing Theory*, ed. Peter C. Herman (Albany: SUNY Press, 2004) 78.

48 Robert Hass, "Meditation at Lagunitas," *California Poetry: From the Gold Rush to the Present*, ed. Dana Gioia, Chryss Yost, and Jack Hicks (Berkeley: Heyday Books, 2003) 235–36.

49 Richard Wilbur, "Epistemology," *The Oxford Book of Short Poems*, ed. James Michie and P.J. Kavanagh (Oxford: Oxford University Press, 1985) 257.

50 Samuel Holt Monk, *The Sublime: A Study of Critical Theories in Eighteenth-Century England* (Ann Arbor: University of Michigan Press, 1960); Portia Weiskel and Thomas Weiskal, *The Romantic Sublime: Studies in the Structure and Psychology of Transcendence* (Baltimore: Johns Hopkins University Press, 1976); Neil Hertz, *The End of the Line: Essays on Psychoanalysis and the Sublime* (New York: Columbia University Press, 1985). For the culture of Ivy League universities in this era, see Jerome Karabel, *The Chosen: The Hidden History of Admission and Exclusion at Harvard, Yale, and Princeton* (Boston: Houghton Mifflin, 2005).

51 Angus Fletcher, *Allegory: The Theory of a Symbolic Mode* (Ithaca, NY: Cornell University Press, 1982); Justus George Lawler, *Celestial Pantomime: Poetic Structures of Transcendence* (New York: Continuum, 1994).

52 Gregory Ulmer, *Applied Grammatology: Post(e)-pedagogy from Jacques Derrida to Joseph Beuys* (Baltimore: Johns Hopkins University Press, 1985).

53 Cathy Caruth, ed., *Trauma: Explorations in Memory* (Baltimore: Johns Hopkins University Press, 1995).

54 Gérard Genette, *Narrative Discourse Revisited*, trans. Jane E. Lewin (Ithaca: Cornell University Press, 1988).

55 David Bleich, *Subjective Criticism* (Baltimore: Johns Hopkins University Press, 1978); Norman Horwood Holland, *5 Readers Reading* (New Haven: Yale University Press, 1975); Peter J. Rabinowitz. *Before Reading: Narrative Conventions and the Politics of Interpretation* (Columbus: Ohio State University Press, 1987); Wolfgang Iser, *The Implied Reader* (Baltimore: Johns Hopkins University Press, 1978); Hans Robert Jauss, *Toward an Aesthetic of Reception* (Minneapolis: University of Minnesota Press, 1982).

56 Paul de Man, *The Resistance to Theory* (Minneapolis: University of Minnesota Press, 1986) 59.

57 Michael Holquist and Katerina Clark, *Mikhail Bakhtin* (Cambridge, MA: Harvard University Press, 1984); Gary Saul Morson, *Bakhtin: Essays and Dialogues on His Work* (Chicago: University of Chicago Press, 1990); Caryl Emerson, *The First Hundred Years of Mikhail Bakhtin* (Princeton: Princeton University Press, 2000).

58 Mikhail Bakhtin, *The Dialogic Imagination: Four Essays*, trans. Michael Holquist (Austin: University of Texas Press, 1982).

59 Michael André Bernstein, *Bitter Carnival: Ressentiment and the Abject Hero* (Princeton: Princeton University Press, 1992).

60 Hans-Georg Gadamer, *Truth and Method*, trans. Joel Weinsheimer and Donald G. Marshall (New York: Continuum, 2005). Early American critical responses to Gadamer were Gerald Bruns, *Hermeneutics, Ancient and Modern* (New Haven: Yale University Press, 1995) and Joel Weinsheimer, *Gadamer's Hermeneutics: A Reading of* Truth and Method (New Haven: Yale University Press, 1988).

61 The Derrida-Austin "debate," as well as the more two-sided one between Derrida and Austin's student J.L. Searle, is well known. But Austin was also mentioned by Foucault in a lecture in Tunisia in 1967, thus signalling the notice the British thinker had already received among continental theorists. See Michel Foucault, *Society Must Be Defended: Lectures at the Collège de France, 1975–1976*, trans David Macey (London: Macmillan, 2003) xix.

62 Fredric Jameson, *The Political Unconscious: Narrative as a Socially Symbolic Act* (1981; London: Routledge, 2002) ix. As can be seen from the subtitle, Jameson did not entirely abandon symbol in favour of allegory. Neither did Angus Fletcher (see note 51), who subtitled his 1964 book on allegory "the theory of a *symbolic* mode" (emphasis mine).

63 Stephen Greenblatt, *Shakespearean Negotiations: The Circulation of Social Energy in Renaissance England* (Berkeley: University of California Press, 1989) 1.

64 Fredric Jameson, *Fables of Aggression: Wyndham Lewis, the Modernist as Fascist* (Berkeley: University of California Press, 1979); Benedict R. O'Gorman Anderson, *Imagined Communities: Reflections on the Origin and Spread of Nationalism* (London: Verso, 1991).

65 Fyodor Tyutchev, "Silentium," *Three Russian Poets: Selections from Pushkin, Lermontov, and Tyutchev*, trans. Vladimir Nabokov (London: Lindsay Drummond, 1947) 5.

66 Jacques Derrida, *Spurs: Nietzsche's Styles = Eperons: Les Styles de Nietzsche*, trans. Barbara Harlow (Chicago: University of Chicago Press, 1981).

67 Balfour, *Late Derrida*, 207.

68 Jacques Derrida, "Circonfession: Fifty-Nine Periods and Paraphrases," *Jacques Derrida*, trans. Geoffrey Bennington and Jacques Derrida (Chicago: University of Chicago Press, 1993).

69 The relation between Derrida and negative theology, often defined very loosely, has been pursued with extraordinary rigour by the notable Australian poet and critic Kevin J. Hart in *The Trespass of the Sign: Deconstruction, Theology, and Philosophy*, 2nd ed. (New York: Fordham University Press, 2000).

70 Gil Anidjar, "Once More, Once More: Derrida, the Arab, the Jew," *Acts Of Religion*, by Jacques Derrida and Gil Anidjar (London: Routledge, 2002) 20.

71 Vladimir Jankélévitch, *Forgiveness*, trans. Andrew Kelley (Chicago: University of Chicago Press, 2005).

72 Antjie Krog, *Country of My Skull: Guilt, Sorrow, and the Limits of Forgiveness in the New South Africa* (New York: Crown, 2005). The work of the commission, as pointed out by Krog, is subject to the same sort of idealization as is Derrida's work on forgiveness itself. Indeed, the idea of a "Truth Commission" eventually seemed to be tantamount to either codified vengeance or a one-time, difference-settling panacea—neither of which were what Derrida was after.

73 Wallace Stevens, *The Palm at the end of The Mind*, ed. Holly Stevens (New York: Knopf, 1971) 316.

74 See Balfour, *Late Derrida*, 211; Balfour says Derrida's "late essays are far more heterogeneous than that."

75 Jacques Derrida, *The Gift of Death*, trans. David Wills (Chicago: University of Chicago Press, 1996).

76 Robert J.C. Young, *Postcolonialism: A Historical Introduction* (Oxford: Blackwell, 2001).

77 Joshua Kates, *Essential History: Jacques Derrida and the Development of Deconstruction* (Chicago: Northwestern University Press, 2005) reaches a conclusion about the nature of Derrida's work that nudges Derrida towards Habermas.

78 Jürgen Habermas, "Modernity: An Incomplete Project," *The Anti-Aesthetic: Essays on Postmodern Culture*, ed. Hal Foster (Port Townsend: Bay Press, 1983).

79 Jürgen Habermas, "Letter to America," *The Nation* 26 November 2002, 10 December 2009 <http://www.thenation.com/doc/20021216/habermas>. As W.J.T. Mitchell points out, Derrida was reluctantly for the *first* Gulf War in 1991, apparently: see W.J.T. Mitchell, ed., *The Late Derrida* (Chicago: University of Chicago Press, 2007) 4. And, by the time of the second Gulf War, approval of the first as a multilaterally sanctioned exercise under UN auspices had become part of the Left's opposition to the second. In any event, Derrida did not put his "approval" of the first war in writing—something important for Derrida. Still, Mitchell's reminder is useful in situating Derrida not as a radical leftist but a sceptical leftist; yet Derrida's difference from Habermas in the early 2000s shows how leftist his scepticism could be.

80 Mitchell, ed., *The Late Derrida*, 9.

81 Maurice Blanchot and Jacques Derrida, *The Instant of My Death, and Demeure*, trans. Elizabeth Rottenberg (Palo Alto: Stanford University Press, 2000).

82 Philip Auslander, *Liveness: Performance in a Mediatized Culture* (London: Routledge, 2008) 181.

83 Both Foucault and Derrida, interestingly, were compared to saints, in the book titles of Halperin and Cixous respectively.

84 See Jacques Derrida, *The Animal That Therefore I Am*, ed. Marie-Louise Mallet, trans. David Wills (New York: Fordham University Press, 2008) 13.

85 Frank Kermode was the first to raise seriously the discourse of secrecy in the context of late twentieth-century criticism, see Kermode, *The Genesis of Secrecy* (Cambridge, MA: Harvard University Press, 1979).

86 Oscar Wilde, *The Soul of Man under Socialism*, ed. Linda Dowling (New York: Penguin, 2001) 237.

87 Jonathan Kandell, "Jacques Derrida, Abstruse Theorist, Dies at 74," *The New York Times*, 10 October 2004: A1. Kandell wrote that "for many Americans" Derrida was "the personification of a French school of thinking they felt was undermining many of the traditional standards of classical education, and one they often associated with divisive political causes." The same could have been said of Heidegger or Foucault, but it was not.

88 See Edward Pike, "Martin Heidegger, A Philosopher Who Affected Many Fields, Dies" *The New York Times* 27 May 1976: 1, 36, and Peter Kerr, "Michel Foucault, French Historian," *New York Times* 26 June 1984: B8. Heidegger's obituary was, for understandable reasons, much longer than Foucault's, and it also made more of an intellectual effort to understand the thought of the deceased (the Foucault obituary well-meaningly but misleadingly called Foucault a "structuralist"). But both articles were appropriately respectful.

89 See Mary Pickering, *Auguste Comte: An Intellectual Biography* (Cambridge: Cambridge University Press, 1993).

90 Derrida, "Letter to a Japanese Friend," 2.

CHAPTER THREE

Deconstructing Gender
FEMINIST THEORY

Academia Before Feminism: The 1950s and 1960s

The theories of Derrida and Foucault influenced and transformed nearly all existing areas of literary study. But they also helped ignite new fields previously unrepresented in literary criticism, fields that focused on certain topics or approaches pertaining to various social identities. These topical movements—feminism, anti-racist criticism, post-colonial theory, and queer studies—will be examined in the next four chapters.

Feminism is one of the most complex and internally differentiated of the various movements in theory. This chapter will look at the prehistory and history of contemporary feminism, examining not only the various episodes in its unfolding—what Foucault might call *epistemes*—but also the considerable debate among feminist critics and scholars. Feminist criticism opened up the canon to literature by women, to the consideration of female characters in books by male authors, and to the inclusion of women as full members of the academic community. These achievements often involved reading against the grain, recuperating possibilities long sidelined by established critical practices, and reading writers who had simply not been considered "literary" or, in some cases, who had not been read at all. We will discuss five distinct historical moments in the history of modern feminist criticism, episodes in a continuing series of crises and revelations that have characterized the unfolding of feminist literary thought.

In the mid-twentieth century, women were not very visible in the literary sphere. If poets are, as Percy Bysshe Shelley said in his *A Defence of Poetry*, "the unacknowledged legislators of the world," then it would be a toss up whether, in the 1950s, there were more actual and acknowledged female legislators in the United States than "unacknowledged legislators" (female poets).[1] While Margaret Chase Smith or Katharine St. George at least served in Congress, imaginative women writers such as Edith Wharton and Willa Cather were faintly patronized in the academy, and Kate Chopin and Sarah Orne Jewett were virtually invisible.[2] As far as women academics were concerned, at as prominent an institution as Stanford University, according to the Victorianist Anne Humpherys, who was an undergraduate there in the 1950s, "there were no women on the faculty."[3] The same is true of African American writers. There were no black literary equivalents of Adam Clayton Powell, Jr.—a Congressman who exercised real power.[4] Notably, Irving Howe read Ralph Ellison's great 1952 novel *Invisible Man* as more of a "protest novel" than Ellison intended it to be, which served to limit its resonance. There were African American academics, but they were largely restricted to the historically black colleges such as Ellison's alma mater, the Tuskegee Institute.[5] We do not understand the manifestation of what seem to be social movements in literary criticism until we realize that the republic of letters was, before theory, well behind the actual US government in giving any kind of proportional representation to women and non-whites.

For whatever reasons, this was less true in Britain and Canada than in the United States. Novelists such as the Canadians Sheila Watson and Ethel Wilson or the British authors Ivy Compton-Burnett and Rose Macaulay had a defined if somewhat limited place in the perceptions of their country's national literatures. Where women were really disempowered literarily was in the United States—where both the "highbrow" and "middlebrow" writers of the 1950s were almost exclusively male—and in the various historical fields of British literature as studied anywhere in the English-speaking world—in other words, when one read eighteenth-century literature, one did not read women writers. Women writers who up until the 1930s had been seen as canonical—for example, Willa Cather and nineteenth-century women novelists such as Helen Hunt Jackson and Harriet Beecher Stowe—were largely dropped from the canon after World War II, on various, largely trumped-up grounds. For instance, Stowe was attacked because her opposition to slavery was seen as too politically activist (and only in the 1950s would that accusation have been politically plausible) while Cather, as Sharon O'Brien has shown, was attacked for being insufficiently left wing and politically committed.[6] And the idea of a woman herself being an academic was still a rather exotic one. It could happen. As we have seen in the preface, Rosemond Tuve played a prominent role in criticism of the Renaissance at mid-century. The character of Emily Brightman (a character based on M.C. Bradbrook, the great scholar of Elizabethan drama) in Anthony Powell's novel sequence *A Dance to the Music of Time* is a woman of great intellectual command, personal willpower, and moral sagacity. But Dr. Brightman does not seem to have a personal life and has apparently accepted a certain genderlessness as the price of her admission into the hallowed cloisters.[7] And this was a relatively recent portrait by a male writer fundamentally liberal on issues of gender and sexuality. Dr. Brightman, though, was an empowered figure compared to some other real-life academics in England. Q.D. Leavis was not only the wife of F.R. Leavis but also his intellectual partner in every sense of the word. Yet the University of Cambridge never offered her a permanent position. This was even though her book *Fiction and the Reading Public* (1932) was highly influential, is still used over seventy years later, and can be seen as a progenitor of the great interest in the quantitative and empirical study of literature and its reception, which will be discussed in Chapter 7.[8]

The medievalist Margaret Schlauch had to spend the final portion of her career in the Polish People's Republic.[9] This was partially a consequence of her left-wing political associations and the problems they caused her in the United States during the era of paranoia about communism. But the comparative neglect Schlauch suffered despite being one of her era's leading Chaucerians surely had to do with her gender. Marjorie Hope Nicolson taught English at Columbia University during what is popularly considered to be the golden age of that institution's English department. But Nicolson is strangely absent from the nostalgia for that period still evinced by many "public intellectuals." Nicolson's subjects ranged from seventeenth- to twentieth-century literature, and she was in many ways ahead of her time in combining literary study with the study of the history of ideas.[10] Her work was also traditional enough in methodology to be thought solid and not meretricious by her (male) peers. Yet Nicolson, though holding a professorial position, was never at the centre of either her university or her field. She was only permitted to teach graduate students, keeping her well away from the young men of the undergraduate college who were being trained to be future leaders rather than mere academics. Cynthia Ozick's famous essay "We Are the Crazy Lady," aptly captures the misogyny and gender anxieties of the academic milieu; it was inspired by an incident that happened when she was a graduate student at Columbia University in 1951.[11] Although Columbia was admittedly more masculinist than most institutions, it was also especially important in the 1950s.

Helen C. White was the long-time chair of the English department at the University of Wisconsin. As a pious Catholic and historically inclined Renaissance scholar, White, notwithstanding her gender, was not going to challenge the 1950s consensus. But it took all of the Wisconsin flagship's well-attested progressive tendencies to employ any woman, no matter how traditional her work, in such a capacity. Undergraduate English departments at co-educational institutions cultivated women students to increase enrolment. Yet they discouraged those same ardent students from going on to graduate work.[12] They did this on the self-fulfilling basis that, with few if any women to supervise them, women graduate students would find themselves in an alienating environment.[13] Many women academics who had significant influence on the field, such as the reader-response scholar Louise Rosenblatt, spent their entire careers in education departments—no intrinsic demerit, but probably not the place many of them would like to have been.

Even those female academics that managed to have careers in this era did not take the work of women writers as their special subject. They did not write "as women"; their attitudes and practices were of the same general sort as their male counterparts. This is not necessarily bad, and it certainly continued to happen even after feminism. There is no rule that women must write about women or that any thinker should have *her or his* intellectual interests constricted to areas of specifically gendered relevance. Yet today there is the *option* to do this. The option for women to write mainly about women did not exist in the 1950s. There was some work *by* female academics. There was some work *on* women authors. But there was no feminist criticism. In fact, women academics often wrote about men, and women authors were often written about by male academics. Why did this change so rapidly? Why did women writing about women authors in an explicitly feminist vein become such a feature of academic literary study by the late 1970s? Incontestably, the empowerment of women across society was a general factor. Women entered law, medicine, business, and, in far greater numbers than in the 1950s, politics as well as academia. But there were particular issues endemic to academia that also played a role. To understand both the obstacles to and the catalysts for this change, we must look at how literary study in the 1950s broke down across specific periods.

When the New Critics slighted Victorian poets, they were doing so largely for aesthetic and political reasons having little to do with gender. When they thought of the Victorians they disliked, they thought of men. Tennyson and Dickens, the most popular writers of the nineteenth century, became just the names *not* to drop at a cocktail soirée in 1950s New York. But this very slighting created a spirit of solidarity and curiosity among students of the slighted period. This feeling of accord among Victorianists occurred in such a way that they inevitably included more women writers and provided a measurably more encouraging atmosphere for female scholars. Victorian studies had a head start over many other fields in terms of interdisciplinarity and openness precisely because it was not privileged within the "resolved symbolic" paradigm.[14] It made a place for George Eliot—grandmothered, as it were, into the canon because of Leavis's advocacy of her moral seriousness. More crucially, it accommodated the Brontë sisters, who had been analysed seriously as novelists for quite some time by the 1970s. Victorian studies, in many ways, became the seedbed of feminism. Just as, in the 1860s, the unification of Italy had to be accomplished from its base in the Piedmont, the achievements of 1970s feminism in Anglo-American literature, to a surprising degree, had their base in Victorian studies (an analogy that the Victorian poet Elizabeth Barrett Browning, a huge enthusiast for Italian national liberation, would have loved).

Medieval and Renaissance studies were other fields in which women, comparatively, flourished. Why? Both areas of study were characterized by an implied conservatism (in which a woman academic could not do too much to upset the apple cart, given the prevalence of Robertsonian and Tuvean paradigms) and genuine rigour. The philological regimen required in these fields meant that those of ability, whatever their gender, were welcome if they proved themselves.[15] Medievalists such as historians Susan Mosher Stuard and Marcia

Colish, as well as Schlauch, and Renaissance scholars such as Tuve herself, Helen C. White, and, slightly later, Rosalie Colie made significant contributions and were well known. In studies of American literature, the situation was less happy. Tillie Olsen—herself a writer reclaimed and properly appreciated only by feminism—said in the early 1970s that only "one out of twelve" writers on the average university syllabus was a woman. If anything, this was an improvement over ten years before and a sign of the first manifestations of the expansion of the canon to include more women. In many classes, it was not uncommon to see only men writers listed on the syllabus and the major figures of a given period as exclusively male.

The study of male writers dominated, for instance, in courses on American fiction of the mid-twentieth century; many books written on the period concentrated on Ernest Hemingway, William Faulkner, and F. Scott Fitzgerald, while Willa Cather's work was marginalized and Zora Neale Hurston's slid into obscurity. But the exclusion of female writers from the canon was not unilaterally true in the study of all literary periods. Virginia Woolf was permitted into the British modernist canon, although faintly condescended to or even sometimes lambasted as a society novelist who could not write convincingly about the lower classes. Even Erich Auerbach's celebrated discussion of her in his "The Brown Stocking" chapter of *Mimesis* was done with a faint air of elegy.[16] It was implied that the modern world had become so disenchanted that women writers examining ordinary experience had come to the fore. But there was a base for feminist criticism to expand on once female perceptions of the everyday became legitimate literary subjects. The inclusion of Woolf in the original postwar modernist canon is definitely one of the reasons Woolf became so central to feminist theory. Other fields, though, were so dominated by men that, when feminist criticism turned its attention to them, there had to be active efforts at retrieval of women writers long ignored or never even heretofore examined. English poetry as read in the universities was almost monolithically male. So was American poetry with the important exception of Emily Dickinson, another writer who became pivotal to feminism both because of her intrinsic quality and because she had been championed by 1950s male critics within "resolved symbolic" paradigms. Drama was similarly an all-male preserve. This was made possible by its restriction to the Elizabethan-Jacobean and modern periods. Few thought then that a Romantic dramatist such as Joanna Baillie would one day draw the attention she eventually did. In other words, the exclusion of women from the canon did not just rest on a purely gendered basis but was in collusion with a certain hierarchy of periods: the very reason T.S. Eliot and Ezra Pound were applauded was that they had ostensibly introduced a modernist vigour and shaken up a nescient and limp-wristed Victorian twilight. (It is no accident that this assertion of literary masculinity occurred just as women were finally getting the vote in both the United Kingdom and the United States.)

Certain other twentieth-century poets, such as the Irishman Yeats, were similarly praised for making their later verse more taut and muscular. This rejection or trammelling of many aspects of the eighteenth and nineteenth centuries occurred partially to navigate round the women writers who would inevitably have been highlighted. In many respects, a look at the dominant tone of criticism in the 1920s, before New Criticism and Leavisism gained strength, reveals a more open sense of gender in the canon. Part of the "innovation" of these two later movements was their masculinization of the canon. Thus, in some ways, feminist criticism of the 1970s was as corrective as it was revolutionary.

In traditional historiography, periods of cultural achievement have been subtly (or not so subtly) gendered. Periclean Athens or Augustan Rome, for example, were seen as manly periods in which artistic greatness and political cohesiveness were fused; other periods, such as the Hellenistic era and late antiquity, were seen as decadent periods in which artistic control was lost, politics became messy and pluralistic, and the former masculine vigour yielded to feminine passivity. In other words, periods with a "good" reputation were gendered male. Those with a "bad" reputation were gendered female. That the second set of periods is as interesting as the first, as Foucault, among others, has shown in his later works, indicates that gender hierarchies did not just subjugate women but were used as a mechanism to privilege certain modes of culture and imagination. In the era of the New Critics, the "manly" periods were the seventeenth century and modernism; all others were merely tolerated. The assertion of feminist critique, by freeing the eighteenth and nineteenth centuries from derogation expressed in gender terms, enriched the study not only of women writers per se but of entire centuries. Nobody looking at learned journals in the early twenty-first century would doubt that the constriction of what was important in history mandated by 1950s masculinity has long since crumbled.

Part of this emphasis on masculinity in the 1950s had to do with the self-justification of English studies in academic terms. Traditionally, the modern languages were not studied in universities. They were supposed to be part of general culture that people of class and taste picked up naturally, whereas, in university, one studied Greek, Latin, and rhetoric. When modern literature did become part of the academic framework, it was clothed in a particularly philological methodology that deliberately distanced it from the kind of impressionistic appreciation largely characteristic of commercial book reviewing and associated with women's consumption of novels and poetry. Much attention has been paid, and rightly, to show that the emphasis on the Anglo-Saxon period in the early twentieth century seemed to come out of a racialist, "Aryanist" rationale, which elevated Northern European peoples over all others.[17] Still, that not only the chosen texts but also the methodology counterweighted the long-established tradition of women as the primary readers of modern fiction all factored into philology's dominance.

This attitude was seen as guarding literature against the frivolity and mere entertainment value associated, rightly or wrongly, with a female readership, and even women authors such as Cather or Wharton, who would never have been associated with populist consumerism, suffered on behalf of this prejudice. Including more women and focusing more on periods or genres in which women were more prominent had the potential to make literary studies seem an interloper in a university setting in which most academic offerings were more objective, more traditionally rigorous, and provided more demonstrable severance between the course of ordinary life and the arcane tools of learning mastered in the ivory tower. Another reason works by women gained exposure in the 1970s is that the literary academy had by this time proven itself sufficiently, so the imputed seriousness supplied by an emphasis on the masculine was no longer thought essential.

Jane Austen seems so much a part of the canon now—the most recognizable canonical literary figure after Shakespeare—that we are in danger of forgetting how recent her pre-eminence has been. Even the classic names in Austen criticism such as D.W. Harding and Stuart Tave are relatively recent figures. Harding was a Leavisite (and Leavis, to give him his due, did see Austen's importance) but one of an independent stripe, who was expert in psychology as well as literature. Tave's understanding of Austen's linguistic resourcefulness and Harding's demolition of the myth of her comedic congeniality began the stream of Austen criticism that still nourishes readers in the twenty-first century.[18] Austen is commonly considered neither a revolutionary nor a feminist. Yet her rise to her current status would have been inconceivable without feminism, and, importantly, this rise triumphed against the same currents that feminism had to combat—anti-humanism, anti-liberalism, and an insistence on political or economic "relevance" as the ultimate criterion of societal or literary seriousness.

As the novelist Millicent Dillon characterizes it, "By the end of the Sixties and certainly by the early Seventies, things had begun to change."[19] The entry of women into the canon, the empowerment of women as academics, and the legitimacy of an actively feminist rationale seemed to arrive overnight in academia. But the discontinuity was not drastic. Indeed, one of feminism's inconspicuous virtues is its stress on continuity in literary history over the theories of catastrophic rupture favoured by the modernists and their disciples. This same logic applies to feminism itself. It did not come out of nowhere. The toehold maintained by a few women writers in certain discrete periods of study was the premise for the rapid overhaul of the canon, and for the admission into it of many heretofore unscrutinized women writers, which ensued over the next decade. The work of male critics such as Tave and Harding and of more obscure figures such as Kenneth Eble was crucial. Eble worked in the far less fertile area of American literature and explored the work of Kate Chopin before she became a feminist icon.[20] These men studied women authors not because they wanted to show that they were "sensitive" academics, not because they wanted to be popular with women or wanted to seem modish and advance themselves on the career ladder. None of these circumstances would have obtained at the time. They studied women authors out of an intrinsic interest in what the subject had to offer intellectually, and, in this, they operated with the genuine sense of aesthetic worth that the New Critics claimed but that too often masked a political, often reactionary rationale. The change that came after them could not have occurred without them. They were the hidden heroes of feminism.

Anglo-American and French Feminisms: The 1970s

Anglo-American Feminism: Pasts, Presents, Futures

Yet, necessarily, it was the heroines of feminism who accomplished the vast majority of the change. Kate Millett's *Sexual Politics* (1970) is a volume now seen as far more part of the feminist movement's heritage than its active agenda.[21] But this underrates what is still a useful and provocative book. Not only was *Sexual Politics* one of the few PhD dissertations to become a bestseller, but it launched the tradition of using readings of literary texts as the germ of a larger, more thoroughgoing gender critique. Millett had a thorough literary training, and it is crucial to understand the core disciplinary background of her generation of American feminists; for example, Alix Kates Shulman studied philosophy at Columbia University Graduate School. Millett's reading of Charlotte Brontë's *Villette* (1853) is a fundamental interrogation not only of patriarchy but also of the literary assumptions that had been premised upon it.[22] Especially eloquent is Millett's response to the passage in which the novel's protagonist, Lucy Snowe, confronts the objectification of women in the sculpture and paintings by men of past ages, art that is displayed in the Brussels museum. Millett showed that feminist rationales did not have to be excavated from earlier texts. They could be seen right on their surface if the critic arrived with a perspective that was open to them. This procedure became characteristic of feminist analysis. Many critics who saw Millett as too political and too unsubtle in her assumptions nonetheless owed her a considerable debt.

Millett turned to psychology and sociology to disestablish the logical inevitability of patriarchy, which had made its sway seem necessary and unalterable rather than contingent and open to revision. Interestingly, mainstream scholars of the "soft sciences," i.e., sociology, psychology, and anthropology, rather than contributors to advances in theory within these disciplines, had a greater direct influence on feminist criticism. Anthropology needed to be passed through a quasi-deconstructive mesh by Clifford Geertz to matter to theory in general. The sociology that mattered to theory was Foucault's and Pierre Bourdieu's, and both thinkers operated outside of the anglophone mainstream. Yet Millett, conversely, frequently cited American sociologists, anthropologists, and psychologists in support of her ideas. Psychoanalysis, in particular, received its second life in intellectual history through feminism. We see this very obviously in the use of the theories of Jacques Lacan by Julia Kristeva and others. But even in a less French, less theoretical, and less iconoclastic mode, work by Millett, Shulman, and Juliet Mitchell gave Freud a new relevance by virtue of his nearly constitutive role in gender theory. The Freud of the fifties—the authoritarian, punitive martinet so epitomized by the work of Philip Rieff and Lionel Trilling or the more benign but still conformist ego-psychological Freud of Erik Erikson and Rollo May—would have been swept out in the tide of sixties radicalism without feminism. Feminists positioned Freud as both the patriarchal norm they wished to overturn and the subversive analyst who provided a warrant for jettisoning myths of male dominance. But feminism also valued the practical, clinical side of psychoanalysis, the way that, even as practised theoretically and linguistically by Lacan and Jean Laplanche, it maintained a concern with the medical case history, the health of the patient, and the exigencies of the body.

Feminist criticism became autonomous from (though never unrelated to) feminist political activity with two developments: the introduction of French feminist theory, which was an aspect of the general theoretical revolution that accompanied the popularity of Derrida and Foucault, and the delineation of the idea of an Anglo-American feminist mode of reading literary texts. *Anglo-American feminism* was at first seen as directly assisting in the struggle for equal rights and pay and the expansion of women's consciousness. The writers analysed were largely canonical figures or even—as in Marilyn French's work on Shakespeare—female characters in canonical male authors. Any sort of text in which "the women question" was pertinent, not just texts authored by women, was fair game. But Millett saw the canon very differently. Her valuation of literary history is exactly the opposite of that favoured by the "resolved symbolic" and has a surprising amount in common with the canon revision proposed by otherwise dissimilar thinkers, such as Harold Bloom.

Millett continues in the vein of those who saw the British nineteenth century as the last time before the 1970s when the literary sphere gave any visibility to women's concerns. Indeed, Millett sees the twentieth century as a time of counter-revolution. More provocatively, she sees as the ultimate counter-revolutionaries the men who were considered apostles of sexual liberation: D.H. Lawrence, Henry Miller, and Norman Mailer. The political right wing has accused feminism of being one of the social movements that came out of the sixties. Yet for all that Millett, at the end of *Sexual Politics*, applauds the youth movement of the day, she strongly rebukes the ethic of "free love," which, in practice, sanctioned unbridled male sexual appetites. For Millett, the sexual liberation dreamt of by erotic prophets such as Lawrence, Miller, and Mailer tends to repeal the incipient sexual revolution glimpsed in the nineteenth century. Feminism, thus, not only involved a reversal of patriarchy. It involved an overturning of historiographic assumptions. Feminism was one of the nails in the coffin of doctrinaire modernism. Modernism had privileged the avant-garde (literally a military term meaning the advanced guard of the onrushing army). The more progressive, the more radical, the better. Feminism, by seeing modernism as a masculine *coup d'état* in the republic of letters that installed the canonical male modernists as a sort of military *junta*, robbed modernism of its hip, with-it justification. In this way, feminism was allied with many strands of postmodernism. Postmodernism tended to question the utopian narratives—or, as Jean-François Lyotard called them, "metanarratives"—of modernity. Postmodernism no longer saw history—including cultural history—as a linear march towards progress. In particular, past idioms were once again found interesting, if only in a partial or ironic way. Whereas a modern artistic breakthrough often took the form of trying to achieve something totally new, a postmodern breakthrough often involved being able to articulate and reshuffle past ways of doing things. This approach was true of Foucault, who, as we have seen, tore down the customary binaries between tradition and modernity in his early work. It is true of Derrida, whose invocation of the "always already" outflanked any transparent assertions of unmediated temporal presence.

Feminism, with its interest in buried pasts and retrieved writers, certainly participated in this decentring of a static present, and in a concomitant and tacit rehabilitation of the idea of a "past." But there were limits for feminism as to how much the past could be rehabilitated. Given that men had dominated society throughout human history, the idea of the past could be no more unequivocally positive than could the idea of modernity—a modernity, in fact, dominated by men. Some feminists tried to posit a time before patriarchy, influenced by the postulation by J.J. Bachofen (a late nineteenth-century Swiss anthropologist) and Marija Gimbutas (a late twentieth-century Lithuanian-born feminist archaeologist) of a matriarchal era before the dawn of recorded time. (This postulation was itself an inversion of the triumphant, patriarchal potency with which "Indo-European peoples" had been endowed by Aryanist accounts.) But most feminists saw the past as, in James Joyce's memorable phrase, a nightmare from which they were trying to awake. Not only was Chopin's *The Awakening* (1899) a widely read text in the early years of feminist criticism, but Adrienne Rich, playing on a title of one of Henrik Ibsen's dramas, used the phrase "When We Dead Awaken" for one of her highly influential feminist essays.[23] Feminist criticism of the 1970s looked to a future time beyond patriarchy and judged the past as insufficient insofar as it did not conform to that future ideal. This positing of the ideal in the future was something not common in postmodernism. Even those postmodernists who seemed at all "futuristic," such as Jean Baudrillard, saw the future as likely to consist of a series of infinitely repeating simulacra, unrelated to any underlying reality. Feminism was more akin to the thought of Hegel or even Marx in seeing the possibility of a realized future, though one utterly unlike the past. It was no accident that science fiction by women writers such as Joanna Russ, James Tiptree, Jr., and Ursula K. Le Guin flourished in the early years of the modern feminist movement or that arguably modern feminism's leading realist writer, Doris Lessing, turned to science fiction at a crucial point in her career.

This 1970s feminist willingness to rebuke the past in light of the hoped-for future is seen in the first major text of Anglo-American feminist criticism that was read more as criticism than as political statement. This text, *The Madwoman in the Attic* (1979), was co-written by Sandra Gilbert and Susan Gubar. Gilbert and Gubar were unafraid to chastise Jane Austen or the Brontës for not presenting woman characters of sufficient strength and independence, for portraying women as overly content to seek fulfilment in relationships with men. This critique led other critics to charge Gilbert and Gubar with "presentism"—with treating the past as an insufficient version of the present. But this was not the critics' goal. Their goal was to unfold the possibility of a future by disestablishing those aspects of past traditions they felt shackling. The two writers had different strengths. Gilbert, an admired poet, was adept at diagnosing the social valence of analogical patterns. Gubar's expertise was more in narrative theory and intellectual history. But the two together staged the most famous collaboration in modern literary criticism. Collaboration itself became a tool of feminist study, as critics combined efforts in recognition of the still-emerging shape of the field and as a gesture against "male" egoism and competitiveness. Gilbert and Gubar took their title from the fate of Bertha Mason, the first wife of Mr. Rochester in Charlotte Brontë's *Jane Eyre*. Rochester had locked Bertha away in the attic, which permitted him to try to "marry" the younger and saner Jane Eyre. It is interesting that, just as Gilbert and Gubar used this character as an image of the repressed agency of women, post-colonial criticism used Jean Rhys's novel *Wide Sargasso Sea* (1966), a prequel to *Jane Eyre* featuring Antoinette Cosway, the "real" Bertha Mason, to symbolize European repression of colonial agency.[24] That the original novel, *Jane Eyre*, was a canonical text nonetheless written by a woman had a lot to do with the influence of this further extension and revision of its fictional world. This dual effort—of rewriting dominant masculinist history and of finding usable elements in the textual heritage bequeathed to them—continued to be a trait of feminist study into the 1990s.

French Feminism: Psychoanalysis and Écriture Feminine

This feminist rewriting of the past, unlike so many of the more rarefied conceptions of theory, was easy to understand and soon gained a manifest place in a wider discursive culture. Feminism, in fact, was the only field of late twentieth-century theory that not only had both a popular and an academic face but whose popular and academic manifestations had a good deal in common. A sometimes overly tendentious insistence on literary characters as three-dimensional figures rather than literary tropes was compensated for by an openness to the future; feminist criticism was not inhibited by the "restorative nostalgia" (Boym's term again) that has often limited literary study and made it stodgy and musty.[25] The use by the previously mentioned science-fiction writers of scenarios of the future and of alternative worlds to explore challenges to traditionally inscribed gender norms had its counterpart in the philosophical abstraction of *French feminism*, whose major figures were Julia Kristeva, Hélène Cixous, and Luce Irigaray. Kristeva was originally from Bulgaria. In fact, she and her fellow countryman, the structuralist and scholar of "the fantastic" Tzvetan Todorov, constituted a significant Bulgarian contribution to French theory. Kristeva's national origin showed early on, when she played a substantial role in introducing the Russian formalists and the work of Mikhail Bakhtin to the West. (As a nation with a Slavic language and, at the time, close political ties to Russia, Bulgaria had a strong cultural connection to Russia.) Later on, Kristeva wrote popular detective stories that sometimes delved into Bulgaria's Slavic and Byzantine heritages. But very soon Kristeva became assimilated to a quintessentially French body of thought, and she married a famous French experimental writer, Philippe Sollers, about whom Roland Barthes wrote a celebratory essay.[26]

Kristeva's career, like Derrida's, was largely occupied with language and philosophy. But she differed from Derrida in the central role psychoanalysis has played in her work. It was, in fact, through Kristeva that the often arcane French psychoanalyst Jacques Lacan (1901–81) became a widely known name within literature. In the 1950s, it was often spoken as a truism that French culture, with its aforementioned Cartesian clarity and rationality, disdained the murky depth of psychoanalysis. Given that, at this very moment, Jean-Paul Sartre was surging to world fame with a body of thought largely influenced by the just-as-murky Hegel and Heidegger, this argument had a very thin basis. Admittedly, Sartre did reject psychoanalysis, and, in the mid-twentieth century, Sartre *was* French thought for many inside and outside France. This Sartrean hegemony, the object of sharp generational challenge from many of the thinkers we see as literary "theorists," makes clear the conceptual barriers that the recognition in the anglophone world of French psychoanalysis faced. Lacan, whose famous credo was "the unconscious is structured like a language," offers an emphasis that stressed conceptual formations over primal drives. Earlier, the French surrealists had embraced what seemed like Freud's regenerative unleashing of the irrational. But the surrealists were more overtly irrational, less "scientific" and "clinical" than Lacan, with a Hegelian, dialectical hominess to their premise of the saving rescue occasioned by the irruption of irrationality and its healing restoration to a conscious level of awareness. Lacan saw various levels of figuration, traceable as different phases of personal psychological structuration, as undercutting rational agency.

For Lacan, the infant first came to consciousness in the imaginary or "mirror stage," when it saw its own image and assumed that its own self was the entire world. Life as actually lived, though, cannot, experientially, be adequate to the idealized image in the mirror. So the mirror stage is "imaginary" in a double sense: pertaining to one's own image and also in its false sense of the adequacy and sufficiency of the self. (The looser use of "imaginary" in theory, such as descriptions of a nation's self-idealization as a "national imaginary," ultimately comes from this Lacanian use of the term.) Later on, the "symbolic" stage occurs when the child realizes it is part of the larger order controlled, in the first immediate instance, by the father, and that it must enter and inscribe itself within this linguistic macro-structure. This is the Lacanian equivalent of the Freudian Oedipal stage. So far, we are very much where we were in the American 1950s, with the transgressive yet overbearing Oedipus in control of the situation, albeit, in Lacan's theory, the situation is laced with a far greater linguistic self-consciousness and an awareness that, in the order of language, unlike that of political authority, revision is always a possibility near at hand. Kristeva sought to go beyond the "symbolic," in a move very similar to the reactions to the Anglo-American "resolved symbolic" that we discussed in the Preface. Instead of privileging the ultimate Lacanian stage, "the Real," which, somewhat as in medieval scholasticism is that which is at once most absolute and least penetrable, Kristeva goes the other direction, away from the absolute, towards the outside, the inchoate, what she styles *chora* (from a Greek word for "the countryside"). *Chora* is used by Plato to indicate a space that bestows ineluctable materiality on the Platonic form, as childbirth does for the soul of the child. In both Platonic and Kristevan manifestations, *chora* is a cloudy, indeterminate sort of materiality that is unable to be neatened, that is anarchic and rife with instability. Kristeva raised the idea of a "semiotic" sphere as an alternative to the symbolic. As terms, both "semiotic" and "symbolic" have to do with representation, but symbolic implies a fixity and coherence not connoted by semiotic, which refers to the idea of "signs" or linguistic markers that admit their own indelible status as representations.

In its Anglo-American reception, the symbolic-semiotic distinction often suffered the unfortunate fate of being read as a simple binary, with the semiotic being seen as a cathartic breakthrough beyond the symbolic. As with all French feminists, and all poststructuralists, the evocation of an alternative linguistic field is not meant to annul or evade the authority of the previously acknowledged nexus. Kristeva does not contest the manifestation of the symbolic order or see it as undesirable. She merely posits the existence of other discourses, and she sees the semiotic as far more anarchic and even inchoate, whereas the symbolic, as described by Lacan, she sees as reassuring in its sense of a structural base for psychic experience, for all its complexity and interdependence. This multivalence is one of the sources of the common tendency to see French feminism as less "essentialist" than the Anglo-American version. In other words, it is seen as less presuming on innate qualities ascribed to men and women.[27] This characterization is true to an extent. French feminism participates in post-structuralism's overhauling of binary oppositions and arbitrary absolutes. Yet French feminism clearly sees women as having inherent qualities in their discourses, if not in their bodies, that cannot simply be exchanged for male modes of production. This view may be an example of what Gayatri Chakravorty Spivak—a post-structuralist, feminist, and post-colonial critic—has called "strategic essentialism." The idea of *écriture feminine*—feminine writing—textualizes gender. But it also genders the idea of writing. *Écriture feminine* is a certain kind of writing that is less methodical, more irrational, less intellectual, and more experiential. In this way, it certainly participates in gender distinctions. What it does not do is value the agency or the self-determination of individual women in the way that Anglo-American feminism does. Anglo-American feminism largely saw the liberation of women as a class as epitomized by the liberation of women as individuals. Thus the character who evades or escapes patriarchal institutions in a novel or the feminist critic who reveals new meanings in women's texts is seen as representing a larger class of emancipatory activity. The transformation of the individual impels the transformation of the type or group, in an all-pervasive practice of what Elaine Showalter influentially termed "gynocriticism."[28] In the French model, it is language as such, not any individual text or personal experience, that must be changed. In fact, language, because of its capacity for density and innovation, can function as a site of resistance to authoritarian practices and ideologies, as advocated by figures such as Barthes and Derrida. And the change in language, though spurred by the revolution against what Irigaray called "phallogocentrism" or patriarchy, is part of a general process of linguistic and even ontological reinvention and rupture. This is a process radically willing to dispense as far as possible with past certainties.

After Kristeva sprung to fame in the late 1960s on the heels of her first significant publication, she was young enough to have several phases in her career ahead of her. In the early 1980s, she became so interested in psychoanalysis that she decided to train as an analyst herself. This sense that using the techniques of another discipline requires full training in that discipline was a recognition all too infrequent in the spree of interdisciplinary borrowing that has characterized recent work in the humanities. But it did mean that Kristeva granted psychoanalysis a certain authority; it was not just a trope, it meant something referential. This referentiality made her work very different from Lacan's, beneath which there was always the potential for the system to reveal itself as a concocted linguistic artefact that was burlesquing psychoanalysis as much as propagating it. This fictive, satiric aspect was especially true when Kristeva's thought was applied in the English-speaking world, where a Lacanian clinical tradition never exerted any sway. Other countries, such as Italy (under the auspices of the publicist and partial con man Armando Verdiglione) and Argentina developed a strong presence of actual Lacanian clinical practitioners, which made the entire idea of Lacanianism less of a conceit.[29] In the anglophone world, the average analyst or therapist down the block was unlikely to be a Lacanian. In fact, Lacan's metaphorizing of Freudian terms was seen as part of the general collapse of the authority of Freud—and of the institution of psychoanalysis itself, towards the end of the twentieth century.

Kristeva's mid-career turn towards what were, in this context, more practical models buttressed her image as someone actually interested in the doing, not just the trumpeting, of psychoanalysis. Kristeva turned to the British "object-relations" school of psychiatry pioneered by Melanie Klein and D.W. Winnicott. These thinkers, who focused on the pre-Oedipal rather than the Oedipal stage, were interested in the fragmented and "immature" emotions that the Oedipal emphasis on maturity, discussed in the Preface to this book, tried to seal off and cap in the service of a normative regimen. Object-relations psychoanalysis was more socially optimistic. It saw the psyche less as a dark, turbulent landscape that had to be governed ruthlessly by a regime of caution and restraint and more as a realm where consensus and trust could be gradually built by a realistic negotiation of the mother-child bond and the inevitable fracturing of that bond as the child grew older. Klein's idea of "reparation"—in which creativity was one of the paths to which the aggressive, depressive, and guilty tendencies constructively direct themselves—opened up for imagination the role of vehicle of emotional health; creativity was no longer just a displacement of untameable energies. This stress on (to use Winnicott's phrase) "the good-enough" in the framing of the individual breaks down the binary opposition between the individual and society. In Kristeva's work, this relation between society and the individual became something more sinuous and interactive, less melodramatic and categorical. Some feminists even saw Kristeva's affirmation of psychoanalytic techniques as ceding too much to master discourses ultimately formulated by men and too little to the individual woman.

Kristeva saw object-relations psychology as a road to a new vision of the political sphere. As a Bulgarian, Kristeva was, from the beginning, essentially anti-communist, despite a youthful flirtation with Maoism. Her use of Klein and Winnicott moved her towards an open, pluralist, constructive vision of a society in which individuals were free to make their destinies yet resided in unavoidable contingency with respect to the wills and desires of others. Even as Anglo-American thinkers saw Kristeva and other French theorists as radicals subverting the hegemony of the bourgeois subject, within a French context, Kristeva was part of an ever-further distancing from the traditional intellectual Left. Nearly every thinker associated with "French theory" represented a swerving away from standard leftist beliefs. Even Sartre, himself often avowing communism, roundly condemned the French Communist Party after the Soviet invasion of Hungary in 1956.[30] And many French thinkers distanced themselves from this party, which had been under the leadership of Maurice Thorez since the 1930s, and from the ideas espoused by communist intellectuals such as Roger Garaudy, who flourished into the 1960s. Only Louis Althusser, of all the big names associated with theory, took a more Marxist approach than his predecessors, and Althusser with Marx, like Lacan with Freud, always had the never-activated potential to reveal his rendition of Marxism as simply an elaborate, hyperbolic burlesque, a feat of linguistic legerdemain.

Although theory was seen in the English-speaking world as a sometimes invigorating, sometimes dangerous new injection into the intellectual bloodstream that, whatever its merits or demerits, was certainly *radical*, it operated in France as a *liberalizing* agent. This difference can be attributed not just to local variations in intellectual history but also to long-established differences between the two worlds. In the English-speaking countries, constitutional traditions had evolved gradually and in such a way as to give ordinary people an unusual degree of rights when compared to those enjoyed by the rest of the planet. Consequently, Anglo-American intellectuals—what Coleridge would call "the clerisy"—were anxious about reserving intellectual power, keeping it separate from this potentially unfettered democracy. This motive was behind the idea of Victorian intellectuals such as Matthew Arnold that criticism could operate as at once an education for democracy and a brake on excessive democratic desires. In France, where political change occurred in a series of dramatic ruptures and constitutional norms were not established until much later, the intellectual had always been more of the visionary conscience of the country than its practical monitor. Kristeva, with her deep concern for both abstract linguistic patterns and the concrete emotional education of the individual, bridged this anglophone-francophone gap in the manner that had been achieved by earlier (and very different) French intellectuals such as Voltaire and Proust. Thus, to reiterate, in France, Kristeva was liberalizing; in the English-speaking world, radicalizing.

Kristeva could not have achieved this impact without her concentration on theories of gender. Her reconception of such a fundamental issue as gender enabled her to reconceive long-ossified ethical and political norms. Luce Irigaray, too, created an entire philosophical system around feminism. In one of her major works, *Speculum of the Other Woman* (1985), Irigaray questioned and even jeered at the supposition that men and women could be distinguished by anatomy alone, as both Freud and the ancients had assumed. Irigaray shows that what seem to be purely scientific definitions of woman are, in fact, highly loaded and categorical distinctions designed to subordinate and sideline women. Unlike non-European peoples, woman could not be simply ignored, put on the edge of the map with the notation of "Here be dragons." She was needed for human reproduction. This necessity, argued Irigaray, infuriated men so much that they developed an entire system of bogus anatomical and biological distinction in order to disguise and alienate women's power as much as possible. But Irigaray does not advocate female separatism as was nearly done by other French feminists, such as the novelist Monique Wittig.[31] Nor does Irigaray conclude that women are the same as men. Her work involves a complex tug of equality and difference, both of which are desire but not exclusively. Difference, according to Irigaray as well as Derrida, is a positive value—not only should men and women not be the same but all women should not be the same. One of Irigaray's principal charges against the metaphysical concept of "woman" was that it had hidden the agency of each woman and the individual differences between women. But Irigaray did not want difference unnecessarily insisted upon. Nor did she favour difference being lodged surreptitiously in definitions that seem to be scientific but are, in fact, spurious.

Of the three major French feminists, Irigaray accomplished the most within professional philosophy, and Cixous (notwithstanding Kristeva's late development as a popular detective novelist) had the greatest achievement as a creative artist. Cixous's plays, poems, and creative non-fiction meditations parallel her academic work. Indeed, some feminists did nearly all their theoretical work in poems and poetic manifestos. It is interesting to think how *écriture feminine*, as practised and as discerned by Cixous and Irigaray, differed from the writing categorized as belonging to past modernist movements, such as Dadaism and surrealism, as well as from modernist fiction, such as the works of Proust and Joyce. French feminists were influenced by these earlier innovators. Cixous's first major book was on James Joyce, and she used Molly Bloom's monologue in Joyce's *Ulysses* as a proof text for the idea of *écriture feminine*, even though that monologue was written by a man and presented "woman" as a rather non-intellectual being.[32] In *Revolution in Poetic Language*, Kristeva wrote lengthily on such male late nineteenth-century innovators as Stéphane Mallarmé and the Comte de Lautréamont, treating them as exemplars of a semiotic whose difference from the symbolic imaged the escape of feminist discourse from patriarchal constraint. On the other hand, the explicitly political agenda of Kristeva and Cixous and their advocating a subordinated group gave them a different relation to history and to ideas about history. This is not to say that their experimentation was more "relevant" in a crudely measurable way. But, decisively, it was unhinged from metanarratives of progress that, as Lyotard had observed, accompanied even modernist ruptures of progress. The very term "experimentation" was adapted from science and seemed to justify linguistic instability only because, in the manner of scientific laboratory work, it contributed to a goal-oriented process of unearthing knowledge. Even if the breakthrough was ostensibly away from mechanistic, quantifiable progress towards a higher stage of consciousness, the rhetoric of progress was still lurking beneath the surface. Feminist experimentation, on the other hand, valued the sheer touch and impact of language itself, its specific gestures as much as its comprehensive implications. Cixous and her peers argued that a male-dominated language had repressed the capacity for play and alteration that a feminist viewpoint could potentially bring, an argument similar to that of Anglo-Australian feminist Germaine Greer, who had contended in *The Female Eunuch* (1970) that women's sexuality had been repressed by socially constructed gender roles. In French feminism, the idea of *jouissance*—ecstatic, unhindered play—in many ways took the place of earlier vocabularies of experimentation and aesthetic advance. And *jouissance* could extend across all genres.

Modernist experimenters had somewhat sundered themselves from the idea of the expository. Although figures such as Walter Benjamin, Elias Canetti,

Maurice Blanchot and (not to be forgotten in this regard) T.S. Eliot valued the essay as a creative form, most of the best-known modernists put all their energy into other forms of creative expression. The Québécoise poet Nicole Brossard and the Latina feminist Cherrie Moraga also worked in hybrid forms, which proliferated between prose and poetry, imagination and meditation. This fictocritical emphasis, this splaying of the difference between exposition and imagination, seemed peculiarly suited to feminist work. The African American feminist bell hooks wrote pieces that were half abstruse meditations and half self-help and consciousness-raising treatises, in a style at once accessible and gnomic. As hooks's work showed, feminist writing also permitted a sense of the personal in literary criticism. The growing willingness of male critics to write personally and autobiographically in the 1990s was a direct response to the influence of feminism. So, more generally, was the rise of the memoir and of creative non-fiction as respected literary genres in which it was prestigious or lucrative to write. The struggle of women to enter the academy, and the way their entrance changed what and how academics read, enabled the introduction of subjectivity into the literary-critical process in a way that, when combined with academic rigour, helped broaden the reach of criticism. As a result, criticism could operate on nearly equal terms with imaginative genres such as fiction, poetry, and drama.

Academic Feminism: The 1980s

Feminism, Difference, and the Canon

Women had been the primary readers of literature, especially the novel, since the eighteenth century. Now they were finally at the core of its study. The 1980s saw the consolidation of what came to be called second wave feminism. The first wave of feminism was usually defined as flourishing in the late nineteenth and early twentieth centuries. In this phase, the idea of the "New Woman" was articulated to aid in the fight for women's suffrage. The second wave was defined as the feminism articulated beginning in the late 1960s and, in Anglo-American criticism, associated with critics such as Millett, Gilbert, and Gubar. After the rise of the third wave of feminism in the 1990s, the second wave often began to be seen as monolithic. In fact, the second wave had very different emphases during the 1970s as compared to during the 1980s.

The academic feminism of the 1980s differed from the 1970s version because it became more centred on the past. Feminism attempted to discover a hidden history, a history of resistance. Though eventually nearly any woman, no matter what her political position, became a permissible object of feminist scholarship and advocacy, the first rescued women writers of the past were often explicit advocates of women's rights. For instance, both the seventeenth-century poet Sor Juana Inés de la Cruz, a Mexican nun, and the fourteenth-century lyric poet Christine de Pisan launched defences of women's intellectual worth and advocated the possibility of female achievement. These were not just women writers, but writers who wrote explicitly about the condition of women. Christine de Pisan, in fact, allegorized the lack of accepted precedents that still worry women writers six centuries later. She did this in her chief work, *The Book of the City of Ladies*, by having the precursors of women's creativity be not people but abstractions: Reason, Justice, and Rectitude. It was to avoid this lack of a heritage that late twentieth-century feminists turned to the past, in many ways inspiring other subordinated groups, such as African Americans and Latinos, to do the same. In the 1980s and 1990s, much Anglo-American feminist work hereby turned to the retrieval of heretofore unnoticed past texts by women.

These texts were authored by writers who had been mentioned in literary histories but left out of print and dismissed as irrelevant—the eighteenth-century novelist Frances Burney, the Romantic-period poets Felicia Hemans and Anna Lactitia Barbauld, and the British "New Woman" novelists of the 1890s. Just as frequently, they were authored by those who had been obscure to all but a few students of the period—the Renaissance dramatist Elizabeth Cary, the Victorian poets Augusta Webster and Mathilde Blind, the Alabaman Augusta Jane Evans, the eighteenth-century British poet and essayist Lady Mary Chudleigh, the seventeenth-century mystic Margaret Cavendish, and the sixteenth-century French poet Louise Labé. These and other previously ignored women writers became the regular subject of courses, conferences, and books. Unlike Sor Juana or Christine de Pisan, these writers could not be termed proto-feminists, and often they did not write specifically about the condition of women. But their very gender made them relevant after feminism in a way they had not been before; also, their texts were considered significant *largely because of the gender of their authors* not because of their intrinsic worth. Women writers who had been admired for their craft but had not been given a place in academic reception, such as the Victorian poet Christina Rossetti, the US novelist Sarah Orne Jewett, and the medieval mystics Margery Kempe and Julian of Norwich, suddenly found their work could be accommodated in the new reconceptualization of literary study. Given that these writers' texts were essentially new to any sort of modern literary analysis, the critical heritage that was there in the case of Austen, Eliot, the Brontës, and even Chopin could not be assumed. Whereas, in the case of the better-known writers, feminism could correct and reorient patriarchal assumptions, in the case of the "noncanonical" writers (who rapidly became canonical, as they were frequently taught and became the object of study and research), feminist scholars had to prepare the literary work as an object of study. Editorial work, textual scholarship that sought to provide definitive versions of the works as originally published, and first-stage critiques that included ample plot summaries for the many unfamiliar with the work were inexorably necessary. None of this had to be done with Jane Austen or *Jane Eyre*. All of it had to be done with Webster or Cavendish.

Literary theory does not lend itself to happy or authoritative endings. The rescue of formerly suppressed texts by women did not end all historical contestation. Adding Cavendish to the seventeenth-century canon or Lady Mary Chudleigh to that of the early eighteenth diversified the canon in terms of gender but made it more elitist in terms of social class. Both Cavendish (definitely) and Chudleigh (more marginally) were of the titled aristocracy by birth or marriage. Many of the rescued women writers were connected to powerful men. This connection may have been a prerequisite for them being able to write at all, and most feminist scholarship acknowledged female versions of Thomas Gray's "mute inglorious Milton" who, tacitly, were (incompletely) represented by the more socially elevated women who, unlike their working-class sisters, *were* able to write and, although less frequently, publish. But there was also a danger that emphasizing rescued texts by women of the past rather than more contemporary work that looked more towards the future risked endorsing the social conditions of that past even as it overhauled latter-day gendered scenarios of what that past was like.

Some feminist theorists, understanding the power of normative social conditions to govern the lives of even the most creative and inspired women, turned to the law as a way of excavating the ingrained prejudice latent in Western social systems. The American feminist scholar Drucilla Cornell engaged many of the same issues as the French feminists, to whose work she frequently responded, but placed her analysis in the context of specific regulatory and governing institutions. After reading Cornell, one can see feminist theory was specifically about women, yet it also mattered to intellectual life generally. Cornell cites Derrida as much as she cites the French feminists, and she endorses his anti-logocentrism in postulating "no ultimate outside referent" to ground gender identity: Derrida, according to Cornell, helps us to "dance differently."[33] Cornell critiques "gender consolidation" as proceeding from a self-enclosed, self-sustaining system whose interest (and goal) is to perpetuate itself rather than disclose external reality.[34] Cornell gets her idea of the "system" from sociologist Niklas Luhmann, who is, in essence, neutral about the idea of systems and whose framework of self-sustaining systems was influential on the "autopoetic" biologists to be discussed in Chapter 7. Cornell is saying not only that the system of gender is biased by its patriarchal content but also that self-sustaining systems can be directed, out of their own properties, in certain ways that disempowered women. Cornell concurs with Derrida that, unlike as in the late modernist celebrations of the auto-referential as wiser or more discerning than the hetero-referential, self-referentiality does not inherently bring with it superior wisdom. Cornell does not deny the neutrality of systems. She does *not* believe that systems are innately tinged by an underlying ideological bias. But she *does* believe that systems can be manipulated to exclude individuals. Cornell, in fact, argues that the metaphysical idea of "woman" functions not only to obscure individual women but also to set off women in competition with each other, as each is trying to incarnate the unattainable ideal designed by men. Feminism becomes an opportunity to reflect on the conditions of intellectual life, all the while unswervingly concentrating on issues of gender. Cornell follows Kant in saying "the right to claim one's person is the basis of all legal rights."[35]

Kant's philosophy is so intimidating and abstract that we often forget that it was the greatest and most systematic product of the Enlightenment's emphasis on human freedom and that Kant's ultimate conclusion, as Cornell suggests, is that it is very nearly impossible for reason to consent to the deprivation of freedom for the infringement of what we would now call "human rights." Cornell uses Kant's looking towards the "ought" as opposed to the "is" to focus beyond the emphasis on merely legal rights espoused by 1970s feminists, as seen in the ERA (Equal Rights Amendment) and various equivalent statutory laws. Cornell opposes none of these early feminist endeavours, but she sees them as insufficiently accommodating the range of rights ideally represented by feminism. Calling for a re-embrace of the radical social ideas of Kant's contemporary, the late eighteenth-century feminist Mary Wollstonecraft (Percy Shelley's mother-in-law), Cornell laments how feminism's acceptance of bourgeois social norms severed it from anti-racist and gay and lesbian causes. Cornell's work not only provided a crucial link between deconstruction, feminism, and law but also canvassed how individuality and meaningful self-expression can coexist with a sense of social equity that can be called civilized. This is not to say that feminism was only valuable when it transcended its own advocacy of women's equality and rights. Feminist concerns are fundamental, not parochial or passing. But Cornell's thought, like Kant's, goes well beyond the immediate social circumstances that at least partially prompted it.

Cornell stood between Carol Gilligan's difference feminism, which emphasized women's biological capacity for nurturing, and the body of work that came to be called "cyborgian feminist" thought led by Donna Haraway.[36] Gilligan's *In a Different Voice* (1982) was probably the single most influential feminist text of the 1980s.[37] Gilligan was a psychologist who sought to expand developmental models so that they did not derogate or give short shrift to women's experiential and cognitive practices. This project led her to come rather near biological essentialism in her emphasis of private over public contexts and her stress on the intimate nature of the mother-child bond. Gilligan viewed women as, for both social and biological reasons, more contextual, empathetic, and relationship oriented, as having strengths that were at once more interpersonal and more private when compared to those of men. This view was well suited to buttress women's self-assertion during the era of what Susan Faludi called the "backlash" of the 1980s. Gilligan's emphasis on a positive difference that sought to complement rather than to imitate or rival male behavioural patterns also had the effect of bringing motherhood, seldom a staple of discussions of women's lives in the 1970s, back into the forefront, and of seeing child-rearing as a pivotal attribute of women's ways of knowing and doing. (Kristeva's move from post-Lacanian semiotics to object-relations humanism, which occurred in the 1980s, was also concomitant with a greater emphasis on motherhood.)

Gilligan's position is easily caricatured. It is important to underscore that her emphasis on relatedness, connection, and context resembles the emphasis on "language games" and "family resemblances" that is found in the later work of the philosopher Ludwig Wittgenstein, or the stress on tradition and conversation in the hermeneutic work of Hans-Georg Gadamer (discussed in Chapter 2). All these thinkers stress groundedness, context, situation, and connectedness; they react against the individual monad. When Gilligan took this approach, people complained it was too feminist—a charge not made against the other philosophers.

In the 2000s, a younger generation of feminist scholars such as Peg O'Connor and Cressida Heyes made connections between feminism and relatedness less biologically grounded than Gilligan's, but the implications of their work were not far from the prevailing viewpoint of Gilligan's *In a Different Voice*.[38] Gilligan's privileging of maternal feeling, empathetic privacy, and relatedness was a counter-statement to the dehumanizing tendency of the mechanical. Diametrically opposite to it was Donna Haraway's cyborgian feminism, which emphasized the unnaturalness over the naturalness of women's bodies. As opposed to Gilligan's generally quietist and apolitical stance, Haraway's counted as a deliberate challenge to the political hegemony of the day. For at the moment of its greatest reach into academia—the 1980s—feminism was facing an array of opponents.

Haraway and Cyborgian Feminism

The failure of the ERA to get sufficient votes for ratification in 1982 seemed to signal that the second wave of feminism had died down in the public sphere. What Faludi described as a backlash against gender equality led to the reassessment of what the women's movement should do. Gilligan's answer was to emphasize women's temperamental and relational difference from men, a difference grounded in biology and long-ingrained habit, in other words, grounded in "natural" or non-mechanistic and traditional views that had been offered previously as rationales for women's subordination. Yet Haraway contended that anything mechanical had the capacity to re-imagine the imbalance of physical strength that lay behind men's traditional dominance. Far from seeing mechanization as a threat—a rationalistic, male discourse running rampant over feminine qualities of feeling and emotional connection—Haraway welcomed technology as a mode whose inventiveness could sweep away the ossified hierarchies of male power.

Yet Haraway was not just a super-cool techno-futurist. Her work called for a rethinking of nature. Women had the "advantage" of not having the sense of distance from and supremacy over nature that male subjects had arrogated to themselves, a distance discernible even in male Romantic poets' deliberately

Haraway

empathetic attitude towards nature. Male Romantics such as Wordsworth and, less successfully, Coleridge sought to fuse themselves with nature because they saw themselves, prima facie, as not fused with it. Without fetishizing the female body as more "natural" than the male, cyborgian feminism saw embodiment as linked with *both* nature and technology in a way that did not uniquely privilege the human subject, as traditional male-oriented anthologies had done. The cyborg had links not only with the robot but also with the tree, with the ant, with the worm. Unlike Gilligan's "difference feminism," Haraway's cyborgian feminism did not see nature as ipso facto nurturing and reassuring. Destruction, appetite, death, and remaking were common attributes of both nature and technology, and feminism, in the view of Haraway, should not shrink from these challenges but negotiate them in a critical and empowered way. Haraway's manifesto was aphoristic, written as a series of terse, well-honed diagnoses. Haraway did not come out of a literary-critical background. Thus, she was independent of the canons and protocols that had quickly developed in literary feminism. That her cyborgian aphorisms lacked literary intent heightened their literary impact.

Haraway reversed many of her initial readers' assumptions. Nostalgic historiographies stressing matriarchy had associated the female with orality rather than literacy. But Haraway pointed out that African American women had used literacy, denied to them as far as possible by racism and patriarchy, to enfranchise themselves. So the acquired (in this case literacy) was as connected with female agency as the innate. The acquired technology of writing is *emancipatory*, not alienating. This view, of course, has echoes of Derrida's strategic privileging of writing. But Haraway's very different valence and her independence from explicitly post-structuralist methods give this point a ground-level salience that would have seemed less compelling had it come readily equipped with a deconstructive warrant. Both Haraway and the science fiction of the African American writer Octavia E. Butler, whose novels often feature bodily change and distortion that is affirmative or matter of fact rather than nightmarish, engage in a rehabilitation of myth and futurity. Both myth and futurity were usually held in low esteem by postmodernists. Kermode, for example, exalts fiction over myth, and Lyotard and Baudrillard privilege reshufflings of the past over utopian imaginings of the future. These orientations are symptomatic of the general postmodernist scepticism concerning the possibility of wresting a meaning from myths of the past or future. Yet Haraway, along with Cornell the most explicitly political of the thinkers discussed in this chapter, was vitally engaged in the present, and, indeed, she was pointing out that her own present was more mythic and futuristic than that of the modernists who had, on different trajectories, elevated both myth and futurity. If Cixous, Kristeva, and Irigaray linked feminism to postmodern theory, Haraway's work linked feminism with the social and cultural conditions of postmodernity itself.

Haraway deliberately wrote her essay as a "socialist feminist" response to the Reagan era. Unlike the French feminists, and for that matter unlike Foucault,

Haraway produced her work in the wake of the revived power of the tradition-alist and free-market paradigms later termed "neoliberalism." Haraway's sense of the political made feminism seem far more engaged in conversation with surrounding intellectual discourse. Feminism became something not only for avowed feminists or for those who concentrated their intellectual work in that field. It became generally conversant with issues discussed across the postmod-ern universe. Feminism was often painted as the establishment, as that against which newer generations reacted. Notably, feminist critics born in the 1930s and 1940s were seen as "old hat" long before male historicist critics born in those decades were: Stephen Greenblatt (as we shall see in Chapter 7) remained *au courant* long after Sandra Gilbert and Susan Gubar were seen as less than chic.

Nor were the feminists who were explicitly or inferentially attacked by this rhetoric the privileged, tenured, rebels-gone-establishment caricatures that they were often alleged to be. It was not just the women who were of college age when feminist criticism began in the early 1970s who entered academia as a result of feminism. Many middle-aged women resumed and completed their education and entered academia. Second wave feminism was experienced not just by one generation but by several—by women of various ages who were denied entrance to intellectual life because of the misogyny of modernism and of other ideologies dominant until the middle of the twentieth century, which saw the most recent manifestation of ingrained patriarchal attitudes. The gender revolution of the late twentieth century was not a mere cathartic breakthrough on the part of baby boomers. It was the realization of social changes that, in retrospect, had certainly become inevitable by World War II. The wartime era saw women entering the workplace in large numbers out of economic necessity. This development was only temporarily forestalled by the reasserted conserva-tism of the 1950s, which, far from being the norm the American Right assumes, was, in many ways, what the political theorist Carl Schmitt (see Chapter 7) termed a "state of exception." The change that saw women assume prominence in fields such as law, medicine, politics, and business, as well as in academia, was no casual will o' the wisp or generational fluke. Although, if anything, the aca-demic world was behind some of these other ones in accommodating women, it assumed a leading role in the feminist movement partially because women in academia could not only do the jobs that once only men had done but also, as a part of being an academic, reflect on the fact that women were now perform-ing these jobs. And this reflection could be done in an atmosphere in which the ornery and intransigent misogynistic male academic was largely a relic. After a certain point in the 1970s or 1980s, there were more women than men in departments of literature, and the default image of a literary academic was more likely to be a woman than a man. This was certainly a dramatic reversal from the era when only one graduate department chair in the United States was female. Yet all was not blissful for women in academia after feminism.

Women got positions in academia only in time to see many academic jobs become part time and to be given, more often than not, administrative jobs or jobs with heavy teaching and grading responsibilities, work that male professors tended to shun. Female academics, even after the visibility of feminist critiques, were regarded by the academic system as much as a "reserve army of labour," useful in order to flood the market with candidates and therefore keep salaries down, as a talented new pool of minds to replenish the rather fallow intellectual resources of the professoriate. Many academic traditions seemed designed to be indifferent to the needs of people with obligations to take care of family members. For instance, the largest annual literary academic meeting, the Modern Language Association (MLA) convention, was held just after Christmas, making it very difficult for mothers and grandmothers to attend the convention and also be with their families during the holidays. Once, the convention had been a place where men could go, entrusting their families to the hands of their wives, sisters, or mothers. When women entered the academy, this framework became out of date, and, when the dates were finally changed in time for the 2011 conference, few objected because changes in society and in gender roles meant that careers no longer took place so independently of family circumstances. More important in creating a "glass ceiling" for women in the academy were assumptions about the nature and course of academic work. Hiring policies and presumed career trajectories often assumed lives uninterrupted by the physical act of childbirth or of being a child's primary caretaker, careers pursued irrespective of what a spouse or partner's career needs or obligations were, and careers pursued upon arrival in adulthood rather than being taken up after one's family was fully raised.[39] The strict division between full-time and part-time positions meant that people whose lives required flexible schedules were often shunted into low-wage and low-recognition adjunct positions, whose main purpose was to save the university money.[40] Adjunct jobs often became a "pink-collar" ghetto where personally and professionally vulnerable women deemed supernumerary by the academic system were placed. A Foucauldian analysis might well see the embrace of feminism as a deliberate ploy by the existing social system to provide a rationale for the creation of this new labour pool, which was comprised of women who so avidly sought out tenuous and ill-paying academic employment.[41]

This could possibly be too dark a scenario. Academia encouraged and fostered the growth of feminist critique, and, in the 1990s, it was as likely that the department chair at any given university would be a feminist as it was that, in the 1950s, he or she would have been a Leavisite or a New Critic. The traditional lag of academia with respect to politics worked wonders here; just as feminism went out of style in the political sphere, it reached new heights of prestige and productivity within academia. Academia's slow, deliberate hiring processes and the carefully managed way in which it produces intellectual knowledge can make it immune to, or slow to reflect, immediate trends, which, although possibly frustrating at a time of dramatic social change, can provide sanctuary and sustenance to ideologies spurned by the public sphere. In the case of feminism, academia had space and time to develop a coherent method that could be insightfully applied to literary texts. The annoyance of certain cavillers that feminism and other theoretical ideologies became "the establishment" in the 1980s belies the fact that, in any organized activity, there must be some sort of "establishment," however pluralistic and democratic the process of management or coordination should be ideally. Moreover, the contemplative mien of academia—its being equipped to mull over and to vet job candidates, their articles, and ideologies—meant that, when feminism at all prevailed (and there were many institutions in which it did not), it came with a sense of self-examination as well as an already developed tradition. And feminism became part of recorded intellectual history within the academy. Putting aside voting rights (and the Fourteenth Amendment's earlier tacit acknowledgement that women were US citizens), one sees that gender issues did not gain explicit mention in the US Constitution. But feminist ideas becoming embedded in university publisher backlists, journal archives, and departmental custom and lore was an accomplishment, although, admittedly, a distant second to the political and legal establishment of equity for women. It meant that feminism was not just a protest movement but also a genuine part of the history for whose previous shortcomings it had assumed responsibility.

In the non-academic world, though, circumstances seemed more problematic, and the viability of the feminist movement itself seemed under threat. Some feminist commentators, without opposing the basics of feminist ideology, began to try to revise it from within. Gilligan's emphasis on women's nurturing and communitarian tendencies had the danger of being essentialist in gender terms.[42] But it also presented a less combative and oppositional model of women than did voices such as Kate Millett's. Barbara Ehrenreich tried to disassociate feminism from "the sexual revolution," pointing out, not incorrectly, that it was dissident men from the Beat Generation onward who agitated for sexual freedom. They did this, according to Ehrenreich, mostly as a way of being socially uncooperative and of reaffirming male potency, which they saw as under pressure in an increasingly bureaucratized society in which the relatively more powerful physical strength of men that had always lain behind male dominance meant less and less.[43] Feminism became not just the triumph of brains over brawn but the unshackling of conscious history from previously inflexible givens, enabling a wholesale reshuffling of history's possibilities. Even explicit critiques of feminist orthodoxy, such as Camille Paglia's boisterous and invigorating *Sexual Personae* (1990), benefited from this bravado regarding reshuffling historical narratives, from a certain confidence that, although women had not had the official status to frame past and present cognitively, they now had gained that right.[44]

Generations: The 1990s

In the early 1990s, feminism reasserted itself. But it was a different kind of feminism. The "third wave" was younger, more comfortable with explicit discussions of sexuality, and less preoccupied with the previous sins of the patriarchy. Third wave feminism distinguished itself from second wave feminism on two different levels. On one level, it positioned itself as less politically dissident, less identified with the social struggles of the 1960s, and more identified with the consciousness of a younger generation of women who had grown up during decades when women's equality in the workplace and in society was accepted and when texts by women were assuming a growing place in the canon. In this context, 1970s feminism seemed strident, insistent, and out of date. Third wave feminism also claimed a very different attitude towards sexuality than the second wave did; indeed, second wave figures such as Andrea Dworkin and Catherine MacKinnon, who vigorously campaigned against pornography, were seen by third wave feminists as inhibiting discourse about sexuality. (Note that, although these two feminists are often reductively grouped into a twinned dyad, they are very different figures and had different lives and careers.) The second wave attitude to pornography became a particular problem in literary circles, where accusations of immorality had long been a tool of political or literary conformists who sought to inhibit free expression. Anti-pornography campaigns also had the potential to be reductive in their flattening out of a text's literary multiplicity to a straightforward registering of whatever sexual referents were present in it. Many felt that literature should be a realm of discourse in which risk and pushing the envelope were permitted or encouraged rather than repressed in the name of even the laudable denunciation of exploitative pornography. Anti-pornography raised the danger of, as it were, a "resolved literal" that made the connotative seem denotative and that occasioned modes of creative expression that might seem pornographic to be read the same way obvious pornography was.

Writers such as the Marquis de Sade or Vladimir Nabokov could be accused of being simply pornographic and excluded from the canon, just as they might have been under a conservative religious regime. Even though feminists for whom anti-pornography campaigns were the main issue were not a huge part of literary academia, the association of feminism with censorship, real or imagined, primed literary academia to be ready for a new iteration of feminism, one that did not see any manifestation of explicit sexuality as menacing and inherently threatening to women. Third wave feminists claimed a more positive attitude towards sex and, indeed, regarded women's sexuality as a key area of power for them, one that could be owned and claimed as a site of resistance without simply rearticulating male fantasies of sexual gratification. The problem with this scenario is that many feminists of the previous generations—Americans such as Marilyn French (1929–2009), the novelist and Shakespeare scholar, and theorists such as Irigaray—had written eloquently of women's need to claim their own sexuality and of patriarchy's denial of women's sexuality in the name of inspirational or domestic ideals as one of its biggest dysfunctions.

Indeed, the third wave of feminism often exhibited a binary preoccupation with the second wave that was equivalent in investment to the second wave's preoccupation with the patriarchy itself. So much time was spent on internecine generational struggles that the overall agenda of feminism was clouded. What Astrid Henry describes as the third wave's insistence that it was "a daughter's movement" was limiting in that it put what should have been an intellectual dilemma within the limiting context of family dynamics and individual self-expression.[45] Nor did the third wave feminists perform a particular set of third wave literary readings—one could roughly sum up the characteristics of a second wave feminist reading of, say, women in Milton's *Paradise Lost*, but what a third wave one would be is hard to grasp, despite feminist academics born after 1960 having written massively on Milton. In a way, this multiplication of feminist approaches to literature is a positive. No longer was there one determinate feminist way of reading but a variety of mutually informative feminisms. Third wave feminism, though, also criticized the whiteness of the second wave and its association with the bourgeois upper-middle class, and, indeed, two of the most common second wave paradigms were the daughter of a privileged family claiming a social and vocational status to equal her father's and the divorced (or divorcing) wife in a failed marriage claiming the status and privilege denied to her but previously possessed by her husband. These privileged socioeconomic circumstances and this "path dependence" on powerful males did not apply to women of the working class or, very frequently, to those of colour.[46] These women often felt marginalized by second wave feminism and more represented by anti-racist advocacy or other forms of activism and critique that were not gender based. In her poem "Women's Liberation," the indigenous Australian writer Lisa Bellear, who died young in 2006, had a ferocious take on this disconnect between feminism and those subordinated by circumstances other than gender:

> Talk to me about the feminist movement,
> the gubba middle class
> hetero sexual revolution
> way back in the seventies
> when men wore tweed jackets with
> leather elbows, and the women, well
> I don't remember or maybe I just don't care
> or can't relate.
> Now what were those white women on about?[47]

The feminism of the 1970s, second wave feminism, was seen as too white. So third wave feminism made a conscious attempt to be less white. Thus, even

Hm— he insisted how w we hasn't elsewhere

figures whose biographies and ideologies were more associated with the second wave, such as Cherrie Moraga, owed their large-scale emergence into discourses of feminism to the third wave and its greater openness to African American, Asian, and Latina voices. Third wave feminism was also far more involved with lesbian, queer, and transgender discourses. In the second wave, lesbianism had been an important but largely autonomous component. But, in the third wave, awareness of queer issues travelled across many more vectors. Third wave feminism gave greater visibility to transnational or global concerns and took more account of migrants, domestic workers, or non-Western women whose experiences had simply not been imagined under the category of "woman" as voices in the academy in the 1970s. Paradoxically, though, what these female subjects possibly needed was a discourse closer to that of the early feminist movement rather than the one offered by third wave feminism. An emphasis on basic rights and an insistence on their right to speak, including as literary producers and analysts, would most likely have been more useful to these women than the more "boutique" (to adapt Stanley Fish's phrase) and post-collegiate agenda of the third wave.[48] Indeed, the third wave often seemed to consist of separate critiques of second wave feminism—on generational attitude and on white privilege—that were seldom conjoined in an overarching, positive rationale.

As one would expect in a feminist movement so heavily coloured by modes of linguistic discourse, the names used for these various ideological tendencies mattered; what the structural linguist Émile Benveniste had termed the *énonciation*, the way things are said, was as important as the *énoncé*, what is being said. The third wave, like the "third way" of former British Prime Minister Tony Blair, often seems too pat a synthesis between contrasting positions, too formulaic a desire to move on from the past. One wonders, indeed, why the opposition to the second wave is so dominant and why the first wave is put safely back a hundred years previous to it. In other words, why not just call the second wave the first wave—because, as far as contemporary feminism was concerned, it was that—and have the third wave be called the second?[49] This is not done because there seems a desire for the third wave of feminism to be a Hegelian synthesis, a concordant reconciliation of discord. This perspective names the second wave as merely the dissenting antithesis, as that which is, in Hegelian terms, sublated or, as the deconstructionist J. Hillis Miller put it, "elated"—that is to say, largely lost in the dialectical shuffle.[50] Numerology and coded implication seem to triumph over substance. There was some talk, by the end of the twentieth century's first decade, of "fourth wave feminism," which may have the capacity to square out what has become a confining triangle and add another imaginative dimension. But "fourth wave" will hopefully not be a code word for Generation Y (born after 1981) as third wave essentially was for Generation X. Generational essentialism lies behind Naomi Wolf's assertion that "all feminist waves are ... peer-driven," which is far less true of the second wave than of the third wave.[51] Second wave feminists included people from Tillie Olsen (born 1913) to Cherrie

Moraga (born 1952).[52] It included women whose ambitions and hopes had been occluded by male dominance during the entire period of modern-era male reassertion, which goes back to the eclipse of the "New Woman" of the 1890s and the letdown after the attainment of suffrage in the late 1910s. Generational identity can be as much of a prison as racial, ethnic, or gender identity, and new feminisms should be able to invent rationales for themselves that are conceptual rather than local and temporal, ones that speak to the broad reach of philosophical and moral concerns addressed by Kristeva, Irigaray, Cixous, and Haraway.

Where did all these successive waves leave the literary canon and the place of women writers within it? In an odd way, third wave feminism dislocated the very idea of "woman" from gender. This dislocation had a salutary effect, permitting, for instance, the evolution of masculinity studies as a full-fledged field— males, after all, had "gender" too. But this stance also led to a certain turning against women writers, especially recently rediscovered writers who were white women. In an astonishing irony, writers who had been rescued by the second wave were attacked for racism and white privilege in the 1990s. Sarah Orne Jewett was chastised by Sandra Zagarell for having one of the main characters in *The Country of the Pointed Firs* characterize a negatively portrayed character, Mari' Harris, as looking like "a Chinee." This use of what is now perceived as a slur against people of Chinese descent, according to Zagarell, is "racist," and this racist slur attaches itself not just to the character who says it but, if not to Jewett, at least to the "implied author" and her social environment (note the utility of Wayne Booth's post-"resolved symbolic" term).[53]

Zagarell makes telling points in her essay. She successfully argues that the text privileges "individual idiosyncrasy" while opposing "racial diversification."[54] This is an important corrective to earlier Jewett scholarship, which somewhat romanticized the isolated, female-dominated rural communities about which she wrote. And Jewett, though a reformist in many ways, had complex and often white supremacist ideas of race. But there is a problem here: Jewett's canonicity. Jewett had been given glancing treatment by male critics of the "resolved symbolic" era, men such as F.O. Matthiessen and Werner Berthoff. Jewett then became popular in the 1980s in the wake of scholarship by such feminists as Marjorie Pryse, Judith Fetterley, and Ann Romines.[55] An accusation of racism against Jewett has a far more maximal effect than one against another liberal, largely reformist writer of Jewett's era—Mark Twain, for example. Twain *is* securely in the canon. Jewett *is not*. There seems to be a kind of "last in, first out" procedure at work here so that it is only the latest writer to be elevated, Jewett, who is delegitimized because she shared some of the almost endemic racism of her time. And it should be noted that it is also highly questionable to reveal the hidden racism of the ostensible liberals of an era while not at all rebuking the far more overtly racist conservatives. Twain's opposition to the US occupation of the Philippines after 1898 may have been as filled with racial stereotypes as President William McKinley's support for the plan. As we have seen in our discussion of Joseph Conrad, racism and anti-colonialism were often arranged in tandem during the age of imperialism. But, for Filipinos and Filipinas who did not want their country to be occupied by the United States, Twain's attitude was preferable. And certainly, as the work of writers of Chinese background such as Sui Sin Far shows, Chinese people trying to make their lives in the United States had fiercer and more reprehensible opponents than Sarah Orne Jewett.

Zagarell's article was one of the markers of a threshold beyond which women writers were no longer seen as inherently virtuous because of their sex. Other variables, such as racial background or political beliefs, superseded gender in more contemporary appraisals, and often this balancing act became very complicated. Sarah Gertrude Millin (1889–1968), a South African writer, was a problematic figure. She was a woman, but she was white. She was a Jew, but she was very racist towards Africans. How was she to be evaluated as a literary figure? Did the critic want to examine her works and assess them within the complexity of Millin's personal and historical context. Critics frequently decide a writer is worth advocating, and therefore they read this writer's works in a critical light that makes them look their best—doing so is an aspect of the subjectivity and interpretive choice present in all criticism. Or did the critic dismiss her as racist and not read her, or read her works only as symptoms of racism? Was Millin fundamentally a white person, a woman, or a Jew? Which identity category was to predominate? In the 1970s and 1980s, "woman" had seemed a strong identity category. In the ensuing decades, the strength of this identity became less obvious.

This displacement of "woman" as an inversely privileged category was one of the most daring moves of third wave feminism. Another, less visible tendency was to begin to speak of "gender" rather than "women" as a variable in texts. This substitution put the whole issue in more neutral and clinical terms. But it also extended the feminist discussion to cover gender and all its variables— touching on the issues of queer theory to be discussed later—and underscored the omnipresence of gender in textual representation. The ubiquitous—and, admittedly, easily parodied—phrase "gendered space" was used to describe the tendency of texts to mark out gender excessively and to reinforce the notion of the "separate spheres" of men and women, which was a dominant concept through most of the history of the West.[56] This idea of space could then be inverted or questioned, and the entire concept of separate spheres could be problematized. It was this use of gender as a variable that enabled such a supple and flexible set of moves.

Thus the third wave saw a kind of normal, institutionalized feminism that went on unobtrusively amid the polemical tumult. These constructive aspects were often offset by the triviality of third wave feminism, with its collegiate or post-collegiate air, its assumption that all younger women were the daughters of feminism who had benefited from and assumed its achievements, and its sense of a boutique dialectic internal to the generational self-definition of privileged whites. The emphasis of second wave feminism on equal pay, social enfranchisement, and fair treatment in the workplace might arguably have been of more benefit to the categories of women the second wave tended not to accommodate in its discourse than were the concerns of the next wave which, to its credit, largely did accommodate these categories of women.

One of the other complications of third wave feminism, indeed, is that it often underestimated not only its foremothers' achievements but also its own. The reassertion of debates over feminism, the emergence of figures such as Katie Roiphe, Naomi Wolf, and Susan Faludi in the early 1990s, was a prerequisite for the continuation of feminism as a way of thought. Without the critique they provided of earlier feminisms, feminism itself would have been at a standstill; it would have met the same fate experienced by the Leavisites and New Critics, an intellectual drying up. What was often on the surface a polemical challenge became in practice an internal renewal. The rhetoric of "girl power" that characterized the 1990s, as evidenced in the "riot grrl" movement in popular music and in a slew of movies and television shows directed specifically at "girls," was culturally important because it partially undid the heavy and hyperbolic emphasis of the 1980s, with its connection between renascent political conservatism and male recrudescence.[57] This issue is important beyond the specifics of those particular decades. As we discussed previously when comparing modernism and Victorianism, eras that were seen positively were described as manly, full of vigour, and self-disciplined; those that were less positively seen were thought of as weak, decadent, nescient, and feminine. "Girl power" feminism, then, can be seen as reacting to one of the principal ways of putting women down, namely, using the symbolism of the female as a derogatory metalanguage and associating this language with a particular era. Thus, "out" decades such as the 1970s and 1990s, those that were not praised at the time as eras of cultural ferment, had, in their counterpoising to the more heralded 1960s and 1980s, a tacit gender. The third wave reintroduced a sense of temporal variety and validated a positive sense of temporal difference. It rescued the ordering of history from being the vehicle of the dominant political tendency, at the time, Reaganesque conservatism. For this service alone, the third wave more than proved its worth.

But the third wave's renewal of feminism was often lost in media coverage, which emphasized polemics and, whenever possible, the repudiation or curtailment of former radicalism. Roiphe's concern about excessive reaction on campuses to the problems of sexual harassment and date rape met widespread acclaim because it was seen as recognizing the limits of "political correctness" and an atmosphere that patrolled inappropriate sexual expression in an overly oppressive way. The tacit contention was that feminism was a form of *ressentiment*, as diagnosed by Nietzsche, and that political correctness was emblematic of feminism's inadequacy, its reactiveness expressed through restrictive social protocols. Stanley Fish, however, saw in the new speech and behavioural codes of academia a sort of politesse, a decorum that helped navigate the risky shoals of communication among individuals and groups in the aftermath of the expansion of academia beyond the white gentlemen's club of the 1950s. Fish was, importantly, claiming an effective virtue in the bureaucratic recognition of gender. By this light, the great victory of theory is that it took the bureaucratic apparatus of academia, with which the New Critics had been so uneasily comfortable, and threw this apparatus full bore in the service of radical change. Theory leveraged the institutional heft of academia and made it provocative and catalyzing. Of course, academic bureaucracies were not always fair, did not always show good judgement, and sometimes exhibited arrogance or prejudice. But this coalescence of radical views and constituted authority did combine academia's own rigorous process of self-evaluation with a new set of dynamic intellectual concerns.

For all its admirable energy and freshness, for all its effects within public culture, the third wave lacked this degree of fructifying connection to larger cognitive and administrative thought bodies, to, as Foucault might put it, "governmentality." Aside from its links to Haraway and cyborgian feminism, the third wave did not have the amplitude of connections to philosophical thought, especially to European theory, that the second wave had.[58] Although the tension between Anglo-American and French branches of second wave feminist criticism was well advertised at the time, much like the concomitant distinction between Derridean deconstruction and the Foucauldian sociology of power, the distinction between the two varieties of feminist theory was largely chimerical and masked many overlapping discourses and concerns. Third wave feminism lacked both the textual and the theoretical orientation of the second wave. European thinkers such as Adriana Cavarero, whose interest in both feminism and public speech would have accorded well with the third wave's critique of the second wave's tendency to emphasize public/private gender binaries, were not consulted.[59]

Long on personally situated perceptiveness but short on a discursive framework, the third wave managed to displace its predecessor but not to supersede it. Feminism was not just a generational manifesto but also a radical critique of much of human history. Generational change should not jettison this critique, especially as history has shown that, just as one generation is fully emergent, another is coming up behind it. Also, as Paul de Man shows in "Literary History and Literary Modernity," little that thinks itself new is ever totally new.[60] Some third wave critics, such as Devoney Looser, took a manifest interest in cross-generational dialogue and, indeed, explored how women writers evaded conventional definitions of the career arc as well as generational identities.[61] But this sort of exploration was far more the exception than the rule.

An additional potential pitfall for many critiques of feminism is that, like some critiques of deconstruction, they present no original ideas or no details about how things should be done alternatively. They just criticize without any hope of an alternative. They are worrisomely parasitic on what they critique. Of course, this is true in a different way of feminists and deconstructionists themselves. Witness Derrida on Plato. But their parasitism is far more self-aware. Thomas Jefferson and Tom Paine may have been right in immediate political terms when they advocated US independence from the British monarchy. But they took the opportunity to delineate larger conceptual principles that mattered centuries later, when the antagonism between Britain and its former American colonies had long since faded. The 1990s critiques of second wave feminism, even if history totally vindicates their polemical thrust, are unlikely to have that staying power. It is the work of the second wave itself, which, in many ways, did for difference what Paine and Jefferson did for equality, that is more likely to endure.

Feminist Metamorphoses: The 2000s

However, nobody doubted that staying within the second wave paradigm would have been intellectually ruinous. There was a vital need to engage in the act of what Janet Halley termed "taking a break from feminism."[62] The third wave made sure that feminist issues and perspectives would continue to be aired in the twenty-first century. And this century, when it came, presented a social landscape that, in terms of gender, had again metamorphosed. Indicative of a clear sense of crisis in gender role in the early 2000s are both Ariel Levy's discernment of a category of "female chauvinist pigs"—women who voluntarily embrace previous male stereotypes of women and display a raunchy, unbridled sexuality more or less congruent with the long-established imaginary of male sexual fantasies—and, on the other side of the spectrum, Caitlin Flanagan's promotion in upmarket general-interest magazines of a resurrected female domesticity.[63] How women live their lives is still a very debatable issue and has come to involve, and to reverberate upon, a whole host of other issues seemingly unconnected with gender. But it a mistake to see this undeniable sense of crisis, which is affecting what seemed decades before to be an unshakeable feminist consensus (at least in urban, liberal areas), as a symptom of the invalidation of feminist criticism itself. In fact, that the sense of crisis was so charged and engaged so many people testified to the continuing importance of questions of gender.

This crisis of the early 2000s brought new urgency and new articulations to dynamics that had featured in feminist debate since the early 1970s. The question of equality versus difference has been a recurring motif of recent feminist discussions. That this question is so fundamental to discourses besides those surrounding gender highlights how important feminism has been to contemporary intellectual debate in general. An intriguing intervention on the equality/difference issue is offered by the feminist philosopher Rosi Braidotti. Braidotti, the sort of global figure all too lacking in third wave feminism, was raised in Australia and established her academic career in the Netherlands. Braidotti is substantially influenced by the thinking of the French philosopher Gilles Deleuze. Though, like Irigaray, this philosopher remained more firmly within the discipline of philosophy than did Derrida, Deleuze notably touched on literature. His essay on Kafka as a "deterritorializing" writer of "minor literature," co-written with Félix Guattari, is seminal. However, although his own work is not without literary aspects, Deleuze has proven even more significant to literary theory through the influence he has exerted on others. Braidotti uses Deleuze to address tacitly one of the conundrums of French feminism. Derrida, for all his foregrounding of writing over speech, the grapheme over the word, did not endorse verbal irrationality. Indeed, American reconstruction of the de Man era, for all its commendation of French feminism—Jonathan Culler famously entitled the first chapter of his acclaimed guidebook to deconstruction "Writing as a Woman"—tended to emphasize the side of Derrida that critiqued Rousseau, rebuked a celebration of the instinctual as an alternative to Cartesian rationality, and saw the centrality of insurgency as something as much to be displaced as the centrality of authority. Deleuze offered a model of irrationality that was not redemptive, unlike the earlier surrealist idea of "automatic writing" premised upon the Romantic notion of tapping the imagination—"that imperial faculty, whose throne is curtained within the invisible nature of man"—and upon the Freudian idea of the irrational as a saving reserve of life understood through "free association."[64] In that way, Deleuze's view was more compatible with feminism's characteristic attitude towards reason, though Derrida was more willing to see himself slightly in the feminist camp than was Deleuze.

Deleuze, a self-proclaimed "anti-Oedipal" figure, spurned goal-oriented trajectories in favour of a more indeterminate sense of motion. When Deleuze spoke of flow or embodiment, he emphasized a dynamic multiplicity and the disorder and anarchy of these multiple states rather than their cathartic or orgiastic fulfilment.[65] Deleuze's use of geographic analogies such as islands and nomads showed that he did not wish to escape reference or fuse individual referents in one monadic entity.[66] Thus, when Deleuze speaks of "becoming-woman" as a part embodiment and part allegory of the processes of the breakdown of unitary rationality, he is not merely reprising a Romantic championship of the "eternal feminine." He scrutinizes a specific unfolding taking place in apprehensible contexts. Braidotti critiques the overly metaphorical nature of Deleuze's idea of woman. She implicitly chastises the very idea of a male critic positing "woman" in some sort of absolute way, even if it is in an absolutely de-universalizing one. But she endorses the privileging of "becoming" over "being" as an analogue for feminist thinking. Braidotti also defends feminism against what Deleuze castigates as the "molar" or narrowly identity-focused outlook, which he contrasts with the more general "molecular" outlook (both terms are adapted from physics). Braidotti counters that feminism is, in its embrace of mutability and applicability, a paradigm of a large, overall process.

Braidotti, though, follows Deleuze in not seeing de-universalization as evading form entirely. Braidotti's "alternative figurations of the subject" are encased, enclosed in ever shifting, ever more indeterminate, but never disincarnate ideas of form.[67] Braidotti's idea of a change of shape into "new fields of perception, affectivity, becoming" is a very different idea of form than the traditional "literary" kind. But the New Critics would be pleased that she does not endorse the utopian, technocratic vision that gained new life as a result of the Internet boom of the 1990s. Braidotti denounces the spectre of "the technocratic takeover of the human body."[68] However, her vision of embodiment, stemming laterally or, as Deleuze would say, "rhizomatically" (like the root systems of plants) from Deleuze's concept of "the body without organs," is a far cry from the organicism of what the New Critic, and notable American poet, John Crowe Ransom called "the world's body."

Braidotti's embrace of the non-human—plant, animal, and mineral—makes her thought analogous to some modes of ecofeminism—feminism with a non-reductive and non-essentialist concern for the earth and for ecological justice. And her interest both in different shapes of the human and in the interface of the human and the non human influenced two growing fields of the early twenty-first century: disability studies and animal studies. In many ways, disability studies in particular, as a consequence of the field's quest to call attention to the repressed and underrecognized, assumed the critique of the normative that feminism had raised. Yet Braidotti's insistence on both materiality and transformation shows that, for her, content does not entirely eclipse form.[69] For Deleuze, nomads do not mean the Scythians, and islands do not mean Greenland; similarly, for Foucault, archaeology and genealogy do not mean excavations and family trees. In the Deleuzian lexicon, "nomads" and "islands" denote modes of transgression that are both abstract and referential. Equally, Braidotti does not oppose form and content in a "hylomorphic" way passed down from Aristotle; in other words, she does not consider form as an abstraction that organizes content. She repositions referents as stealth abstractions. Her perception that content, when foregrounded, can be form emblematizes how unhinged from its previous certainties literary thought has become, and, by implication, how this is paralleled by the concrete empowerment of women, whose consequences are far from just material. Feminism can also be formalism. Bodies can also be mirrors or tropes. The material can be where imagination can declare itself the most boldly. In a sense, if difference is allowed to be thoroughly different, to be artificially partitioned into binaries, difference can foster a sense of equality, what Braidotti calls a "bio-centered egalitarianism" that, in its sheer inclusiveness, avoids the hierarchies of domination as well as the counter-hierarchies of insurgency, revolt, or special pleading.[70]

Another feminist thinker who emerged in the 2000s, Kelly Oliver, also separated feminism from identity politics while maintaining and even sharpening its efficacy as a mode of resistance. Just as Braidotti took Deleuze's notion of becoming and sculpts a fresh feminist ontology out of it, Oliver was influenced by the late nineteenth-century work of Friedrich Nietzsche with its jettisoning of the ostensibly solid philosophical ground on which many encrusted philosophical positions are professedly built. In *Witnessing: Beyond Recognition* (2001), perhaps the most important work of feminist theory to be produced in its decade, Oliver enriched the public sphere by bringing into it aspects of life that Carol Gilligan and the object-relations psychologists had seen as private, such as the mother-child bond. By seeing this bond as a social relationship, Oliver metamorphosed the formulations by which those aspects of feminism having to do with personal rights had been made to seem merely trivial, dwarfed by the more collective struggles easily recognizable because they strove for such an easy form of recognition, a convenient badge of identity. Oliver suggested that "witnessing" replace the Hegelian-sounding concept of "recognition."[71] She preferred that a radical openness to the other replace a dialectic that strives, through subjectivity, to find a voice by means of overcoming antagonists or rival contestants for recognition. "Witnessing," as limned by Oliver, provides a way out of the gender essentialism of second wave feminism. It also evades the Hegelian bind of third wave feminism, which saw enunciations of generational, racial, and ethnic identities usurp much of feminism's original transformative drive. Oliver's work makes impossible any reduction of feminism to merely subsiding in unimaginative gender distinction.

Yet neither Braidotti nor Oliver scanted the fundamental importance of gender. At the beginning of *Speculum of the Other Woman*, Irigaray quotes Freud: "When you meet a human being, the first distinction you make is 'male or female?' and you are accustomed to making the distinction with unhesitating certainty."[72] French feminism, beginning with Simone de Beauvoir's famous dictum that "one is not born, but rather becomes a woman," has sharply challenged this binary. Yet nobody would doubt that gender, as a variable, even if not necessarily a rigid, constituted category, is very nearly constitutive of the way we perceive and engage the world.[73] Beyond the bare fact of life itself, gender is arguably the most inescapable human experience. It is impossible to separate literature from an awareness of gender, whether in Homer, the Bible, Shakespeare, or Jane Austen. Literature is different from all the other disciplines because it is the place where people can tell and discuss stories of how we feel and describe the channels through which we feel, and gender subtends a significant amount of our affect.

What Cressida Heyes has termed "feminism's need to use gender as a basic category of analysis" is a truly, comprehensively humanistic vision of literature.[74] Even as feminism continued to receive more than its share of polemical brickbats, in the widest sense, this overlap with humanism was conceded, as when US intervention against the Taliban in Afghanistan after the World Trade Center terrorist attacks of 2001 was partially justified by the need to free Afghan women from a strict patriarchal control that regarded women as property and discouraged girls from attending school. That, as Drucilla Cornell pointed out, this raised troubling questions about the exploitation of feminism in the service of war, as well as a potentially Eurocentric idea of women's rights, does not gainsay the conceptual acknowledgement of feminist concerns by a political establishment often deeply resistant to them in earlier decades.[75] That the policy of the US government embraced an agenda that decades ago would have been seen as rather parochial in emphasis illustrates how feminism has transcended any put down of it as merely representing a special interest. US foreign policy and a "Western feminism" newly conscious of its ties to historic discourses of "Western civilization" (much as discussed with respect to Derrida and *laïcité* in Chapter 2) were now structural allies! This happenstance may not have been authoritative in its implications. But it does sketch the ability of feminism to diagnose the human in all its capacities and identities. Indeed, feminism brought the idea of "the human" beyond the constrained version that was held by male academics until the middle of the twentieth century. As Haraway might put it, feminism provided an idea of the post-human that did not entirely relinquish the human.

NOTES

1 Percy Bysshe Shelley, *A Defence of Poetry* (Indianapolis: Bobbs-Merrill, 1904) 90.

2 For the women in Congress in the 1950s, see Karen Foerstel, *Biographical Dictionary of Congressional Women* (Westport: Greenwood, 1999).

3 Anne Humpherys, e-mail to the author, 18 August 2008.

4 Charles V. Hamilton, *Adam Clayton Powell, Jr.: The Political Biography of an American Dilemma* (New York: Cooper Square, 2002).

5 For more on Ellison and liberalism, see Michael Nowlin, "Ralph Ellison, James Baldwin, and the Liberal Imagination," *Arizona Quarterly* 60 (Summer 2004): 117–40.

6 Sharon O'Brien, "Becoming Noncanonical: The Case Against Willa Cather," *American Quarterly* 40 (1988): 110–26. As far as Stowe is concerned, Ruth Wisse's comparison of Stowe and George Eliot and her assessment that Eliot "faced a tougher task" comprise a latter-day reflection of the dominant attitudes of the previous generation. See Ruth Wisse, *The Modern Jewish Canon* (Chicago: University of Chicago Press, 2003) 423.

7 Anthony Powell, *Temporary Kings* (New York: Little, Brown, 1973).

8 Q.D. Leavis, *Fiction and the Reading Public* (London: Chatto and Windus, 1995).

9 Christine M. Rose, "Margaret Schlauch (1898–1986)," *Women Medievalists and the Academy*, ed. Jane Chance (Madison: University of Wisconsin Press, 2005) 523–39.

10 Marjorie Hope Nicolson, *Mountain Gloom and Mountain Glory* (Ithaca: Cornell University Press, 1959) is an intellectual history of the early modern aesthetics of nature, which, long after the author's death, found some popularity among literary environmentalists.

11 Cynthia Ozick, "We Are the Crazy Lady and Other Feisty Feminist Fables," *Ms.* (Spring 1972): 40–44.

12 The academic Anne Humpherys (born 1937) wrote the following in an e-mail to the author dated 18 August 2008: "I graduated with my BA from Stanford in 1959. In my four years there, I had only one woman instructor: I took a humanities seminar from the wife of a Chinese specialist and remember being puzzled about why she wasn't on the faculty. I was told, 'No women on the history faculty'— despite the fact that she was the better scholar of the two of them. She could only get a research appointment at the Hoover Institute while he got the professorship, and she was only allowed to teach because the humanities courses 'didn't really count.'... As it happens, I went to Columbia [for graduate school] where again, except for [Marjorie] Nicolson, I had no women faculty members. There was another husband and wife team there [the Nobbes] but, as I remember it, he was the senior professor. He taught Chaucer, and she taught the novel, which was not considered a serious subject."

13 The novelist Millicent Dillon (born 1925) recalled the era this way in an e-mail to the author, 21 August 2008: "When I started going to graduate school in English—or creative writing—at San Francisco State at the beginning of the sixties, I knew of two women in the department. There may have been more, but I wasn't looking on that basis. They were Ruby Cohn, who was an expert on Beckett, and Kay Boyle, known of course for her fiction. That's all that I knew of my own experience. As for women authors who were talked about—Woolf, of course, Katherine Anne Porter, Katherine Mansfield, and Flannery O'Connor. The men, of course, predominated, and I think were thought of as models for us to rely on.... As I was finishing my master's at San Francisco State, my professors urged me to apply at Stanford to get a PhD. I went to see the head of the department at Stanford. He looked at my recommendations and said, 'Very impressive, but I do not suggest you apply.' And why? I asked. 'You're too old,' he said. I was then 41. He said. 'We just don't take people that old.' I should also add that there were no blacks that I knew of in either department. That was the way things were then."

14 The vitality of the Victorian field even in the 1950s and 1960s can be witnessed in two comprehensive books that are still staples of Victorian studies a half-century later in a vastly changed world—Walter Houghton's *The Victorian Frame of Mind* (New Haven: Yale University Press, 1963) and Jerome H. Buckley's *The Victorian Temper: A Study in Literary Culture* (Cambridge, MA: Harvard University Press, 1961). A glance at random issues of the leading periodical in the field, *Victorian Studies*, for 1962 and 1963, reveals articles by U.C. Knoepflmacher, Philip Collins, and J. Hillis Miller—three scholars who were professionally active into the twenty-first century and who achieved widespread fame as opening new areas of inquiry. A look at comparable journals in the field of seventeenth-century literature would reveal far more epigones of the New Critics who never made their own way in the academic world.

15 This relative gender openness was true even at the height of technically oriented philological approaches, see Helen E. Sandison, "Spenser's 'Lost' Works and Their Probable Relation to His *Faerie Queene*," *PMLA* 25. (1910): 134–51.

16 Erich Auerbach, *Mimesis: The Representation of Reality in Western Literature*, trans. Willard R. Trask (Princeton: Princeton University Press, 1953).

17 See Allen J. Frantzen, *Desire for Origins: New Language, Old English, and Teaching the Tradition* (New Brunswick: Rutgers University Press, 1990).

18 See D.W. Harding, "Regulated Hatred: An Aspect of the Work of Jane Austen," *Scrutiny* 8 (March 1940): 346–62 and Stuart M. Tave, *Some Words of Jane Austen* (Chicago: University of Chicago Press, 1973).

19 Millicent Dillon, e-mail to the author, 21 August 2008.

20 Kenneth Eble, "A Forgotten Novel: Kate Chopin's *The Awakening*," *Western Humanities Review* 10 (Summer 1956): 261–69. Eble was also very interested in pedagogy, which, in a sense, is unsurprising as much of the overhaul of the canon in the late twentieth century took place in the classroom by virtue of what texts teachers began to assign; feminism was not simply handed down by bureaucratic apparatchiks in the mode of a mandatory fiat.

21 Kate Millett, *Sexual Politics* (Urbana: University of Illinois Press, 2000).

22 Millett, *Sexual Politics*, 240–47. A comparable study of American literature took place in Annette Kolodny's two volumes *The Lay of the Land: Metaphor as Experience and History in American Life and Letters* (Chapel Hill: University of North Carolina Press, 1975) and *The Land Before Her: Fantasy and Experience of the American Frontiers, 1630–1860* (Chapel Hill: University of North Carolina Press, 1984). Both explored how the feminine images of the North American landscape infiltrated the language that was used to describe it and thus deflated the machismo of the pioneer ethos in much the same way as Millett debunked its partial successor, the macho avant-garde.

23 Adrienne Rich, "When We Dead Awaken: Writing as Re-Vision (1971)" *On Lies, Secrets, and Silence: Selected Prose, 1966–1978* (New York: W.W. Norton, 1979) 33–50, and Kate Chopin, *The Awakening* (1899; Mineola, NY: Dover Publications, 1993).

24 See Nicola Nixon, "*Wide Sargasso Sea* and Jean Rhys's Interrogation of the 'nature wholly alien' in *Jane Eyre*," *Essays in Literature* 21.2 (Fall 1994): 273–84.

25 Svetlana Boym, *The Future of Nostalgia* (New York: Basic Books, 2001).

26 Roland Barthes, *Sollers Écrivain* (Paris: Editions du Seuil, 1979). Indeed, the journal Philippe Sollers helped launch in 1960, *Tel Quel* (which continued in the 1980s as the less influential *L'Infini*) provided the principal forum for the later work of Barthes, and *Tel Quel* became, in many ways, the signature journal of structuralism and, to a degree, post-structuralism, though Derrida was not particularly associated with it.

27 However, this association of French feminism with anti-essentialist thought was only made when French feminism was contrasted with Anglo-American feminism; when contrasted with Marxist or deconstructive approaches, French feminism was, as Kelly Oliver points out, seen as "invalid and essentialist." See Kelly Oliver, ed., *Ethics, Politics, and Difference in Julia Kristeva's Writing* (London: Routledge, 1993) 81.

28 Elaine Showalter, "Towards a Feminist Poetics," *Women's Writing and Writing About Women*, ed. Mary Jacobus (London: Croom Helm, 1979) 22–41.

29 On Argentina, see Mariano Ben Plotkin, *Freud in the Pampas: The Emergence and Development of a Psychoanalytic Culture in Argentina* (Palo Alto: Stanford University Press, 2001).

30 Sartre's comment on the French Communist Party, delivered in the context of the 1956 invasion, is relevant here: "Each sentence they utter, each action they take is the culmination of thirty years of lies and sclerosis." Translated from *L'Express*, 9 November 1956.

31 Monique Wittig, *Les Guérillères*, trans. David Le Vay (Boston: Beacon, 1969).

32 Hélène Cixous, *The Exile of James Joyce*, trans. Sally Purcell (London: John Calder, 1976).

33 Drucilla Cornell, *Beyond Accommodation: Ethical Feminism, Deconstruction, and the Law*, rev. ed. (Lanham: Rowman and Littlefield, 1999) 83.

34 Drucilla Cornell, Michael Rosenfeld, and David Gray Carlson, *Deconstruction and the Possibility of Justice* (London: Routledge, 1992) 7.

35 Drucilla Cornell, *Just Cause: Freedom, Identity, and Rights* (Lanham: Rowman and Littlefield, 2000) 68.

36 Donna Haraway, "A Manifesto for Cyborgs," *Socialist Review* 80 (1985): 65–108. Some of Haraway's ideas had been anticipated by Shulamith Firestone's work of the early 1970s.

37 Carol Gilligan, *In a Different Voice* (Cambridge, MA: Harvard University Press, 1982).

38 See Peg O'Connor, *Morality and Our Complicated Form of Life: Feminist Wittgensteinian Metaethics* (University Park: Pennsylvania State University Press, 2008) and Cressida J. Heyes, *Line Drawings: Defining Women Through Feminist Practice* (Ithaca: Cornell University Press, 2000).

39 See Rachel Hile Bassett, *Parenting and Professing: Balancing Family Work with an Academic Career* (Nashville: Vanderbilt University Press, 2005).

40 Rudolphus Teeuwen and Steffen Hantke, eds., *Gypsy Scholars, Migrant Teachers, and the Global Academic Proletariat: Adjunct Labour in Higher Education* (Amsterdam: Rodopi, 2007).

41 This agenda, however, is far from the actual one of feminist Foucauldians such as Ladelle McWhorter, who find feminist potential in Foucault's sense of the omnipresence of power and his equally strong scepticism about its benevolence. See Ladelle McWhorter, *Bodies and Pleasures: Foucault and the Politics of Sexual Normalization* (Bloomington: Indiana University Press, 1999).

42 Gilligan, *In a Different Voice*.

43 Barbara Ehrenreich, *The Hearts of Men: American Dreams and the Flight from Commitment* (New York: Doubleday, 1983).

44 Camille Paglia, *Sexual Personae* (New Haven: Yale University Press, 1990).

45 Astrid Henry, *Not My Mother's Sister: Generational Conflict and Third-Wave Feminism* (Bloomington: Indiana University Press, 2004).

46 The term "path dependence" was first coined by Kenneth J. Arrow in *Social Choice and Individual Values* (New York: John Wiley, 1951). "Path dependence" explains how the choices one faces in the present are dependent on the decisions one has made in the past, and it was often expressed by seeing what feminism enacted as the "feminization" of earlier male discourses, if this was all that needed to happen and the existing discourses could, as substrates, be "feminized" without being fundamentally changed themselves.

47 Lisa Bellear, "Women's Liberation," *Anthology of Australian Aboriginal Literature*, ed. Anita Heiss and Peter Minter (Montreal: McGill-Queen's University Press, 2008) 179.

48 Stanley Fish, "Boutique Multiculturalism, or Why Liberals Are Incapable of Thinking about Hate Speech," *Critical Inquiry* 23.2 (Winter 1997): 378–95.

49 In French feminism—that is to say, feminism in France, not just the "French feminism" of Kristeva, Cixous, and Irigaray—the "first wave" seems, more sensibly, to be associated with the 1950s and 1960s and the work of Simone de Beauvoir. See Lisa Walsh, "The Swell of the Third Wave," *Contemporary French Feminism*, ed. Kelly Oliver and Lisa Walsh (New York: Oxford University Press, 2004) 1–12.

50   J. Hillis Miller, "Stevens' Rock and Criticism as Cure," *Georgia Review* 30 (1976): 5–31.

51   Naomi Wolf, *The Beauty Myth: How Images of Beauty Are Used against Women* (New York: William Morrow and Company, 1991) 281.

52   Henry, *Not My Mother's Sister*, 9.

53   Sandra A. Zagarell, "*Country's* Portrayal of Community and the Exclusion of Difference," *New Essays on* The Country of the Pointed Firs, ed. June Howard (New York: Cambridge University Press, 1994) 39.

54   Zagarell, "*Country's* Portrayal," 47.

55   See Josephine Donovan, "Sarah Orne Jewett's Critical Theory: Notes toward a Feminine Literary Mode," *Critical Essays on Sarah Orne Jewett*, ed. Gwen L. Nagel (Boston: G.K. Hall, 1984) 212–25; Ann Romines, *The Home Plot: Women, Writing & Domestic Ritual* (Amherst: University of Massachusetts Press, 1992); Marjorie Pryse, "Sex, Class, and 'Category Crisis': Reading Jewett's Transitivity," *American Literature: A Journal of Literary History, Criticism, and Bibliography* 70.3 (1998): 517–49; and Judith Fetterley, "Reading *Deephaven* as a Lesbian Text." *Sexual Practice, Textual Theory: Lesbian Cultural Criticism*, ed. Susan J. Wolfe and Julia Penelope (Cambridge: Blackwell, 1993) 164–83.

56   See, for instance, Nicole Pohl, *Women, Space, and Utopia, 1600–1800: Imaginary Spaces* (Burlington: Ashgate, 2006). The vocabulary of "gendered space" made feminism able to exist as what Thomas Kuhn, in *The Structure of Scientific Revolutions*, called "normal science"; this language was a symptom of a continuity and durability that surpassed the ins and outs of critical fashion.

57   Marnina Gonick, "Between 'Girl Power' and 'Reviving Ophelia': Constituting the Neoliberal Girl Subject" *NWSA Journal* 18.2 (Summer 2006): 1–23 takes a more politically pessimistic view of the "girl power" trope than is evinced here. Kathleen Hanna of the rock group Bikini Kill, on the other hand, has concertedly emphasized links between third wave and second wave feminist perspectives.

58   Drucilla Cornell's use of Kant to go beyond second wave legal formalism, discussed previously, is just the sort of connection the third wave could have made to its advantage.

59   See Adriana Cavarero, *For More Than One Voice: Towards a Philosophy of Vocal Expression*, trans. Paul Kottman (Palo Alto: Stanford University Press, 2005). Similarly, the third wave was disconcertingly unaware of feminist thinkers with similar agendas but working in very different contexts, such as the Peruvian poet and critic Rocio Silva Santisteban, who pursued the more overtly political agenda that the third wave intermittently seemed to desire.

60   Paul de Man, "Literary History and Literary Modernity," *Blindness and Insight: Essays in the Rhetoric of Contemporary Criticism*, rev ed. (Minneapolis: University of Minnesota Press, 1983) 142–65. His essay has long been recognized as undercutting the claims of cathartic breakthroughs; it may be as sagacious in undercutting the complacency of premature syntheses or reconciliations.

61   See E. Ann Kaplan and Devoney Looser, *Generations: Academic Feminists in Dialogue* (Minneapolis: University of Minnesota Press, 1997), as well as Devoney Looser, *Women Writers and Old Age in Great Britain, 1750–1850* (Baltimore: Johns Hopkins University Press, 2008).

62   See Janet Halley, *Split Decisions: How and Why to Take a Break from Feminism* (Princeton: Princeton University Press, 2006).

63   See Ariel Levy, *Female Chauvinist Pigs and the Rise of Raunch Culture* (New York: Simon and Schuster, 2006) and Caitlin Flanagan, *To Hell with All That: Loving and Loathing Our Inner Housewife* (Boston: Little Brown, 2006). That there was, in an allegedly "post-feminist" age and in a decade so concerned with traditional political history such as wars and elections, such an investment in debates about gender suggests that, whatever the perspectives of individual polemicists, gender retained and even expanded its role as a seismic register of social tension and debate. As McKenzie Wark illustrates in *The Virtual Republic* (Sydney: Allen and Unwin, 1997), cultural debates about an issue cannot only stake out alternative positions on that issue but put that issue, as such, front and centre in the public sphere, a process facilitated by the celerity with which information travels in the Internet age. Future ages may see the "post-feminist" debate as at once introducing the idea of gender to a wider discursive space and liberalizing and ramifying the entire idea of gender itself; this perspective parallels the dynamic earlier observed with Julia Kristeva, that she represented a radicalizing, in one sense, and a widening and liberalizing of previous revolutionary tendencies, in another—an accommodation of both these tendencies to the humanist mainstream.

64   Percy Bysshe Shelley "A Defence of Poetry, 1821" *English Literary Criticism: Romantic and Victorian*, ed. Daniel G. Hoffman and Samuel Hynes (New York: Appleton-Century-Crofts, 1963) 164.

65 See Michael Hardt, *Gilles Deleuze: An Apprenticeship in Philosophy* (Minneapolis: University of Minnesota Press, 1993) 12. Deleuze's critical revalidation of pantheist or pan-evolutionary thinkers such as Spinoza and Bergson marks him out as very different from Derrida, who was more interested in ironically bouncing off canonical philosophers (whose assumptions he questioned) rather than reframing out-of-favour past philosophers in a distinctively personal way. Nor would Derrida exult in immanence, however redefined, as Deleuze does; for Derrida, both the immanent and the transcendent would be equally questionable as sanctuaries for the metaphysics of presence. But both Derrida and Deleuze are opposed to an overarching Hegelian dialectic, and both can inform feminism insofar as they can keep its horizons open beyond the premature, practical reconciliation offered by the third wave.

66 For nomads, see Gilles Deleuze and Félix Guattari, *Nomadology: The War Machine* (New York: Semiotext[e], 1986). On islands, see Gilles Deleuze, *Desert Islands and Other Texts* (Cambridge, MA: MIT Press, 2004).

67 Rosi Braidotti, *Metamorphoses: Towards a Materialist Theory of Becoming* (Cambridge: Polity Press, 2005) 268.

68 Braidotti, *Metamorphoses*, 256.

69 Braidotti, *Metamorphoses*, 147.

70 Braidotti's inclusion of animals and other non-sentient forms brings the inclusiveness well beyond any anthropocentric "third way" synthesis.

71 See Kelly Oliver, *Witnessing: Beyond Recognition* (Minneapolis: University of Minnesota Press, 2001).

72 Luce Irigaray, *Speculum of the Other Woman*, trans. Gillian C. Gill (Ithaca: Cornell University Press, 1985) 13.

73 Simone de Beauvoir, *The Second Sex*, trans. H.M. Parshley (New York: Vintage, 1974) 1.

74 Cressida J. Heyes, *Line Drawings: Defining Women Through Feminist Practice* (Ithaca: Cornell University Press, 2003) 19.

75 See Drucilla Cornell, *Defending Ideals: War, Democracy, and Political Struggles* (London: Routledge, 2004) 99.

CHAPTER FOUR

Deconstructing Privilege
ANTI-RACIST THEORY

Up to the 1970s: Race in Pre-Theoretical Criticism

Race and the Conditions of Criticism

Perhaps the most visible effect of literary theory was in bringing the issue of race and past racial prejudice to the forefront of literary awareness. Expansion beyond the "resolved symbolic" opened the canon to consideration of works by African Americans and other minorities that had long been excluded and enabled books by current writers of colour to be appreciated and analysed swiftly within the contours of academia. Anti-racist criticism, though, not only advocated for attention to be paid to certain books but also asked the readers of literature what structural issues of racism had historically been at work in the institutional body known as "literature."

In 1993, Toni Morrison became the first African American writer to win the Nobel Prize for Literature. Five years earlier, a previous American literary Nobel Prize winner had asked this question, "Who is the Tolstoy of the Zulus, the Proust of the Papuans?" Saul Bellow, who trained as an anthropologist and wrote *Henderson the Rain King*, an acclaimed novel set in a fictionalized Africa, was no racist, and, in context, his question suggested that he would not be averse to such a Papuan or Zulu figure appearing and gaining recognition.[1] But it was still an execrable, crude, and regrettable remark, and one that crystallized the institutionalized prejudice facing writers of colour even in the 1990s, decades after the achievements of the civil rights movement and the martyrdoms of Malcolm X and Dr. Martin Luther King, Jr.

Bellow, or whoever attributed the quotation to him, was also wrong empirically. Proust might well have been interested in how Russell Soaba's novel *Maiba* chronicles rapid social change taking place across one lifetime. Soaba has forged a sustained career in a Papua New Guinea, which faced nearly constant crisis in its first several decades of independence but whose national perseverance is subtly reflected in Soaba's fiction, as France's is in Proust's. And the late

Mazisi Kunene's poetry had an epic reach that might have made the author of *War and Peace* and *Hadji Murad* proud. But the remark was not meant to insult certain peoples in South Africa and the South Pacific. The thrust was not against people outside the United States at all—it was meant as a gesture of resentment against African Americans and reflected the perception that literature by African American writers was being studied as part of an enforced multiculturalism that served a compensatory purpose.

The contention, in other words, was that writers such as Morrison, Richard Wright, and Ralph Ellison were being promoted by the academy only because of their colour. The reality was more complex. They were being promoted by the academy because they were great writers who wrote about the African American experience, among other things, and they were writing during a time when that experience was of interest because of the civil rights movement and its aftermath. Similarly, Yeats and Joyce and J.M. Synge and Sean O'Casey were promoted by the academy in the twentieth century because they were great writers touching upon, among other things, Irish life in the era of Irish independence and national struggle. And writers such as Faulkner, Flannery O'Connor, and Eudora Welty were great writers writing at a time when the US south was entering rapidly back into the mainstream of national cultural life from which it had been largely sundered since the Civil War. (The New Critics also exemplified this re-entry of the southern states.) That there was such vociferous objection to the entry of African American writers into the canon and so little to the entry of these other writers indicates that there was racism within the literary-critical establishment and that anti-racist criticism was needed in order to combat this institutionalized prejudice.

We may take it as a matter of course in the twenty-first century that a history of American poetry would include, among others, Langston Hughes with his pithy, plangent lyricism; Countee Cullen, with his grave, balladic melancholy laced with mordant humour; Sterling Brown, for his colloquial, satiric bite; Gwendolyn Brooks, for her rough-hewn sagacity; and Claude McKay, for his defiant eloquence. Yet a 740-page book on American poetry, published in 1968—the year of Dr. King's assassination—contained references to nary a one of these poets.[2] Indeed, *no* African American was included in this history of American poetry, which took the reader "from the Puritans to the present." That this book was *not* written by a truculent southern formalist, still not quite over General Lee's surrender at Appomattox, but by a visionary, Emersonian northern liberal was all the more proof that the twenty-first century consensus about the value of black writers had to be dearly won. Furthermore, looking at the past like this may make us see that what happened in the intervening years was not "politicization." It was simply being able, finally, to look at the full range of literature produced in America and judge this literature on its merits. It was the 1968 book that, in fact, was politicized. Though the critic under discussion was a man of considerable gifts and insight, the book is debilitated by the exclusions it makes. The book would have suffered as well if it had excluded Walt

Whitman and all the poets influenced by him. The point is that literary history that deliberately excludes a key part of its terrain is an irretrievably compromised one. Toni Morrison studied American literature in the 1950s at Cornell, and she knew well the world of the New Critics and the myth-and-symbol school. In her book of literary criticism *Playing in the Dark* (1992), Morrison expanded the traditional horizon of American literature by arguing that great American novels written by whites are haunted by race even when they seem to have only a white cast of characters.[5] Criticism of novels with a similarly pigmented cast is, in this case, haunted by race as well. While Morrison suggests that novels can seethe with these contradictions and still be great novels, criticism may, in this respect, be a more fragile art.

This chapter will concentrate on critical discourses surrounding race and literature in the United States. The dividing line between anti-racist and post-colonial criticism can be arbitrary. For instance, descendants of immigrants to the United States from China, Japan, or Korea are analysed as "Asian American writers," whereas an analogous writer of Indian or Bangladeshi descent is likelier to be seen as a "post-colonial writer." The nations of Latin America were products of the first full-fledged exercise in European colonialism, but, within a US-based framework, Latino literature is seen as representing racial and not colonial discourses. A Filipino American writer living in Hawaii is seen as a minority American, whereas a Filipino writer living in Australia would be seen as post-colonial. Any writer of African descent is seen as post-colonial, no matter in what language they write, but people descended from Africans with heritages of long family residence in the United States or Canada are part of the national literatures of those countries. The dividing line seems arbitrary, much like the imaginary meridian in the Treaty of Tordesillas by which Spain and Portugal theoretically divided the non-European world in 1494.

Generally, it seems as if countries that actively threw off the colonial mantle centuries ago, such as most of the nations of the Americas, are deemed to have national rather than post-colonial literatures, whereas colonies less quick to jettison the mother country (Canada, Australia, or New Zealand) or former colonies whose independence was gained from European countries within living memory (India and most African nations) are said to have post-colonial literatures. Even this, though, is not a totally reliable metric, and there is inevitably some arbitrariness in what writing is covered in this chapter and what is assayed in the next. Furthermore, in some countries that were originally English colonies, such as Canada and Australia, a writer of Italian or Jewish descent would be considered an ethnic minority; whereas, in the United States, he or she would not. Philip Roth and Don DeLillo are seen as part of the American mainstream, whereas Nino Ricci or Venero Armanno and A.M. Klein or Judah Waten are or were seen as "ethnic" writers in their home countries (in each pair above, the first is Canadian, the second Australian). Obviously, this is not categorical with respect to US literature. Chaim Potok, who wrote largely about rabbis and pious Jews, and Mario Puzo, who wrote largely about Italian-Americans involved in organized crime, were associated with more ethnic specificity than, say, Samuel R. Delany, the African American (and gay) science fiction writer, whose fans frequently did not know of his racial background until he began to be studied by African American criticism in the 1990s. But still, the generalizations already outlined were largely true in US culture. In defining the prejudice that anti-racist criticism had to overcome as principally one of colour, this chapter will necessarily follow a US-based paradigm.

The people who first started this conversation rolling may have been practising novelists from the 1930s to the 1960s. Richard Wright, in his commentary on his novel *Native Son* (1940), "How Bigger Was Born," deliberately ties his story of "an American ... who was not allowed to live as an American" to the mainstream of white American literature, in fact, tacitly seeing his novel as the embodiment of a depth that white writers could only approach through hint and implication. Bigger Thomas epitomizes "a past tragic enough to appease the spiritual hunger" of a Henry James and with enough "horror" so that Edgar Allan Poe would not have to go looking for more; horror would surround him.[4] What Wright was speaking to here is the difference between criticism of the American and the British novel. Whereas someone like Leavis, despite not being a Marxist or a revolutionary, certainly wrote about the English novel with the sense of a social context, the American novel was seen as more formal and symbolic, more "romance" than "novel." Indeed, American novels were eligible for the intrinsic analysis promoted by the "resolved symbolic" in a way that only a few English novels, such as *Wuthering Heights*, were. (In this way, going back to our discussion of Foucault and *Don Quixote* in Chapter 1, "the novel," as a concept, introduced a level of heterogeneity into critical discourse, especially when novels were read with full attention, a sentiment with which Mikhail Bakhtin might heartily agree.) Wright suggested that the American novel could not be talked about socially *not* because of the predominance of its formal patterns but because having this discussion would entail bringing up race. The next major African American novelist, Ralph Ellison, demanded even more of a place in the middle of American culture; his *Invisible Man* (1954) was such an undeniable achievement as to impinge even upon the world of the New York Intellectuals. The stirring and provocatively tentative closing line of this novel— "Who knows that but, on the lower frequencies, I speak for you?"—presented the white reader with a sense of the African American writer as someone who could speak for everybody, not just for her or his own race.[5] James Baldwin took the next step; as both an African American and a gay man, Baldwin experienced the condition of belonging to a double minority, and his novel *Another Country* (1962) presented a vision of a bohemian world positioned at the interstices of race, class, and gender, before and beyond what later became termed "identity politics." In Baldwin's novels, the general air of an active dissent from establishment social norms included those who were outsiders because of discrimination, but these dissenters were defined by their lifestyle not by how the social mainstream discriminated against them. Baldwin came very close here to the fluid interchangeability presumed by deconstruction.[6]

Building a Criticism of Black Literature

It took a while for academic literary criticism to catch up to the achievements of these creative writers. Indeed, history, as an academic discipline, was ahead of literary criticism. As the autobiography of the historian John Hope Franklin reveals, he was sent as a Fulbright professor to Australia in the late 1950s, a gesture really remarkable in light of the racial history not only of the United States but also of Australia.[7] At that time, there would not have been an African American literary critic of sufficient stature to send. Nor would there have been any understanding of the need to send one. But even in the days before African American writing was studied in the academy, it was discussed and evaluated by polymathic intellects such as the well-known W.E.B. Du Bois and by the lesser but still imposing figure of Benjamin Mays, president of Morehouse College and a teacher of Dr. King. These writers were, of necessity, interdisciplinary in their approach. Yet the earliest criticism of African American writing to be consciously written as academic literary criticism was actually, as Houston A. Baker Jr. has pointed out, not far from New Criticism. Its mission was to read texts by black writers and explicate them in more or less their own terms.[8] Stephen Henderson was one of the most accomplished of these critics. He spent most of his career at Howard University. Howard was, like Morehouse, one of the historically black colleges and universities without which the large-scale study of African American literature with and after theory would not have been possible. Like the New Critics, Henderson studied poetry, for the most part. But unlike them (and despite basically remaining in a formalist framework), he studied the complicated relationship of African American poetry to black speech patterns and to music, especially the blues.[9] If the New Critics had been more in touch with the vernacular music of their own culture, such as bluegrass, they would have been different: less stodgy, less stuffy, less assimilable to the Ivy League punctiliousness of the establishment institutions in which most of them eventually taught. Henderson characterizes words used in blues lyrics and poetry, words such as "rock," "jelly," and "jook," as "mascon" words, words of "massive concentration of black experiential energy." Had one of the New Critics coined "mascon," it would probably be a byword in every English class in college—and extolled by defenders of the old ways against newfangled critical jargon such as *différance*. Henderson was born in Florida and went to college in Georgia. Notably, it could be argued that Henderson kept more of the south with him than the New Critics, who all too soon adopted the cultural norms of states like Connecticut where they taught and dwelled. Henderson got his PhD at the University of Wisconsin, which, as we saw in Chapter 3, had one of the most liberal English departments of the early 1960s, with a woman, Helen C.

White, as chair. In a sense, the very fact of Henderson's practice as a critic was politicization enough. It spoke for itself, which permitted him to concentrate on issues of language and form.

Robert Bone, on the other hand, was a more traditional literary historian. His *The Negro Novel in America* (1958) is important not only for giving a sustained account of the African American literary tradition but for representing the sort of solid literary history that was still produced amid the attempted purification of New Criticism. In African American studies in many other fields, this sort of work lay behind the more theoretically ambitious achievements of later generations, which relied on earlier scholarship's casing of the historical field.[10] Not surprisingly, Bone's four "major" writers were all male, although he included a woman novelist, Zora Neale Hurston, in the next-best or "superior" category. Both Bone and Henderson are figures of historical importance, but Henderson, as a critic, tried to innovate more.

Henderson was allied with the Black Arts Movement of the early 1970s in aesthetic terms. Most other members of that group, though, wrote far more about political issues than did Henderson. In the wake of the civil rights movement, politics could hardly be avoided. The Black Arts Movement later had a reputation as being ethnocentric and merely a vehicle for restrictive racial affirmation. But this was not really the case. (Nor, in the context, would this necessarily have been bad.) Larry Neal, the figure most associated with the phrase "Black Arts Movement," operated out of a desire for existential wholeness that, again, dovetailed with New Critical ideas of organic form. Neal saw the West as not just guilty but exhausted, in ways that have much in common with white writers such as the T.S. Eliot of *The Waste Land* and the John Barth of "The Literature of Exhaustion." Amiri Baraka (originally LeRoi Jones) wrote compelling poetry as well as criticism that was racially oriented but that, partially as a result of Baraka's Marxist leanings, also sought broad connections with world literature. Baraka's occasional penchant for extremist remarks should not obscure his importance; he was one of the first contemporary examples of an African American literary intellectual operating deftly in various cultural registers. Another poet who changed his name as an anti-racist gesture (and as part of his conversion to Islam) was Haki R. Madhubuti, formerly Don L. Lee. Madhubuti's poetics can be seen in the frequently anthologized, "Black Again, Home."[11]

In Madhubuti's poem, a man who tries to assimilate into the white, corporate culture finds himself stifled and, in the end, returns to his own community and a less oppressive lifestyle: "back again. Black again, home." As with Baldwin, though in a more polemical way, Madhubuti espouses bohemianism as well as black consciousness. He provides a rejection of monochromatically taking on the culture of the white man but also a countercultural questioning of conformity and the normative in general. This questioning of conformity was extended back through time by the novelist Ishmael Reed in *Mumbo Jumbo* (1972).

Reed's postmodern conspiracy novel features, as its villains, the "Atonists." In the history, Atonists were followers of the monotheistic Egyptian Pharaoh Akhenaten (14th century BC). Akhenaten was often lauded by white suprem-acists as a proto-rationalist, Proto-Indo-European figure who broke from the backward paganism of his Egyptian milieu and introduced dynamic "European" agency in the form of a single transcendent deity.[12] Reed turns the tables, castigat-ing "Atonism" as repressive and conformist, and opposing it with the alternate ideology of "Jes Grew," which, in its proliferation and pluralism, is reminiscent of Derridean *différance*. Indeed, Reed's structural critique of Western reason—not just of European ethnocentrism—is, in general, remarkably parallel to Derrida's. Other African American theorists had a very different profile. Nathan A. Scott, Jr., was a long-time professor of religious studies at the University of Virginia. Scott, though, largely wrote about literature, addressing ethical dimensions in the work of such figures as Saul Bellow, T.S. Eliot, W.H. Auden, and Albert Camus, as well as writing on African American authors such as Ralph Ellison and Richard Wright. Scott was one of the first American critics to take the work of Martin Heidegger seriously, although he did so in a far less radical way than did Derrida.[13] Although Scott did write substantially about African American writers, many people who read and cited his work, such as the acclaimed British poet Geoffrey Hill, clearly did not know Scott was black. After Scott's death, this largely accidental omission of him from the African American critical canon was rectified.[14]

Despite all these achievements, African American criticism had reached a kind of impasse in the mid-1970s. Black studies programs were established in many major universities, but they were seen as a release for the energies of protest as much as places where serious academic thought took place. It was rare for a white student to enrol in a class on black literature. Once the gesture of racial pride had been made, there seemed no second act. The sec-ond act, though, came, and came quickly, from a different direction. In fact, it arrived from two different directions—African American women's writing and deconstructive literary theory. When writers such as Toni Morrison and Alice Walker began publishing in the 1970s, their fiction, rather than being about race relations or the racial issue, concentrated more on relations within the black community. This focus suggested that the black community, in and of itself and as much as any other community, could be the locale for important fiction. Although many black male writers, such as Ishmael Reed and the music and cultural critic Stanley Crouch, saw these women writers as conducting a deliberate vendetta against the black man, Walker and Morrison made racial as well as gender connections in their work and life. When Walker discovered the burial ground of the important novelist Zora Neale Hurston (1891–1960), she had engraved on the new tombstone the legend "A Genius of the South"—a quotation from the lyric chorus "Georgia Dusk" by the acclaimed black male poet of the early twentieth century Jean Toomer. In anchoring Hurston in terms of race and region, as well as gender, and in acknowledging the precedent of the experimental and mystically inclined Toomer, Walker was being the opposite of narrow and parochial.[15]

Walker's story "Everyday Use" illustrates how her agenda differed from that of some of her black male counterparts.[16] It concerns a mother in Mississippi and her reactions to her two daughters: Dee, who has left home and become educated and politically radicalized, and Maggie, who has stayed at home and continued in more or less the ways of her mother. The story is very reminiscent of the New Testament parable of the prodigal son, except, here, the privilege given to the returned exile in the biblical story is not necessarily bestowed. "Everyday Use" is not about race relations; rather it is a story about tensions within the black community and among African American women—all the major characters are black and female. And, interestingly, the story does not champion what might be assumed to be the radical or "politically correct" perspective. In the 1960s and 1970s, the adoption of African names was a key gesture in the affirmation of Black Power, done by everybody from Baraka, Madhubuti, and the politician Kweisi Mfume to the boxer Muhammad Ali and the basketball players Kareem Abdul-Jabbar and Zaid Abdul-Aziz. But Walker seems to share the mother's combination of incredulity, incomprehension, and mockery at Dee assuming the name "Wangero." Her narrative use of the parenthetical in the name "Dee (Wangero)" is actually a very cunning rhetorical move; it holds both names in place, adjoining them and layering the old and the new. The mother may not have gone beyond second grade (which again presents the denial of literacy to black women that the feminist work of Donna Haraway made into a crucial issue, as we saw in Chapter 3), but that does not prevent her from being rhetorically very conscious. But note that the mother actually volunteers to use the name "Wangero" even though the daughter says that doing so is not necessary. The mother adjusts; she puts the name *to everyday use*. It is Wangero who expects the renaming to be disruptive, a kind of theatrical distance.

Is Walker coming out against blacks adopting African names? Not necessarily. After all, the mother not only uses Wangero as a name, but, when Wangero's partner Asalamalakim is introduced, she knows that the phrase "*Asalaam 'Alaykum*" is used as a greeting in Arabic and, as such, is employed in many African countries; she has heard it before. Most likely, indeed, Walker means the reader to realize that this is probably not the real name of Wangero's partner, that the mother is probably assimilating it to a phrase she already knows and recognizes as African. She is integrating it into her practice of everyday use. In many ways, the division is not between African and American. It is between the theoretical and the practical, the theatrical and the absolutely ordinary. This story actually could not take place in the twenty-first century, as, by that time, there were in the United States so many Africans—people born in Africa—and so many people with Muslim names that the drama of the unusual name would not be possible even in the most rural town in Mississippi. Walker seems to be saying that the child who goes away and becomes educated may seem to be the more successful, but, sometimes, the one who stays home and seems to live the more restricted life may have values worth admiring as well. However, the sisters are not utter contrasts: both have potential husbands. Walker is often accused (for instance, by Ishmael Reed) of being anti-male. But in "Everyday Use" she presents marriage to men as part of the expected trajectory of both younger women.

The metaphorical effect of the story with respect to African American discourse is to place a renewed stress on vernacular traditions and their continuity. Walker propagated this ethic of continuity in another way with her rescue of Hurston's reputation. Hurston's combination of the vernacular, the experimental, and the culturally and philosophically venturesome in many ways launched the mix for which African American critical discourse came to be known. In "What White Publishers Won't Print," Hurston writes about the "mainstream" and its "lack of curiosity about the internal lives of Negroes."[17] She wrote this essay just when the works of Joyce, Woolf, and Faulkner had made the revelation of the inner life in stream of consciousness and interior monologue all the rage. Hurston's example showed that the sources of "experimentation" in fiction and literary thought did not have to be European. Because of Hurston's influence on Walker, her writing was, in a way, more "deconstructive" than Morrison's, which could be characterized, nevertheless, as more complicated and challenging. (We have already seen this pattern in our discussion of Nabokov, Borges, and the Yale school.) Though Morrison drew deeply from the well of African American experience, her principal influences were established, canonical white modernists, Woolf and Faulkner. The anchoring role that Woolf played for feminist criticism was, in many ways, performed by Hurston for African American criticism (and, for that matter, for African American critiques of feminism). Hurston combines discourses of blackness with formal and structural experimentation. Her *Their Eyes Were Watching God* begins with an oracular pronouncement about ships at a distance carrying men's lives on board with them; then the language shifts abruptly, and man as "humankind" becomes man as "gendered male" when Hurston writes about women that their hopes are not so rhetorically distanced, that, for them, "the dream is the truth." This writing takes down the principles of opposition in general, not just those concerning race or gender. The very idea of a plausible "universality" is questioned. But the idea is questioned, not demolished. As suggested by Barbara Johnson (1947–2009), a white feminist and deconstructive critic who gave crucial theoretical readings of texts by African American women, de-universalizaton does not arrive as a fixed point; it is an ongoing process, keeping both the vestige of the universal and contrary subversive energies differently in mind.[18]

As a novelist, Morrison, too, questions universality on the basis of an African American female discourse of blackness, but she also bases this questioning on the rhetoric of earlier twentieth-century avant-garde high literature. As a critic, Morrison in many ways opened the way to "whiteness studies." Critics such as Maurice Berger studied whiteness as whiteness, as something specific and contingent, not as a majoritarian norm.[19] Noel Ignatiev, in his book *How the Irish Became White* (1995), discussed how whiteness was, in a sense, invented; in the United States, for example, the category of whiteness was constructed to provide a covering identity for all peoples of European descent, even those like the Irish who had originally faced fierce religious and class-based discrimination.[20]

The 1970s and Early 1980s: The Emergence of African American Criticism

The second change that the 1970s saw in African American literary studies came from the influence of post-structuralist theory itself. The pivotal figure here was Henry Louis Gates, Jr. Yet, as so often in the history of recent literary theory, Gates could not have taken this step without the foundation built by important predecessors. When Gates was a student at Yale, the African Americanist Robert Stepto was on the faculty there. Though Stepto's interests as a critic were not exclusively theoretical, it matters that he was on the same faculty as Harold Bloom and Paul de Man, in what was then the nation's flagship English department, just as the work of Robert Farris Thompson on cross-Atlantic aesthetic influences in black America had particular significance because it took place at Yale. Robert Bone, by comparison, taught at the Teachers College of Columbia University. This institution was respected but, because of its pedagogical emphasis, not necessarily in the academic mainstream. This does not discount the importance of Bone's work. Indeed, it magnifies it. But without the presence of African Americanists such as Henry Louis Gates, Jr. at prestigious departments that embraced deconstruction, conversation in this field would not have entered general academic discourse so quickly.

It was Gates's work that first brought together these two discourses. His most influential idea was that of "signifying." Gates noted that "signifying" in African American parlance consisted of remarks, taunts, gestural responses, or other varieties of rhetoric that reverberate, in echo or in retort, with previous discussions, both sympathetic and antagonistic. Signifying can be the art of fighting back, using language to subvert an unjust oppressor, to throw the hateful words of persecutors or arrogant power wielders back in their face. It can be the gentle, companionable, but verbally alert teasing of a friend; the paradigmatic example of this is "playing the dozens," which means playing verbal games of perpetually increasing verbal stakes, a kind of ritualistic badinage of simulated castigation, such as a man telling another man "Yo' mama does___" (something obscene or unlikely), which inspires a hyperbolic riposte even more outrageous. Signifying can also be call and response, as seen in the black church, where hearing the message of the preacher is only part of the experience, and the empowered congregations' affirmation or expansion of the preacher's words is key to the overall meaning. Gates, being at Yale, points out that the *practice* of signifying, which is an African American rhetorical tradition, has a kissing cousin in the idea of the signifier and the signified, as first explained in Saussure's linguistics. Also, he notes a parallel between the use of the term "signifying" to describe a linguistic practice that creates meaning within a culturally specific context and form and its use as a literary term to indicate the arbitrary nature of the relationship between the signifier and the signified. African American discourse had this term, yet within the white Anglo-American mainstream "signifying" sounded new, trendy, "sublime," advanced. Only in African American discourse did Saussure's linguistic terms find a spontaneous echo. There is something tremendously moving here, and it goes beyond the example of an African American using European theory as part of his intellectual ensemble. After all, in the 1770s, Phillis Wheatley had used Enlightenment universalism to justify her right to speak as a black woman, and, in the early 1900s, W.E.B. Du Bois had used the thought of Hegel to undergird his crucial idea of "double-consciousness" in *The Souls of Black Folk*. Richard Wright and James Baldwin had both gone to Europe to escape the cauldron of US racism and work in a less charged environment, as had many singers and jazz musicians. What was new here was not the European influence but that Gates was bringing together black American vernacular and European philosophical discourses *in the academy*, and doing it in such a way that it constituted an ongoing, reusable methodology, not just a brilliant one-off performance. Gates stages not just a momentary encounter but also a recognition scene between the two discourses, one guaranteed to mark the beginning of an ongoing relationship.

It is of special salience that Gates's theory of signifying presumed a history, a chain of verbal interaction, that did not exist in monumental invulnerability like the Western canon as conceived by, say, T.S. Eliot and Erich Auerbach. Gates did not junk any idea of tradition entirely, as had radicals from modernism—think Ezra Pound's slogan "make it new"—to the 1960s, with its generally contemptuous attitude towards the very idea of a past. Like, in their different ways, Derrida, Foucault, Gadamer, and Bakhtin, Gates linked texts together to form a tradition that, although not dependent on invariable chronological sequence or observable causality, was more than a meaningless, amoral series of fragments subsisting amid emptiness. Gates, like the others mentioned above, showed that criticism could subvert "the metaphysics of presence" in the Derridean sense and still not only have values—the entire idea of anti-racism depends on having values—but also understand those values as existing in some sort of historical continuum.

In the 1970s, people, of whatever ethnicity, took courses on black American literature to learn about the heritage and history of the black community. In the 1980s, they took these courses to be familiar with the literature that was inspiring some of the most exciting debates in current theory. In the 1990s and after, they did so in order to be generally literate. One hopes that this progression was inevitable. That it happened so quickly was due both to Gates's intellectual accomplishment and to the fact that his presence at Yale made his work almost immediately audible.

Another slightly older and, for a time, equally influential critic of African American literature was Houston A. Baker, Jr., who taught at the University of Pennsylvania. Baker was deeply learned in the general literary and cultural history of the United States. He can, in many ways, be seen as the African American equivalent of what Leslie Fiedler was in Jewish American criticism (though, of course, the impact of both scholars resonated beyond the biographical ethnicity of each). Baker insisted on the importance of symbolic patterns within African American culture. Texts, he argued, cannot simply be assessed or diagnosed by external criteria. He pointed out the condescending quality of Marxist criticism, which recognized the oppression of African Americans in a way less politicized discourses did not but insisted on judging their achievements by a European metanarrative.

Eventually, Gates and Baker were seen as antagonists. Baker scolded Gates for being too assimilationist and establishmentarian. Thus, it is useful to remember that, in the early 1980s, Baker and Gates seemed to be operating on roughly parallel trajectories. Baker, for instance, was quite friendly to theory, and many academic administrators probably first heard of Jacques Derrida when Baker, in a prominently placed article in *The Chronicle of Higher Education* in the fall of 1985, called for the application of Derrida's theories to black women's writing.

Baker rejected what he saw as Gates's neo-formalism and, later, his apparent eagerness to cooperate with and become a part of the literary and academic establishment. It must be said that this (undeniable) establishmentarian tendency is most likely just what, say, the twenty-second century will *not* see in Gates, if he is still read at that point. Wordsworth and Coleridge were condemned for their apostasy by their younger contemporaries, Shelley, Byron, Leigh Hunt, and the like, but, by the end of the nineteenth century, it was the poetry of Wordsworth and Coleridge that was valued, and, even today, their politics and morals, despite getting some historicist traction during and after the 1980s, are seen in a more complex vein than their younger contemporaries imagined. In the early 2000s, some critics saw Gates as being too aligned with traditional academia, as having an apolitical or even neoconservative orientation. Gates, to adapt the terms of the cultural debate in nineteenth-century Russia, was seen as a Westernizer to Madhubuti or even Baker's "Slavophile." Gates was seen as making African American literature accessible and palatable to a mainstream white audience, while Madhubuti or Baker were more concerned with addressing a black audience. But, if future scholars compare Gates to, say, James Baldwin as a thinker, they might see Gates as speaking more to an idea of African American identity. (And when Gates was controversially arrested by the Cambridge police while he was trying to enter his own home in the summer of 2009, he certainly did not feel a member of the mainstream.) On the other hand, Gates "organizes" blackness into a category far more than Baldwin did. Baldwin's black-gay-urban-female-bohemian hybridity was, in a sense, the synthesis that consciously post-modern and diasporic critics such as Paul Gilroy and Kwame Anthony Appiah came to, within the mesh of theory, thirty to forty years later.

In one sense, Gates was using deconstruction strategically. By applying it to African American literature, Gates was taking a very European, albeit subversive, body of thought and applying it to a very different set of texts than those that had lain behind it originally. He also was taking the most acclaimed and difficult critical method of his day and showing that it could be applied to African American texts. He thus validated them not only as objects of ethnic pride and parochial championship but also as an academic field whose internal complexity was the same as any other. This mixture had a hothouse quality, which perhaps accounts for it not immediately producing any sustained work after Gates himself stopped practising it upon his turning to more popular and public modes of non-fiction writing in the 1990s. (For example, Gates wrote for *The New Yorker*, was on television, and wrote companion books to TV shows.) On the other hand, the kinship Gates discerned between, say, Derrida and Hurston, the way he outlined how both used new modes of language to escape from binary oppositions, promote difference, and overturn hierarchies—this scholarship was genuine. And it is very important work both for African American studies and for theory in general, as it showed the catalyzing and emancipatory effect that theory was capable of having on a new academic field. It also showed that theory, which Yale school critics had applied mostly to canonical texts, could speak to works without a long tradition of formal academic commentary. As we have seen, J. Hillis Miller proudly boasted that he was a reader of canonical texts. Gates, though, argued that theory could yield insights on texts new to academic study as much as to those that had already been subject to a sustained tradition of earlier readings. Yet part of Gates's mission, as we have discussed, was to stress that there was a *tradition* of African American culture, both learned and vernacular, that could complement theory in providing an abstract rationale for literature rather than just serving as a material base on which theory could intervene.

Even at the time, just as Gates was attacked from the Left for being too conventional and having too much truck with the halls of ivy, he was also attacked from the Right for advocating African American literary tradition in ways some found threatening to traditional academic standards. Giving these critics the benefit of the doubt as to their motives—and in an area as sensitive as this one it is wise to be as generously minded as possible—one wonders why they were so upset by Gates. D.G. Myers, for instance, in the neoconservative journal the *New Criterion*, says the resemblance between the Saussurean use of "signifying" and the African American practice of "signifyin(g)" is an "accident—that the two words are mere "homonyms." Gates would agree that the two "signifyings" are radically different. But to say "homonyms"—as if these words pertained no more to each other than turkey (the animal) and Turkey (the nation)—is clearly an effort to ward off the very interpenetration of the European and the African American vernacular Gates is embracing.

Other than some vague appeals to the greatness of Shakespeare (reeking of what Eric Hobsbawm and Terrence Ranger termed "the invention of tradition"), literature by whites, en masse, was not defended as aesthetically superior to literature of people of colour, en masse, because such a distinction simply has no ground. When it was acceptable to make such distinctions, they were only made on categorical claims of European "dynamism," which were so much folderol. Reading literature by people of all races and making a special effort to pay renewed attention to earlier literature by African Americans, such as novels by Charles Chesnutt, Sutton E. Griggs, and Pauline Hopkins, novels that had been neglected because of racism, is simply part of acknowledging the equality of all people. The study of texts by African Americans and other racial minorities brought books into the canon that had not been previously studied with the old methods—so this literature was not only about previously underrepresented experience but also a perfect testing ground for new and invigorating theoretical approaches. This marriage of a newly appreciated literature and a new method of literary analysis should not have been in any way controversial. Political correctness did exist, and it did become a sort of unofficial civil religion of the academy. At times, it was nettlesome not only for its ideological dogmatism and its tendency to see anyone not willing to subscribe to regnant academic dogma as automatically maleficent but also for the way it tended to provide a simple set of affirmations that repressed or at least counterbalanced any original ideas. But this same phenomenon had happened before. It was, for instance, politically incorrect to like Romanticism in the era of the "resolved symbolic." Before Foucault and the historian Peter Brown, it was politically incorrect to like any Latin or Greek literature after roughly the time of the first Roman emperors.

The same repressive consensus, the same collusion of the intellectually mediocre with the status quo, happened in these cases as it did later on with race and gender, and it is probably a perennial and, in the ultimate instance, tolerable if regrettable aspect of collective academic life. Indeed, as Foucault might argue, intellectual history is, in many ways, a series of successive exclusions; the difference between *epistemes* is found in what they exclude. The critics of political correctness made an additional mistake in supposing that race was the only reason writers of colour were read. It was *partially* that. But it was partially also a need for new material, a delight in not just having the same old books to talk about in the same old ways. Intellectual life needs such stimulus. When one is working in a past period whose intellectual lineaments are perceived to have been sketched long in advance, the need for rediscovered writers or new approaches becomes like oxygen. Also, race as an orientation to literary analysis and the retrieval of neglected African American writers served to variegate the academy more generally. We have to remember that, in 1960, there were very few texts or authors thought "major" enough for an academic to bother to publish a significant book about. In the case, for example, of Scandinavian literature, the greatness of Henrik Ibsen and (in a far more restricted way) August Strindberg was granted, but Scandinavian literature was seen as a minor field that only those who studied the language could or should pursue. That, in 2008, the respected critic Arnold Weinstein could publish *Northern Arts: The Breakthrough of Scandinavian Literature and Art, from Ibsen to Bergman* was a testimony to the rehabilitative effect of looking at literature under national and ethnic rubrics shorn of any rhetoric of racial superiority or invidious distinction. African American literary studies helped reinvigorate this more equitable approach to literature in general.[21] African American literary studies showed, in addition, how comprehensive and internally variegated looking at national or ethnic literature could be. Between 1920 and 1940, for instance, "African American literature" included both the domestic novels of manners of Jessie R. Fauset and the savage satire of George Schuyler, as well as the mixture of aesthetic modernism and political consciousness more usually associated with the Harlem Renaissance. Grouping authors together because of their racial background, in this case, foregrounds not the unanimity but the diversity that these sorts of rubrics can bring into literary discourse.

The 1980s: Building the African American Canon

Gates advocated this diversity in his important general foreword to all the books in the series "The Schomburg Library of Nineteenth-Century Black Women Writers." This advocacy was done not just in the light of cultural or archival importance but also in that of theory. As Gates pointed out, "For reasons unclear to me even today, few of these marvelous renderings of the Afro-American women's consciousness were reprinted in the late 1960s and early 1970s."[22] The fact that Gates does not automatically impute this neglect to gender prejudice and attribute the new visibility of these texts totally to the rise of feminism implies that he suspects a post-structuralist influence is also at work here. When Richard Yarborough, in his introduction to Pauline Hopkins's *Contending Forces*, describes the book as a "sentimental romance" filled with "embodiments of white bourgeois values,"[23] he is sharply revising canonical norms and expectations. During the heyday of the Black Arts Movement, a book with the "sentimental" trappings Yarborough discerns in Hopkins's work would no doubt have been dismissed as inauthentic, as only a halfway step to a true black voice in fiction. This dismissal of sentimentality is the other side of the coin of the New Critical exclusion of anything at all social and political. In both cases, it was deconstruction that enabled the tolerance of a dialogue between form and content, authenticity and genre, where neither totally prevailed.

In Pauline Hopkins's text, the contending forces are not only those of racial pride and intolerance—not just those generated by the plangent awareness that "there is something very wrong in our world" or by the urgent hope of glimpsing a horizon of redemption—but also those of readerly expectations and authorial goals. Consequently, Derridean concepts such as difference and supplementary, which advance beyond an either-or towards a provisional and tentative both-and stance, make this text and others like it more comprehensible than they would have been in an age divided between New Critical aesthetic self-sufficiency and Leavisite moral relevance. Too decorous for the confrontational Leavis and far too discursive and political for the New Critics—the novel, in fact, contains extended speeches and historical accounts that have little role in its dramatic action—*Contending Forces* is a book that, even had it been written by a white person, might well have needed to wait until the 1980s to be found aesthetically pardonable. By bringing various modes of discourse into the idea of what could be permissibly termed "African American literature," Gates emphasized the way writers called upon representations of experience in models provided largely by other writers to whom they felt akin. It is through this mode of literary revision, one amply evident in the texts, that Gates's idea of canonicity defines itself.[24]

Gates opposed an ethnocentric essentialism that saw racial identity as subsisting in an extra-textual space rather than in a carefully handed down and performed sequence of literary protocols. But Gates's warning is also just as salutary against previous traditionalist ideas of European literature that attributed literary achievements to some innate cultural prowess evident in European history. Gates's view of tradition also reveals the heavy influence of his critical contemporaries and immediate predecessors. His insistence that the text itself matters is inherited from the New Critics while the creative potential of revisiting tradition is impossible to conceive of without the work of Harold Bloom. His sense of language both problematizing and facilitating the process of literary transmission is from Derrida while the key concept of "intertextuality," which is latent in Gates's theory, was coined by Julia Kristeva. In Gates's use of the word "revision," one may see a double tribute—to Bloom's ideas of the revisionary ratio by which the new writer deals with the burden of a precursor and to Adrienne Rich's idea of writing as "re-vision," a way to renew—not reinvent!—a tradition from a feminist vantage point.

Nor, contrary to many antagonistic claims, do Gates and the critics who paralleled and followed him insist that any writer is important because he or she is a writer of colour, or that there is no process of canonization. In selecting the Schomburg Library, Gates presumably eliminated many texts from consideration. Moreover, among those he eventually selected, some have attained widespread academic popularity in the intervening twenty years, others a graspable foothold in critical circles, and others were scarcely studied at all. Pauline Hopkins, Harriet Wilson (whom Gates rediscovered), and Frances E.W. Harper would fall into the first group; Emma Dunham-Kelley, Alice Dunbar-Nelson, Mary Seacole, and Elizabeth Keckley into the second group; and the remainder would fall into the third. (Harriet Jacobs was rediscovered concurrently with Wilson, though not by Gates; Phillis Wheatley was already famous.) For all the seeming multitude of candidates, in the end, F.R. Leavis himself could not have devised a more stable canon.

An analogous library of male nineteenth-century African American writers would have included, among others, William Wells Brown and Martin Delany, whose works contributed crucially to the prehistory of the "Black Atlantic" concept discussed below. Yet, of all these figures, Jacobs, Wilson, and Wheatley became the best known among the general run of literary academics, though Hopkins came close. The already well-known Frederick Douglass aside, the only pre-twentieth-century African American writer who became, in the wake of the achievement of African Americanist criticism, an English-department house-hold word was the eighteenth-century autobiographer Olaudah Equiano. He, of course, was not included in the Schomburg Library series because he was both male and too early. Equiano was the only pre-Hurston black writer to become a superstar; every practising academic knew his name. Partially this was because he could be claimed as a figure in both English and American literature. Also, he was relevant both to scholars of what Paul Gilroy called the "Black Atlantic" as well as to the coalescence of Enlightenment and imperialist courses that Srinivas Aravamudan labelled "tropicopolitanism."[25] In any event, the canonicity of these revived and revalued works sorted itself out in a way that, for better or for worse, did not seriously discommode existing notions of literary merit.

Female African American literary critics also participated vigorously in these new theoretical conjunctions, which texts by African American women writers had done so much to start. Hortense Spillers tried to address the resentment held by some African American male writers against the centrality of Morrison, Walker, and, retrospectively, Hurston in the African American canon by arguing that the African American male must regain the female as part of his heritage, that, in effect, the denial of the feminine was a trauma wrought by racism. Spillers was prepared to use theory, but others, such as Barbara Christian, denounced theory as hegemonic. This attitude was part of the general reaction, among people of all colours, against the tyranny of theory. Joyce A. Joyce was even more overtly hostile to theory. There was perhaps a difference between the white conservatives' objections to theory and those of Joyce and Spillers, however.

African American critics could plausibly argue that "their" literature had not yet been fully studied "on its own terms," whereas Shakespeare and Milton, for example, had. Consequently, theoretical modes, when applied to the Western canon, made sense because reams of more practical and immediately helpful criticism had been completed. But even the opposition to theory was intellectually interesting in the 1980s and was part of the mix of that era. It was not just the content of theory but the way it excited and challenged even those who disliked it to mount strong and trenchant arguments that made the 1980s an important episode in intellectual history. Barbara Smith saw the possibilities of such a theory-ignited environment. She adopted black feminism as a critical posture, as compared to Mary Helen Washington who diligently catalogued and did first-order research into the texts of black women writers. Hazel V. Carby used theory in a distinctive way. Carby's work took advantage of the feminist and psycho-analytic theory described in Chapter 3. Carby's criticism also had a different feel to it because she received her academic training in Britain and was influenced by the specific articulations of theory and critique that happened there in the 1970s. bell hooks was not formally theoretical. But her use of the personal voice as a standpoint of critique presumed the work of Derrida and Kristeva, as well as that of Anglo-American feminism, as a baseline.[26] Her recognition as a distinctive, broadly recognized "brand name" anticipated Gates's recasting of himself in the 1990s and, indeed, the breakout from theory in general.[27]

The 1990s: Questioning Race in the Public Sphere

In 1990, people began to use the term "African American" instead of "black." This switch marked a turning point not only in nomenclature but also in assumptions and procedures. John Callahan, a white critic who was Ralph Ellison's literary executor, was one of the first to use this term in a book title, *In the African-American Grain.*[28] This play on William Carlos Williams's book title (*In the American Grain*) signified that "black" was no longer seen as "other," that, as Ellison suggested in the final lines of *Invisible Man*, African Americans had the potential to speak for all Americans, if at first only "on the lower frequencies." But, as if to counterbalance the potential trend towards subsidence into a unitary national identity, the conscious link to Africa, the unavoidable terminological acknowledgement of African origins, also operated in this term, and it did so as an agent of plurality rather than as an assertion of a monolithic ethnic identity. All that was implied in the term was epitomized in the frequent collaboration between Gates and Appiah, two close colleagues who could not have had more different origins. Kwame Anthony Appiah was the grandson of a British Labour Party politician famous in his day and the son of a high-ranking leader of the Akan people of Ghana. Henry Louis Gates, Jr. was from West Virginia, traditionally a working-class state. West Virginia, in terms of the convergence of racial and social justice, was one of the saddest stories of post-Civil War America. The counties that comprised the state specifically separated from Virginia because of their citizens' anti-slavery views, yet, still, when Gates was born in 1951, West Virginia was a practitioner of Jim Crow discrimination laws.[29] Ghana and West Virginia would be considered polar opposites on any comparative cultural spectrum. Yet Gates and Appiah, who were colleagues at several different institutions through the years, formed the nexus of a group of intellectually ambitious, interdisciplinary African American thinkers. They were soon joined, and perhaps even exceeded in public prominence, by Cornel West, an ordained minister who drew on both the traditions of the black church and American pragmatism, supplemented by a wide range of European philosophical discourses, mostly of the Left.

After moving through a series of prestigious academic appointments at Yale, Cornell, and Duke, Gates arrived at Harvard in 1991 as the head of a revamped African American studies program. West and Appiah joined him there, adding to a group of already well-known African American academics at Harvard, such as the sociologists William Julius Wilson and Orlando Patterson and the political scientist Martin Kilson—the first African American to be granted tenure at the prestigious university. (A white scholar who was almost like a member of this group was the German-born thinker Werner Sollors, whose stress on "consent" and not "descent" in the construction of ethnicity chimed with the anti-essentialist view of race held by most of his African American colleagues.) At Harvard, Gates took several important steps that would shape African Americanist theory into the 2000s. Gates assumed editorship of the journal *Transition*, which, in its original Ugandan location, had been highly influential during the first decade of African independence. But as Uganda slipped into dictatorship, civil war, and the forced exile of its East Indian diasporic population, the journal had shut down. Under Gates's editorship, the journal's focus shifted substantially to the United States. But it maintained the cosmopolitan reach that its tradition enabled it to claim, and it created a textual forum centred on but not restricted to African American discourse. Moreover, Gates, along with Appiah and West, began to publish widely in general interest magazines, appear on television in various contexts, and write books substantially more accessible to a non-academic audience than *The Signifying Monkey* had been.[30] Consciously modelling this approach after that of the New York Intellectuals, Gates and his colleagues achieved more than their role models because they had already fashioned a substantive, theoretically informed body of academic work whose conclusions sustained and nurtured them even as the scholars necessarily simplified and popularized their insights in order to have them resonate with a wider public.

Of Appiah, West, and Gates, only Gates was deeply influenced by deconstruction. West came more out of Marxism, the black church, and American pragmatism, whereas Appiah's philosophical influences were much more British (analytic) than continental (speculative). Nonetheless, the climate in which the three men functioned and flourished was one enabled by theory. The sense of an interdisciplinary project that was at once idealistic and specific, abstract and political was liberated from an overly polemical or utilitarian identity by deconstruction's sense of instability and plurality. This is different from saying that the three thinkers' philosophy of non-ethnocentrism and cosmopolitanism came from deconstruction. Such an outlook could have come from any of the other sources delineated previously. But the fact that this non-ethnocentrism did not congeal into an ideology just as constraining as ethnocentrism (in this case, Afrocentrism) was partially attributable to the deconstructive influence measurable in Gates's work and present, at least implicitly, in the approaches of the other two scholars.

This popularization of Gates's scholarship again came with a cost. Gates's work of the 1990s and after is unquestionably less interesting than his work of the 1980s. *Thirteen Ways of Looking at a Black Man*, his book profiles from *The New Yorker* on figures ranging from the military and political figure Colin Powell to the singer and activist Harry Belafonte, was a skilled example of its genre. Its second chapter did much to promote the reputation of novelist and essayist Albert Murray, who was (along with Ellison) one of the first to contend that African Americans are, in a way, the most "representative" Americans. Gates did a good job on the *Encyclopedia Africana* originally dreamed of by Du Bois (and, of course, more necessary when Du Bois dreamed of it) and on the television documentary *Wonders of the African World*. But others would have done nearly as good a job as Gates, whereas only Gates could write books of not only the calibre but also the particular intellectual and personal synthesis of his 1980s work, such as *The Signifying Monkey* and *Figures in Black* or even the essay on Albert Murray in *Thirteen Ways of Looking at a Black Man*. This is different, though, from criticizing Gates merely for being famous and successful; and he received a lot of criticism on this score. This criticism points to one of the elements in the reaction against theory as a whole: part of this reaction was simply vocational sour grapes, resentment against the theory star not for being a theorist but for being a star.[31] But Gates's public prominence was part of a broadening of African American discourse in the 1990s, one that included Oprah Winfrey's TV book club, which, for the first time, brought Morrison's work to a mass audience, as well as the emergence of a middle-class black female constituency for the work of Terry McMillan and of a fledgling popular gay African American constituency epitomized by the extensive sales of the fiction of E. Lynn Harris (1955–2009).

What we have been calling "African American literature" did not confine itself to the territorial United States. In the nineteenth century, US-born thinkers Alexander Crummell and Edward W. Blyden were active in the African nation of Liberia, set up to repatriate freed American blacks. The Caribbean, too, had already made many contributions to African American literature, such as the poet and novelist Claude McKay. But its pre-eminent intellectual product in the pre-civil rights twentieth century was the Trinidadian C.L.R. James, whose reach was as polymathic as that of Du Bois (even encompassing writing superbly on the game of cricket) and who wrote even more discerningly on literature. In 1952, James produced the only serious work on Melville in the 1930–70 period that did not adhere to the "myth-and-symbol" paradigm favoured in that era's American literature criticism. *Mariners, Renegades, and Castaways: The Story of Herman Melville and the World We Live In* also portended the more political tack taken by later Melville criticism without losing sight of the fact that the contradictions of Melville's writing are essentially literary ones. James's *The Black Jacobins* (1938) told the story of Toussaint L'Ouverture's slave rebellion in Haiti of the 1790s, which had set up the world's first African-ruled modern state. Though sidelined in the United States by America's highly Eurocentric Marxist tradition, this text surged back into prominence in the 1980s. After 1945, though, Caribbean literary activity outside the West Indies became centred in Britain and fell largely under the rubric of post-colonial criticism. Two exceptions substantially affecting black American discourses are Stuart Hall and Paul Gilroy. Hall, born in Jamaica and influential in founding the Birmingham School of cultural studies in Britain, became well known in America as a leading practitioner of cultural studies. This was even though his form of criticism was very specific to British institutions. It called upon a particular tradition of dissenting British cultural criticism whose only widely known representative in the United States was Leavis, although Raymond Williams became appreciated in America near the end of his life partially due to the advocacy of Hall and Edward Said.

Hall linked critical analysis with socio-cultural phenomena in ways later emulated by North American cultural studies, although the latter had a very different social and academic context. Paul Gilroy, of partially Guyanese ancestry, pioneered the idea of the "Black Atlantic" in his 1993 book of that name. Even before that, though, he had, in the memorably titled 1987 *There Ain't No Black in the Union Jack*, pointed out that, although semi-official British identity presumed a white, European country, Britain, in reality, had grown increasingly multicultural. In the past, those outside the United States had seen race as "only" an American problem or one confined to countries such as South Africa or (Rhodesia) Zimbabwe, which were ruled by white minorities at the time. After the work of Gilroy and of scholars in other nations with similar projects, such as the "Africadian" poet and critic George Elliott Clarke in Canada, the idea of race itself circulated outside national boundaries. This was what the "Black Atlantic" meant, not just the vile "middle passage" across which slaves were hauled from Africa to the Americas but the circulation of ideas, practices, and, as Gates might put it, modes of signification across and around the Atlantic— with everything touched by cultural idioms associated with those of African descent in Africa, the Americas, and even in Britain and other parts of Europe. After Gilroy, "Atlantic" became a critical concept.[32] Historically, the Pacific had been the interesting ocean. The term "Pacific" indicated the many island peoples in the middle of that ocean as well as the Asian-European encounter converging from the rims. The Pacific had always seemed multicultural; the Atlantic had either seemed empty or had pertained to North American-European diplomatic relations; in other words, the meaning of "the Atlantic" was restricted not just to the North Atlantic but to the *white* North Atlantic. It must be remembered that most people heard this phrase only in the context "North Atlantic Treaty Organization," the alliance formed in 1949 specifically to oppose the Soviets. Gilroy's approach coloured in the Atlantic and made it interesting, not just a blank or white space.

The term "Black Atlantic" followed very much upon the term "African American," not just chronologically but conceptually. Africa informed the conception, in both cases, but it was an Africa in transit, dispersed, and productively interlocking with other discourses. In his subsequent work, Gilroy came nearer to advocating a post-racial approach than any other prominent theorist of the African diaspora. In *Against Race* (2000), Gilroy sharply criticized essentialist theories of race that were, in his view, no longer enabling, if they ever had been. This book was received differently in the United States than it was in Britain. In the United Kingdom, it was generally seen as helping enable integration by tearing down ossified discourses of race. In the United States, it was, both for good and ill, seen as an abandonment of the claims to a substantive black identity that had been so prominent among both activists and academics in the post-civil rights era. And this perceived abandonment resonated all the more loudly because of the sentiment that the turn of the millennium had seen the resurgence of conformism and an acceptance of a neoliberal, capitalist ideology (see the discussion of Hardt and Negri in Chapter 5). Cornel West firmly dissented from Gilroy's and other analogous views by maintaining that "race mattered." Even though race as a concrete biological identity was a fiction, because people had been wounded and traumatized in the name of race and had formed, in counterpoise, affirmative identities that endowed racial belonging with positive attributes, society should not be so anxious to dispose of race, as a category, entirely and precipitously. Yet West did not see race as an eternal substantive that would endure throughout all forthcoming history. For West, race *should* end. The question for him was whether it currently *could* end.

Asia, America, and Anti-Racist Discourse

In this era, discussions of race also widened beyond the categories of "black and white." Other minorities in the United States and worldwide had, by this time, articulately engaged in academic literary discourse. Still, even in the late 1990s, the mandate of President Bill Clinton's important Commission on Race, headed by the aforementioned John Hope Franklin, was restricted early on to African American questions. Nevertheless, anti-racist discourse was broadening to include the voices of various groups who had faced prejudice. Asian Americans had experienced a particularly paradoxical racial history. They were discriminated against far more than was any other immigrant group. The effort to exclude or limit Chinese and Japanese immigration to the West Coast in the early 1900s, even though Asian labour was crucial in setting up the mines, railroads, and businesses that enabled this region to prosper, was a prodigious one and unfortunately consumed much of the region's intellectual energy. Later in the century, Asian Americans became seen by whites as "the model minority," one that was hard-working and self-effacing rather than angry or recriminative, which many whites perceived African Americans and Latinos as being. Unlike

African Americans, who, wherever their ancestors were from, became one over-all group in the United States, Chinese Americans and Japanese Americans did not simply melt into each other; there was an irreducible heterogeneity between them. Indeed, at least until the middle of the twentieth century, the prejudice against Japanese people was not so strong as that against the Chinese, who were often described as "coolies." This anti-Chinese prejudice caused different reactions in two Eurasian sisters who immigrated to Canada in the 1870s: Edith and Winnifred Eaton. Edith assumed the Chinese name Sui Sin Far, moved to Los Angeles, and gained fame by writing articles and stories critical of the racist treatment of Chinese Americans. Winnifred, perhaps to take advantage of the era's interest in "Japonica"—think *Madame Butterfly*—adopted the Japanese pen name Onoto Watanna and wrote narratives with elements of the romantic and exotic. The most important point of this story: the adoption of these two different racial identities by sisters points out that, in some ways, race is a fic-tion, a performance—it is what people want it to be.

Concepts of race are also frequently formed in association with assessments of various nations or continents. The different degrees of prejudice experienced by Japanese and Chinese Americans, for example, can be traced to historical valuations of their two countries of origin. As late nineteenth- and early twenti-eth-century racial attitudes among whites were being formed, China and Japan were in very different positions. Japan was a rising power and became, in 1905, the first Asian power to defeat a European power, Russia, in a contest of roughly equal militaries. China, on the other hand, was an empire approaching its final collapse, and exploited by European powers. And it had sent many more of its people as economic immigrants to the United States than had Japan.

During this period, Japan took over Korea (an event whose repercussions are chronicled in perhaps the most experimental Asian American literary work, Theresa Hak Kyung Cha's *Dictée*). This forced occupation was very much in the same spirit as that of the European countries' colonization of Africa, and it was because of Japanese imperial expansionism that Japan became an hon-ourary European power. Korea remained under harsh Japanese rule from 1910 to 1945. In the 1930s, however, once Japanese power and immigration were perceived as threatening, attitudes in the United States shifted somewhat. In 1937, Japan invaded China, which, at that time, was not expansionist and was riven by internal strife. In some quarters, China was idealized if faintly patron-ized, especially by an American missionary tradition that produced such white-written works, totally set in China, as Pearl S. Buck's *The Good Earth* (1931). When Japan attacked Pearl Harbor in 1941, Chinese Americans celebrated in the streets, as the United States was now at war with China's enemy, Japan. This enmity between two peoples grouped together as Asians was a far cry from the views of Zora Neale Hurston, who, in her 1940 autobiography *Dust Tracks on a Road*, had some good things to say about the Japanese as a non-white power. There was little Chinese American protest about the unjustified internment of

Japanese Americans in twelve camps in the western and southern United States, which transpired while other Japanese Americans from Hawaii were fighting valiantly on the European front for the United States in World War II. The internment experience was memorialized in the poetry of Janice Mirikitani, herself a child in two of the camps, as well as in Jeanne Wakatsuki Houston's cowritten *Farewell to Manzanar* (1972), set in one of the most populated camps in eastern California.

Later incarnations of heterogeneity occurred. In the years after 1945, when China became, under the Communist Party, first an ideological and then an economic and military competitor of the United States and postwar Japan renounced its military aspirations and became an economic powerhouse, the valences again changed.[33] The overall point is that, although "Asian Americans" experienced a shared history of discrimination in the United States, the nature and severity of this discrimination varied as a consequence of the very different national histories of China and Japan generating different Euro-American responses. Also, Chinese and Japanese people defined themselves as distinct. Despite these differences, an Asian American literary movement emerged in the early 1970s, with activists such as Frank Chin spurring awareness of the heritage of the various immigrant communities. Earlier Asian American literature was rediscovered, and it was found that the great American road novel, usually ascribed to Jack Kerouac or Vladimir Nabokov, might well have been published in 1932 in the form of Filipino writer Carlos Bulosan's *America Is in the Heart*. This rescue work was followed quickly by the pivotal research and criticism of such academics as Stan Yogi, Sau-Ling Cynthia Wong, and Elaine Kim. Asian American writing was quickly represented in English departments, and a thriving field of conferences and journals began to percolate, as had happened on a larger scale with African American studies slightly earlier.

Two tragic murders in 1982 illuminated the dual challenges of Asian Americanist critical work. In November of that year, Chinese American Vincent Chin was mistaken for Japanese and murdered by Michigan whites who held Japan accountable for the decline in auto-industry employment. That same year, Theresa Hak Kyung Cha, a young Korean American conceptual artist and writer, was randomly murdered in New York City. Cha's experimental prose piece *Dictée* (1982) is a consciously difficult work, with multiple, competing structures: for instance, the European frame of the nine Muses organizes the text, yet this frame is also subverted and shattered by the text. The title of *Dictée* comes from the idea of directed dictation letters in French, assigned as academic exercises, and Korea was indeed proselytized by French Roman Catholic missionaries in the later nineteenth century. But this technique of dictation becomes emblematic of other compulsions—those perpetrated by the imperial Japanese over the colonized Koreans, by Americans over Asians, and by men over women. Cha's subtle collage comes, for all its experimental trappings, surprisingly close to being a testimony to lives that were consumed by racism and misunderstanding, lives such as Chin's.

Native American Literature and Literary Theory

Native American discourse, like that of Asian Americans, called attention to the existence of Native American literatures and of criticism about these literatures and called for advocacy of and insight into these newly recognized traditions. Yet writers and scholars of Native American literature were also attendant to the ironies and complexities of their context and highly self-conscious about their mode of articulation. This introspection was evident among others whose literature and literary scholarship was, in part, a response to racism. Asian Americanists, for instance, worried in the early 2000s that the tone of their discipline had become too "elegiac" and had fallen into a prefabricated mould that, in lamenting discrimination, downplayed possibilities for transformation and empowerment.[34] It is important, though, to distinguish modern Native American writing and criticism from collections of and scholarship about the traditional tales and religious narratives of Native peoples. Ever since the aborted efforts of the Cherokee in the early 1800s to participate fully in Western society on equal terms while retaining a sense of their own traditions, Native Americans have struggled against being seen as "other," as hopelessly quaint or primitive peoples to be either memorialized, exterminated, or subjected to a rhetorical combination of both strategies. And even some of the well-intentioned Europeans or Euro-Americans who initially recorded Native American narratives not only viewed Native people as "other" but also wrote down their stories with an Anglo-American audience in mind. Expanding English literacy among Native peoples changed this situation. The emergence of a group of talented novelists and poets of Native American background who wrote in English could not have occurred without the efforts of people such as Ned Hatathli, the mid-twentieth-century Navajo educator who worked tirelessly to disseminate English-language literacy and an awareness of the importance of learning. Such efforts had been occurring, as they were permitted, since the beginning of colonization. Indeed, the warfare and religious conversion attempts that accompanied colonization often necessitated the spread of European languages among Native peoples, who learned early on to write letters of negotiation in French or English, for example. Native American writers expressed themselves in writing from nearly the beginning of cultural contact, with earlier writers, such as Samson Occom and William Apess, often having religious motivations. Between the nineteenth century, and its effective quelling of any Native resistance, and the late twentieth century, and its renewed interest in Native empowerment, an obdurate trickle of writers helped to keep the idea of Native expression alive: Zitkala-Sa (Gertrude Simmons Bonnin), Mourning Dove (Christal Quintasket) and D'Arcy McNickle. These writers were from the northern part of the United States; an earlier focus on the southwest would have oriented Native American literature more towards a Latin American model in which settler and indigenous interests were more aligned, as opposed to a North American model in which they were inherently oppositional.

In the wake of the civil rights movement, American Indian writing became more overtly political and made a far greater impact on mainstream readership. As always in literary history, unusual connections manifested themselves. N. Scott Momaday, who was the first Native American writer to win the Pulitzer Prize with *House Made of Dawn* (1968), had been a student of Yvor Winters's at Stanford, and his poetry (though not his fiction) adhered to Winters's severe formalism. Winters, in turn, had been an advocate of indigenous rights, perhaps the only "liberal" aspect of his public temperament. This comingling of traditional values and Native American advocacy was actually not unusual, as the indigenous presence could, in the same gesture, be acknowledged and fetishized, whereas coming to terms with African American, Asian American, and Latino identities entailed confronting the stark realities of subordination and white privilege in a way that disrupted a tidy metanarrative of colonization and progress, even one in which regret for the mistreatment of the Native people could be articulated.[35] It was the need to dispel the inevitably patronizing air of any unitary characterization of "natives" or "Indians" that led the Anishinabe (in other words, "Chippewa") writer Gerald Vizenor, an influential theorist as well as a creative writer, to propose that indigenous individuals be described first as members of their immediate people rather than as members of the category "Indian." This term, he argued, was historically defined only by resistance to European invasion, and, discursively, it tended to be susceptible of being fossilized into an "otherness." Australian Aboriginal activists paralleled Vizenor's ideas, in that, in the wake of the 1992 *Mabo* High Court decision acknowledging indigenous land rights, one saw Aboriginal writers refer to themselves in the first instance as Koori, Wiradjuri, or Yorta Yorta, for example. This practice involved both an articulation and a deconstruction of identity, and its fostering of difference and supplementarity showed how deconstructive practices could inform immediate matters such as the national and cultural identity of peoples historically dispossessed.

Mestizaje and Latino/a Criticism

If the Native American experience was often commoditized by the literary mainstream and the African American experience, which was perceived as central in fields such as popular music, was acknowledged in literature but, until the civil rights era, insufficiently articulated by it, the US Latino experience was often not even acknowledged as something at all germane to literary analysis. The racism faced by Latino writers and critics in the United States came from a slightly different source than the racism facing Native Americans, Asian Americans, and African Americans. For these three groups, the issue was colour, accompanied by a history of subordination and exploitation; in the case of Latinos, it was language. Canada early on in its history faced the fact that it was a bilingual country, even if bilingualism entailed, until the 1970s, a patronizing relegation of the francophone to second rank. Yet the United States, even though its Constitution carefully did not specify an official language, made no attempt to acknowledge the linguistic practices of the French- and Spanish-speaking people living in the territories it annexed or, in the case of the present-day American southwest, conquered (in the US-Mexican War of the late 1840s). When, in the twentieth century, large-scale immigration occurred, all immigrants were encouraged to learn and speak English. The flourishing of Spanish as a second language in the United States, to the point that, in the early 2000s, the United States was nearly as much an unofficially bilingual country as Canada or New Zealand were officially so, presented particular issues to *English* departments. Moreover, not only were there racial prejudices operative from New World history but also cultural and religious ones stemming from the Old World. The national pride of England was intimately associated with the built-in ideology of English literature. Often, the English department, was associated with opposition to Catholic Europe and, particularly, to Spain. The golden years of Elizabethan England, the time of the early work of Shakespeare, coincided with the defeat of the Spanish Armada and the Catholicism and authoritarianism it was thought to portend. The *leyenda negra* or "black legend" characterizing Spanish rule (and inferentially culture) in the Americas as cruel and unenlightened had its roots in these prejudices and stemmed from internecine European disputes as much as from any actual experience in the Americas, notwithstanding the very different political histories of Anglo-America and Latin America.

Yet American authors, from Washington Irving to Ernest Hemingway, have expressed positive sentiment towards Spain and the Spanish. US writers such as Richard Henry Dana, Jr. and Maria Gowen Brooks had considerable interaction with the Spanish-speaking parts of the Americas that were, at the time, beyond US sway. Many isolationists, those who wanted no traffic with Europe, urged the United States to seek its destiny in conjunction with Latin America, in a way that was not necessarily imperialistic but that did ally with the values of its own hemisphere. But these were always a minority when compared to the Eurocentric sophisticates of the East Coast. Some prominent American writers did evince respect for Latin America, however. William F. Buckley, Jr. (1925–2008), the US conservative commentator, made a point of stressing the history of his family's involvement with Mexico and of linking his own Roman Catholicism to the Catholicism of much of Latin America. (By then, being a Catholic was acceptably "conservative" in the English-speaking world in a way it had not been from 1580 to 1930 or so.) And, when the peoples south of the Rio Grande were not seen as racial others, they could even emerge as true-blue Americans. The strange 1966 film *Alvarez Kelly* features a Mexican Irishmen who eventually fights for the South in the Civil War, a choice pictured more or less affirmatively even though it involves not just fighting for racism that would have discriminated against many Mexicans but fighting, in effect, against the United States. No more than three or four years later, this movie would have been impossible to make, as Latino and African American interests, in the wake of the civil rights movement, had become closely identified in the quest for a more multicultural America. To think that Derrida was making his first American appearance, in the once-slaveholding state of Maryland, the year *Alvarez Kelly* was released is to see how staggering the changes heralded and mirrored by theory truly were. It is also to re-encounter the Foucauldian truth that so many discourses can be alive at one time and yet be contained by that time.

Thus, there is a clear connection between the status of Latinos as a minority within the United States and discourse about the Americas as a whole, one that gets very close to what is commonly called post-colonialism. Again, the "Treaty of Tordesillas" analogy comes in handy here. The reason the Latino material is in this chapter and the anglophone post-colonial material is in the next has to do with traditions of the US academy and not with any gigantic difference in the underlying material. One striking difference, though, is the role of the indigenous in Latino criticiom. Whereas, as we shall see in the next chapter, anglophone indigenous writers (in other words, the Maori, Aborigines, and Native North Americans) have tended to shy away from post-colonial labels because they occlude the historical reality of the indigenous people's prior tenancy of the land, *indigenista* discourses in Latin America have been permeated, though not entirely suffused, by ideas of mixture and heterogeneity.

Most Latin Americans are *mestizos*, descendants of both Europeans and indigenous American peoples. Latin American critics have tended to celebrate this *mestizaje*, or mixture, rather than seeing it as embodying a tragic conflict (as can be seen even in Canada with the *Métis* leader Louis Riel, whose championship of both indigenous and French speaking rights in Manitoba was deemed off the main path of Canadian national development by the ruling Anglo elite.) *Mestizaje* is not automatically liberating in Latin American terms. *Mestizaje* has not eliminated racial prejudice, but historical demographic differences between Latin America and North America led to a different valuation in each culture of those who had mixed blood. The majority of Latin Americans are partially or entirely of indigenous descent (other than in Argentina, although even there the *gaucho* legend, as well as later immigration from Europe and other parts of the world, fostered cultural mixture). Thus to be *mestizo* is to be privileged, as it means one has *some* European "blood." Unlike people constrained by the "one-drop" rule in the United States, which denoted as non-white anyone with even a little non-white ancestry, Latin Americans could be *mestizo* and still part of the elite. *Mestizaje* has become the virtual national ideology of many South American states. Yet the celebration of *mestizaje* among twentieth-century Latin American critics presaged an emancipatory and socially minded agenda that tallied with anti-racist discourses in North America. Whereas, for North American critics, a multiracial conception of literature was a breakthrough possible only after decades of cultural shifts and canonical re-engineering, for Latin American critics, it was simply the given assumption of their practice and outlook.

This was not always true. Nineteenth-century Latin American cultural figures often were highly European in perspective. The Uruguayan writer José Enrique Rodó, in his 1900 treatise *Ariel*, formulated ideas of Latin Americans as the superior Ariel as opposed to the soulless Calibans of the United States. This analogy from Shakespeare's *Tempest* was exactly reversed by the more recent, and more typical, post-colonial claim to Caliban as the subjugated and exploited victim, as opposed to Ariel, the cocky and sprightly intellectual. (For instance, the Cuban thinker— and close associate of Fidel Castro—Roberto Fernández Retamar employed Caliban in just this way.) It is important to note that Rodó's belletrism had a political twist, as his stress on aesthetics distinguished Latinos from North American imperialists; gunboat belletrism, as it were, confronted gunboat diplomacy. Some Latin American writers, however, called for literary appraisals that were less nationalistic. The Cuban poet and visionary José Marti, in the hortatory 1892 text "Our America," urges Latin Americans to cast off both a nostalgic cringe towards Europe and the disdain and disregard of their great northern neighbour, and he calls for a surge not only in political awareness but in creativity. Like Rodó, Marti valued the imagination, but he saw it as actively political rather than political by implication. Rodó's purist ideals were also mirrored and subverted by the Mexican José Vasconcelos's far-out spectres of a "cosmic race," one more in touch, partially due to its indigenous heritage, with primal forces of energy than the soulless shopkeepers to the north.[36] But Vasconcelos saw all peoples as being able to attain cosmic awareness, and, indeed, his vision of a state being at once modernist, populist, and enlightened is what a lot of European and North American modernist intellectuals were striving for less systematically when they tried to join quantum physics with avant-garde aesthetic attitudes. Vasconcelos's prodigious reach and flagrant eccentricity should not gainsay his achievement, which continues to influence many thinkers across the Americas, those belonging to various schools and persuasions of thought. (Vasconcelos's ideas were later refined by the work that Argentine Néstor García Canclini did on hybridity; García Canclini formulated the model in far more concrete and material terms.)

Rodó was a perfectionist; Vasconcelos a prophet. But, in both cases, it was attitude, not descent, which mattered. In that way, both Vasconcelos and Rodó were closer to the United States ideal of "the melting pot" than they would have cared to admit. Although *indigenista* writers such as José Maria Arguedas made more substantive claims for the uniqueness of local indigenous identities, their work does not exclude anyone who lives in Latin America from necessarily participating in their discourses. This inclusivity is, no doubt, an effect of how much of the population of the region (excluding Argentina) identifies itself as at least partially indigenous in descent. With numbers comes confidence, as well as a tendency towards synthesis and amalgamation rather than the preservation of a distinctly indigenous as opposed to European culture. As Juan E. De Castro has recently reiterated, the very term "Latin America" has an ideological valence.[37] In the spirit of Rodó's Ariel-Caliban dichotomy, the term "Latin America" signifies both a European and a New World grounding. "Latin" is associated with the Spanish- and Portuguese-speaking countries of the Western hemisphere and with France, as all Romance languages descended from Latin. France, as the unofficial seat of what Pascale Casanova has called "the world republic of letters" and as the then-dominant antagonist of Anglo-American pragmatism, represented a kind of aesthetic purity unsoiled by commercial ambition.[38] Rodó and *modernista* poets such as the Nicaraguan Ruben Dario (who supplied Rodó with the Ariel-Caliban trope) were formalists whose aesthetic theories were not too far away from those later espoused by the New Critics, although their thinking was far more imaginative and less "resolved" in nature. (Dario was also actively interested in politics.) They reaffirmed the idea that intellectuals constitute what Coleridge called a "clerisy" whose function was at once to instruct the masses and remain aloof from them.

The Peruvian José Carlos Mariátegui was a very different kind of figure. Committed to the indigenous identity of Latin America—as seen in the title of his most famous book, the 1928 *Seven Interpretive Essays on Peruvian Reality*—he was interested, however, in modern phenomena as disparate as Joyce and Charlie Chaplin. The "interpretive" aspect of Mariátegui's work has been honoured worldwide far less than his attention to "reality." To an extent that scholars outside Latin American studies have not recognized, Mariátegui was an intellectual of world stature who did not exclude regarding the world from his articulation of a renewed *mestizo* consciousness.[39] Much like his contemporary (and eventual adversary), the visionary Peruvian politician Victor Raúl Haya de la Torre, Mariátegui's potentially pan-American vision would have had powerful echoes had it been properly appreciated by *norteamericanos*. José Maria Arguedas, a Peruvian of the next generation after Mariátegui, seems a more narrowly *indigenista* figure, but his work was neither "parochial" nor "ethnocentric." Arguedas wrote within the norms of the Western novel, and he saw the local struggle for identity as emblematic of a worldwide hope of liberation. Arguedas's goal was to seize the language and culture of the colonizer for his own indigenous identity, and this project involved negotiating both spheres not just rejecting one for the other, although (commendably) it did not involve assigning equal virtue to both spheres. Works such as Arguedas's *Yawar Fiesta* (1941) certainly took the Derridean side in terms of conceding the infiltration of speech by writing, whereas Ecuadorian novelist Jorge Icaza, in *Huasipungo* (1934), took an even more overtly avant-garde tack that still remained *indigenista*.

The Uruguayan Ángel Rama, on the face of it, seems to be the opposite of these indigenist thinkers. Urbane and cosmopolitan, he was the Latin American equivalent of perhaps an Erich Auerbach or a George Steiner. His signature concept of "the lettered city" was both a descriptive label and an imaginative ideal, pointing out the largely urban nature of the Latin American intelligentsia as well as aspiring to a realm where literature was accessible to all citizens and all citizens potentially had or could have literary aptitude. Indeed, Rama's idea came close to the concept of the "public sphere" made famous by Habermas; both were notions of civil society based on an elevated common discourse, which could yet encourage creativity.[40] Rama had a much darker vision of the public sphere than Habermas. As the Uruguayan critic pointed out, "the lettered city" was initially planned by the Spanish colonizers to structure the intellectual life of their realm in a mode compliant to themselves, and it only later became a plausible structure for free and humane thought. But Rama was not another Rodó. Urban life meant give and take, political dissent, progressive thinking, and an embrace of the plurality of the continent. Rama, indeed, was crucially influenced by the thought of Arguedas, who was stereotypically seen as a more "parochial" thinker and writer. Rama's final major work published in his lifetime, *Transculturación narrativa en América Latina* (1982) was, in many ways, a reading of Arguedas's texts. As seen in the title of this book, Rama expanded upon a term, "transculturation," first used by the Cuban Fernando Ortiz.

Ortiz, who was of substantially African descent, introduced the term "transculturation" to define how elements of one culture were inherited, appropriated, and transformed by another. This idea parallels Homi Bhabha's theories of mimicry, to be discussed in the next chapter.[41] It must be remembered that Ortiz was writing when cultural relativism, derived from anthropology, was granting each culture its own autonomy but was also seeing cultures as unified and somewhat distant from each other. For instance, Oscar Lewis's empathetic portraits of Mexican peasant life had an unintentional but discernible patronizing air to them.[42] Ortiz's transcultural model premised itself on the exchangeability and potential cross-fertilization of elements from different cultures. Cultural cross-influence not only attended or enabled creativity but also constituted it.[43] As Silvia Spitta has pointed out, transculturation is a potentially endless process—and endlessly disruptive of many constituted norms. This mobile yet enduring process can constitute a powerful critique of encrusted absolutes and previously unquestioned norms. But, as Spitta implies, it can also unfold into a hollow celebration of a jolly, everything-under-the-Christmas-tree multiculturalism that attempts to smooth out all contradictions even as, rhetorically, it hails an all-encompassing pluralism. We are back to Derrida's idea of *différance*, and we need to remember that it was not just an inverted Hegelian synthesis—*différance* embodies not just mediation but plurality.

Borderlands

The Peruvian critic Antonio Cornejo Polar's ideas of heterogeneity may seem to resemble Ortiz's "transcultural" model superficially. But, in fact, these ideas introduced another dimension into the discourse of *mestizaje*. So far, the construction of *mestizaje* that we have discussed has emphasized the affirmative side of mixture, the way it gives us two (or more) for the price of one. But Cornejo called attention to the friction involved in heterogeneity, to the idea that the various included discourses could contradict one another and that contradiction could be fruitful, rather than worrisome, without necessarily leading to a triumphant coalescence. Cornejo's heterogeneity has also been compared to Bakhtin's idea of the multitracked nature of our perceptual categories, as displayed in literary thought, in combining not just different ethnic discourses but different levels of space and time. Like Vasconcelos, Cornejo sees *mestizaje* as not just a new mode of ethnicity but a new ontology, although Cornejo, like Bakhtin, is fundamentally critical rather than idealistic even as he admits—as Derrida perhaps would not—the idea of levels of being in his discourse. Unlike Vasconcelos, Cornejo did not seek to found a new ideology on the basis of his idea of heterogeneity, nor did he see it as leading to a higher and more evolved consciousness. Rather, he saw heterogeneity as democratic, as opening up the gates to previously underrepresented voices. Cornejo, like many other politically minded critics of his generation, did not take deconstruction seriously, and his work should not be deployed as the portal to theoretical carnival or license. Yet, as Estelle Tarica has pointed out, the common, garden-variety idea of North American multiculturalism—of giving play to different voices in a way that did not relinquish literary sophistication—has its nearest (and far more theoretically formulated) equivalent in Cornejo's work.[44]

It is notable that so many of the South American theorists of *mestizaje* are Andean, from a region with an inescapable demographic reminder of the continent's indigenous background; more Europeanized nations such as Argentina, though of enormous artistic and intellectual achievement, have contributed less to this discourse. Similarly, the Caribbean was prominent in this area, and theorists of *mestizaje* include Cubans such as Marti, Fernández Retamar, and Ortiz, as well as Dominicans such as Pedro Henríquez Ureña (whose analysis of spoken language in the Western hemisphere mirrored what the other theorists were doing with literature). This focus is natural enough given the inherent transculturation of the Caribbean; even though the indigenous heritage had been largely effaced there, a heavy African influence pushed interracial discourses to the foreground.

The case of Brazil is interesting in this respect.[45] Brazilian history and society parallels that of the United States more than that of most other Latin American countries, with its importation of slaves from Africa, its early post-independence sense of itself as a world power, and its geographical size and diversity.

However, Brazil, of all the countries that have made a serious contribution to literary and cultural theory, has, unfortunately, remained outside the North American purview. (Some Spanish-speaking Latin Americans, in turn, felt that Brazilian thinkers did not take their countries' intellectual life seriously enough.) A smattering of North American intellectuals, admittedly, would, somewhat hyperbolically, privilege Brazilian or Portuguese-speaking writers over Latino or Spanish-speaking ones; this was especially true in New England because of its relatively large Portuguese-speaking population and the presence of so many prestigious colleges employing influential thinkers in that region. The influence of the radical pedagogy of Paulo Freire on many politically minded US teachers was a broader manifestation of US-Brazilian dialogue, which, unfortunately, did not proliferate too extensively beyond this lone example. Not only did Brazil produce Antonio Candido's disciplined and literarily sensitive Marxism, it also, in the work of J.G. Merquior (1941–91), produced one of the first and most insightful analyses of Foucault. Merquior may well have achieved world fame if not for his premature death, although many discerned that the later Merquior, like Foucault, was taking a rightward political turn. Roberto Schwarz's work, in many ways, represents the course that criticism in North America might have taken if Foucault and Derrida had not influenced the North American academy so much. Schwarz (for whom issues of race and ethnicity were not a major concern, despite his Brazilian location) pursued a more politically tinged and overtly radical trajectory that was influenced by Marx and the Frankfurt School but that was not haunted by irony and rupture, unlike de Manian deconstruction. Many in North America would have welcomed the alternative. Yet, in a way, what made deconstruction in the United States so radical is that it attracted the ire of both the Right and the Left.

Marxism provided a ready-made context within which intellectuals such as Schwarz could mix the indigenous and the European. But the mixture made within this context tends to privilege the European, or at least to separate the two as uneasy allies, in ways that fundamentally do not solve the problems of racism. The ideas of *mestizaje* that most influenced North American thought were those that did not have a Marxist backbone or rationale. Later thinkers such as Gloria Anzaldúa were much more politically radical than Rodó and the *modernistas*, and saw literature far more as a form of political protest. In rejecting attitudes like Rodó's as precious and elitist, they were, in fact, espousing values very close to those of the general culture of the United States. Indeed, Latino criticism in the United States injected a needed dose of populism into the intellectual discourse of the country. Unlike Europe-influenced criticism, which had the same aesthetic selectivity as urged by Rodó, or even African American criticism, which was often influenced by the idea of a "talented tenth," (the percentage of the black community that Du Bois had said would lead the rest by the example of their intellect and creativity), Latino criticism emphasized the voice of the people. As Jimmy Santiago Baca said in one of his *Black Mesa Poems*,

> There would be no tomorrow,
> no mountains, no *llano*,
> no me,
> and my drum softened, its speech to whisper
> sleeping to the shores,
> singing us all together.
> I heard rattling branches
> crackle
> as thousands of *la gente* pushed through the bosque
> lining the Rio Grande shore.[46]

The identification of the poet with the collective here is the opposite of the modernist defensiveness, which saw poets immuring themselves in high castles and abandoned towers. In a North American humanities academy that was often snobbish and filled with the legacy of various past cultural elitisms, the insistence of Latin American writers and critics that all the people have something to contribute in terms of imagination and the cultural or critical project is a welcome one. For all the vulgarity of reductive Marxist characterizations of literature as an elite activity, too many intellectuals have acted as if this were, in fact, so. This was why the accessibility of Anzaldúa's voice was so important; her voice was the Latina version of what Wordsworth called "A man speaking to men." Anzaldúa's criticism made little separation between literature and lived experience. If she shared Vasconcelos's conception of mixed-race Americans representing a new kind of hybrid identity, she did so without the Mexican writer's utopianism and messianism. Sometimes, characterizations of this mixed-race, Latin American identity were so fervent as to denigrate excluded cultures. In his meditation *The Bow and the Lyre*, the Nobel Prize-winning Mexican poet Octavio Paz dismisses the cultural achievements of the indigenous peoples north of the Rio Grande.[47] Does providing an alternative to Eurocentric models of Latin America require slamming the Apache or Navajo? This question raises a difference between Latino criticism practised within Latin America and that practised within the United States, a difference as important as that which political borders mandate. Anzaldúa and her US Latino and Latina peers had to do without the monumentality of their southern counterparts' references to past Aztec and Inca grandeur, a looking back that was not that far in mode from Europeans hankering for the glories of ancient Greece. Remember that, for the West, this classical heritage was one of the primary guarantors of what Derrida labelled the logocentric metaphysics of presence.

Anzaldúa's *mestizaje*, however, did not need an exalted pedigree; it was the discourse of the proletarian, the ordinary, and the mundane. For this reason, it included women's and queer subjectivities far more than did the Anglo and South American examples already mentioned. It thus had the potential to add ideals of citizenship to the sense of empowerment that the previous discourse of *mestizaje* proposed. Anzaldúa's criticism was human in scale. It had a down-to-earth quality that was refreshing. Anzaldúa rejected any kind of racial purity. Her major concept—"the borderlands/*la frontera*"—was based literally on the US-Mexican border. Rather than seeing this border as a fixed demarcation, she saw it is a liminal threshold that allowed people and energies to permeate both sides of it. Given that Spanish-speaking people had lived in some US states, such as New Mexico, as long as or longer than any English speakers had lived anywhere near the borderland, the encounter of the Spanish and the Anglo is not one between the old versus the new. This paradox is compounded by the attendant ironies of medical care often being better (or at least more affordable) on the Mexican side and of the Mexican states bordering the United States often being, in demographic terms, the "whitest" in Mexico while the states of the American southwest are among the least "white" in the United States. Yet the character of the population and the rhythms of daily life on each side are growing increasingly convergent. It is not just the juxtaposition or mutual infiltration of identities, however, that is at the heart of borderlands theory; the paradoxes and contradictions of these interrelationships are also central. Borderlands theory contends that these contradictions pose a direct challenge to the unitary models of identity on which both traditional and revisionary models of ethnicity and the nation are based.

Importantly, Anzaldúa's term was bilingual: "the borderlands/*la frontera*."[48] (Even this bilingualism, it could be argued, privileges English; a US Latino text, virtually by definition, must have at least some English in it, and, consequently, these texts are already sundered from the mainstream of intellectual discourse south of the Rio Grande, or, to give the river its Mexican name, the Rio Bravo.) Latino writing and criticism confronted, in a way other minority literatures did not, the US ideology of the "melting pot," which assumed that people of all sorts of background would come to the United States—and speak English there. Even less mainstream ideas of cultural interrelations, such as the post-colonial theories discussed in the next chapter, often assumed that English was the permanent language of world discourse, that it would be subverted, redefined, and transformed in various ways but that the intellectual commerce of literature would be transacted in one particular linguistic coin. The persistence of Spanish among the Latino community pointed to an irreducible plurality in the number of languages and introduced, or solicited, a kind of practical *différance*, a dislodging of any one form of language from anything more than a supplementary position. On the ground level, this linguistic supplementarity paralleled Derridean ideas of how languages would operate deconstructively.[49] (Even in their French versions, so many of Derrida's texts are, in practice, bilingual or multilingual.) Those interested in Anzaldúa's ideas often scorn Derrida as too theoretical; those interested in Derrida's thought see Anzaldúa as someone oriented solely towards a particular situation.

Anzaldúa's embrace of the ordinary was made possible by her simultaneous stress on queerness and heterogeneity. Theory could allow for and even sanction the ordinary if the ordinary was heterogeneous and heterolingual; witness "*la gente*" as used in Santiago Baca's poem sounding more apt, to a theoretical ear, than "people," which would have evoked memories of an outdated proletarian folk song of the 1930s. In such a way, Anzaldúa calls attention to how theory, for all its opacity and elitism, has the potential to open up new vistas on the everyday, a category that had been occluded since the critical heyday of Leavis's beloved George Eliot, who wrote sympathetically of the unheralded, those whose ambitions did not change the world. Anzaldúa's exploration of the everyday could also be seen as cognate to developments in French theory, which moved from Henri Lefebvre's Marxist-influenced documentation of the modern everyday as a forum for the objectification and degradation of human agency to Michel de Certeau's sketching of practices of resistance in the everyday, how individual play and contingent circumstances made tactical inroads into the purportedly hard-and-fast division Lefebvre's objectification rendered. Although French theorists from Lefebvre to de Certeau at once foregrounded and decentred the everyday, it was Bakhtin, with his stress on the vivifying and divided nature of the "prosaic" as opposed to the "poetic," who comes closest to Anzaldúa's vision of the mundane *mestizaje*. Bakhtin's sense of the body and of the release of social energies signalled by a multiplicity of discourses is trying to arrive at the same mixture of complexity, possibility, and canny acknowledgement of residual social limitations as appears in Anzaldúa's work. Foucault also called attention to how ordinary individuals can govern and can be governed, but, like Derrida (who was comparatively uninterested in the everyday), Foucault privileged the world of classical antiquity in his thought in a way fundamentally European.

Octavio Paz and José Carlos Mariátegui tried to proffer the Aztecs and Incas as American equivalents of the Greeks and Romans. (José Marti even labelled the Aztecs as the Greeks of the Western hemisphere.) But Anzaldúa has little to do with these monumental precedents, and neither does Bakhtin. We should not idealize this situation too much, however. Paul Allatson reminds us that seeing people like Anzaldúa as "exemplary subalterns" will blind us to how privileged anybody with the access and status of a writer nearly invariably must be.[50] Moreover, many inhabitants of the border, who, in either Catholic or Protestant terms, are traditional Christian believers, would find Anzaldúa's New Age beliefs difficult to take. Many of the theoretically inclined might join their pious counterparts in this scepticism, perhaps wishing that Anzaldúa had followed de Certeau and, rather than evoking positive and alternative realities, had seen tactical, everyday resistance as staged "from nowhere" and "on the enemy's ground."

Yet, despite its occasional verbal overload and conceptual flaccidity, there remains something genuinely challenging about Anzaldúa's model. Borderlands are not simply "coming to America." The concept is not a redo of the old-fashioned immigrant odyssey of assimilation. It is a permanent reciprocity, a deeply instilled mutual conversation between two sides of a border that is, at times, impermeable, at times, utterly actual. Gustavo Pérez Firmat's idea of "life on the hyphen," of what is in between in a term like "Hispanic-American," also explores the borderlands. This idea captures the sense of liminality (from *limen*, the Latin word for border) that values in-betweenness in itself and sees it as more than the product of a gap between two identities.[51] Pérez Firmat may even go further than Anzaldúa; heterogeneity is, for him, somewhat of a transitional phase, potentially to disappear completely after a few generations and become something even more fluid and indiscernible. Pérez Firmat's concept has the potential to take Latino discourse beyond binaries and synthesis, to make it attentive to third, fourth, and fifth presences. Other critics have been conscious of the languages and literatures beyond the "Latin" or the "American." Roberto Ignacio Diaz has written of the presence, real and suggested, of other languages—European languages other than Spanish—in the literature of Latin America. Ignacio López-Calvo has stressed Asian migrant literatures in Cuba and Peru, and Edna Aizenberg has studied the rich and comparatively neglected tradition of Jewish writing in Latin America.[52] Observers north of the Rio Grande make a mistake when they presume that the population mix of Latin America is what it was in, say, 1600, albeit multiplied by time and growth. The southern part of the hemisphere experienced immigration of a kind and scale in the late nineteenth and early twentieth centuries similar to that of the United States and Canada in that era. In some cases, these emigrant groups made far more of an impact on Latin American culture than they did on that of the Anglo-American lands to the north. (For example, Lebanese, Palestinian and, arguably, Japanese emigrants to Latin America had this effect.) This multilingual aspect took Latin American cultural debates far from a simple reliance on either a Spanish or indigenous heritage. Indeed, the cosmopolitan heritage that North America takes for granted as an option was often the object of quest by Latin American critics who attempted to claim their entire world heritage, free from the constraint of a parochialism imposed on them by outside stereotypes.

Mestizaje and Style

Yet *mestizaje* still had to do with blood. It talked about heterogeneous ancestry coming from intermarriage, but it was still an ethnically defined identity and thus faced, at the very least, problems of translation when it came to the cultural sphere. Anzaldúa acted as if *mestizaje* was automatically critical of unitary formations, as if its opposition to purity made it inherently liberating. When one sees how many ideologies of the previous era relied on ideas of purity, Anzaldúa has a point. The "resolved symbolic" insisted on purity of form, and, in their political mode, the New Critics privileged an agricultural past shorn of

any connections to external, industrial modernity. The Rousseauistic primitiv-
ism that Derrida critiqued used modern anthropology as the way to stress difference from the West, not convergence. In this way, the impurity introduced
by *mestizaje* was indeed provocative. But *mestizaje* was ultimately about the
promotion of an identity, and identities can conceivably become unitary, despite
having a pedigree of mixture, if they become simply slogans.

One of the ways to ramify the concept of *mestizaje* is to extend it to style. A
book like José Antonio Villareal's *Pocho* (1959) is seemingly inadequate when

one remembers the criteria mooted by the New Critics for the few novels that
were permitted into the formalist canon. It is not polished; it is not seamlessly
organized. It is stylistically lacking if one judges it by the unitary idea of style
that, as we have seen in Chapter 2, Derrida and Stanley Fish critiques because
of its nearly unconscious assumption of an affective persona. Yet the stylistic
lurchiness of *Pocho* is, in many ways, what gives Villareal's story its integrity
and liveliness. The rough quality blocks, on the stylistic level, the ability of its
protagonist, Richard, to feel as American as he might want when distinguishing himself from his totally "Mexican" parents or from feeling as irredeemably
the Mexican "other" when he faces discrimination in the United States as a
young adult. *Mestizaje*, here, is the cultural mixture Richard wants in contrast
to his father's desire for purity, but it is also what mainstream American society
threatens to deny him. It thus becomes less a property of blood and more one
of consciousness. Indeed, Villareal was often accused of being assimilationist, so
anti-essential was his conception of Latino identity—as when Richard, whose
father had, we are told on the novel's first page, fought with Pancho Villa and
his rebels, at the end of the novel joins the United States Navy.

Furthermore, although Villareal convincingly establishes a proletarian persona for his narrator, the author himself was not a complete outsider. He studied at the University of California, Berkeley in the late 1940s. There, he might
conceivably have taken classes from Mark Schorer (see the preface) whose
"Technique as Discovery" came closest to a New Critical theory of fiction
and who favoured the close, limited third-person narration that Villareal, like
Flaubert, Henry James, and Joyce, tends to favour. Like Louis Chu's *Eat A Bowl
of Tea* (1961), a charming novel of the "bachelor culture" of Chinatown in
New York and of its transformation by the arrival of a young woman, *Pocho* is
intriguing precisely because it introduces roughness and friction into the finished
sheen of the modernist short novel. (Incidentally, both books were initial fail-
ures and only became well known after the beginning of "ethnic studies" in the
1970s.) Neither *Pocho* nor *Eat A Bowl Of Tea* is, to use Henry James's famous
characterization of Tolstoy's work, a loose, baggy monster. They are clearly
influenced, at however many removes, by Flaubert and Joyce. Yet both authors'
execution of this form is one of inflection rather than the simple adaptation of
received paradigms to new forms of life. (For instance, the lengthy masturba-
tion scene in *Pocho* would have been quite risky in 1959 and is far more literal

than the equivalent in Joyce's *Portrait of the Artist* involving Stephen Dedalus.) Experimentation in form and in content went hand in hand.

This was also true of Tomas Rivera, whose 1971 novel *This Migrant Earth* took advantage of modernist experimentation in fictional technique, being influenced by Joyce, Faulkner, and Woolf in roughly analogous ways to Toni Morrison's work of that decade.[53] All these literary developments took place in the context of the La Raza and Aztlán movements, which organized Chicanos in protest and consciousness-raising activities, and amidst the quest for civil and human rights exemplified by César Chávez's leadership of the United Farm Workers union. "Alurista" (the pseudonym of Alberto Baltazar Urista Heredia) connected these political movements with literary practice; in both his fiction and non-fiction, he embodied a sense of the need for political self-determination to manifest itself in literary expression. Alurista can perhaps be considered the Chicano (Mexican-American) equivalent to such Black Arts figures as Baraka and Madhubuti. It is important to understand that, when figures such as Alurista are studied in the context of a literature department in a university, it is not just because of their politics, though political importance has, in the past, not been a bar to being studied in universities. It is because they wrote in literary forms using literary techniques that their work can be best explicated by literary scholars trained in literature. To study Chicano protest writers in a literature class is a very different experience than to study them in a history, political science, or ethnic studies class. A greater realization of this would have allayed the fears of such figures as Myers, whose *New Criterion* piece on Gates did not at all reject the idea of non-white writers *per se* but was troubled by the prospect of the wholesale replacement of the traditional canon by new, ethnic, and political writers. Wilfrido Corral, a far more sophisticated critic, is right to conclude that slathering about on literary texts of theories of *mestizaje* often slights the oeuvres of important individual authors, but one of the consolations of the academic-critical machine is that the cream very often *does* rise to the top. As shown by the fate of the African American women writers resurrected in Gates's Schomburg series, there are always canons, even canons among revived minority writers. People always pick and choose; texts attract readers and intellectual conversations, some more than others. And people still read and loved Shakespeare even in the midst of all this.[54] Alurista is studied because literary scholars have found it productive to study him. An analogous figure in Puerto Rican migrant literature is Eugenio Maria de Hostos. Both Hostos and Alurista were nationalists whose work was a focal point for ethnic pride and anti-hegemonic consciousness, although Hostos is not at all comparable to Alurista in chronology or mode of production. Hostos wrote in the late nineteenth century; was a contemporary of Rodó, Marti, and Darío; and had a vision of cultural fusion more level headed than that of Vasconcelos. And there is inevitably a "Victorian" aura about his writing that is very different from Alurista's hip, vivacious experimentalism. Yet Hostos was still looked to for inspiration by the Puerto Rican migrant population that flowed into New York in the decades after World War II, the people called by some "Nuyoricans." Also, Hostos and Alurista, along with being activists, were writers worth studying for their literary style as well as their political significance, just as Winston Churchill, America's founding fathers, and Julius Caesar are worthy of both literary and historical notice. When literary critics speak of "discourse" or "discursivity" in the work of these figures, they are calling attention to the status of their work as writing, in the sense that these texts must be studied as literature. Alurista and Hostoz were literary figures in a way that other political activists such as César Chávez and Pedro Albizu Campos were not. And often a political agenda can awaken or expedite an awareness of new possibilities in literary style or form. By the early 1970s in the US Latino community, formal and linguistic innovation went hand in hand with political assertiveness.

This juxtaposition of new form and new content became even more ramified in the work of Anzaldúa. Anzaldúa was openly lesbian and also had a mystical streak. In her work, one can perhaps glimpse an ontological *mestizaje*— a *mestizaje* of being that is, however, not as monumental or as ambitious as Vasconcelos's construct. This redescription of being has the potential to introduce the blended, permeable quality that these thinkers have most immediately talked about in terms of ethnicity into other areas. We have seen with Derrida the sense that *différance* can tear down the borderline between life and death. Can *mestizaje* do this as well? Helena Maria Viramontes's "The Moths," a tale of a dying grandmother in the Latino community in East Los Angeles, tells a story that is equally Latino and American, equally at home with the matrilineal Latino traditions of the family and with American brand names like Pine-Sol. Indeed, the arresting—if not exactly appetizing—combination of Pine-Sol and vomit (the two smells that accompany the grandmother's demise) may be the most immediately striking aspect of the story. This story deals with material that has the potential to be creepy and gross, and the author braids the multicultural story with something close to the horror story. In fact, this combination can be said to be something of a tradition in American minority writing, going back to Wright's evocation of Poe in *Native Son*. The creepiness is a deliberate effect on Viramontes's part—she wants to bring home our culture's discomfort with death. When physicality is linked with sex, we find it titillating; when materiality is linked to nature, we find it evocative; but when physicality and materiality are followed through to their eventual terminus—death—we find what is, ironically, one of the most natural aspects of existence to be unnatural, uncanny. By having the narrator experience the death of her *abuela* in such an explicit manner, Viramontes is not permitting us to conveniently sentimentalize it.

Equally, although she uses the magical realist techniques popularized by Latin American novels successful in the US market, which has the potential to be highly formulaic, Viramontes does not permit us to sentimentalize or exoticize the cultural milieu of the story. Spanish words such as *abuela* are left untranslated: Viramontes had an artistic reason for doing this; she wanted to create a thick cultural texture that was written in English, open to English-speaking readers, yet, for those readers, containing a degree of friction and blockage because of the untranslated Spanish, which reminded readers that they were engaging in an act of cultural translation. The additional elements of plurality in the fictional works of Viramontes suggest that an identity-based *mestizaje* will be ultimately as limiting as an ideology of oppositional racial purity. One of the issues with any critique is that it is potentially parasitic on what it critiques. Feminism can be parasitic upon patriarchy, anti-racism on racism, and deconstruction on referential theories of language. These critiques have resonated with such force because that which they oppose is not going away any time soon. Yet one worries whether this potential parasitism will give these ideologies a limited shelf life. Equally, the ideology of *mestizaje* seems premised on the unitary racial identity opposing it. When this unitary identity is no longer there, *mestizaje* will no longer seem as provocative. And indeed *mestizaje* has appeared in forms that many might deem more "conformist" than Anzaldúa's. Richard Rodriguez, the well-known memoirist and essayist, was unabashed about his Latino identity although he insisted that writing as a Latino did not mean that he could not be fully assimilated into the US mainstream. De Castro states that Rodriguez was willing "to leave race and ethnicity behind."[55] Rodriguez operated outside academia and wrote for a reasonably mass audience—he was not at all a theorist, nor was he trying to be one—but this approach had its academic versions as well.

Ilan Stavans, a Mexican of Jewish background, reached a wide academic audience in the 2000s with his essays, which covered the gamut from comic books to experimental European literature to linguistics. Stavans, who professed his admiration for Lionel Trilling and in many ways exemplified the most admirable traits of the New York Intellectuals of the 1950s, felt free to inhabit one part of his background and context and then leap to another. He did not see himself as giving voice to a predetermined ethnicity of which he was but a representative. Ethnicity, for Stavans, was performative and provisional. It was also something that the intellect at once constituted and evaded. Both Rodriguez and Stavans were political centrists, and they should not have their politics confused with those of someone such as the San Diego-based columnist Rubén Navarrette, Jr. Navarrette, though actively identifying himself much more as a "Latino" than Stavans did, was conservative leaning in politics. Stavans and Rodriguez, on the other hand, represented different articulations of urbane, cosmopolitanism liberalism, in the nineteenth-century sense of that word. Stavans's championing of "Spanglish," the tendency of US Latinos to speak both English and Spanish in the same sentence or speech act, is indicative here. With both Stavans and Rodriguez, though, there was the issue of whether they were just telling their audience what it wanted to hear? Did they not just provide reassurance that ethnic minorities were not so angry any more and were prepared to play ball with the establishment? This is the easiest and often the most callous criticism one can make of a serious thinker, and it should be undertaken very reservedly and with the utmost reluctance. But it should also be noted that the theorists who take up the most space in this book are those who have created their own audiences and assembled a disparate set of readers whose coalescence around them one might not have predicted. Derrida and Foucault were two such writers, and, as we will see in the next chapter, so was Edward Said. And Henry Louis Gates, Jr., in presuming a reader at once interested in Africa and intertextuality, was also one. Thus far, neither Stavans nor Rodriguez has exhibited the ability to reshuffle intellectual givens creatively the way Gates has. Stavans also presents the point that any stretching of the canon, no matter how inclusive it is, also presumes privilege. Just as the Leavisites and New Critics got away with their small canon because they were perceived as educating first-generation college attendees, Stavans's wide canon presumed a cadre of already literate students ready and willing to either ramify and diversify their tastes or have the confidence to build a personal canon knowing that, if they did not know certain culturally indispensable works, others did.

Stavans and Rodriguez represented the Hispanic intellectual fully willing to function in English and to address a general English-language readership as well as a readership specifically interested in the writer's Latino background. Stavans wrote frequently and polymathically for general-interest journals and, in his public profile, was not far from the post-theoretical literary journalists to be discussed in Chapter 7. But in his evocation of an identity partaking of multiple backgrounds and contexts, Stavans's thought paralleled ideas about the "Black Atlantic" that we have seen given voice in the work of Paul Gilroy. Both Gilroy and Stavans moved from the paradigm of minorities critiquing "universalism" to that of minorities critiquing allegedly ethnocentric paradigms within minority studies.

The 2000s: Oprah, Obama, and the Legacies of Theory

The visions of hybridity that Gilroy and Stavans sketch are appealing ones, in political, ethical, and cultural terms. Their call for an eschewal of racial exclusivity and for a dialogue among and between cultures is both liberating and inspirational. Race was an ideologically invented category, so the end of racial discourse is certainly conceivable. Race is not a fact of nature, does not really exist. But there are still some, as Wordsworth would say, "obstinate questionings" at the end of race. As Cornel West has pointed out, "race matters." Even if race is an artificial and often malign construct, so many people have lived their lives in the crucible of racism that one cannot expect the idea of race to wither away. One also wonders what might happen to anti-racist and race-based criticism when race is dissolved into proliferating discourses of hybridity. If race is still a principle of the critical framework, is this fact just something to be reformed?

Is anti-racist criticism a giant repair job with a built-in expiration date? It is as if formalist criticism were to exist until the form-content distinction could be erased entirely. (Interestingly, given how much racial, ethnic, and political issues are linked to content, here they would be playing the role of form.) On the other hand, anti-racist criticism is criticism that addresses a particular social problem, and that problem has temporal limitations and is not an eternal verity.

Indeed, the idea that literary theory can be relevant to particular times, circumstances, and peoples is part of the legacy of race-based criticism—that criticism can matter when it speaks of matters at hand, that it does not always have to be conducted in an ideal rhetorical universe unaffected by the imperatives of historical circumstance. What one wants to avoid is the acclaim of hybridity or *mestizaje* to the extent that either becomes another consensus, a substrate that literature ritualistically affirms. Neither should hybridity be preferred over discourses that trumpet identity politics in a more uncompromising way just because it is considered a safer mode of political reconciliation or moderation. Most Americans, from any country in the Americas, would most likely vote for a candidate who embraced hybridity over racial purity—whatever her or his race. But this does not mean that we should unilaterally throw on the scrap heap of history the more uncompromising figures, the ones who, even though they often advocated synthesis or commingling between traditions, would have objected to simply relinquishing indigenous or ethnic heritage in the name of hybridity—say Baraka or Madhubuti or Baker in the African American tradition and Arguedas or Fernández Retamar in the Latino. Most intellectuals, no doubt even most contemporary Russian intellectuals, would prefer the "Westernizers" in the classic nineteenth-century debates between the "Westernizers" and the "Slavophiles," who called for the fostering of a uniquely Russian identity based on that nation's Slavic ethnolinguistic roots. But this does not mean that Slavophile-tinctured thinkers such as Ivan Kireevsky, Aleksey Khomiakov, Nikolai Berdyaev, and Dostoyevsky himself are not interesting to read. If the Slavophile Dostoyevsky had not had his works widely read in the Western world, Ralph Ellison would never have been inspired by the narrator of Dostoyevsky's *Notes from the Underground* (1864) to create the analogous narrator of *Invisible Man* (1952). Anzaldúa's vision of *mestizaje* should be combined with Cornejo Polar's complementary but not identical principle of heterogeneity. And the combined theoretical concept should not exclude what Homi Bhabha termed "cultural difference"—it should not be a unitary credo.

No discussion of race and hybridity in contemporary America can be complete without an assessment of the political success of Barack Obama and what it portends for our discussion. Literary-intellectual thought about ground-level political issues has not had a distinguished history. And what follows is admittedly and manifestly only a series of improvisatory thoughts, which may or may not have permanent value. But some contours of the situation are already clear. The cultural sphere played an important role in preparing the conditions that made Obama's election possible. Obama wrote two books himself, books which operated a couple of steps above the level of the boilerplate campaign biography. But there were two other important literary prerequisites for the Obama phenomenon.

As discussed previously, the emergence of Gates, Appiah, and West as public intellectuals in the 1990s, even though their fame diluted the previous theoretical emphasis of their work, introduced to the thinking public discourses of race that were still inflected by theory. These discourses fit squarely within the tradition of an Emersonian, transformative-reformist vision of the American people, and they affected public thought in a more practical and variegated way than the attempts of Richard Rorty to do the same. In addition, Oprah Winfrey's book club played a role in generating a new reading public and a new audience for African American literature. (It was not until Winfrey's championship of Toni Morrison that Morrison's writing was widely read in the African American community.) Obama's appeal was disseminated along literary and cultural channels that arose as a result of the widening of public discourse, a widening made possible by theory and by the reconsideration of the canon that theory prompted and abetted. Moreover, Obama himself was interpreted in light of anterior literary paradigms. When Winfrey acclaimed Obama as "the One" in a December 2007 campaign appearance in North Carolina, it was explained to the general public that this was a reference to Ernest Gaines's 1971 novel *The Autobiography of Miss Jane Pittman*.[56] Gaines's novel was a chronicle of black life in the southern states over several generations, as seen through the prism of its long-lived title character; Winfrey had chosen the novel for her book club. Although many comprehended that this acclamation had a half-messianic, half-transformative connotation, what few noted was that, in the novel, "the One" was Jimmy, a young political activist who arose in the 1950s and finally catalyzed African Americans into actively rejecting the indignities of segregation that had plagued them for so long. The novel ends inspirationally but also tragically. Whites kill Jimmy, in a fashion that reminds the reader of Dr. King's assassination.

But Jimmy's spirit is inextinguishable; the people still carry a part of him within their hearts and minds as they irrevocably march into freedom and empowerment. This mingled aspect of optimism, mysticism, and tragedy was seldom mentioned in the public sphere, even as the appellation "the One" was, often sarcastically, attached to Obama. This oversight occurred because very few white intellectuals had read the Gaines novel. Gates's point that African American literature has developed and sustained its own tradition, one that does not exclude external influence but can communicate meanings in light of a series of textual encodings, was illustrated by the way Winfrey's citation of Gaines resonated for her African American audience. Most white members of what Coleridge famously called the "clerisy" did not apprehend Winfrey's message because they had not bothered to read Gaines's book. Their teachers had not taught it to them; they had not been required to teach it; their teachers had not taught them to teach it. This novel was no obscure work. It was a book that, long before its selection for Oprah's book club, had been made into a movie starring Cecily Tyson. *The Autobiography of Miss Jane Pittman* had been assigned reading in many high schools, though, apparently, only high schools to whose intellectual trajectories the clerisy was deaf. Oprah had generated an intertextual allusion that her *extra-academic audience* comprehended far more than did the professoriate. To compound this sense of internal allusion, when Obama spoke on the night of his election, November 4, 2008, he paid tribute to a 106-year-old woman who had lived through all the tumult of the twentieth century—a veritable non-fiction version of Miss Jane Pittman herself.[57]

We face the interesting paradox that Obama received nearly 53 per cent of the vote of the entire eligible citizenry of the United States; yet, in many English departments a decade or so previously, many professors, even liberal or Democratic-voting ones, had been sceptical that there were literary works produced by non-white writers that had permanent literary value and should be taught. Some of the people who voted for Obama must have been intellectuals who opposed the expansion of the canon to include works by writers of colour. Before Obama, many leading African American figures were stalwart defenders of the traditional canon. Consider the second Bush's second Secretary of State Condoleezza Rice in her role as provost of Stanford University. Obama, though, seems far friendlier to multiculturalism and to theory. In his personal writings, he has gone out of his way to associate himself with theory. In his 1995 auto-biography *Dreams from My Father*, he speaks of deliberately hanging out with "the structural feminists" in college.[58] Of course, Derrida would have preferred Obama to say "post-structural feminists." Possibly Obama was deliberately get-ting it slightly wrong to show that he had outgrown these affiliations, although, as he made clear, they were still part of him. Furthermore, when Obama was asked to name his favourite books, he included among them Morrison's 1977 novel *Song of Solomon*.[59] This was an uncontroversial choice, certainly, but he also named as favourites two Shakespeare tragedies. How many times had there been laments that Morrison was elbowing Shakespeare out of the curriculum? Obama's list of favourite books presaged a truce in the culture wars that had been a long time coming. One wonders why the traditionalist faction had felt the need to wage these wars so fiercely in the first place. The twenty-first century saw, very quickly, the unravelling of the polemical resistances of the late twentieth.

This sudden truce in the culture wars occurred across the board. In 2002, Laura Bush, then the first lady, convened a National Endowment for the Humanities event at the White House that hailed Willa Cather as a great American writer. During the course of this event, Laura Bush commended Cather in terms of diversity and multiculturalism, two characteristics that the dance critic and literary journalist Joan Acocella had denounced as indicative of left-wing politicizing that infringed on aesthetic prerogatives. Acocella's book, published two years earlier than the White House event honouring Cather, reflected the sentiments of the anti-theory camp, which were popular in the mainstream press.[60] Thus circumstances had changed faster than the duelling culture warriors cared to admit. Indeed, the Bush administration's appointment of African Americans and Hispanics to high positions had prepared the way for Obama, as the novelist Walter Mosley pointed out. (Mosley was one of the African American writers most early and active in his support of Obama.) Historians assessing this period will see as much continuity as discontinuity between the Bush and Obama administrations, if their assessment is made in the Foucauldian spirit of recognizing both non-obvious continuities and radical discontinuities between *epistemes*.[61] But what is important for our purposes here is that the literary sphere, for all that theory was accused of politicizing literature, was reluctant to embrace what the political sphere embraced far less timorously. The desire to keep literature as it was; the nostalgia for the bygone age of Leavisism, New Criticism, and the New York Intellectuals; the wish for all the politicizers and theorists and jargon mongers to go away suffused the popular literary journalism of the 1990s and 2000s. These were the so-called halcyon days when even Ellison was chided for being too particularistic, and a phony "universalism" was foisted on his work that would never have been asked of a white writer. A nostalgia for this sort of past and for the canon it had privileged—perhaps for no reason other than that it was the canon certain critics were used to and had been schooled in—scarred the literary sphere in such a way as to leave it a step behind its political counterpart, despite the valiant work of all the critics and theorists mentioned previously and all the less-heralded classroom teachers who diversified education without succumbing to cant or simplistic slogans. The strengths Obama displayed in the campaign—his unstinting advocacy of a reformist agenda that also heeded the lessons of tradition, his unabashed intellectuality, his association with urban and diverse milieus, and his separation of the enabling from the restrictive aspects of group identity—were perfected by him politically, but they already existed in the cultural sphere. The work of Gates, Winfrey, and others in the 1990s had prepared the way for him in terms of discourse and of representation. (Obama's strong defence of Gates in the wake of the latter's arrest in the summer of 2009 underscores this point.) And scholars who rescued African American texts from neglect and condescension and insisted that they be taught in the same department as Shakespeare and Yeats and Dickens prepared the way for Gates and Winfrey.

Obama could also be described as a "post-colonial" as much as an "African American" candidate. Aijaz Ahmad has asserted that the fight for decolonization worldwide and the fight for racial equality within the United States helped fortify each other and contributed to the convulsive social change of the 1960s.[62] This intersection is certainly seen in the way the coming of Obama's Kenyan father to America coincided with the beginning of civil rights mobilization. Furthermore, Obama was born in Hawaii, a state consisting of islands in the Pacific with an originally Polynesian culture and a large Asian American population descended from various Asian migrant groups—Chinese, Japanese, and Filipino. In his ancestry and identity, he was part of both the "Pacific Rim" as well as Gilroy's idea of the "Black Atlantic." Hawaii practised tolerance and pluralism in racial and cultural matters long before most of the mainland United States did. In fact, Hawaii's admission to the Union had been delayed in the 1950s by that decade's fears of the racial tolerance and pluralism already prevalent there. Not only his African father but also his Indonesian stepfather, in whose country Obama lived and studied for several years as a child, make Obama an appropriate subject for discussion in this book's following chapter as well as in this one.

In terms of Bellow's crass remark, we may not have found the Papuan Proust or the Zulu Tolstoy, but a half-Luo man became the president of the most powerful country in the world. Indeed, the very fact that Obama's Kenyan father spoke and did scholarship in English is a by-product not just of colonialism but also of the creative "mimicry" outlined by Homi Bhabha; it is also a by-product of the proliferation of an "Anglosphere," an idea championed by Bush-era conservatives. And, with respect to the Obama phenomenon, academic intellectual paradigms can be deployed as a "hermeneutics of suspicion," to use Paul Ricoeur's phrase, as well as one of acclamation.[63] Whiteness studies scholars might note, for instance, that much was tacitly made of how old-line Anglo-Saxon Obama's white heritage was, and whether or not he would have represented a different kind of hybridity had that part of his background been Italian American, say, or Jewish American. Some clearly use the rhetoric of post-racism to hope that Obama represents the end of race as a subject—one they would rather not discuss. It is as if he were a political version of the *pharmakon* in Derridean terms, the exception that is excluded—or in this case elevated—so that discussion of a phenomenon can be sealed off. Some, like the Peruvian novelist Mario Vargas Llosa, who has been associated in the later portion of his career with the libertarian right wing, laud Obama as the culmination of "the American dream" and as someone whose individual appeal allowed him to transcend race.[64] Vargas Llosa clearly sees Obama as a figure whose politics of hope do not necessarily depend upon what the Canadian philosopher Charles Taylor calls "the politics of recognition."[65] Even Obama cannot, in and of himself, provide a happy ending to the tragic course of racism in American life. But he represents the aspiration of his countrymen to transcend their lamentable racial past.

The legal scholar Patricia Williams is thus sagacious when she observes that Obama's election altered but did not terminate discourses of race. As Williams says, "it is naive to think that the urgently worrisome accumulations of racial inequality, ghetto isolation, horrendous rates of incarceration, or economic disparity will evaporate overnight."[66] Race and racism are not so easily discarded because, as Walter Benjamin argues, "there is no document of civilization that is not also at once a document of barbarism"—an aphorism more lately reaffirmed by Foucault's discussions of biopower and governmentality.[67] Many acted as if Obama's election solved conclusively all issues of racial discrimination—that far from jump-starting discourses of cultural plurality, the reality of an African American president came close to obviating them. This is the sort of convenient sloganeering that it is theory's task to disperse. Literary criticism of any cogency, as the examples of de Man and Achebe show, can only operate by asking questions and keeping matters as open as possible. But Obama's 2008 victory was an historic testimony to how long-ingrained racial prejudice can be overcome. It is therefore important to reiterate that the values of the Obama campaign were, in many ways, the values of theoretically inflected anti-racist critics from the 1970s onward. US literary scholars can be proud to say that their discipline played a substantial role in their country's ability to bring about what Misha Kokotovic, citing Cornejo Polar, called "a modernity compatible with their nation's cultural heterogeneity."[68]

NOTES

1   John Burt Foster, Jr., "'Show Me the Zulu Tolstoy': A Russian Classic between 'First' and 'Third' Worlds," *The Slavic and East European Journal* 45.2 (Summer 2001): 260–74 gives a sensible and level-headed account of the entire incident and its repercussions.

2   Hyatt Waggoner, *American Poets: The Puritans to the Present* (Boston: Houghton Mifflin, 1968). Again, Waggoner was neither a racist nor a conservative but rather an optimistic albeit mystically inclined liberal. But the only non-white he mentions is the Bengali poet Rabindranath Tagore, and the only African he mentions is Roy Campbell—a white South African. To his credit, Waggoner does mention quite a few women, which a more conservative critic writing ten years earlier would not have done. Indeed, such a critic might not have written a book about American poetry at all, but stuck to John Donne.

3   Toni Morrison, *Playing in the Dark* (Cambridge, MA: Harvard University Press, 1992).

4   Richard Wright, *Native Son* (New York: HarperCollins, 1998) 451, 462.

5   Ralph Ellison, *Invisible Man* (New York: Modern Library, 1994).

6   James Baldwin, *Another Country* (New York: Vintage, 2003).

7   John Hope Franklin, *Mirror to America: The Autobiography of John Hope Franklin* (New York: Farrar, Straus, and Giroux, 2005).

8   Houston A. Baker, "Generational Shifts and the Recent Criticism of African American Literature," *Black American Literature Forum* 15 (Spring 1981): 3–21. Baker's historical stocktaking of the field was itself the signifier of a greater self-reflexivity that paralleled the overt emergence of Derridean discourses in African Americanist criticism of the 1980s.

9   Stephen Evangelist Henderson, *Understanding the New Black Poetry* (New York: Morrow, 1973). The very title of Henderson's volume echoed that of Brooks and Warren's *Understanding Poetry*.

10   Robert A. Bone, *The Negro Novel in America* (New Haven: Yale University Press, 1970). Books like Bone's necessarily had a double mission: to analyse a concrete body of work and to show non-specialists that there *was* indeed a body of work to be analysed. This latter imperative may have made ranking more of a part of the book's agenda than it otherwise would have been.

11   Haki R. Madhubuti, *GroundWork: New and Selected Poems of Don L. Lee/Haki R. Madhubuti from 1966–1996* (Chicago: Third World Press, 1996).

12   See Claudia Breger, "Imperialist Fantasies and Displaced Memory: Twentieth-Century German Egyptologies," *New German Critique* 96 (2005): 135–59.

13   William D. Buhrman, *Nathan Scott's Literary Criticism and Fundamental Theology* (New York: Peter Lang, 2006).

14   Nathan A. Scott (1925–2006), spec. issue of *Callaloo*, forthcoming.

15   Deborah G. Plant, *Zora Neale Hurston: A Biography of the Spirit* (Westport: Greenwood, 2007) 58.

16   Alice Walker, *Everyday Use*, ed. Barbara Christian (New Brunswick: Rutgers University Press, 1994).

17   Zora Neale Hurston, *Their Eyes Were Watching God* (Urbana: University of Illinois Press, 1977).

18 As Barbara Johnson says on page 171 of *A World of Difference* (Baltimore: Johns Hopkins University Press, 1988), "the process of de-universalization is never, universally, completed." No better credo than this for a deconstructive, anti-racist, feminist criticism could have been enunciated in the 1980s.

19 Maurice Berger, *White Lies: Race and the Myth of Whiteness* (New York: Farrar, Straus, and Giroux, 1999).

20 Noel Ignatiev, *How the Irish Became White* (New York: Routledge, 1995). As we have seen, European migrants in Canada or Australia were not necessarily perceived as "white" the way they are in the United States.

21 Arnold Weinstein, *Northern Arts: The Breakthrough of Scandinavian Literature and Art, from Ibsen to Bergman* (Princeton: Princeton University Press, 2008).

22 Henry Louis Gates, Jr., foreword, *Contending Forces: A Romance Illustrative of Negro Life North and South*, by Pauline Hopkins (New York: Oxford University Press, 1988) xix.

23 Richard Yarborough, Introduction, *Contending Forces*, xxx–xxxi.

24 Henry Louis Gates, Jr., *The Signifying Monkey* (New York: Oxford University Press, 1988).

25 Srinivas Aravamudan, *Tropicopolitans: Colonialism and Agency, 1688–1804* (Durham: Duke University Press, 1990). In *Equiano, the African: Biography of a Self-Made Man* (Athens: University of Georgia Press, 2005), Vincent Carretta argues that Equiano was not born in Africa but that this does not disqualify him as a producer of "Black Atlantic" discourse.

26 Marjorie Prysse and Hortense J. Spillers, eds., *Conjuring: Black Women, Fiction, and Literary Tradition* (Bloomington: Indiana University Press, 1985); Barbara Christian, *Black Women Novelists: The Development of a Tradition, 1892–1976* (Westport: Greenwood, 1980); Joyce Ann Joyce, *Black Studies as Human Studies* (Albany: SUNY Press, 2005).

27 Hazel V. Carby, *Race Men* (Cambridge, MA: Harvard University Press, 1998).

28 John F. Callahan, *In the African-American Grain: Call-and-Response in Twentieth-Century Black Fiction* (Urbana: University of Illinois Press, 1988).

29 Ira Katznelson, *When Affirmative Action Was White* (New York: Norton, 2005); this text includes West Virginia in its list of Jim Crow states.

30 Henry Louis Gates, Jr., *Thirteen Ways of Looking at a Black Man* (New York: Norton, 1997). Gates's use of Wallace Stevens's poem title was an implied nod to critics such as Harold Bloom and J. Hillis Miller, who quoted Stevens frequently.

31 David R. Shumway, "The Star System in Literary Studies," *PMLA* 112 (January 1997): 85–100.

32 Paul Gilroy, *The Black Atlantic: Modernity and Double-Consciousness* (Cambridge, MA: Harvard University Press, 1992). Note the deliberate echo of Du Bois's famous phrase in Gilroy's subtitle.

33 Christina Klein, *Cold War Orientalism: Asia in the Middlebrow Imagination, 1945–1961* (Berkeley: University of California Press, 2003) is a good overview of the cultural politics of the mid-twentieth century Pacific as viewed through a white US lens. Because of the racial stereotypes of this period, David Palumbo-Liu's suggestion that the hyphen in Asian-American be seen as a gap or a negotiable space as much as a stable linkage is concomitant with a less fetishized idea of the "Asian." See David Palumbo-Liu, *Asian/American: Historical Crossings of a Racial Frontier* (Stanford: Stanford University Press, 1999).

34 Mark Chiang, rev. of *National Abjection: The Asian American Body Onstage*, by Karen Shimakawa, and of *Race and Resistance: Literature and Politics in Asian America*, by Viet Thanh Nguyen, *American Literature* 76.1 (January 2004): 189–91. This review provides an instance of the term "elegiac" as it is used here. See also Anne Anling Cheng, *The Melancholy of Race: Psychoanalysis, Assimilation, and Hidden Grief* (New York: Oxford University Press, 2001).

35 Gerald Robert Vizenor, *Manifest Manners: Narratives on Postindian Survivance* (Lincoln: University of Nebraska Press, 1991). "Postindian" is Vizenor's term for the condition after the emancipation of individual Native discourses from the umbrella term "Indian"; as Kwame Anthony Appiah would point out, it does not mean the same thing as "post-" in "post-racial." Vizenor's use of the term "survivance," often associated with Canadian francophone (Québécois) nationalism, is notable.

36 José Vasconcelos, *The Cosmic Race/La Raza Cósmica*, trans. Didier Jaén (Baltimore: Johns Hopkins University Press, 1997). Vasconcelos's book was a major source for the term "La Raza" in the Latino civil rights discourses of the early 1970s, and "Aztlán," a term often used in that era, which referred to what Anzaldúa would later term "the borderlands" but put in more mythic, Aztec-nostalgic garb. The idea of "Aztlán" was fundamentally nationalistic while that of "the borderlands" was post-nationalist and contingent on, or at least congruent with, post-colonial ideas of hybridity and diaspora.

37 Juan E. De Castro, *The Spaces of Latin American Literature* (New York: Palgrave, 2008).

38 José Enrique Rodó, *Ariel*, trans. Margaret Sayers Peden (Austin: University of Texas Press, 1988).

39 José Carlos Mariátegui, *Seven Interpretive Essays on Peruvian Reality*, trans. Marjory M. Urquidi (Austin: University of Texas Press, 1971).

40 Ángel Rama, *The Lettered City*, trans. John Chasteen (Durham: Duke University Press, 1996).

41 Fernando Ortiz, *Cuban Counterpoint: Tobacco and Sugar* (Durham: Duke University Press, 1995). Ortiz's analogy of "counterpoint" is, in general terms, not far from Bakhtin's idea of polyphony, and it confirms Bakhtin's unwitting utility as a precursor, or monitor, of *mestizaje*.

42 Oscar Lewis, *All About Pedro Martinez: A Mexican Peasant and His Family* (New York: Random House, 1964). One wonders—and this is more than an aside, having everything to do with visibility and empowerment—what Lewis would have made of the famous baseball player, Dominican Pedro Martínez (1971–).

43 Although, as often is the case in these sorts of discourses, the theoretical was in advance of the practical; Ortiz celebrated Cuban blackness, but he opposed the immigration of West Indian blacks to Cuba on the grounds that they were "foreign." See Aviva Chomsky, "'Barbados or Canada?' Race, Immigration, and Nation in Early-Twentieth-Century Cuba," *Hispanic American Historical Review* 80.3 (2000): 415–62 and also the work of Alejandro de la Fuente on race relations in Cuba and Afro-Cuban culture.

44 Estelle Tarica, *The Inner Life of Mestizo Nationalism* (Minneapolis: University of Minnesota Press, 2008) 24.

45 Antonio Cornejo Polar, *The Multiple Voices of Latin American Literature* (Berkeley: University of California Press, 1994).

46 Jimmy Santiago Baca, "Voz de la Gente," *Black Mesa Poems* (New York: New Directions, 1989) 84.

47 Octavio Paz, *The Bow and the Lyre*, trans. Ruth L. Simms (Austin: University of Texas Press, 1987).

48 Gloria Anzaldúa, *The Borderlands/La Frontera: The New Mestiza* (San Francisco: Aunt Lute Books, 1987).

49 This conjectural connection between deconstruction and *mestizaje* is seen more overtly in the title of José David Saldivar and Héctor Calderón's important collection *Criticism in the Borderlands: Studies in Chicano Literature, Culture, and Ideology* (Durham: Duke University Press, 1991); the book's title paid conscious homage to Geoffrey Hartman's 1980 book *Criticism in the Wilderness*, one of the first serious expositions of post-structuralist thought in the United States.

50 Paul Allatson, *Latino Dreams: Transcultural Traffic and the U.S. National Imaginary* (Amsterdam: Rodopi, 2002) 43.

51 Gustavo Pérez Firmat, *Life on the Hyphen: The Cuban-American Way* (Austin: University of Texas Press, 1994).

52 Roberto Ignacio Diaz, *Unhomely Rooms: Foreign Tongues and Spanish American Literature* (Lewisburg: Bucknell University Press, 2002); Ignacio López-Calvo, *Imagining the Chinese in Cuban Literature and Culture* (Gainesville: University Press of Florida, 2008); Ignacio López-Calvo, *The Dragon and the Condor: Literary and Cultural Representations of the Chinese Diaspora in Peru*, forthcoming, 2010; Edna Aizenberg, *Books and Bombs in Buenos Aires: Borges, Gerchunoff, and Argentine-Jewish Writing* (Boston: Brandeis University Press, 2004).

53 Tomas Rivera was also one of the principal shaping forces in the institutionalizing of Chicano studies in the United States.

54 For instance, at Boricua College in New York, an institution oriented towards the Puerto Rican community although it provides instruction largely in English, there has never been a semester during which the works of Shakespeare and other traditional writers of the Western canon have not been taught. Hostos Community College, a college in the City University of New York system named after Eugenio Maria de Hostos, most likely has had the same history.

55 Juan E. De Castro, *Mestizo Nations: Culture, Race and Conformity in Latin American Literature* (Tucson: University of Arizona Press, 2002) 108. As De Castro points out, Rodriguez—who has openly discussed his homosexuality, has spoken positively of Roman Catholicism, and has praised the Amerindian contribution to *mestizo* identity—cannot simply be categorized as seeking acceptance by the mainstream.

56 Ernest J. Gaines, *The Autobiography of Miss Jane Pittman* (New York: Dial, 1971); for the messianism comment, see Ben Smith and David Paul Kuhn, "Messianic rhetoric infuses Obama

rallies," *Politico*, 9 December 2007, 28 November 2008 <http://dyn.politico.com/printstory.cfm?uuid=C1276B28-3048-5C12-00914D91CF0A11E0>.

57 Lynn Sweet, "President-elect Obama's Grant Park speech: Text and video," *Chicago Sun-Times* 5 November 2008, 29 November 2008 <http://blogs.suntimes.com/sweet/2008/11/obamas_grant_park_speech.html>.

58 Barack Obama, *Dreams from My Father* (New York: Three Rivers Press, 1995) 99–100.

59 Barack Obama, Facebook page, 13 December 2008 <http://www.facebook.com/barackobama>.

60 For the Bush-Cather connection, see Marilee Lindemann, Introduction, *The Cambridge Companion to Willa Cather*, ed. Marilee Lindemann (New York: Cambridge University Press, 2005); the case against a multicultural Cather was expressed by Joan Acocella, *Willa Cather and the Politics of Criticism* (Lincoln: University of Nebraska Press, 2000).

61 Walter Mosley, qtd. in Jayne Ann Phillips and Patrick McGrath, "The State of America after Bush," *The Observer* (London), 2 November 2008, 2 November 2008 <http://www.guardian.co.uk/books/2008/nov/02/george-bush-legacy-usa>.

62 Aijaz Ahmad, *In Theory: Classes, Nations, Literatures* (London: Verso, 1993).

63 Paul Ricoeur, *Freud and Philosophy* (New Haven: Yale University Press, 1970).

64 "Peruvian literary great Vargas Llosa applauds Obama," *FOX 43 News*, 2 November 2008 <http://www.fox43.com/pages/landing/?blockID=31743&fcedID=14>.

65 Charles Taylor and Amy Gutmann, eds., *Multiculturalism and "The Politics of Recognition"* (Princeton: Princeton University Press, 1994).

66 Patricia Williams, "A Nation could be on the Verge of its Mandela Moment," *The Observer* (London), 2 November 2008, 2 November 2008 <http://www.guardian.co.uk/world/2008/nov/02/us-elections-2008-barack-obama>.

67 Walter Benjamin, "Theses on the Philosophy of History," *Illuminations: Essays and Reflections*, ed. Hannah Arendt (New York: Schocken, 1968) 266.

68 Misha Kokotovic, *The Colonial Divide in Peruvian Narrative: Social Conflict and Transculturation* (Eastbourne: Sussex Academic Press, 2007) 1.

CHAPTER FIVE

Deconstructing Centrality
POST-COLONIAL THEORY

Up to the 1980s: Decolonization and Its Aftermath

Fighting Colonialism

From the time of Columbus until the mid-twentieth century, European nations colonized much of the world. Operating out of mercantile, ideological, and religious motives; differently spurred by economic survival and great-power rivalry; sometimes pursuing their goals unsystematically and sometimes as a deliberate instrument of policy—European states controlled, directly or indirectly, virtually the entire planet by 1900. Even those countries that were not formally colonized experienced the heavy influence of the West and were irreversibly changed by it. Colonial attitudes became deeply braided into the Western way of thought. Post-colonial criticism, arising in the aftermath of the political independence of many non-Western states, sought to diagnose and remedy the effects of this colonialist mentality.

Kwame Anthony Appiah, one of the leading African American public intellectuals to emerge in the 1990s, asked the question "Is the Post- in Postmodernism the Post- in Postcolonial?" In fact, this was the title of his 1991 article, which was published in the prestigious Chicago-based journal *Critical Inquiry*.[1] The answer on Appiah's part was generally no. Postmodernism pertained to the subtleties of intellectual history. It addressed the collapse, in the terms of Jean-François Lyotard, of the "grand narratives" and their replacement by more pluralistic and ironic discourses.[2] Post-colonialism, on the other hand, dealt with the liberation of the culturally subordinated in the wake of colonialism. Postmodernism *could* be political. But post-colonialism was *necessarily* political. Similarly, Homi K. Bhabha, a major post-colonial theorist, distinguished between "cultural diversity" and "cultural difference."[3] Diversity is a term associated in the United States with affirmative action programs. It was used most prominently by Supreme Court Justice Lewis Powell in the 1978 *Bakke* decision. This US legal judgement permitted racial preferences but only to increase the "diversity" of the workplace or educational setting, not explicitly to make up for past prejudice. Difference, as we have seen in Chapter 2, is associated with Derrida, and pertained to a more radical fissuring and reframing of identity. Diversity advocates inclusiveness but in the name of an existing norm and in a fashion that liberalizes but does not sever links with the previous era of hierarchical domination. Difference asserts an indelible heterogeneity that does not resolve into modifications of an existing consensus, and it juxtaposes various identities in such a manner that all bets are off. Post-colonial theory has aligned itself with issues of both diversity and difference. It advocated the literature of lands formerly colonized by European powers and, in more general terms, the writing of those previously ignored on the basis of their previously "marginal" status. In other words, it has increased literary diversity. But, more generally, it has introduced a principle of radical difference into the subject as well as the formal mode of literature, taking the critiques of Derrida and making them far more material and thematic.

What we now call post-colonial thought first seriously began in the French-speaking world. As early as the 1930s, poets such as Aimé Césaire (1913–2008) from Martinique in the French Caribbean and the Senegalese Léopold Sédar Senghor (1906–2001) from West Africa propagated the doctrine of *negritude*. This valorized the previously denigrated or undervalued idea of blackness, making it a positive quality. As Césaire put it,

> my desire a throw of tigers caught in the sulphurs
> but the stannous awakening gilds itself with infantine deposits
> and my pebble body eating fish eating doves and slumbers
> the sugar in the word Brazil deep in the marsh.[4]

Literary innovations—the free-verse mode, the surrealistic imagery, and eulogistic diction such as "stannous"—mime the energies of a renovated representation of human reality in Césaire's work. Although these poets mastered the rigorous art of writing well in the highly formalized French language, they did not take the assumptions of the colonizer as given. If anything, in fact, they inverted them too much, valuing just what the metropole rejected in a way that, to later Derridean eyes, might seem overly binary or Romantic. (Recall Derrida's characterization of the thought of Rousseau or Lévi-Strauss, which was discussed in Chapter 2.) This view that both poets were opponents operating within French culture and politics was heightened by the way that Césaire and Senghor, though determined advocates for the full civil rights of Martinicans and the independence of the Senegalese respectfully, were also pillars of the French literary establishment, respected and laurelled even by academicians who strongly suspected the wild theories of the young Barthes or Derrida. Both men also became active political figures, Césaire as mayor of Fort-de-France, Martinique's chief city, and, concurrently, as member of the French National Assembly, and Senghor as the founding president of Senegal.

Another post-colonial theorist born in Martinique, Frantz Fanon, was of a younger generation and a more radical stripe. Fanon, who became an African revolutionary, was a transnational figure more interested in fomenting revolution across the African diaspora than in becoming an elected political figure in or for a particular constituency. However, it would be a mistake not to understand that Césaire, Senghor, and Fanon shared the same ideals fundamentally. Yet there are moments when Césaire or Senghor might seem "essentialist."

Thus it is striking that Fanon was so influenced by Sartre's existentialism. "Existentialist" used to be the antonym for "essentialist." After a point, "existentialism" stopped being chic. But "essentialist" remained as a term of opprobrium for doctrines such as deconstruction, whose practitioners also thought that existentialism was essentialist! Sartre understood ethnic identities as possible locales of existential authenticity, a point he argued in his essay on anti-Semitism. This argument provided the ground for Sartre's influence on Fanon. Fanon was also influenced by psychoanalysis. In fact, the three major francophone thinkers who in many ways initiated what we now call post-colonial discourse—Octave Mannoni (1899–1989), Albert Memmi (1920–), and Fanon himself—were either psychiatrists themselves or were influenced by psychoanalysis. Of these, only Fanon was strictly speaking a "Third Worlder." (Memmi is a Tunisian Jew and is thus in a situation analogous to that of Derrida, and Mannoni was a white Frenchman who wrote about the pathologization of self amid colonialism and was variously hailed and castigated by later anti-colonial thinkers.) This association between post-colonial theory and psychoanalysis continued even into later anglophone post-colonial thought; Homi Bhabha published his famous essay on mimicry in a 1984 special issue of the journal *October*, which was devoted to psychoanalysis. Much as we have seen with feminism, post-colonial thought turned to psychoanalysis to discover new routes for the articulation of the self that often felt (in Kristeva's terms) abjected by the assumptions of colonialism or patriarchy. But the flexibility of Bhabha's and Kristeva's thought was lacking in Mannoni's and Memmi's. Although Mannoni and Memmi virulently denounced colonialism, they did so in a way that depicted the subject in the aftermath of colonialism as being disempowered, a victim capable of little. The irony and double-sidedness associated with later post-colonial thought are potentially there, but both are whelmed in a sea of essentialism.

Actually, even Fanon often seemed essentialist to later eyes; this judgement may have occurred, in part, because his early death (in 1961, at the age of thirty-six) kept his thought from explicitly engaging post-structuralism. Fanon was not only within a year of Foucault's age but had similar intellectual influences; both men studied medicine and psychiatry but were unable to accept orthodox articulations of them. Unlike Foucault, though, Fanon did not eschew direct revolutionary action.

In fact, Fanon's political activities, which took him mostly to Africa as well as to Europe and his home country, made him an odd combination of Foucault and, say, Che Guevara. Fanon's explicit advocacy of violent resistance in *The Wretched of the Earth* (1961) and his tacit conclusion in *Black Skin, White Masks* (1952) that black people who succeed in the terms of white society have somehow lost their real personality seemed overly declarative and unironic to later theorists who espoused more indirect and textual strategies of resistance. But it must be remembered that Fanon was writing this work in the face of racism and oppression, which, by the time of the rise of the more ironic approaches, had lessened. In 1952, for instance, only two black African countries were independent. Even after the independence of India and other Asian states, Africa was thought destined to be in European hands for much longer. Yet ten years later, scores of African countries were independent states.

Fanon was more an anti-colonial than a post-colonial thinker. He advocated decolonization rather than post-coloniality. Homi Bhabha, very much on the other side of the equation, goes to great lengths to stress the continuity between Fanon's ideas and his own in his 2004 introduction to the reissue of *The Wretched of the Earth*. Defending Fanon against accusations of being "lost in a time warp" and having a "vain hope," Bhabha does, revealingly, link Fanon to "the lost rhetorical baggage of the daunting quest for a nonaligned postcolonial world inaugurated at the Bandung Conference in 1955."[5] The limitations of Fanon's thought had mostly to do with the limitations of what might be called the Bandung mentality.

What was Bandung? The conference itself (held at the Indonesian site of Bandung) was, according to Robert Young, "the first major conference of independent African and Asian states, represented a coming together of recently decolonized nations and a strategic decision of nonalignment with respect to the major two powers of the cold war."[6] This sense of nonalignment and shared values lay behind the classification of these states as "Third World," as contrasted to the "First World" of Western Europe and the United States and the "Second World" communist states, such as the Soviet Union and its allies. The Bandung mentality was broadly anti-colonialist, involving a coalition between many peoples of different racial, cultural, and religious background. Bandung also originated processes that, according to Robert Young, sought to make "a concerted attempt to readjust the exploitative economic relations between the West and the rest."[7] It was felt that Europe, after departing in colonial-political terms, had, in the phrase used by the German economist André Gunder Frank and the Guyanese historian Walter Rodney, "underdeveloped" its former colonies, especially Africa—depriving them of the means to launch a successful economy. Thus the Bandung outlook partook of a broad resentment of Western arrogance and indifference. But it was also strongly influenced by nationalism. It was, after all, a coalition of states, of governments with political agendas concerned to promote their national interests. However, nationalism was more than a pragmatic political and economic agenda at Bandung; it was a quest. National rights, the righting of past and present injustices, and self-determination were also claimed—a more ideological and even in some ways a Romantic nationalism. The very concept of nationalism was associated with romanticism; the common styling of independence struggles as "wars of national liberation" was reminiscent of the German term *befreiungskriege* used of the struggles against Napoleonic rule and against entrenched internal power at the height of romanticism in the nineteenth century. This vision of nationalism as a just quest matched the romanticism of what was often a racially essentialist stance.[8] Whites had attempted to endow their colonial efforts in racial terms. The critique of white power also involved racial claims and assertions.

National independence for African countries from European colonialism, as well as the earlier independence of Indian and other former Asian British colonies, forced people to take stock of the literature of these countries. Nations able to send diplomatic representatives to the United Nations now were no longer automatically deemed to have no literature: again, we see the relationship between acknowledged and unacknowledged legislators. The young American writer Paul Theroux, for instance, who taught at the University of Makerere in Uganda, wrote a brief but influential essay on early post-independence African literature. He later wrote an early book on his then-friend V.S. Naipaul, a Caribbean-born product of the Indian diaspora. Individual post-colonial writers such as Naipaul, R.K. Narayan, and, as we have seen in the preface, Chinua Achebe were known and published and positively reviewed in the West. These writers had very different personalities and views: Naipaul was often seen as excoriating his fellow non-Europeans for not having sufficiently high cultural standards; Narayan was serene, charming, and apolitical; and Achebe explicitly engaged in a mission of anti-colonial challenge. There was the beginning of a due recognition of writing from outside Europe. This recognition, though, was affected by the precise political evolution of the new countries and their relation to the West.

Britain and France had a chance to make the inevitable process of decolonization orderly and to exit from their overseas domains with a modicum of grace. But Britain, in its brutal suppression of the Mau Mau rebellion in Kenya, and France, in its vain attempt to hold on to Vietnam and its rear-guard defence of the French settler population in Algeria, made anti-colonial sentiment seem a matter not just of theory but also of urgent practice. Anti-colonialism was exacerbated in the Suez Crisis of 1956, when newly installed Egyptian President Gamel Abdel Nasser nationalized the Suez Canal, threatening the commercial and military privileges of Britain and France. The two European countries and Israel launched a military operation to regain control over the canal, which ended in fiasco. Importantly, the United States opposed this venture. Had it supported its European allies, the United States might well have lost the cold war, so unpopular would it have been in Africa and Asia. As it was, even despite its manifest posture, the United States sustained a kind of guilt by association, and anti-Western sentiment soared in the Third World. With Suez still firmly in the hands of the Egyptians, the West could no longer hope to exercise unitary commercial and military suzerainty over the world. This situation inevitably led to a certain decline in the swagger of European culture and in its automatic assumption of superiority over that of the rest of the world.

The Failure of the Third World Project

Bandung-era literary culture was both nationalistic and internationalist in ways that went stale after a point. The internationalism began to be tarnished in the early 1960s after the Soviet Union and China had their ideological split and the leading anti-capitalist power and the leading non-European country were no longer on the same side. Benedict Anderson began his seminal book *Imagined Communities*, which redefined nations as built on shared linguistic and media spaces rather than representing an ideologically cognate Romantic sense of peoplehood, by pointing out that the 1979 war between China and Vietnam, both communist states but the latter then a Soviet ally, shattered many assumptions on the left about how Third World nationalism and socialist internationalism would harmoniously combine.[9]

Nationalism itself underwent a downturn after so many newly independent African and Asian states ended up being one-party dictatorships or democracies dominated by corruption and family dynasties. The analysis of Third World literature that hailed this literature as the product of a new post-independence mentality inevitably lost morale because of these political developments, even though, for instance, African novelists had been sharp internal critics of their countries' governance from early on, as seen in the Ghanaian Ayi Kwei Armah's *The Beautyful Ones Are Not Yet Born* (1968) and the Malian Yambo Ouologuem's *Le devoir de violence* (1968).[10] Much later, the Ivorian writer Ahmadou Kourouma, in *Allah n'est pas obligé*, would write a horrifying novel of child soldiers, which no one could accuse of idealizing life in contemporary Africa.[11] The Nigerian novelist, dramatist, and memoirist Wole Soyinka sharply criticized the "leftocracy" of his country's intellectual life, but the work of his fellow national Chinua Achebe was more cautious in its criticism of post-independence rule until belatedly criticizing it in *Anthills of the Savannah* (1987). Soyinka was a Yoruba, Achebe an Ibo. Though the two writers did not take partisan sides when their peoples largely opposed each other in the Nigerian civil war over the Biafra province in 1967–70, the war was yet a symptom of the sundering of the idealized unity of the immediate period after decolonization.

Other African writers decided to use this crisis to declare themselves more African. While he was jailed for political dissent in the late 1970s, the Kenyan novelist Ngugi wa Thiong'o, formerly James Ngugi, announced that, after writing successful and widely hailed novels in English, he would henceforth write only in his native language, Kikuyu (Gikuyu).[12] This achieved the outcome of rejecting the language of the colonizer. It also liberated Ngugi from having to represent Africa to the West, which was a major contributor to the burden felt by both political and literary liberation movements in this era, something which should not be underestimated. But it did not do much to enable Ngugi to communicate with Africans, the vast majority of whom did not speak Gikuyu.[13] Even in Kenya itself, for instance, members of the Luo people, including the ancestors or relatives of President Obama, may have felt more alienated by a Gikuyu text than an English one. At least English could serve as a bridge between the two often-rivalrous groups. Writing in Gikuyu became something that was half novelty act and half vanity project, meaning as little outside Kenya as a book written in the failed international artificial language of Esperanto would have meant. Even in India, English provided a language of national unity, although it was spoken only by a minority of the nation's elite and far more people were literate in Hindi or Bengali or the Dravidian languages of southern India—languages that, unlike most African tongues, had long-established literary traditions predating colonialism. Still, English provided India with a lingua franca in which people of different castes or ethnicities could speak across traditional divides of social class, region, and religion. And certainly the novelist or poet writing in English could potentially command a broader range of audiences across India than a writer who wrote solely in Telugu or Malayalam. The same paradox applied to Africa. Ngugi was writing in greater solidarity with his own immediate group, but the pan-African rationale was hard to see. This initial isolation may be the cost of national freedom. After all, Martin Luther and Shakespeare and Dante, by not writing in Latin, similarly gave up a broader international audience, for the short term at least.

Despite this stress on indigenous identities, what might be called the Bandung ideology was strongly affiliated with European ideologies—various ideologies on the European left. The Third World's critique of the West was performed in Western terms. The cold war and its rivalries both made and unmade Bandung-era generalities. Because both superpowers courted the newly independent nations, the Third World—as distinct from the capitalist and the communist worlds—became a kind of global "swing vote"; Third World opinion and good will mattered. In practice, most of the newly independent states were more interested in what the Soviet Union had to offer ideologically than what the United States represented. Despite American rhetoric of anti-colonialism, in the early 1960s, America's strongest allies were Britain and France, which were still perceived as colonial powers. France was still actively seeking to retain some control over Derrida's native Algeria. Even after the split between the Soviet Union and China had made the former appear less inherently friendly to non-Western powers, Marxism, as an ideology, and other forms of socialism were very appealing in Africa and southern Asia. This meant that many of the Western states were opposed for their residual imperialism or, in the case of the United States, their "neo-imperialism" but that post-colonial theorists of this time generally did not make the more abstract critiques mounted by Foucault and Derrida, of Western modernity and Western logocentrism, respectively.

From 1975 onward, the force of the Third World critique attenuated. African and Asian nations became less enamoured of socialist economics and looked to the newly prosperous capitalist nations for support and sustenance. In addition, many Third World Marxists, who earlier had seemed to be voicing independent nonaligned critiques of potentially emancipatory reach, were revealed to be working more or less in tandem with Soviet ideology or were too intellectually close to those categories to adapt to a changing world.[14] With the implosion of the USSR after 1989, there was no more Second World, and the Third World, as a term, lost its original meaning and much of its subversive panache. Resistance to Western hegemony continued. But, by this time, it was couched in very different terms, and the fundamental mechanisms if not the overall goals of the critique had changed.

As George Steiner's *In Bluebeard's Castle* (1971) asserts, the Holocaust raised fundamental questions about "Western civilization," which deflated and undermined the boastful, self-buffeting narratives of European accomplishment that had been at the core of school and college humanities curricula.[15] Not only the Holocaust but also the intra-European violence of both world wars as well as the invention of nuclear weapons, and their use against Japan, raised a long-term perspective. They constituted a fundamental blow to Europe's own sense of its moral rectitude. It is not often remembered how much the *négritude* of Césaire and Senghor had its crucible in World War II, when Senghor was actually a German prisoner of war for two years and Césaire did battle with the collaborationist Vichy-appointed administration in Martinique. These experiences, seeing at first hand the violence Europe had brought to itself and the world, certainly enhanced their intellectual self-confidence as thinkers of African descent. These violent events also raised the awareness of other genocides and atrocities, which were committed on a mass scale and concomitant with colonialism and European expansion. The self-promulgated allure of Europe and its arrogant claims to greater "civilization" were far more arguable in the wake of these circumstances. This example lays out the difference between a critique of specifically Western political liberalism, a critique largely motivated by Marxist or pro-Soviet political views, and a longer lasting and more philosophical awareness of what Gianni Vattimo called the *Verwindung* (unwinding or decline) of abstract European claims to a kind of innate superiority, which was cultural if no longer literally racial.

The Bandung/Third World perspective was expanded by this broad and long-term critique. It was also challenged by anti-communist activity in Africa and Asia. Once it became clear that who held power in the Third World was an important question to the United States, the American Right became interested in Africa. While the Left acclaimed Sékou Touré, the first president of Guinea, and Kwame Nkrumah, the first president of Ghana, the Right acclaimed Congolese politician Moise Tshombe and the Angolan guerrilla leader Jonas Savimbi. In the United States, the Right's support of Tshombe and Savimbi was a marked departure from the previous racialism and isolationism of American conservatives. In the 1980s, Savimbi was even touted by the US Right for having darker skin, and therefore being more authentic, than the Marxists he was trying to overthrow in Luanda, the country's capital. US right-wing politicians made pilgrimages to Jamba, Savimbi's remote hideout, the same way that radical Marxists had visited Nkrumah's capital of Accra or Touré's capital of Conakry. The views of the Right were not, however, those of typical Afrocentrists. This was, to say the least, not your father's Afrocentrism.[16] Still, the father of President Obama was able to come to the United States during this period and marry a US resident because America was courting the nations of black Africa, now that they were independent, and trying to ensure that they did not turn to communism. As we recall from the views of Aijaz Ahmad, presented in the last chapter, pressure to look good in independent African eyes also hastened the arrival of civil rights for African Americans within the United States.[17] And this enabled a multiplicity of perspectives to attach themselves to the adjectives "African" and "Asian." Naipaul, following to some extent the example of Nirad Chaudhuri, tried to be more English than the English, but he always maintained a sense of his Indian diasporic origins. Naipaul offered a critique of Third-World leftism that could not be accused of racism or vestigial colonialism because Naipaul was of Indian descent. Naipaul served as an indication that critiques of Europe based on colour and politics had the potential to be countered in the same coin. Naipaul was, in a way, the literary equivalent of Tshombe and Savimbi, though, happily for him and his readers, he had far more success in his chosen career.

The 1980s: From Commonwealth to Post-Colonial

In the academic world, conditions were more placid. Even in 1970 or so, literature was more of an export to the former British colonies, now part of the Commonwealth of Nations, than an import. Many British professors came out to universities in Australia, Canada, and post-colonial Africa to teach about the English novelistic canon, as seen by F.R. Leavis (see the preface). Some of them came back with an enhanced idea of what was actually happening in the literature of the countries where they were teaching, but many did not. Even as writers like Caribbean poets Derek Walcott and Edward (later Kamau) Brathwaite were formulating sophisticated challenges to dominant European paradigms in their poetry, comparable innovation in criticism did not occur. Even as Derrida and Foucault became household names during the 1970s, what was then called "world literature in English" or "Commonwealth literature" existed in a state of calm and obscurity, presided over by diligent but largely untheoretical scholars such as Bruce King, Joseph Jones, and William Walsh, who prepared the canons that, in later decades, would be the premise for the theorizing that overtook them. This nascent criticism considered as its subject what was then called, at least in the English-speaking world, "Commonwealth literature," after the Commonwealth of Nations that replaced the British Empire after 1947. Scholars in the field of Commonwealth literature, such as Walsh, King, and Jones, did not excite much interest among graduate students in any era.[18] Yet these critics laid the groundwork. They did the first-order tasks, the identification of important writers and themes that later academics, who gained far more fame and currency, crucially depended on.

One of the patterns established early on by these critics was that criticism (and later theory) and primary literature were regarded side by side. Anna Rutherford, an expatriate Australian, published the influential journal *Kunapipi* from the University of Aarhus in Denmark.[19] Rutherford published fiction and poetry by post-colonial writers and criticism about them in her journal. In this milieu, "white" and "black" writers were colleagues, in a way often underappreciated outside the United States. In the United States, post-colonial criticism became associated with racial diversity, and it was seen as mainly concerned with South Asian or African issues. (Other non-white areas of the world, e.g., Samoa, Fiji, and the other island nations of the South Pacific, were, as Juniper Ellis has argued, scanted by typical US post-colonial accounts.[20]) But, even in the United States, the dialogue between the creative and the critical established by Rutherford and her generation of scholars and editors remained. As compared to US minority or feminist studies, which, especially after the 1980s, concentrated on retrieving previously marginal texts, post-colonial studies concentrated far more on the literature of the present. Lay readers exploring current fiction from India, Africa, and, to a lesser extent, Canada and Australia, which became very popular in the 1990s, ended up unintentionally reading writers either in dialogue with theory or under analysis by theorists. Therefore, curiously enough, post-colonial studies, one of the latest and initially most arcane areas of theory, might well have made the maximum impact of any theory school on the lay reader.

One of the early centres of post-colonial study was the University of Leeds in England, where A. Norman "Derry" Jeffares trained an entire generation of post-colonial scholars who went on to teach the world over.[21] It might seem incongruous that a city located in the country that formerly ruled the British Empire became an incubator of post-colonialism. But it actually raises two important points. Post-colonialism, as contrasted to Bandung-era "Third World" thought, was never about national independence per se. It was not just a coalition of nationalisms, although it was at its most fruitful when certain nationalisms informed the discourse. Rather, post-colonialism partook in a general sounding of the aftermath of colonialism, the damages inflicted by the colonial mentality and the possibility of a critique of hegemonic dominance—dominance as such, not just the dominance of a particular nation or political tendency. Second, the fact that Leeds was in the industrial north of England, not the more elite-dominated south, raised the possibility of a commonality between working-class consciousness and the reparation of global inequality. This potential was tacitly raised by Leavisism but never fulfilled because Leavis had a very limited canon and was relatively incurious about new works, from anywhere. But in the next generation, these discursive walls came tumbling down, and Leeds, like Aarhus, was as vital to what became post-colonialism as Sydney, Calcutta, Port of Spain, Vancouver, Dhaka, or Accra.

King, Walsh, Jones, and Jeffares were largely conventional scholars who wrote about style, theme, and technique, as critics of European literature would have at the time. Their importance was in writing about world literature in English at all; they got the idea of studying these writers into the curricula and bibliographies of institutions. But other scholars realized the need to use different methods in recognition of the different qualities in some of the new literatures. In both the Caribbean and the "Celtic fringe" of the United Kingdom, poetry retained songlike, oral qualities, and these literatures were replete with the excitement of the transition between oral and written culture as had occurred in the times of Homer, the Hebrew Bible, and the Arthurian romances and in various places during the early nineteenth century.[22] Post-colonial scholars coined the word "orature." Orature emphasized the sophistication of oral expression in narrative and lyric without succumbing to the hierarchical assumption that the printed word was all that mattered.[23] The idea of orature functioned to enhance people's notions of what a text could be, and it emancipated texts from dependence on the written word. Yet the written word was necessarily the medium in which even analysts of orature responded to the works they studied.[24]

And it was the written word that provided the most attention-getting aspects of the new literatures. Nobel prizes were won by the Australian Patrick White (who was, however, unlike his younger compatriot Peter Carey, always seen as too modernist to be really post-colonial), the South African novelist Nadine Gordimer, the Nigerian playwright and memoirist Wole Soyinka, the St. Lucian poet Derek Walcott, the Irish poet Seamus Heaney, and, later, the British writer of Indo-Trinidadian descent V.S. Naipaul. These prizes testified to the institutional recognition of world literature in English. Literature in English that originated outside of England or the United States was not, as pre-1970s' thought had tended to judge it, inevitably second rate and derivative. Importantly, a good many of these writers were also critics or advocates of the idea of new national and diasporic literatures; the Canadian novelist Margaret Atwood, for instance, early in her career was a Canadian literary nationalist who asserted autonomy from both British and American precedents and called for understanding Canadian literature within its unique territorial and political situation. Even a writer such as Naipaul, who often took provocatively unorthodox, often conservative-sounding positions, called attention to the importance of Africa, the Caribbean, and the Muslim world in contemporary society, and he did so in a way that posited it not just as novelistic subject-matter but as a set of social and cultural circumstances that demanded world attention.

These writers were part of "international English literature," and their work resonated because of both their individual achievements and their common participation in a project of non-metropolitan enfranchisement. But these writers also profited from and were succoured by national frames. Walcott could not have emerged as a poet, for instance, had there not been an anglophone Caribbean institutional structure, just developing in his youth, represented by the poet Frank Collymore and his editorship of the journal *BIM*.[25] Similarly, the New Zealand novelist Janet Frame received support. Frame spent much of her life in the United States and the United Kingdom, and, although her books were often set in New Zealand and dealt with the dissociations and dislocations of consciousness, they could have been set anywhere in many respects. Still, Frame would not have become a writer had not Frank Sargeson, a locally prominent New Zealand fiction writer, taken her into a cottage on his property and offered her moral support.[26] Also notable was that both Walcott, in some of his earlier poetry, and Frame, in her memoirs and in some of her earlier fiction, were intensely autobiographical writers—not naively or invariably so, but their self was at the centre of their work. Soyinka also devoted much of his literary career to writing acclaimed autobiography.[27] The growth of the self echoed the growth of post-colonial assertiveness. This did not always happen in a direct expressive linkage—often the axis of individual growth and the axis of political circumstances were at cross purposes. But individuality, the self, was always more a part of the post-colonial project than it was for the discourses of race, ethnicity, and even sexuality, for which group identity seemed to be at least the first step in carving out a space of critical awareness.

There was an appreciable difference between how English and French functioned worldwide. Other than the Congo Republic (known as Zaire in the era of high post-colonialism), Rwanda, and Burundi, all of which were colonized by Belgium, all francophone post-colonial nations had at one point been colonized by France, and, in many cases, had similar historical and institutional relationships to their colonizer. This situation did not pertain in the English-speaking world: the Philippines, for instance, is a populous country with English as one of its several literary languages, yet it had been an American rather than a British overseas possession, and its writers could not readily be seen as part of "Commonwealth literature."[28] Similarly, writers such as the Somali Nuruddin Farah, whose nation had been colonized by Italy, wrote in English by choice, without necessarily having a "colonial" or even "post-colonial" relationship to the language the way others might—the reverse of how Ngugi, living in the country just to the south of Farah's, saw his relationship to English.[29] Neither all nations nor all new post-colonial literatures had the same story. Nationality or locality made a difference.

The fruitful role played generally by notions of national space in incipient post-colonial criticism can be seen in an exemplary way in the case of Canada. Until the mid-1960s, both the world and Canadians considered Canadian literature to be provincial. Those within and outside of Canada knew that the country produced literature, but this literature was taken, by definition, to be not up to world standards. It was not so much that the literature was weighed in the balance and found wanting by a series of accredited critics but that Canada itself was found wanting, was not seen as worthy of the honour of producing notable literature. It did not matter that Canada produced remarkable writers with the capacity to speak to readers who were not Canadian and had no personal stake in the growth of Canadian literature; the narrative poetry of E.J. Pratt, the distinctive realism of Sara Jeannette Duncan and Sinclair Ross, and the home-grown experimentation of Sheila Watson and Howard O'Hagan all burst well beyond the stereotype of the staid, parochial, behind-the-time desuetude in which the literature of Canada was classified by outsiders, if they thought about it at all.[30] Thus, Canadian literature could only be valorized once Canada itself had been valorized by, in a word, nationalism. The anglophone Canadian nationalism that emerged during the 1970s had many problems. Its literary criticism had a thematic focus that was inherited from Frye and seen in the critical thought of the novelist Margaret Atwood, the poet Dennis Lee, and, slightly later, the critic Gaile McGregor. This focus was at first edifying, but it later became a straitjacket.[31] Frye's discernment of a "garrison mentality" in the Canadian mindset, a hunkering down in the cities and fortresses along the thin strip of populated land at the southern edge of the country, led to a privileging of the wilderness as the place that would answer the fundamental Canadian question—not "who are we?" (as in the case of the United States) but "where is here?" Canada needed to embrace its own landscape as a resonant symbol for fiction. Thus, criticism became preoccupied with nature and its archetypal significance in a way that ignored the fact that Canada was an urban nation and one that, as Frank Davey suggested, was a "post-national" polity because of its heterogeneity and lack of mobilizing patriotic rhetoric.[32] Though Atwood, both in her early novel *Surfacing* and in her influential critical tract *Survival*, gave a complex view of the landscape whose strangeness had to be embraced and yet not surrendered to or fetishized, often, Canadian literary explorations of the landscape ended up being what T.D. MacLulich characterized as "Northerns," Canadian versions of US Westerns in which the landscape was used as a metaphor for discovery, growth, and psychological enlargement or bafflement.[33] This approach produced some interesting works of fiction. But, by and large, it tended towards the apolitical, for instance, by not taking sufficient and specific account of the Inuit and other First Nations Canadian peoples.

The entire issue of whether indigenous peoples were "post-colonial" at all was taken up by the popular First Nations Canadian novelist and media personality Thomas King, who rejected the term because it "organizes Native literature progressively," cuts Native people off from "traditions that were in place before colonialism," and "supposes that contemporary Native writing is largely a construct of oppression."[34] Besides, King felt that to be a token strand

in the large fabric of post-colonialism would slight the specificity of his people's historical experience, their decimation, suffering, and perseverance.[35] The
French-speaking population of Canada could mount similar observations about
viewing Québécois literature in terms of anglophone Canadian post-colonialism. Although French language and culture were threatened in "post-colonial"
and predominantly English-speaking Canada, especially when diversity issues
and multiculturalism began to challenge official bilingualism, to see Québécois
literature as "post-colonial" organizes it according to the advent of English
dominance and disregards what that literature is in and of itself—a literature
distinct from Canadian literature in English.

It was felt that English and French-speaking literature were "two solitudes,"
the title of Hugh McLennan's famous novel, and that the same critic could not
be competent in both.[36] This seems a bit absurd, as certainly a Victorian critic
such as Matthew Arnold kept up to date on people like Hippolyte Taine and
Ernest Renan. Why could an appreciative reader of Lee and Atwood not read
Roch Carrier or Réjean Ducharme in the same spirit? There was more here than
just mere intellectual timidity, though. As Christian Champion has pointed out,
the Anglo-Canadian nationalism of the 1960s, though seemingly speaking out
against Canada's marginalization by its British colonizers and by the cultural
arrogance of the United States, its colossal neighbour to the south, was also
intended to marginalize the French-speaking aspect of Canadian culture.[37] That
this same era saw the "Quiet Revolution" during which Québec transformed
itself from a deliberately backward bulwark of old-fashioned rural Catholicism
to a dynamic and diasporic liberal and, eventually, post-liberal society meant
that the rhetoric of Canadian and Québécois nationalism produced a palpable
sundering between the two sides. Francophones were embracing the city while
anglophones, at least symbolically, were going back to the land.

Yet 1970s nationalism enabled Canadian writers to be respected worldwide
in ways that had never happened before. Canadian writers wrote about Canada
instead of attempting international settings, as had earlier writers such as
Morley Callaghan (acclaimed charmingly if somewhat quixotically by Edmund
Wilson, in the classic instance of a US critic granting a seigniorial nod to a
lucky writer from another country.)[38] Alice Munro and Robertson Davies were
valued precisely because of their quirky Canadian qualities. They were willing
to set their stories in remote small-town Ontario and let the significance of their
vision be communicated by the excellence of their writing rather than make any
deliberate appeal to being international, as might have occurred in the modernist era. However, although Canadian writers were properly appreciated, many
contemporaries and counterparts of theirs from other former colonies were not
known outside their home countries. In a way, Canadian nationalism was also
responsible for this. Bookselling practices, such as having a separate section
of bookstores for Canadian books, were symptomatic of a sense of reserve,
of using Canadian books to fill a quota that took national identity more into

account than literary quality. Canada's entering into a free-trade pact with the United States in the late 1980s augured, or at least paralleled, a freer migration of books across the US-Canadian border.

Open Borders

The idea of open borders became more heard in literary circles in the 1980s. Partially enabled by the implementation of neoliberal economic policies, partially a product of non-European literature in English finally feeling free to be ambitious and to ventilate its concerns on the largest of scales (a circumstance that was itself inspired, in part, by the Latin American "boom" of the 1960s, which made the mode of magic realism widely popular), a sense of release and expansion accompanied post-colonial writing in the 1980s. Perhaps the quintessential figure in this regard was Salman Rushdie, whose *Midnight's Children* (1981) linked the growth of a young boy with the history of India and Pakistan after independence and partition in 1947.[39] Rushdie's protagonist and surrogate, Saleem Sinai, is "connected to history," in both literal and metaphorical ways, and this connection enabled Rushdie to write a book that could present India (and, for that matter, Pakistan) to a global audience yet resonate at the same time with the South Asian reader in intensely local ways.

Rushdie showed that, both on the lower and higher frequencies (as Ralph Ellison might say), postcolonial literature could make news. He also showed that, even if one accepted Iser's dictum (see Chapter 2) about the text positing just one sort of reader, the condition of post-colonialism raised the spectre of this reader perhaps having more than one face. Rushdie shows a keen sense of European tradition—*Midnight's Children* revels in its overt address to European precursors such as Cervantes, Laurence Sterne, E.M. Forster, and James Joyce. But these gusto-filled allusions were not just intertextual engagement or even Bloomian "misreading." They were also a kind of critique. By knowing so much about Western literature yet performing it in his own South Asian terms, Rushdie was paying tribute to the European tradition as well as satirizing and burlesquing it. This simultaneous practice of emulation and parody was picked up on by many post-colonial critics. Bhabha's theory of creative mimicry was one of the foremost articulations of this feeling.

Key here was a short book by three Australian-based academics. *The Empire Writes Back* (1989), by Helen Tiffin, Gareth Griffiths, and Bill Ashcroft, was an overview of all of post-colonial literature and theory that, for the first time, presented a methodical prism to conceptualize the landscape of the new literatures. For Ashcroft, Griffiths, and Tiffin, literature in a post-colonial context was an act of resistance but also of rearticulating; the colonized did not simply rebut or refute the colonizer but rather took the colonizer's game and replayed it on the former colony's turf.[40] The genealogy of the title *The Empire Writes Back* is an interesting one. Its basis is the 1980 movie *The Empire Strikes Back*, the second (eventually the fifth, counting the prequels) film in the *Star Wars* series. In this fictional universe the "Empire" is the villain (a clear debt to traditional US anti-colonialism, whose advocates taught in US elementary school classrooms that British imperialism was villainous—and taught this just as fervently as did anti-colonialists in, say, post-independence Ghana). George Lucas's title had become such a fixture in popular culture that, in 1982, after Argentina had invaded the British-held Falkland Islands, claiming (only half-truthfully) that this was an anti-colonial move, the British decision to try to retake the islands (which was eventually successful) was heralded on the cover of the April 10, 1982 *Newsweek* magazine as "The Empire Strikes Back." This usage, interestingly, saw the "Empire" as Britain, still determined to exercise its military power. But it was meant positively. The US media supported Britain, both because America and Britain shared a culture and because the United States preferred to support a democracy against a dictatorship.

That same year, Paul Gilroy used the same title for a co-edited anthology on black British identities, *The Empire Strikes Back: Race and Racism in '70s Britain*, a book that examines the construction of an authoritarian state in Britain being fundamentally intertwined with the elaboration of popular racism in the 1970s. This usage, though contrary in meaning, anticipated in thrust how the three Australian critics would use and amend the slogan by the end of the decade. In the Ashcroft, Griffiths, and Tiffin usage, the "Empire" was not, as it was for both Gilroy and those who wrote about the Falklands, Britain but the *former British colonies*. But the positive valence for "Empire" remained. In a sense, the British Empire was fighting back, against itself. This sense of post-colonial literature being a redefinition as much as a refutation of that of the colonizer was a persistent strand in *The Empire Writes Back*. Also notable was how the focus was shifted to the English-speaking world, and the stress was on literature in English. The three critics spoke many methodological languages and put them to ingenious use in analysing and theorizing an astonishing multiplicity of contexts. Occasionally, they mention critics working largely outside of anglophone literatures, such as the Haitian-Québécois academic Max Dorsinville. Their work was certainly potentially applicable to other world languages, and its paradigm was frequently so applied. But the only language that seemed to be spoken in practical terms was English.

Appiah's question, with which this chapter began, tended to be answered negatively. The "post-" in "postmodern" and in "post-colonial" were not the same. Postmodernism tended to focus on fictional and linguistic innovation whereas post-colonialism had to do with concrete political conditions and the psychological scars of racism and marginalization. What the two had in common, though, Appiah suggested, was a sense of an unresolved relation to their predecessor. Jean-François Lyotard, who had early on sketched the difference between modernist avant-garde progressivism and postmodern scepticism, nonetheless warned that the postmodern could not entirely afford to jettison the

modern and that much of what postmodernism could achieve consisted of refin-
ing a new non-modernist perspective—which nonetheless took the modern into
account. Post-colonialism had a similar connection with colonialism although,
in concrete terms, a far less felicitous one. But what was that connection? Did
post-colonialism mean after colonialism, in the wake of colonialism, or bearing
the impact of colonialism? Used in denotative political terms, post-colonialism
originally meant "after national independence." Indeed, much early analysis
of post-colonial literatures focused on the emergence of national literary institutions. This could, for instance, involve the role of crucial precedents who
paved the way for later writers (such as Amos Tutuola in Nigeria or Sargeson in
New Zealand) or the way literature could operate to strengthen what Benedict
Anderson called the "imagined community," which was often constituted by
print culture and articulated by the media within a specific national space.

But there was a problem here. Nations that had achieved independence
from European colonization often harboured secession movements themselves.
Nigeria, one of the largest and potently one of the most prosperous and important African nations, experienced the catastrophically bloody rebellion of the
eastern region of Biafra. The South Asian nation of Bangladesh could be said to
have waged three anti-colonial struggles: against its British colonizers; against
the Hindu India with which it, a Muslim nation, did not want to combine; and
against Pakistan, when this country tried to privilege religion over language
and rule Muslim Bengal from a thousand miles away. A neat organic analogy,
whereby the national literature can blossom in a fashion complementary to the
nation's emergence onto the world stage cannot be applicable here. Moreover,
is "anti-colonial" and "post-colonial" the same thing? Is postmodern the same
thing as anti-modern? Lyotard and most theorists of the postmodern would say
no, and this is why a frankly realistic painting or a bestselling novel is not routinely considered postmodern, even though it may be produced in the postmodern era and even though it has no claim to being modernist; postmodernism has
to show some formal awareness of modernism before doing something new, in
the view of most. Similarly, post-colonialism may involve less lashing out against
colonialism and more understanding of its complicated legacy. Further, many
argued that colonialism was not yet over. Even the emancipated former colonies
were still economically dependent on the former colonizer, a circumstance especially true in francophone countries that were once colonies. The omnipresence
of American economic power or that of multinational corporations constituted
a sort of "neocolonialism." All this meant that the celebrations of unambiguous
national freedom had to be postponed.

A question cognate to Appiah's, but far less frequently asked, was, "Is the
post in post-colonial the same as the post in post-structuralism?" Here the
answer may, paradoxically, be more positive. Even though structuralism, in the
person of its most famous exponent Claude Lévi-Strauss, had preoccupied itself
with non-Western peoples and how their units of linguistic meaning operate

in ways applicable to Western subjects as well, Derrida early on accused Lévi-Strauss of romanticizing the non-European "other" much as Rousseau had done in his eighteenth-century ideas about the "noble savage." Derrida articulated a historicity, an admission of change and fragmentation into structuralist binaries that rendered non-Western subjects not just as static complements but also as dynamic formulators that spoke within a flexible and uncontrollable series of signifiers. As a Jew from Algeria who made his career in France, Derrida was, of course, a quintessential post-colonial and diasporic figure. Even more crucially, post-structuralism advocated the tearing down of cultural walls and the abandonment of taboos about what was canonical and what was not, what could be inside the house of literature and what could not. As with anti-racist and feminist critics, advocates of post-colonial literatures needed Derrida in order to make their field visible within the anglophone academy. One would think that the existence of independent former European colonies would be enough, in political terms, to make literatures and theories emanating from these new countries viable. Indeed political and literary recognition did coincide in the aftermath of the collapse of the Soviet Union between 1989 and 1991; the world understood that this event had produced a set of regional and national literatures that now could speak freely. But post-colonialism involved more than a renewed nationalism, and this was why, as the question was inevitably asked and answered after 1991, the "post-" in "post-Soviet" was indeed different from the "post-" in "post-colonial" (with the arguable exception of Central Asia).[41] The invisibility not only of Asian and black African literatures in English but also of white settler literatures was not just a reflection of political nearsightedness. It was a product of a deep and complex series of intellectual investments. It took post-structuralism's overhaul of settled assumptions to shake up these investments.

Said, Spivak, and Bhabha: Major Post-Colonial Theorists

The arrival of post-structuralism in the field of Commonwealth literature made it "post-colonial." No longer was the purpose just to read and celebrate world literature in English; it was to question the hierarchical and even metaphysical assumptions that had lain behind colonialism itself, as Derrida had questioned the assumptions of logocentrism. Post-colonial criticism brought a large and heterogeneous body of texts and ideas into literary study. But, as with deconstruction, star theorists emerged who attracted attention to the larger set of discourses they represented. Of these, Edward W. Said (1935–2003) was the best known, although the least "theoretical" in the formal sense. Of Palestinian descent (Christian, not Muslim), Said and his family left their homeland upon the establishment of Israel in 1948. Said's family was well off, and he went to exclusive schools both in Egypt and in the United States, where he did his undergraduate and graduate work. Said started out as a scholar of Joseph

Conrad, whose role both in the established canon and for post-colonial studies we have discussed with respect to Achebe in the preface. Early on, though,
Said wrote *Beginnings: Intention and Method* (1975), a work notable for how
perceptively it connected with what was just beginning to be called "theory." A
particular inspiration for Said in this book is the eighteenth-century Italian philosopher Giambattista Vico.[42] Vico concentrated on "gentile history" as opposed
to "sacred history." He assumed this focus both to keep out of controversy and
also to understand how institutions originated out of history rather than simply
being handed down from above.[43] In the modernist era, Vico was often seen as a
figure who urged the cyclical as opposed to the linear view of history. This was,
roughly, how James Joyce had used him in *Finnegans Wake*. But, in the postmodern era, Vico's interest in history, not only in its content but in its making,
became important. From Vico, Said got the idea of truth emerging from human
agency, not inspiring it. Thus, Said speaks of "contingent authority," the kind
of power established by an author in the course of her or his work.[44] In a sense,
"contingent authority" was like the authority wielded by newly independent
states, a power that had to be striven for, carved out.

Yet, despite these analogical potentials, Said had thus far written more or
less as a Western critic sharing his interests might have. This changed with
Orientalism (1978). *Orientalism* was one of the most important books of the
late twentieth century. It made an immediate impact on how people thought
and spoke. *Orientalism* was a critique of the derogation of the East by the
West, of the designation of the East as "other" (Said borrowed the term "alter-
ity" from the psychoanalytic thought of Jacques Lacan, and it became more
widely used in its new context than in its old). But *Orientalism* was not written
about the non-Western world. It was written about Western discourses *about*
the non-Western world. Those hoping that Said's book would afford them positive knowledge of the world outside Europe ended up very disappointed. What
they learned about was how past Western scholars, such as Louis Massignon
and Raymond Schwab, constructed the East. Said was not just muckraking here,
not just exposing cultural prejudice; he was providing a Viconian history of the
making of knowledge. But this knowledge was not actually "about" the non-
Western world. Indeed, one of the unfortunate by-products of Said's book is
that, by analysing Western interest in the non-Western (begging the question of
the highly debatable nature of that distinction in the first place), it facilitated the
easy castigation of any curiosity about the non-Western "other" as "Orientalist."
Said did not mean to do this, but he did mean to demonstrate that knowledge
created in the West about the East was not disinterested, that it had an agenda,
both in what it said about "the other" and in its use of power to say anything
about "the other."

Nor was Said himself disinterested. Indeed, he thought it very important for
people to understand that intellectuals have affiliations or, in an even deeper
sense, are "filiated" (from *filius*—son in Latin) with ideologies to which, in

a mode familiar to us from our discussion of Foucault, they have a virtually archaeological or genealogical relation. Said did not vilify or defame European thinkers whom he called "Orientalist" (which was originally a neutral term denoting people who studied the Orient, much as astronomers would study the stars). He merely wanted the student to know where they were coming from in order to assess their thought in its full scope. Said spoke of the "secular" as something he valued. This term meant the non-religious, the sphere of civil society. But Said did not partake in the metanarratives of secularization that were also eschewed by the later Derrida. He meant "secular" in the sense of another favourite term of his, "worldly." The worldly critic, for Said, was willing to be acquainted with institutions, to mix it up with them, neither to be totally co-opted by them nor to become locked in a fruitlessly oppositional posture. The worldly intellectual became familiar with institutions without becoming their creature.

Said sympathized with Antonio Gramsci's concept of the "organic intellectual," the thinker whose thought did not transcend the social horizons from which it emerged but ministered to that context. Aimé Césaire, for instance, is a perfect example of what an organic intellectual would be. Said was *not* an organic intellectual. Despite participating in Palestinian political activity (sometimes outrageously, as when he symbolically threw a stone at Israeli-occupied territory, doing his cause no good in the minds of people already suspicious of him), Said did not live in Palestine or anywhere in the Arab world. He lived in New York. Indeed, in many ways, he became in manner and range of interest the quintessential New York Intellectual, far outstripping someone like Trilling by not only being acquainted with a broad range of literature and culture but also excelling in fields such as music, into which the word-centred Trilling would have never assayed. But the point here is that his New York self was non-resident with respect to his own presumptive identity, that of an "Arab." Said, in fact, closely associated the idea of the intellectual with the figure in exile, with thinkers who may well have loyalties but who did not subsume themselves into a concrete adherence to such loyalties which might well have proven constricting.

Being such an intellectual example does not always jive with doing concrete intellectual work. Said, though, also excelled as a reader of texts. He was an admirer of R.P. Blackmur as well as Raymond Williams, and he was as fascinated by language and inference as he was by culture and society. Indeed, perhaps the most influential single reading of the theoretical era may well have been the treatment of Jane Austen's *Mansfield Park* he gave in *Culture and Imperialism*.[45] As we have seen, Jane Austen, though always a popular favourite, had only become the object of wide critical study after feminism. But a vestigial image of Austen as apolitical or perhaps as being vaguely concerned with preserving a certain existing social order but otherwise acquiescent to patterns she did not subvert or challenge still ruled the day. Said, though, points out that *Mansfield Park* "connects the actualities of British power overseas to the domestic imbroglio within the Bertram estate."[46] When Sir Thomas Bertram comes back from the West Indies he surprises his children and their friends who had, without his warrant, staged Elizabeth Inchbald's quite free adaptation of August Friedrich Ferdinand von Kotzebue's play *Lovers' Vows*. The conventional reading, done most famously by Lionel Trilling, sees Austen as endorsing Sir Thomas's dislike of the play, which causes him to look with new favour upon his previously neglected ward, Fanny Price, who had participated only reluctantly and minimally in the theatrical project. Austen, suggests Trilling, is suspicious of the fakery and inauthenticity of the theatre, and Sir Thomas operates as a kind of cultural enforcer in restoring sobriety and the expected. That Austen would also be interrogating her own fakery, her own art, was a tacit part of this argument. And part of the undertone of the entire 1950s New York Intellectual approach to literature was how deeply uncomfortable creativity, in all its aspects, made it. Said turns our attention not to Sir Thomas's return but to where he had been—the family's estates in Antigua. In that era, owning property in the West Indies must have meant owning slaves. Thus, all the wealth of Mansfield Park is built on slavery, and the entire lifestyle is, in a sense, a play in that it disguises its fundamental dependence on racial inequality. This reading enabled the mainstream English canon to be opened up to post-colonial discourses.

Said was not telling people not to read Jane Austen, however; he was not throwing her on the trash heap as a racist. He was, in fact, reinvigorating the reading of Austen, giving it a new rationale. Indeed, *Mansfield Park* became what Said called "a traveling text" in the wake of the slavery reading, a text that gains new meaning as it manifests itself in different contexts. Although the 1990s Jane Austen film boom was seen, in some quarters, as a return to traditional values, the 1999 adaptation of *Mansfield Park* had to include the slavery aspects—the director was one who would not have resisted such a reading, but, even if a different filmmaker had made the film, the presence of slavery in it was now unavoidable. And other readings could radiate out from these. Some might note that Kotzebue, the original playwright whose work was subversive in the context of the Bertram family, was, in fact, so conservative that German radicals assassinated him in 1819 for being too much a stanchion of traditionalism. Some feminists, such as Susan Fraiman, questioned Said's reading. Fraiman usefully cautioned against seeing post-colonial readings as a panacea or as a monolithic determinant of what the text "really meant." In Fraiman's analysis, doing either privileged a cool, subversive but still patriarchal masculinity.[47] But Fraiman's critique was occasioned by Said's, as were other responses questioning Said's assumption that an English gentleman who owned property in the West Indies would automatically own slaves. Said's reading of Austen did become a cliché, and one that was often used as a kind of votive offering to the imperative of listening to the oppressed, after which the oppressed could no longer lay a claim upon their oppressors. This is the fate of nearly all ideas that become popular, though; they become convenient ideological slogans, and theory's task is to continue to problematize them. In Said, these approaches find an ally. Far from closing off reading with politically correct mandates, Said opened it up, enlarged the circle of interpretation. Many ideas can radiate out from Said's approach to literature, and the work of William D. Hart, among others, has already shown its fecundity in this respect.

Said inspired general critical approaches as well, approaches having to do with more than post-colonialism or the presentation of Islam. His idea of "late style" suggested that the late works of various writers and composers had a distinctive style or set of styles to them. Said drew the circle of how literature could be appreciated ever wider. Whether within the global political economy or within the intimate circumstances of an individual author, Said opened up new space for understanding, inquiry, and appreciation. Said made another important move in counting William Butler Yeats as a post-colonial writer. Whereas, as we have discussed, most other US-based critics defined the post-colonial category in racial terms, Said did not. For example, he saw Yeats, who was not only white but also part of the Protestant elite of Ireland, as an oppositional, post-colonial intellectual because Yeats supported the cause of Irish independence. This perspective opened the way in the 1990s for a vigorous convergence between Irish studies and post-colonial theory, as seen in the work of Elizabeth Butler Cullingford and Joseph Lennon. It also allowed for consideration of what Michael Hechter had, as early as the 1970s, called the "internal colonialism" of England with respect to Wales and Scotland, largely Celtic parts of Great Britain. Recognition of this form of colonialism led to substantial work emerging in the 1990s on Welsh and Scottish post-coloniality by such scholars as Ian Duncan, Caroline McCracken-Flesher, and Kenneth McNeil, work that coincided with the political re-emergence of Wales and Scotland as nations with limited self-rule. (The process of devolution followed a referendum in 1997 and ended in the creation of two devolved national legislatures in 1999.) This work on "internal" post-colonial literature in the United Kingdom complemented that done by Hall and Gilroy on black and diasporic British identities (see Chapter 4). Indeed, it could be argued that the United Kingdom itself, as a political unit, was consummately post-colonial, including in the 1990s not only the English, Scottish, and Welsh but also people of Irish, South Asian, African, and Caribbean descent as part of one civil commonwealth. What the United Kingdom had by tradition is in many ways what other nations were desperately trying to acquire by more formal means. But the overall point is that the presence of these debates in US post-colonial criticism was tremendously facilitated by Said's liberality. Another major contributor here was Katie Trumpener, whose *Bardic Nationalism* (1997) saw Celtic local and regional discourses of the Romantic era as providing the template for later assertions of national plurality within the English-speaking world and for the consummate expressions of national identity through the historical novel, a genre so often associated with later post-colonial writing.[48]

But the point of post-colonialism was not just a plurality of nations but also a plurality of modes and systems of thought. Said's theoretical orientation was Foucauldian, although Said did not share Foucault's scepticism about agency and the possibility of individuals making history, which is much like being influenced by Søren Kierkegaard (about whom Said wrote brilliantly in *Beginnings*) without sharing Kierkegaard's Christianity. The connection between post-structuralism and post-colonialism, however, is located most pivotally in the work of Gayatri Chakravorty Spivak (1942–) and Homi Bhabha (1948–). And Bhabha and Spivak were Derrideans. Spivak was a deconstructionist before she was a post-colonialist. Spivak got her start in the academic world as the translator of Derrida's *Of Grammatology*. Spivak, as we have discussed, also wrote a lengthy introduction to this book, which was many people's first exposure to the ideas of Derrida.

For his part, Bhabha published his reputation-making article in a 1984 special issue of the journal *October*, a quarterly with post-structuralist inflections that focused on the visual arts. The special issue was on psychoanalysis, especially Lacanian psychoanalysis. The point is that both Spivak and Bhabha connected post-colonial criticism to theoretical approaches to literature. It was not enough to read novels from India and Africa, decide that they were good or at least interesting, and write criticism on them. If this were all that was needed, Walsh, King, and Jones would have been famous critics, and Spivak and Bhabha would not have needed to emerge. But the curriculum and canon and training of English professors was doggedly conservative, and, even after the methodological opening that occurred in the wake of Derrida and Foucault, the liberalized methods were largely being applied to the same old texts. It took the theories of Spivak and Bhabha to make novelists like Rushdie readable in academia.

Spivak's "Can the Subaltern Speak?" asks a very Derridean question: Is it ever possible for the subaltern—the subordinate, the underprivileged—to master a discourse that, by its very articulation, is most likely controlled by whomever is in power? Is it ever possible to get outside of a master language? "Subaltern" was originally applied to subordinate officers in the British Army, then later to native administrators within India. The term "subaltern" was used in India to describe those who were subordinated or routinely dictated to, those who were the objects of the attempted control of others. "Subaltern" as a word was very much a product of "British English" as a language as opposed to "American English." However, Spivak's essay probably had its greatest audience in the United States, precisely where, for linguistic reasons, the term "subaltern" would not resonate and where, indeed, it was as much a neologism as *episteme* or *différance*. In many ways, post-colonial criticism not only represented Asian and African homelands in the West but also enabled components of the West to understand their own diasporic and fragmented heritage.

In "Can the Subaltern Speak?" Spivak asks about the conditions under which those oppressed by colonialism can manifest literary self-awareness;

she contends, in other words, that post-colonial writing is not an ideal speech situation, that there are conditions and contingencies against which many who attempt to make them known must struggle. Spivak herself unabashedly avowed membership in the elite Brahmin caste and described herself as being of upper middle-class background; she had a keen understanding of the combination of privilege and of elevated racial status that her background gave her in the various spheres in which she moved, both in India and the metropolitan West. Spivak was also uncompromisingly intellectual, and she was indispensable in establishing post-colonial studies as a field of the most exacting and self-questioning thought, a field that did not flinch from facing its own contradictions and enigmas. Spivak was conscious both of her upper middle-class origins and her elite status within the North American academy, and she constantly drew attention to the Bengali writer Mahasweta Devi, who wrote of oppressed women's lives, and the historian Ranajit Guha, who pioneered "subaltern studies" as a formal discipline.

Spivak, like Said, was also known for practical readings of widely read, frequently studied canonical texts. Spivak produced an influential reading of *Jane Eyre*, but she read the text in a very different way than had the feminists Sandra Gilbert and Susan Gubar. For her (and for the novelist Jean Rhys, whose 1966 *Wide Sargasso Sea*, a prequel to Brontë's book, became highly canonical in the post-colonial era), "the madwoman in the attic" was not a woman scorned but a colonial subject exploited and alienated. In both the feminist and the post-colonial readings, we see criticism making fiction discursive, making its characters and plots into modes of interpretive statement. This approach diverged from the New Critical emphasis on technique, but Gérard Genette's structuralist narratology and Mikhail Bakhtin's dialogic theory are comparable. Genette's focus on narrative function and the Bakhtinian emphasis on dialogical texts with a rich plurality of voices—most post-colonial readings were nothing if not dialogic—supported the idea that the "post-colonial" mode of reading was as viable as any other for interpreting narrative prose. Spivak also gave a pivotal analysis of Mary Shelley's *Frankenstein*, giving a post-colonial tilt to a work that had already been claimed and popularized by feminism and historicism. Spivak saw the monster in the novel as an emblem of Europe's anxiety about colonization, as a symbol of European knowledge that a domain seemingly securely under control might rise up and seek to rival and destroy its "master." This kind of reading, as Fraiman pointed out in her response to Said's reading of Austen, does have a certain prefabricated, smoothed-out quality. Spivak, despite her deconstructive rigour, was able to assay when necessary and useful what she termed "strategic essentialism," an approach that enabled deconstructive critics to suspend temporarily their awareness of the prison house of language without eternally confining themselves to a literalized world without textual awareness.

Spivak set the pattern for the many post-colonial critics, largely from South Asia, who made their reputation during the 1990s. Although able to write on specific works or contexts, they were at their best when they wrote on large themes or issues both within literature itself and within wider spheres of discourse. There were other prominent India-based and diasporic South Asian intellectuals. Ashis Nandy was somewhat comparable to Appiah in being largely influenced by analytic rather than continental philosophy. Also, his interest in Gandhian doctrines of nonviolence made him somewhat more "rooted" in recent Indian tradition than his counterparts. S.P. Mohanty championed a sceptical cosmopolitanism and the possibility of communicating across discursive mindsets, somewhat palliating the excessive cordoning off of spheres done in the wake of Said's work. Partha Chatterjee limned the coherence and fragmentation of national identities, making them unpredictable of essentialism yet cogent enough to inform models of reading. Dipesh Chakrabarty's *Provinicializing Europe* provided the needed historiographical basis for many of the enabling assumptions of post-colonial thought. Gauri Viswanathan called attention to the origins of English literature as a discipline in the nineteenth-century historian Thomas Babington Macaulay's program for Indian education, which was in contrast to the largely classical educational program undertaken in England itself.[49] The English department, according to Viswanathan, originated in India!

Homi K. Bhabha, another major post-colonial critic, was highly influential in theoretical circles long before his first official book was published in 1994.[50] He exemplified a new and model non-European intellectual, one very different from the protest-minded figures of the previous generation. Despite being professedly leftist, Bhabha was not a "Third World" intellectual, as were Césaire, Fanon, and even, to an extent, Said. The difference is difficult to define, but it had something to do with Bhabha and Spivak being from India. Despite his pivotal role in the formation of the Bandung ideology at the 1955 conference, Indian Prime Minister Jawaharlal Nehru and other Indian political and cultural leaders of the twentieth century had strong ties to the reformist Western Left because of the British Labour Party's long advocacy of Indian independence. In other words, Indian intellectuals were linked to Western social democrats, which made their opposition to Western hegemony more internal and incremental than that of intellectuals of African and, in Said's case, Palestinian descent, who felt that the established hierarchies, even of the reformist West, were less friendly to their inclusion in and access to the corridors of political and academic power. This did not mean Bhabha was prone to either compromise or co-optation. But it did mean that, when compared to, for instance, Achebe, he was more willing to let opposites come into play rather than abruptly oppose them to each other. In addressing Achebe's reading of Conrad (see the preface), Bhabha does not minimize the colonialism of the European writer, but he places the stress on how Achebe and Conrad were both articulating different aspects of the same discursive terrain. The colonized could outwit and outflank the colonizers not by warring against or upending them but by subtly renegotiating the terms of the colonial context. The means by which this was accomplished, according to

Bhabha, was "mimicry." Bhabha's theory of mimicry proposed that, although the colonized often imitated the colonizer and regimes of education (such as Macaulay's advocacy of English in India) often proposed to blindly reproduce colonial models without envisioning any inflection by the native recipients, what happened was really more complex than imitation or reproduction.[51] In reality, Bhabha argues, the colonized subjects imitated the colonizer but consciously so, turning mimicry into an active, ironic dissent.

Mimicry at once serves, parodies, and exposes the colonizer. Bhabha's model went well beyond Fanon's in that it did not merely invert black-white oppositions or call for racial pride to counteract assertions of white supremacism. Mimicry, by permitting irony and linguistic refraction into the process, acknowledged both the inertia left in the wake of colonization, which prevented a full-bore assertion of an anti-colonial agenda, and the creativity and ingenuity of colonized subjects who wrested for themselves, in linguistic and conceptual terms, far more imaginative space than the mandate that the colonizers would have permitted them. What emerged was what Bhabha termed a "third space" of mixture, hybridity, and difference. Like Derrida, Bhabha is not positing this difference as a stable outcome, a finished product, or a fungible commodity. He does not necessarily even see it as ever fulfilled or consummated. Bhabha enunciates a kind of slow history, in which colonizer and colonized do not confront each other in one cathartic encounter but dilate, negotiate, bicker, and barter across lengthy expanses of time and constructions of space. Bhabha was famously reviled for his obscurity. But this obscurity was a consequence of attempting to think out ideas that had seldom been pointed to before and also of his making connections between fields such as linguistics, psychoanalysis, and politics, which had long been thought independent of each other. Bhabha's approach enables one to analyse Naipaul, even if adversarially; all Fanon's would yield is calling Naipaul out. From a Fanonist viewpoint, Naipaul was a traitor, a Judas, a Benedict Arnold, or he was simply a bewildered and alienated lost soul, much like the character Santosh in Naipaul's own novella "One out of Many." In many ways, however, Bhabha derived his idea of mimicry from Naipaul's novel *The Mimic Men* (1967), in which Naipaul asserts that the ruling class of the newly independent "Third World" states are mimics of a Europe they are emulating without truly understanding, all the while failing to set their own course. Naipaul sees this mimicry as sterile, Bhabha as productive; but, Bhabha is seizing ground already occupied, making it less polemical and binary. Bhabha's difficulty perhaps came from the way his work gave equal voice to theory and practice—which sounds like a wonderful compromise but which came close to being considered the "aesthetic ideology" that Paul de Man warned against. But, when done rigorously, the marriage of theory and practice is the most difficult accomplishment of all in humanistic study, and Bhabha's opacity is, in a circuitous way, proof of his enormous success in this duality of modes. His form and mode of expression also mitigated any sense of establishmentarianism or bourgeois smugness; the style was adamantly, and gloriously, rebellious.[52]

The 1990s: Diaspora and Hybridity

After Bhabha, "hybridity" and "diaspora" became the dominant keywords of late 1990s post-colonial study. These words turned post-colonial study away from reliance on a monolithic national identity. As Ien Ang pointed out in her 2001 book *On Not Speaking Chinese*, one could be identified as "Chinese" but speak no Chinese and know little about China. Ang, for example, was born into a *peranakan* Chinese family in post-colonial Indonesia; the term *"peranakan"* signifies that her ancestors had migrated to South East Asia from China long before the formation of the Dutch East Indies. She relocated with her family to the Netherlands when she was twelve, was educated there, and eventually went on to teach in Australia.[53] She spoke no Chinese. Ang belonged to all of these contexts, but none could totally claim her. The Ang example shows the potential for diaspora and hybridity to explain concretely how many people were living their lives at the turn of the millennium; they were beyond conventional expectations of what national or ethnic identity could be. A downside of these words is that they both imply some natural source in the homeland. "Diaspora," as a term, stems from the Jewish diaspora of the ancient Mediterranean world, the dispersion of the Jews that exiled or removed them from a land that their religion privileged as a site of potential return, at least in the metaphorical sense. Equally, diaspora could be read as privileging those with the mobility to leave their homelands, for whatever reasons. Just because hybridity and diaspora seemed inclusive ideas did not mean that they did not elevate a certain kind of identity to a position of privilege and magnitude.

Many different spheres wanted in on the post-colonial action. Now that the Soviet-dominated "Second World" was gone, the Canadian critic Stephen Slemon re-appropriated that term to refer to former settler colonies, such as Australia and New Zealand.[54] Others spoke of "micro-states," usually small island nations, whose sovereignty challenged that of the reigning idea of the conglomerate or federation. Theorists within the Hispanic world (Antonio Benítez-Rojo) and French-speaking lands (Édouard Glissant, a student of Césaire's) were seen to have theories that resembled those of the major anglophone post-colonialists, and the colonial histories of their languages were similar enough to make post-colonial literary criticism potentially an easy fit. This circumstance did not lead, though, to many critics involved in anglophone and francophone studies reading texts in the other languages. In this regard, post-colonial literature was well behind the old "comparative literature." Also, formerly colonizing nations that spoke languages other than English or French were less obvious fits for the post-colonial model: Germany, with its belated unification and come-from-behind attempts at imperialism; Italy, as a colonizer presenting a smaller scale but similar profile to Germany's; and Russia, with its colonialism being performed entirely by expansion on the Eurasian land mass and less immediately detectable. Still, scholars in Germanic and Slavic languages nonetheless delved into paradigms of race and domination, which revealed hidden histories.

Nonetheless, post-colonial theory remained heavily tethered to the anglophone world. This was its strength. It had the potential for all the English-speaking peoples of the world, European-descended and not, to communicate with each other. The eruption of post-colonial theory was coeval with that of the Internet, which made it appreciably easier for speakers of world languages to feel their global linguistic reach. But this focus on the English-speaking world was also post-colonial theory's weakness. The monolingual aspect of post-colonialism fostered a parochialism dwelling uncannily at the core of all the rhetoric about extending the scope of letters. Discourse about the "Transatlantic," strongly boosted initially by Gilroy's theories about the Black Atlantic, became characterized by a sometimes rote stitching together of British and American referents, which was often done with a sense of naïveté about whether or not criticism had ever braided them before, as happened in the case of the reception of nineteenth-century British authors in the United States, for example. Transatlanticism, in other words, became whitened and more establishmentarian than its original emancipatory potential had heralded. The fading, after the end of apartheid in South Africa in the early 1990s, of anti-racist activism in the anglophone world furthered the increasingly antiseptic tendencies in this drift. Some even went so far as to see the United States as a post-colonial country, which was certainly justified by some aspects of its history, although here some important questions had to be asked. Could a country so powerful be called post-colonial? And did classifying the United States as post-colonial thus vitiate the effectiveness of the term?

The "anglophone world," as a concept, also carried inherent baggage. In the 1990s, it was liberating that the Internet facilitated quick and easy contact between speakers of the same language; in New Zealand or Newfoundland, the Transvaal or Tacoma one could e-mail back and forth in English, and the same could happen in other languages. After the communication advances of the 1990s, Spain's cultural role in Latin America only increased, as Juan E. De Castro has shown in *The Spaces of Latin American Literature*. But the idea of the anglophone also had the potential to reinforce traditional hierarchies within the English-speaking world. As Elisa Tamarkin pointed out in *Anglophilia* (2008), even the United States, with its early assertions of rambunctious independence from the mother country, deferred heavily to British precedent in practice during the nineteenth century, and the same tendency was observable in 1990s post-colonial criticism and literature, despite the rhetoric of subversion and dissent. It could hardly be otherwise as long as the English language was the only practical currency in which post-colonial thought could be circulated. This monoglot emphasis is reinforced in its potential conservatism by what Tilottama

Rajan has called "the Anglo-American concern with practice," which, by a kind of tidal drift, took post-colonialism away from provocative theory and towards the reassuring and practical.[55]

A more productive move was when post-colonial criticism was extended *backward*. Medievalist scholars turned to the representation of the East during the Western Middle Ages, a study that was particularly fascinating because continuity could be shown between patterns from that era, which had comparatively little geographical knowledge, and, say, the Enlightenment, patterns that would have interested Foucault and Adorno. The ancient world also had empires and practices of imperial subordination. As we have seen, the modern Western prejudice against the creative works and history of late antiquity and, by implication, of the Byzantine Empire was so normative it was the object of Foucault's concerted critique.

The ancient world was also the object of later Europe's imperialistic fantasies. In the multiple volumes of *Black Athena* (published 1987 to 2007), Martin Bernal, a British scholar teaching in the United States, concentrated his criticism on the idea that the cultural achievements of ancient Greece were utterly distinct from those of earlier cultures in the nearby portions of Asia and Africa, an idea much prized by later Europeans.[56] He turned sharply from this notion, from what he saw as the nineteenth-century tendency to see classical Greece as largely Indo-European in linguistic and cultural influence, and he revived the earlier tradition of seeing substantial Egyptian and Phoenician influence on Greek culture. As remote as this dynamic might have seemed to contemporary eyes, Bernal was aligning the non-European peoples of the ancient world with those of the modern world, a comparison that was performed as early as Vico's eighteenth-century comment that, in Homer's time, "the Greeks ... had long since opened up their country to commerce with the Phoenicians, whose tales no less than their merchandise the Greek peoples had come to delight in, just as Europeans do now in those of the Indies."[57] The direct comparison between ancient and modern exoticisms was being made in *the eighteenth century*. All Bernal did was to return to Vico's position after intervening periods of modernity and Eurocentrism. Bernal was not saying that the Greeks were not what we would call today "white," although certainly Greeks and other southern Europeans have been on the receiving end of many northern European prejudices through the ages. Nor was he saying that there was substantial black African influence upon ancient Greece. The Phoenicians were ethnically and linguistically akin to the ancient Hebrews. The Egyptians, though African geographically, are generally not considered black Africans in "racial" terms although they had heavy commerce with black Africans and were, for a time, ruled by them. Notwithstanding Bernal's limited claims about race, many classicists were shocked, and some were extraordinarily concerned that Bernal's assertions meant the end of their discipline. Some of Bernal's claims about the ancient Egyptians were outlandish and were deservedly rejected. For instance, he spoke of the accomplishments of the Pharaoh Senworset (Sesostris) I in ways that even that Pharaoh's mother might well have found exaggerated. Yet Bernal, after losing many battles, won the war in the end. In the twenty-first century, no serious scholar denied that Greek culture had been influenced substantially by the regions of ancient Africa and Asia nearest to Greece.

That Bernal's theories, which were not about race or blackness, were often read as such is attributable to the racially charged nature of US society, as discussed in the previous chapter. This racial charge led post-colonialism to be defined differently in the United States than in other countries: as having to do with people of colour, particularly English-speaking ones, from abroad. Because US post-colonial theory was racially defined, it ignored post-colonial writers who could not be seen as objects or agents of racial critique. The problem may not have been *just* race but also relevance. If Canada and Australia had bigger armies, the US intellectual establishment, for all its peace-loving rhetoric, would heed their literature more. It is not surprising that Indian literature, even Indian diasporic literature, began to gain world popularity only when India, as a polity, began to show it was a global force in geostrategic terms.

But if US academia did not embrace Australian or Canadian writers, there was an alternative solution—the US commercial publishing industry. Indeed, after the success of the 1996 film of Michael Ondaatje's 1992 novel *The English Patient*, Canadian and Australian fiction, some even with Canadian and Australian settings, began to be snapped up by US publishers. The Canadian literary agent Denise Bukowski created a mini-boom of young Canadian authors getting huge contracts in the United States. Unfortunately, writers such as Andrew Pyper, Gail Anderson-Dargatz, Kerri Sakamoto, and Frances Itani could not reap quite the commercial success expected of them (though they often garnered good reviews and made an impact on discerning readers). An even more unfortunate circumstance was that the publishing aspect of this fiction was entirely severed from a theoretical ballast, which a greater appreciation of the post-colonial potential of Australianist or Canadianist criticism would have enriched. To some extent, this severance was true even of Indian fiction. When average consumers read books by Pankaj Mishra, Amit Chaudhuri, or Arundhati Roy, they did not necessarily read them in light of post-colonial theory. But scholars studying these writers did and were encouraged to do so by US literature departments. If post-colonialist scholars had not critiqued these books, if only people within India had bought these books and read them for pleasure, the traffic in ideas about Indian post-colonial literature and the histories chronicled in it would have been far poorer—and this is what happened in the case of Canada and Australia. So the commercial success of the authors of these two countries was not matched by a willingness of US academia to take them up in the thoroughgoing way that had been afforded Indian or Indian-diaspora writers. Canadian literature has made great strides in world visibility over the last fifty years; but, as is the case for other post-colonial literatures, to be Canadian could be an advantage if international readers thought this origin was somehow new and exotic but a disadvantage if they thought it took them too far away from where the main cultural action was. What gave the metropolitan reader this right to choose, to decide whether countries such as Canada could be fully post-colonial?

The Late 1990s and 2000s: From Post-Colonial to Global

The aforementioned sense that everything could be potentially post-colonial led to a recession of the previously attested notion that post-colonialism involved an historical relation to British colonization in the nineteenth and twentieth centuries. Post-colonial theory thus ceased to be primarily about the anglophone world or about the literature produced from former colonial states. Instead, it became about the global, metropolitan centre and its ability to absorb, appreciate, and adapt to these new literatures. The "post-colonial" became the "global"—and lost a lot in the process. In the 1960s and 1970s, the adjective "global" evoked a vaguely humanistic Third World utopianism, an outreach to Fanon's wretched of the earth. In the 1990s, though, it came to signify the absorption of the whole world into a refurbished and gentrified but fundamentally First World, US-led, and neo-capitalist framed. Academic treatments of the "global" did attempt to take a wider and more variegated perspective. Scholars such as David Damrosch and Wai-Chee Dimock gave global accounts of world and US literary history that followed Chakrabarty in "provincializing Europe." But global literary approaches tended to lose sight of the historically specific relation of modern colonialism that post-colonial theory had, despite its penchant for abstraction, very concretely addressed. Even the ideology of anti-globalization protest, which crested in the late 1990s, was animated by a resentment against the hegemony of a centre, whose existing power it unquestioningly, in rhetorical terms, accepted; there was no attempt to find other, more marginal nodes of power. As Seamus Heaney (not unironically) put it,

> I could feel at home inside that metal core
> slumbering at the very hub of systems.[58]

Subverting globalization at its centre did not necessarily mean more recognition for literature produced outside the centre.[59]

Empire (2000), a spectacularly influential collaboration between the American scholar Michael Hardt (whose first book had been on Deleuze) and the Italian communist and political prisoner Antonio Negri (a generation Hardt's senior) did not consider "empire" in its residual political sense.[60] In political terms, empire was a concept transferred from the Roman imperial tradition to describe the overseas dominions of European countries, countries that could not hope to constitute a single empire in their home continent. But for Hardt and Negri, "empire" was used very much in the Foucauldian sense of "governmentality"—it meant mechanisms of control and coercion that did not need formal government to operate. What Hardt and Negri were ultimately talking about was the economic and political power of the United States and of the multinational corporations headquartered there or in pro-US countries. Even more specifically, they addressed multinational institutions such as the World Bank and the International Monetary Fund, whose financial strictures had imposed the "Washington Consensus" upon many countries that had formerly espoused socialist economics. But empire for them was not incarnated in or exhausted by any one of these institutions; rather, it was a vast, pliable, protean set of hegemonic interests that operated through controlling "biopower"—another Foucauldian term, which, this time, Hardt and Negri used explicitly. Biopower was the conversion into force of the energy of subject populations that were dominated, manipulated, or commandeered to serve the interests of these powerful and unchallenged institutions. Hardt and Negri saw the United States as so much at the centre of this universe that meaningful change could only happen there; the hope of Sargeson or Collymore that literary change could come from New Zealand or the Caribbean was dwarfed by the dominance of this new empire, this all-seeing, hydra-headed behemoth. So pressing was Hardt and Negri's sense of the omnipresence of this visible and invisible global governmentality that *Empire*'s hysteria verged on exultation; indeed, only a few changes in vocabulary would have sufficed to make the book a report issued by a centrist, pro-globalization think tank in Washington or a corporation wishing to blind observers to its vicarious misdeeds and exploitations by giving a sense of global sweep and interdependence. If, to use the Ngugi example, books in the Gikuyu language were published in New York, things would have been different. But they were not. The rhetoric of globalization had to it some of the hype and drama that the rhetoric of the sublime had in the deconstructive 1980s. The observer could not quite be sure whether the discourse of either wanted to promote or subvert the term in question, and, in both cases, a sense of awe and grandeur seemed to aspire both to being menacing and to being somehow motivational.[61]

Pascale Casanova, in her highly influential *The World Republic of Letters*, contends that the world community only notices novels when they come from the right country. Casanova is sceptical that literary merit alone makes people pay attention to literatures previously unnoticed; she contends the literatures are noticed when the metropole has its own reasons for doing so.[62] Often, however, post-colonial novels are acclaimed on the purported basis of literary merit alone, leading the current "stars" to be lauded well above the more inconspicuous pioneers who had the misfortune to write when the metropolitan elite was not interested in literature from their countries. Casanova exaggerates the centrality of France, and she castigates individual writers, such as the Indian novelist Vikram Seth, in ways that, whatever the commoditization of his work by "the culture industry," seem reductive in an almost "vulgar Marxist" way. Indeed, Casanova's book, with its magisterial survey of various world literary phenomena and of how the metropole gives or takes away its approval of them, is reminiscent of vintage Marxist histories, such as that of Barrington Moore Jr., which explained why various societies did not become capitalist in the way England did. Both, in other words, tend to assume that what may well be an exception is, in fact, the norm.[63] Casanova shows that the centre *thinks* it is the centre. But she does not show that it *is* the centre.

The discourse of globalization had, near the end of the first decade of the twenty-first century, become unexpectedly monochromatic and conservative. Its anglophone emphasis seemed to make it incurious about other languages and overly aligned with two very traditional ideologies, Anglophilia and American exceptionalism. The story of globalization in literary studies is at first exhilarating—it tells how a largely European canon expanded and made room not only for texts from all parts of the world but also for interpretive approaches premised on the experience of subordination and exploitation felt by the world's colonized peoples. This mode of thought was not just about these particular texts or nations. It was about the idea of no longer doing things from the centre, no longer accepting the literary judgements of London or New York as automatic—saying that literary judgements could come from Auckland or Calgary or Dar es Salaam or Port Moresby. But, after a point, the story becomes more sobering—it shows how a worldwide gaze became more and more a centring point for the reassertion of privilege; particularly, globalized literary criticism confirmed the dominance of the US publishing and academic industries and of other allied metropolitan interests. In the early 2000s, writers from these "post-colonial" places could only matter if, say, they had been shortlisted for the (Man) Booker Prize and received a lucrative contract from Knopf or Farrar, Straus, and Giroux.

A certain image of India, especially, was part of the problem. India was, as it were, still the jewel in the post-colonial crown that it had been in the colonial, even though the celebration of the anglophone and globally adept India, which was plugged into world technology by outward migration and outsourcing to American high-tech corporations at home, was well beyond the "Raj nostalgia" for the period of British control, a nostalgia that waxed in the 1980s. The post-colonial concentration on British India has been likened by the anthropologist Ann Laura Stoler to the Marxist exaltation of industrial England. Every other country follows a *Sonderweg* or "special path."[64] A *Sonderweg* is a separate way of development that deviates from a main path. Just as a certain neoconservative rhetoric seized upon the Marxist assumption of England as norm to postulate an Anglocentric progressivism that the rest of the world, from France to Iraq, has to "reach up to," so did the post-colonial privileging of the subaltern experience become inverted by imperial revisionists such as the British historian Niall Ferguson. Ferguson's basic postulate was to argue that the British imperial experience was far more benign than post-colonial critics had alleged. What had been proposed, by post-colonialism, as a divergent set of reactants "writing back" to the centre of world power became a network of globalization emanating from the centre of world power. James Bennett's term "the Anglosphere" emerged in the early 2000s as a conservative equivalent of the post-colonial idea of the empire writing back.[65] The Anglosphere was constituted by metropolitan countries such as the United States and the United Kingdom as well as by settler colonies such as Australia and Canada and, importantly, by former subject colonies such as India—all united not just by the English language but by a common opposition to fundamentalist Islam that involved active or supportive participation in the war on terror.

As long as globalization meant a relatively benign US monopoly, critiques of this formation seemed more like grumbles from malcontents. But this situation hanged after 2001 as globalization began to seem linked to either Islamic terrorism or the aggressive US response to that terrorism. But post-colonialism did not return. Once the English-speaking world became conceived of as connected by a tradition of democracy and liberalization, the idea of globalization turned from one of critique or even co-operation to one of an actual reaffirmation of the centre, which was spruced up by tacking on adornments provided by the periphery. After 2008, the United States may have sought deliberately to move from a unipolar to a multipolar world. But to riff once again upon Appiah's irresistible formulation, the "multi-" in the post-2008 "multipolar" was not the same "multi-" as it would have been ten years earlier.[66] Literatures from non-European nations were well established at this point, in both the Western academy and publishing markets. Writers from any part of the world found it far easier to make an impact than they would have fifty years before. Yet post-colonial criticism did not just aim to improve communications among different parts of Casanova's "world republic of letters" but to create a league of republics rather than one republic. Ironically, the idea of "one world republic" was the vision of both the Bandung Third Worldism advocates in the 1960s and the neoconservatives planning for a "league of democracies" in the 2000s. Both were inadequate because they were insufficiently plural.

The previous two chapters of this book, on feminist and anti-racist criticism, have chronicled success stories, odysseys from the narrowness of the 1950s to the expansive terrain of the twenty-first century. But the end of the post-colonial story will have to sound a more bittersweet and elegiac note, one expressing something akin to Anne Cheng's idea of "racial melancholia."[67] After so many non-European countries achieved national independence, colonialism, as a formation, seemed fragile, a mere political configuration compared to deeply ingrained prejudices such as those relating to gender and race. Yet the colonial mentality still seemed present, defining and subverting many of the attempts to move beyond it. The colonial aspects of thought and of circumstances were certainly subject to change, yet that change occurred both more seismically than might have been expected and less thoroughly than might have been desired. The biggest mistake that the rhetoric of both post-colonialism and globalization made was underrating the persistence of nationalism and how the nation, despite being "imagined," may be productive of meaningful discourse.

In fact, after the 1990s, "empire" became a more valued term than "nation," even for the Left. Empire was seen as federative, plural, and not involving nationalistic claims that led to ethnic cleansing. Empire, in its vast scope, gave a space for dissent, whereas the nation did not. This underrating of nationhood foretold that interesting developments might come in the future (when the nation was allowed to come a bit more back into fashion) from a sharpened idea of what a national literature was. And a renewed nationalism might be necessary for globalization not to be just a parade of the winners, for it to become what (to return to the francophone beginnings of our post-colonial story) Michel Le Bris and Jean Rouard called a "littérature-monde" in which there would be no centres, no places where reputations were made or literary currents vetted.[68] That this decentred situation was so far from what was evident when Le Bris and Rouard wrote suggests that the days of post-colonial criticism may not be over if only because the need for post-colonial criticism certainly is not.

NOTES

1 Kwame Anthony Appiah, "Is the Post- in Postmodern the Post- in Postcolonial?" *Critical Inquiry* 17 (1991): 336–57.

2 Jean-François Lyotard, *The Postmodern Condition* (Minneapolis: University of Minnesota Press, 1984).

3 Homi K. Bhabha, *The Location of Culture* (1994; London: Routledge, 2004).

4 Aimé Césaire, "Serpent Sun," *The Collected Poetry*, trans. Clayton Eshleman and Annette Smith (Berkeley: University of California Press, 1984) 105.

5 Homi K. Bhabha, foreword, *The Wretched of the Earth*, by Frantz Fanon, trans. Richard Philcox (1961; New York: Grove Press, 2004) ix.

6 Robert Young, *Postcolonialism: A Historical Introduction* (Malden, MA: Wiley-Blackwell, 2001) 213.

7 Young, *Postcolonialism*, 192.

8 Eric J. Hobsbawm, *The Age of Capital, 1848–1875* (New York: Vintage, 1996).

9 Benedict Anderson, *Imagined Communities: Reflection on the Origin and Spread of Nationalism* (London: Verso, 1983).

10 On Armah, see the criticism of Neil Lazarus, *Resistance in Postcolonial Fiction* (New Haven: Yale University Press, 1990)—another book that helped establish the term "post-colonial"—and, on Ouologuem, see the criticism of Christopher L. Miller, *Blank Darkness: Africanist Discourse in French* (Chicago: University of Chicago Press, 1986).

11 Ahmadou Kourouma, *Allah n'est pas obligé* (Paris: Editions du Seuil, 2000).

12 See Kingsley Bolton and Braj R. Kachru, *World Englishes: Critical Concepts in Linguistics* (London: Taylor and Francis, 2006) 54.

13 Compare the approach of the South African poet and educator Ezekiel (Es'kia) Mphahlele, who was as liberating and prophetic a figure as Ngugi but who, for better or worse, wrote in English.

14 Dorothea A.L. Martin, *The Making of a Sino-Marxist World View* (Armonk, NY: M.E. Sharpe, 1990) 103.

15 George Steiner, *In Bluebeard's Castle: Some Notes Towards the Redefinition of Culture* (New Haven: Yale University Press, 1974).

16 Nina J. Easton, *Gang of Five: Leaders at the Center of the Conservative Ascendancy* (New York: Simon and Schuster, 2000) 171–72.

17 Mary L. Dudziak, *Cold War Civil Rights: Race and the Image of American Democracy* (Princeton: Princeton University Press, 2002).

18 William Walsh, *Commonwealth Literature* (Detroit: St. James Press, 1985); Bruce Alvin King, *The Commonwealth Novel Since 1960* (London: Palgrave, 1991); Joseph Jones, *Terranglia: The Case for English as World-Literature* (New York: Irvington, 1965). These scholars were, though not theoretical, remarkable in their range; King was a seventeenth-century scholar as well as a post-colonialist, whereas Jones was a great admirer of Ralph Waldo Emerson as well as the first American to write seriously about many other literatures in English.

19 On Rutherford, see Hena Maes-Jelinek, Gordon Collier, Geoffrey V. Davis, eds., *A Talent(ed) Digger: Creations, Cameos, and Essays in Honour of Anna Rutherford* (Amsterdam: Rodopi, 1996). This press, Rodopi, is a book-publishing version of *Kunapipi*, and it produces much seminal post-colonial work away from the theoretical glitz.

20 See J. Ellis, "Tatau and Malu: Vital Signs in Contemporary Samoan Literature," *PMLA* 121.3 (2006): 687–701.

21 On the importance of A. Norman Jeffares, see Leigh Dale, *The English Men: Professing Literature in Australian Universities* (Toowoomba: Association for the Study of Australian Literature, 1997) 177. I am also grateful to my colleague Elaine Savory, who was a student at Leeds in the Jeffares era, for her detailed recollections of the man.

22 On orality and literacy, see Brian Stock, *The Implications of Literacy: Written Language and Models of Interpretation in the Eleventh and Twelfth Centuries* (Princeton: Princeton University Press, 1983).

23 See Annette Henry, *Taking Back Control: African Canadian Women Teachers' Lives and Practice* (Albany: SUNY Press, 1998) 115.

24 In so many cases, theory mediated, or meditated upon, transitions between modes of expression—whether oral and literate, or print and digital—and it was no coincidence that thinkers such as Brian Stock, Marshall McLuhan, Walter J. Ong (SJ), Jack Goody, and Paul Zumthor, who meditated the disjunctures and continuities characterizing these medial transitions, flourished in the era of theory. It was a recognition of the continuities between these modes that provided the plausibility for the range of materials examined in post-colonial studies.

25 On the importance of Collymore for Walcott, see Paul Breslin, *Nobody's Nation: Reading Derek Walcott* (Chicago: University of Chicago Press, 2001) 17.

26 Michael King, *Wrestling With the Angel: A Life of Janet Frame* (New York: Basic Books, 2001). King (1945–2004), who also wrote a biography of Frank Sargeson, was himself a figure in the expanding New Zealand discursivity that he chronicled, and his example shows that post-colonial writing included non-fictional forms as well as the standard genres of imaginative literature.

27 Wole Soyinka, "The Critic and Society: Barthes, Leftocracy and Other Mythologies," *Black Literature and Literary Theory*, ed. Henry Louis Gates, Jr. and Sunday O. Anozie (London: Routledge, 1984). Both the fact and the tenor of Soyinka's contribution made this pivotal anthology not only cosmopolitan but politically plurivocal. On the general question of the relation of post-colonial theory to standard-issue anti-colonial Third-Worldism, the Cameroon-born thinker Achille Mbembe remarks cogently that post-colonialism "derives both from anti-colonial and anti-imperialist struggles on the one hand, and from the heritage of Western philosophy and of the disciplines that constitute the European humanities on the other." See the interview with Mbembe, "What is postcolonial thinking?" *Eurozine*, 9 January 2008, 8 March 2009 <http://www.eurozine.com/articles/2008-01-09-mbembe-en.html>.

28 See Luis Francia, ed., *Brown River, White Ocean: An Anthology of Twentieth-Century Philippine Literature in English* (New Brunswick: Rutgers University Press, 1993).

29 Nuruddin Farah, *Maps* (London: Penguin, 2000).

30 W.H. New, *A History of Canadian Literature* (Montreal: McGill-Queen's University Press, 2001).

31 Margaret Atwood, *Survival: A Thematic Guide to Canadian Literature* (Toronto: Anansi, 1972). The name "Anansi" (a Ghanaian spider god) for this publishing house, which issued many of the early Canadian literary and nationalist manifestos, itself bespeaks the inclusion of Canada in the "post-colonial"—an inclusion that this chapter seeks to stress. Dennis Lee, the co-founder of Anansi, tried, with mixed success but admirable intentions, to incarnate this vision in literary terms in *Civil Elegies* (Toronto: Anansi, 1972). See also Gaile McGregor, *The Wacousta Syndrome: Explorations in the Canadian Landscape* (Toronto: University of Toronto Press, 1985) whose unfairly negative reception (because the "thematic" paradigm had passed) is a perfect example of the "Don Quixote" syndrome to which theory has too often fallen prey.

32 Frank Davey, *Post-National Arguments: The Politics of the Anglophone-Canadian Novel since 1967* (Toronto: University of Toronto Press, 1993). See also Cynthia Sugars, ed., *Unhomely States: Theorizing English-Canadian Postcolonialism* (Peterborough: Broadview Press, 2004). For a similar perspective on Australian literature, see Nicholas Birns and Rebecca McNeer, eds., *A Companion to Australian Literature Since 1900* (Rochester, NY: Camden House, 2007).

33 T.D. MacLulich, "The Alien Role: Farley Mowat's Northern Pastorals," *Studies in Canadian Literature* 2.2 (1977): 226–38.

34 Quotation is from page 11–12 of Thomas King, "Godzilla vs. Post-Colonial," *World Literature Written in English*, 30.2 (1990): 10–16.

35 Thomas King, "Godzilla vs. Post-Colonial," *World Literature Written in English* 30.2 (1990): 10–16.

36 Hugh McLennan, *Two Solitudes* (1945; Toronto: McClelland and Stewart, 2003).

37 See, for instance, C.P. Champion, "A Very British Coup: Canadianism, Quebec, and Ethnicity in the Flag Debate, 1964–1965," *Journal of Canadian Studies* 40.3 (2006): 68–99.

38 Edmund Wilson, *O Canada! An American's Notes on Canadian Culture* (New York: Macmillan, 1965).

39 Salman Rushdie, *Midnight's Children* (New York: Knopf, 1981).

40 Bill Ashcroft, Gareth Griffiths, Helen Tiffin, *The Empire Writes Back: Theory and Practice in Post-Colonial Studies* (London: Routledge, 1989).

41 David Chioni Moore, "Is the Post- in Post-Colonial the Post- in Post-Soviet? Toward a Global Postcolonial Critique," *PMLA* 1161 (2001): 111–28. Also see the work of Mark von Hagen of Arizona State University in this respect, as well as, from another perspective, Spivak's about her trips to post-Soviet Armenia: Gayatri Chakravorty Spivak, *Other Asias* (London: Wiley-Blackwell, 2008).

42 Giambattista Vico, *New Science*, trans. Thomas G. Bergin and Max H. Fisch (Ithaca: Cornell University Press, 1948).

43 Stephen Bonnycastle, *In Search of Authority* (Peterborough: Broadview, 1996) provides a good general overview of Viconian reverberations in contemporary theory.

44 Edward W. Said, *Beginnings: Intention and Method* (New York: Columbia University Press, 1985) 86.

45 Edward W. Said, *Culture and Imperialism* (New York: Knopf, 1994).

46 Said, *Culture and Imperialism*, 95.

47 Susan Fraiman, "Jane Austen and Edward Said: Gender, Culture, and Imperialism," *Janeites: Austen's Disciples and Devotees*, ed. Deidre Lynch (Princeton: Princeton University Press, 2000) 206–22. See William D. Hart, *Edward Said and the Religious Effects of Culture* (New York: Cambridge University Press, 2000) for an analysis of Said (but not specifically of the *Mansfield Park* reading) that strays as far from "the literal" Said as does Fraiman's; Hart's analysis is supportive and exfoliating rather than corrective, however.

48 Michael Hechter, *Internal Colonialism: The Celtic Fringe in British National Development, 1536–1966* (London: Taylor and Francis, 1975); see also Katie Trumpener, *Bardic Nationalism: The Romantic Novel and British Empire* (Princeton: Princeton University Press, 1997).

49 On Spivak, see Donna Landry and Gerald Maclean, eds., *The Spivak Reader* (London: Routledge, 1995). Ashis Nandy, *Traditions, Tyranny, and Utopias: Essays in the Politics of Awareness* (New York: Oxford University Press, 1987); Partha Chatterjee, *The Nation and its Fragments: Colonial and Postcolonial Histories* (Princeton: Princeton University Press, 1993); Satya P. Mohanty, *Literary Theory and the Claims of History: Postmodernism, Objectivity, Multicultural Politics* (Ithaca: Cornell University Press, 1997); Dipesh Chakrabarty, *Provincializing Europe: Postcolonial Thought and Historical Difference* (Princeton: Princeton University Press, 2000); Gauri Viswanathan. *Masks of Conquest: Literary Study and British Rule in India* (New York: Columbia University Press, 1989). Viswanathan's book was originally a Columbia doctoral dissertation, supervised by Edward Said.

50 See David Huddart, *Homi K. Bhabha* (London: Routledge, 2005); Homi K. Bhabha, ed., *Nation and Narration* (London: Routledge, 1990).

51 Homi K. Bhabha, *The Location of Culture* (1994; London: Routledge, 2004).

52 Edward W. Said, *On Late Style: Music and Literature Against the Grain* (New York: Pantheon, 2006).

53 Ien Ang, *On Not Speaking Chinese: Living Between Asia and the West* (London: Routledge, 2001).

54 Stephen Slemon, "Unsettling the Empire: Resistance Theory for the Second World," *The Post-Colonial Studies Reader*, ed. Bill Ashcroft, Gareth Griffiths, and Helen Tiffin (London: Routledge, 1995) 104–10.

55 Tilottama Rajan, *Deconstruction and the Remainders of Phenomenology: Sartre, Derrida, Foucault, Baudrillard* (Stanford: Stanford University Press, 2002) 304.

56 Martin Bernal, *The Fabrication of Ancient Greece, 1785–1985* (New Brunswick: Rutgers University Press, 1987), vol. 1 of *Black Athena*. This book contained the material critical of the Aryanist consensus; subsequent volumes, published in 1991 and 2007, focused on archaeology and language and advanced more positive—and more debatable—theses.

57 Vico, *New Science*, 299.

58 Seamus Heaney, *The Haw Lantern* (New York: Farrar, Straus, and Giroux, 1987) 18.

59 See Daniel T. O'Hara, *Empire Burlesque: The Fate of Critical Culture in Global America* (Durham: Duke University Press, 2003).

60 Michael Hardt and Antonio Negri, *Empire* (Cambridge, MA: Harvard University Press, 2000).

61 See Nicholas Birns, "'Thy World, Columbus!': Barbauld and Global Space, 1803, '1811', 1812, 2003," *European Romantic Review* 16.5 (2005): 545–62. Even the very canny Gayatri Chakravorty Spivak, in *The Death of a Discipline* (New York: Columbia University Press, 2003) seems to leap on this bandwagon: she extols "planetarity" as a virtue ripe to replace the universalism of comparative literature and the area studies perspectives that depend on the world as regarded from Washington during the cold war. Yet specificity has its virtues and can manifest local resistance, whereas planetarity, while exhilarating in its promise of diversify and multiplicity, has the danger of becoming monolithic and monologic. Graham Huggan, following Ellen Meiskins Wood and James Petras, has referred to the hyperbole over globalization as "globaloney" (Huggan, "Globaloney and the Australian Writer," Australian Literature in a Global World: 30th Anniversary Conference of the Association for the Study of Australian Literature, Wollongong, New South Wales, Australia, 29 June 2008). This term may well be the equivalent with respect to globalization as Sianne Ngai's idea of "stuplimity" (see Chapter 7) is to that of the sublime.

62 Pascale Casanova, *The World Republic of Letters*, trans. Malcolm DeBevoise (Cambridge, MA: Harvard University Press, 2007).

63 Barrington Moore, Jr., *Social Origins of Dictatorship and Democracy: Lord and Peasant in the Making of the Modern World* (1966; New York: Beacon Press, 1993).

64 Ann Laura Stoler, lecture, New School, New York, 8 November 2007.

65 James C. Bennett, *The Anglosphere Challenge: Why the English-Speaking Nations Will Lead the Way in the Twenty-First Century* (Lanham: Rowman and Littlefield, 2007).

66 Parag Khanna, *The Second World: How Emerging Powers Are Redefining Global Competition in the Twenty-First Century* (New York: Random House, 2008). Khanna speaks to this multipolar recasting of globalization, which contrasts not just to Bennett's but, more saliently, to Hardt's and Negri's. Intriguingly, Khanna, in using "second world" to mean "new multipolar challengers to US hegemony" provides yet a third use of the term, after the Soviet-bloc one and Slemon's settler-colony designation.

67 Anne Anlin Cheng, *The Melancholy of Race: Psychoanalysis, Assimilation, and Hidden Grief* (New York: Oxford University Press, 2001).

68 Michel Le Bris and Jean Rouard, *Pour une littérature-monde* (Paris: Gallimard, 2007).

CHAPTER SIX

Deconstructing Normativity
QUEER THEORY

Up to the 1990s: Introducing Queer Theory

"Queer theory" is the umbrella term applied to critical discourses arising out of gay and lesbian studies and other inquiries into the relationship of literature to sexuality and sexual identity. The term "queer" began to be used in the 1990s and largely replaced the "gay" and "lesbian" labels. "Queer" did not refer just to literal homosexual relations or identities. The term applied to the entire panoply of discourses and modes of imagination opened up by a vision of sexuality not tethered to traditional heterosexual assumptions.

What became queer studies started out for the same reasons as the body of criticism focusing on other previously marginalized groups but quickly took a different trajectory. Whereas feminist and anti-racist criticism often specialized in retrieving writers forgotten by the "mainstream" canon, gay and lesbian studies often focused on revealing different sides of writers thought to be mainstream. Wayne Koestenbaum's early work, for instance, focused on the collaboration between male poets such as Samuel Taylor Coleridge and William Wordsworth and on the homoerotic implications of this undeniably complicated relationship.[1] Gay and lesbian criticism plausibly explained the emotions of writers whose sexuality was presumed absent or a mystery—Henry James, Willa Cather, Walter Pater, Emily Dickinson—as in fact directed towards their own gender.[2] It is stunning to realize that the now seemingly obvious interpretation of the first 126 of Shakespeare's sonnets as motivated by homoerotic passion was only given *sub rosa* attention in Shakespearean circles until the publication of Joseph Pequigney's *Such Is My Love* in 1984.[3] Until then, it had been argued that the professions of love on the part of the poet for the young aristocratic male addressee were the products of conventional rhetorical figures of the sort that Rosemond Tuve loved to explicate (see the preface) and did not translate into any inner passion or manifest desire.[4]

262 THEORY AFTER THEORY

It was also only in the 1980s that Marcel Proust's thin disguise of his own homosexuality in his seven-novel sequence *À la recherche du temps perdu* was lifted, a disguise that was maintained by most of his critics for many decades. Only then was perhaps the greatest novel of the twentieth century, one read by critics from Gérard Genette to Paul de Man for its rhetorical mastery and extravagance, seen as also an avowedly gay text when it was read with the slightest attempt at depth.[5] Even such an acclaimed master of modern fiction as André Gide, universally known to be gay, had frank discussion of his work inhibited by reservations about his sexuality. Writers known to be gay or lesbian—Oscar Wilde, Gertrude Stein, Paul Verlaine, Radclyffe Hall, Djuna Barnes, and Christopher Marlowe—also came far more into the foreground. They were no longer saddled with the marginality or even derision that had inhibited their presence in literary discourse. Wilde, in particular, became a very important figure in the late twentieth century. He assumed the cultural prominence that the organs of society had so zealously tried to deny him a century earlier. As someone whose trial in 1894 led not only to his personal disgrace and imprisonment but also to the public demonization and pathologization of the homosexual, Wilde became a posthumous hero for gay liberation in the "post-Stonewall" era.[6] This era, named after the riots in a New York City gay bar in 1969, saw gays and lesbians able to articulate themselves publicly in a way unprecedented in Western social history.

In fact, the aforementioned negligence of the gay aspects of Shakespeare's sonnets may well have to do with the repression of Wilde's playful identification of the London youth "Willie Hughes" as the mysterious "Mr. W.H." to whom the dedicatory page of the sonnets was addressed. But Wilde became more than a gay icon in the age of theory. His importance in social history combined with the highly aestheticist and non-objective bent of his critical outlook to create a site where historicism, deconstruction, and sexuality studies could meet. Wilde, long scorned for most of the twentieth century as having a suspect outlook, was, by its end, a kind of a cosmopolitan consensus figure upon whom several different critical lines could converge. He became to postmodernism what T.S. Eliot and Joseph Conrad were to modernism, combined. Similarly, Gertrude Stein had the aesthetic effect of her work expanded by the more open celebration of the lesbianism that, in her case, had always been known. Her rigorous and unstinting linguistic experimentation received a human face in the light of the many accounts of her long-time love for her companion Alice B. Toklas.

As with feminist and anti-racist criticism, gay and lesbian studies—or "queer theory" as the field began to be known from the early 1990s—had its conservative detractors. These, though, focused less on delegitimizing the literary quality of the writers queer theory advocated, who, after all, were often privileged in the canon. The critique ran more along the lines that queer theory was reading sexual scenarios into texts where they did not manifestly exist or polluting innocent stories with perverse agendas. Queer theorists, for example, often read as gay the relationship of the sleuth Sherlock Holmes and his sidekick and narrator

Dr. Watson in Sir Arthur Conan Doyle's famous detective stories. This reading disturbed those who wanted to see the two men as merely cerebral collaborators with a strong intellectual affinity or who wanted to read the stories as pure entertainment without having to think about social issues. Those opposed to queer theory often felt as if this sort of interpretation irretrievably coloured the text, whereas advocates of queer theory, those who saw queer theory as an approach more than a doctrinal reclassification, tended to see this reading as a strategic intervention that broadened the possibilities of reading. To them, adding a queer dimension to the characters of Holmes and Watson enriched the range of possibilities that reading Conan Doyle's text offered.

Yet this sort of reading ran into another obstacle, one that was, in many ways, on the other side of the ideological fence. Historians such as John Boswell had tried to prove the existence of practices we would now call homosexual in medieval Christianity, and the widespread practice of sexual relations between men in Greece was well known.[7] Yet Foucault contended that each historical concatenation possessed a mutually unintelligible framework and that to read sexual practices across time according to present-day ideas would be ahistorical. In particular, Foucault recognized a difference between the acts of sex between men (or women) and an identity that proceeded from these acts. It was nineteenth-century medicine that first created the label of "homosexual" that became an inclusive rubric for characterizing all individuals who performed same-sex acts. This label was later claimed affirmatively by gay liberation movements in the twentieth century. But there still existed a gap between it and conditions in past eras or outside the West, when and where practising same-sex acts did not lead to a fundamental reclassification in terms of identity as "homosexual"—in other times and places, then, it was the sex act, not the ascribed identity of the person who performed it, that mattered. Thus, paradoxically, Foucault, the most visibly gay theorist, was often used to tamp down the enthusiasm on the part of queer theorists for making categories of the present, such as gay or lesbian, unproblematically retroactive. Consequently, in the 1990s, at the time when historical approaches were favoured, the even newer discourse of queer theory was often held at bay or ramified by this insistence on the inapplicability of present-day terms to past circumstances.

Queer theory reacted against this insistence by noting a certain inflexibility in historicist approaches, a dour and staid unwillingness to probe beyond accepted ideas of what was thinkable in the past. Queer approaches were often accused of being "anachronistic," out of synch with the time they were analysing. Scholars such as Valerie Rohy, though, made an argument for the utility of conscious anachronism in reading.[8] Any act of reading, they argued, is disruptive of the settled circumstances upon which it intervenes. A knowing and self-aware anachronism can be enlightening and is able to open up new possibilities. (We are in similar territory here to the issues surrounding the "denial of coevality," discussed in Chapter 1, or to the speculation about counterfactuals to be canvassed in Chapter 7.) It may be hazardous to brandish "what was possible historically" in terms of sexuality, argued queer theorists, as these perhaps imagined and no longer extant possibilities could become another subtle form of repression today and an attempt to circumscribe the alternatives available in the present. Queer theory was symptomatic, or determinative, of the loosening of hard-and-fast period definitions. These prescriptive definitions, such as "the Augustan Age" or "romanticism," were replaced by more descriptive and elastic labels, such as "the early modern," "the long eighteenth century," and "the long nineteenth century."

Queer theory, though, did not just read epochs. It also read texts. The pivotal move in the queer reading of texts was made by Eve Kosofsky Sedgwick (1950–2009), whose *Between Men: English Literature and Male Homosocial Desire* (1985) graphed homoerotic elements where many would not expect to find them—in nineteenth-century novels written by avowed heterosexuals and centring on a marriage plot.[9] Sedgwick demonstrated that those areas of life—hunting, politics, finance—that seemed most quintessentially sexually normative in male terms were in fact "homosocial," premised on male friendship whose emotional tug went more towards the homoerotic than was consciously acknowledged. In trading in women to ballast homosocial desire—the classic instance of the friend marrying the sister of his closest comrade—male-male desire used heterosexuality as a signifying system to satisfy its unstated needs. (Leslie Fiedler had noticed a similar dynamic in American literature decades before in his book *Love and Death in the American Novel*, which postulated that American men sought out interracial homoerotic relationships as a way of escaping from domestic obligations associated with heterosexuality.[10] But Fiedler did not really position this observation in terms of gender theory.) Sedgwick dramatized how male-male relationships set off or counterpoised male-female ones. She thus provided a grammar for reading sex unconventionally in fiction. Sedgwick made it possible to discern gay affect in ground-level fictional relationships while still situating it in the sort of interpretive, plot-based reading customarily practised on the novel, eschewing technical narratological jargon and reading novels largely as three-dimensional interactions between embodied characters, much as Leavis or Booth in their different ways did. Gay and lesbian literary studies at first tended more than other theoretical approaches to the study of plot and character. This focus may have occurred because plots and characters in novels showed love, loyalty, altruism, fixation, caring, and investment between persons of the same sex, and these relationships had not been properly ventilated in the canon previously. Because of this emphasis, queer theory kept in surprising contact with traditional modes of analysis. Similarly, work on homosexuality in the English elegy helped itself by adhering recognizably to critical conventions of commentary on this form. The English elegy's tradition was to have one young man lament the death of another: Milton elegizing Edward King in the stately *Lycidas* (1637), Shelley lamenting Keats's death in the bitter *Adonais* (1821), and Tennyson meditating on death after the passing of his friend Arthur Henry Hallam in the searing and agonized *In Memoriam* (1849). Gay-inflected work on these great poems choreographed gay approaches in ways that manifested themselves as convincing and largely internal readings of the poems.[11]

The 1990s: Masculinity, Femininity, Performativity

The growing prominence of queer theory introduced a new kind of masculinity into the academy. There are some historical determinants for this. Many of the male academics who held jobs at mid-century were veterans of the two world wars. In these wars, a persona of invulnerable masculinity was often necessary, both tactically and psychologically. And this persona was upheld despite the manifest presence of homosexual feeling among the male soldiers, as was revealed in countless novels and stories, not the least of which was the last volume of Proust's *À la recherche du temps perdu*. Still, for the male academics born between 1890 and 1930, seriousness and a deeply internalized hyper-masculinity were mandatory. In later eras, as the wars of the West became more virtual, less labour intensive, and more optional, views of masculinity changed to present an expanded repertoire of masculine academic roles. The gay male professor paralleled the sensitive heterosexual man—a type memorably parodied in the character of "Orshee" in Richard Russo's *Straight Man* (1997), the young heterosexual male professor who bends over backward to say "or she" in any conceivable circumstance. As the playful notation in the comically self-reflexive front matter of Dave Eggers's *A Heartbreaking Work of Staggering Genius* (2000) noted, Eggers described himself as a 3 on the Kinsey scale, where 1 meant totally straight, 9 meant totally gay. This identification certainly did not impair Eggers's heterosexuality, though, which indicates that masculinity was less inhibited by paranoia about being gay. Yet it also hinted that male privilege had sinuous ways of incorporating dissident elements in this less staid organization of gender. The permissibility of discourse about male homosexuality, in other words, was a new strand in an already well-ensconced figuration of masculinity. Admitting a queer aspect to the spectrum did not squelch masculine braggadocio.

Lesbian critics were less accommodated in this manner, although they began to come into the academy in large numbers at the same time women in general did. Their fight was harder, and it took slightly longer for lesbian approaches to enter visibly the general run of critical discourse the way gay male approaches did. Given that the idea of women academics teaching above the high-school level was so often associated with a loss of femininity, those lesbians who called attention to lesbian interpretive possibilities in literature enabled opportunities for heterosexual women as well to contribute their talents fully to the literary-critical sphere. The Canadian writer Jane Rule's *Lesbian Images* (1975) was a pioneer in this regard. Often reductive and lacking any connection to linguistic theory, Rule's book nonetheless affirmed that literature could and did represent

lesbianism and that lesbian approaches could be productive of literary meaning when used in scrutinizing texts.[12] That writers such as Radclyffe Hall and
Djuna Barnes were known as lesbian and could be read as such was largely
due to Rule's path-breaking efforts. Rule epitomized the generation of dissident
academics that was not rewarded by academia and had to make its way, coura-
geously and perilously, on the margins.

Lillian Faderman and Bonnie Zimmerman also made key contributions to
lesbian literary theory in the 1980s. Faderman focused on friendship between
women as a social relation that could be and often was lesbian or proto-lesbian
in inclination, whereas Zimmerman insisted both on the interaction between
feminism and lesbianism and on a specifically literary aspect to the appreciation of past lesbian writers. Zimmerman's idea of the "metaphorical lesbian"
allowed lesbian subtexts to be seen in many ostensibly heterosexual situations
in literature, and it also freed the idea of lesbianism from a reductively literal
definition.[13]

Lesbian criticism had already been given a great boost by the presence of
a theorist who was also among the foremost poets of her time: Adrienne Rich
(1929–). Rich posited a theory of the lesbian continuum. There was not a firm
demarcation between "straight" and "gay," as was said to exist more frequently
in the case of males. In fact, there existed a variety of woman-centred practices
that might or might not be termed manifestly lesbian but that represented an
evasion of the control of "compulsory heterosexuality." This idea gave insight
into many literary texts—such as Elizabeth Gaskell's *Cranford* (1853) or Sarah
Orne Jewett's *The Country of the Pointed Firs* (1896)—where relationships
within communities of women dominated. These relationships, in the aftermath
of Rich's work, were not so much "exposed" as lesbian as understood to be
part of a general weave of sexual complexity. Acknowledging this complexity
redefined "lesbian" as a fluid field of identity and self-rendering rather than
a rigid label. Rich's magnificent poem "Transcendental Étude" (1977) linked
seemingly ephemeral practices such as quilting with the tectonic geology below
the ground, anchoring the minutiae of women's relationships within a layered
perspective of deep time: the "rockshelf further / forming underneath everything
that grows."[14]

Though at times queer theory ran the risk of sexualizing all phenomena and
thus depriving the sexual and the non-sexual equally of their distinctness of
affect, it largely revealed a richer vision of the sexual, one in which desire could
not simply be mechanistically turned on or off. Queer theory arose amid the
AIDS pandemic, which became widespread in the early 1980s and decimated
the worldwide gay community until its control as a treatable disease in the
mid-1990s. Besides, the general public did not accept homosexuality nor was it
legal in many nations at the time. In 1986, for example, the US Supreme Court's
Bowers v Hardwick ruling reaffirmed sodomy as a prosecutable crime.[15] So
homosexuality was not fully approved or tolerated, and its very existence was a

matter of political controversy. This situation was different from that in which anti-racist or feminist theories emerged. These literary approaches were largely constructed on an anterior body of socially emancipatory practices. Queer theory, however, had an active role in shaping the social empowerment of the group for whom it spoke. As Rick Perlstein has shown, several US court decisions expanding homosexual rights relied on queer theorists for precedents.[16] Although the usual stereotype of theory involves academics bantering about obscure, recondite questions in an atmosphere of comfortable, unassailable liberalism, queer theory has helped give protection and dignity to a population historically stigmatized and denied equality. One suspects that critics of theory who despise what they see as its social ineffectuality would be made even more unhappy by this example of its social effectiveness.

The rise of "queer" approaches coincided with a second phase in the history of literary theory as a whole, a phase contemporaneous with the emergence of third wave feminism (Chapter 3) and the nascent popularity of post-colonial studies (Chapter 5). This second phase involved theory turning away from being the application to canonical texts of the approaches advocated by big names from France and towards the scrutiny of various dissident subject positions, taking into account the experiences and orientations of students who had been drawn to the first generation of theory. But just as "queer" made "gay" or "lesbian" theoretical, so also did "queer" make "theory" sexy. Despite its rhetoric of play and game, deconstruction, especially in the version professed by Paul de Man, has often seemed ascetic and monastic, much like, to use the image from Homer made famous in critical theory by Theodor Adorno, Odysseus lashing himself to the mast in order to resist the sensuous call of the Sirens. Queer discourses shared the freedom and subversiveness of deconstruction, but they enabled that freedom to be less purely cerebral, more embodied. Queer theory also inevitably made instability more pragmatic and more applicable, and it was thus, at least within the academy, a shade less exciting and subversive in cognitive terms than de Man's thought had been, at its first unfolding.

The rise of the term "queer" occurred at about the same time as Judith Butler's theories of gender performativity began to be popular. This is no coincidence, as Butler is the figure who augured and monitored the change that was announced by the reclamation of the previously derogatory epithet of "queer." This reclamation was done in order to turn an insult against those who used it. But it also took discussion of sexuality beyond sexual orientation or practice, as such, and guided it into a far larger range of stances and desires. Gay and lesbian theory necessarily had to be referential or reductive, in order to stake its claims to speak in the first place. Queer theory, laced with linguistic and theoretical self-awareness, saw the avoidance of categorization, the recognition of the gossamer nature of all identities, as the ultimate liberation from restrictive gender norms.

Butler was heavily influenced by continental philosophy and linguistics; her first book was on twentieth-century French readings of Hegel, such as those by Jean Hippolyte and Alexandre Kojève that so influenced Foucault. Butler's work participated unreservedly and with great perceptiveness in deconstructive rhetoric and patterns of thought. In *Gender Trouble* (1990), she asserted that gender was not inherent either in biological or conceptual terms. It was the result of a series of iterated roles or practices. In other words, gender was "performative."[17] Although Butler certainly meant to allude to the idea of performance in the theatrical sense, she also meant to indicate the idea of the performative that was explicated in J.L. Austin's theories of linguistics. There, the performative was opposed to the constative.[18] The constative asserted that things were, whereas the performative actually brought those things about, at least in linguistic terms, by speaking them. Noam Chomsky's similar distinction between linguistic "competence" and "performance" also helped structure Butler's use of the latter term.[19]

"Performance," then, in Butler's discourse related to gender, may at first seem a weakening of sexual identity. If gender is only a role, only put on, a disposable fiction, then it must be only a game, a lark, and an improvisation. But if performing gender is understood in the linguistic sense, sexual identity is arguably strengthening. It is something done, a statement made, and a manifest gesture. Performance has to do with *repetition*. For Butler, gender, even if it is not biological or essential, if repeated a sufficient number of times acquires an *ontological* identity—one that has to do not with *seeming* but with *being*. Individuals, in other words, do not just get to choose their gender nor is gender simply "socially constructed," to use the easy parlance often adopted by cultural relativists. Rather, it is a complex repertoire of repeated performances mixing individual expression and collective articulation.

Performativity thus has much in common with Derridean repetition or iterability, as discussed in Chapter 2. Performativity, for Butler, means an articulation of gender within a claiming and owning of gender as a worldly idiom. But Butler certainly means to insist that there is no such thing as something inherently "male" or "female." She suggests that even the totally heterosexual man or woman behaving in the most normal way that society commends is still performing gender, even if the ascribed dominance of these roles makes their performance seem natural. Although Butler herself was not specifically associated with the rise of the term "queer," the deconstructive inflection of her work is temporally and discursively cognate with the broader application of "queer" as a category. Indeed, some worried that "queer" had become too wide a label. In some uses, it came to extend well beyond specifically gay and lesbian identities: the celibate, the sexually uncommitted, the disabled, even those who were too old, too young, too unconventional, or otherwise judged ineligible for the narratives of heteronormativity. Anyone who did not adhere to conventional scenarios of sexuality or behave in conventional sexual modes could potentially be termed "queer." This broadening of the category had some very interesting ramifications. For instance, it led to many attempts to link queerness and spirituality as states of being that reached beyond the materiality of the given world. "Queer" was as much an attitude of nonconformity as it was a specific manifestation of sexual identity.

Queer Affects

Queer theory also addressed states of feeling and sought to explore new modes of affect in literature; it attempted to ramify and diversify the psychological states that had become established in a compulsorily heterosexual world, or the literary accounts of these psychological states. Butler demonstrated this aim in her 2003 book *Antigone's Claim*, a book about Sophocles' fifth-century BC drama in which a woman asserts the right to bury her slain brother against the wishes of Creon, the new king of her city, Thebes. In the high-school classroom, this conflict is usually boiled down to a New York Intellectual–style opposition between the "individual and society." This view, as Butler shows, is a diluted version of a famous reading of the play by Hegel, which asserts that the drama is a contest between two goods, that of personal conscience and that of the polity. But Butler, once again counter-writing Hegel, asserts that Creon not only represents the state but has a familial role as well; he is the brother of Antigone's mother, Jocasta (who, since Jocasta famously married a man who turned out to be her own son, Oedipus, is both Antigone's mother and grandmother). Creon is thus not just an impersonal statesman but Uncle Creon, and he is not relating dispassionately to Antigone; he sees her as more than a rebellious citizen, and his own personal interest and emotions are involved. Furthermore, Butler argues, Antigone is acting not for herself as an individual but on behalf of her slain brother—to see *him* secretly and securely buried. It is not individuality in the sense of "express yourself" or "be all that you can be" that moves Antigone. It is family loyalty. Furthermore, Creon's opposition to Antigone may be rooted in his own family interest. There is nothing explicitly "queer" in Butler's reading of *Antigone* in that nothing in the play relates literally to same-sex relations. But Butler's questioning of what it means to be an individual and a society partakes of the destabilizing effect of queerness, of its creative ability to imagine new relations (and give fresh readings of texts).

The queer entailed a redefinition of the boundary between public and private. The only gradually diminishing inadmissibility of same-sex feelings led to a covert quality, a surreptitiousness that made feeling—affect—often a surrogate for the public civil rights that were not accorded queer subjects. Queer affect extended to feelings that were not primarily sexual. Kant, in his *Critique of Judgment* (1790), also distinguished between the passions and the affects, limning the affects as a world of feeling where erotic or choleric passion was absent and leaving affect as an intermediate zone of normality between sexual charge and affectlessness, a zone that became repositioned with respect to the agency of

270 THEORY AFTER THEORY

queer subjects. As Ann Cvetkovich—perhaps the scholar most associated with the phrase "queer affect"—put it, "affect is a way of charting cultural contexts that might otherwise remain ephemeral because they haven't solidified into a visible public culture."[20] Whereas, in the paradigms of Freud or even Lacan, sexuality had been an occult reservoir that had to be carefully mediated into public life by the privileged psychoanalytic interpreter in order to both gain insight into the human subject under scrutiny and maintain the stability of the culture, queer affect used private feeling not just as a good in itself but as an expression of unrealized social emancipation by other means.

In this manner, queer theory served to make literature departments, really for the first time, the haven for the full panoply of human affect that undergraduates who majored in literature had traditionally assumed it was. Was not literature the most open sphere of discursive activity, one in which possibilities and not just actualities, alternatives and not just givens could be explored? But, too often, as we have seen in the preface, literature departments emphasized a vision of "life" that not only excluded individuals because of their gender, race, or sexuality but also, even more lamentably, denied imaginative access to ranges of experience that were potentially in any given person. Queer theory also had a different relationship with contemporary creative writing. The fact that, unlike in the Victorian novels discussed by Sedgwick, homoerotic relationships were free to be acknowledged as such by living authors ramified the fabric of narrative in such a way as to make it far less formulaic. The collapse of compulsory heterosexuality in novel plots gave, at a stroke, the freedom from conventional scenarios that modernists had laboured so hard to achieve through extra-social and supra-sexual means.

Where this difference also manifested itself was in the relation of contemporary novels about homosexuality (those written in the age of theory) with the scholarship about homosexuality in novels of the past. Contemporary feminist novels, which often advocated a feminism aligned with radical or egalitarian political ideas, had an uneasy relationship with "rediscovered" early feminist work, such as that by Margaret Cavendish, Lady Mary Chudleigh, and Augusta Webster (discussed in Chapter 3). For contemporary feminists, the earlier women writers often seemed too approving of inequitable social arrangements. The relationship between anti-racist literature of the past and present could also be strained. Despite the presence of practising authors such as Alice Walker and Toni Morrison, there was a certain discontinuity, in style and outlook, between contemporary African American writers and those of the past, such as Charles Chesnutt, Harriet Wilson, and Pauline Hopkins. Partially because most writers reclaimed as gay were well known and canonical and had been taught in school to writers growing up in the 1950s and 1960s, there was a more seamless relationship between contemporary and retrieved queer literary production.[21] Even a novelist as calculatedly outrageous as James McCourt could be described as writing in an acknowledged tradition of letters in which his works provocatively participated. Similarly, canonical writers had made direct or oblique reference to homosexuality for centuries. For example, Tennessee Williams's use of the climactic stanza of Hart Crane's poem *The Broken Tower* (a poem that is a major touchstone in Harold Bloom's work) as an epigraph for his 1947 play *A Streetcar Named Desire* codes the play's action as gay even if it is not declaratively so on the surface. There is a sense of a tacitly articulated continuity of allusions and implications even in one of the most popular, audience-friendly works of modern American drama. The easy coexistence of homosexuality and the mainstream, even amid a near complete lack of overt mainstream acknowledgement of homosexuality, is striking. Moreover, gay male writers, despite their greater manifest social exclusion, tended to have an easier relationship to dominant discourses of popular culture, as seen in the work of Manuel Puig and Ethan Mordden. Once the idea of homosexuality could be articulated, the continuity provided by the public approval of less radical forms of the masculine was able to provide a paradoxical accommodation. Queer readings thus did not operate as a total disjuncture with what preceded them, whether straight or gay.

How does a queer reading differ from a gay reading? Let's examine Willa Cather's well-known short story "Paul's Case" to find out. The story can be (and has been) read as hinting at the homosexuality of its hero. Paul flees his home in bourgeois Pittsburgh because he cannot fit in there. He has an inconclusive encounter with a young man in New York that may or may not be sexual in nature. Finally, Paul dies, flinging himself on the railroad tracks not out of an absolute desire for death but because he lacks any viable alternative. Paul ultimately feels that the world as it is cannot accommodate him. A gay reading might try to use the biography of Cather, her known lesbian orientation (now conceded by all but a few), to reveal homosexuality as the "secret." Paul cannot live because he cannot live as the gay man that, beneath the level of allowable articulation, he is. Butler, though, who wrote about Cather's *My Antonia* in *Bodies That Matter* (1993), might give a queer reading by pointing to the interest Paul has in the theatre—he's not interested in writing or acting in plays but in hanging around playhouses—as a indication that he is performing a certain mode of masculinity. The performativity of gender—the non-naturalness, the conscious pose of it—might be what makes Paul so inassimilable to his milieu. A similar observation could be made of the 9th Marquess of Queensberry's famous accusation that Oscar Wilde, his son's lover, was a "posing somdomite (sic)." Was the felicitously named Marquess more irate at Wilde for performing acts of sodomy or for acting as if he might?

This is the realm opened up by Butler's talk of performing gender. Inevitably, a theory this provocative and popular became easily debased. "Gender performativity" became as much of a rote phrase as any academic mantra of the past generation. But this is a testament to the normalizing power of the academy and not a bar against the continuing productivity of Butler's arguments. Butler was a particular target of the spleen of those who thought all theory ridiculous. She

272 THEORY AFTER THEORY

was criticized for her obscure style and "bad writing." She was, in a situational sense, vulnerable to these criticisms because she was an American and a woman and did not have the intimidation factor that Europeans such as Derrida and Foucault would have had in the same circumstances, although, certainly, the latter two were similarly reviled. Butler's style was definitely obscure. However, throughout her career, Butler has written on very public issues relevant to a variegated swath of intellectual and social interests. These include not just queer theory but also academic speech codes, personal identity, and reconciliation and contest in the political sphere. Butler's obscurity may have been all the more provocative to people because of the visibly consequential nature of the issues she addressed. In addition, she was trying to juxtapose many discursive spheres that her opponents would have preferred cordoned off as separate.

Transgendering Discourse

Judith Halberstam, in *Female Masculinity* (1998), took Butler's theories a step further by explicitly taking on the question of transgendered people.[22] In discussing drag kings—women who persistently perform in male identities but who have not transformed themselves biologically from female to male people—Halberstam shows that female masculinity is something different from the norms of either gender. Gender and biology can dramatically not conform to each other and be symbolically complementary at the same time. Masculinity can be unhinged from maleness and from a discourse of dominance. Yes, masculinity can be subversive. Female masculinity is a viable category. It provides a stable anthropological identity for those who practise it and is, at the same time, an inventive idiom flagrantly violating socially postulated gender norms.

The increasing frequency of students at women's colleges in the United States identifying as transmen, thus problematizing the very category of "woman" or of a binary division between genders as ruling public spheres, has given a fillip to the increased role of transgender issues in feminist theory.[23] Male-to-female transgender theory has been harder to find than its female-to-male counterpart, which perhaps had an easier entrée via lesbian theory than male-to-female theory did via gay studies. In addition, many strands of feminist thought, such as the overtly transphobic work of Janice Raymond and the guardedly sceptical stance of Bernice Hausman, tended to be somewhat suspicious of transgender identities. They regarded transgendered women as men trying to appropriate female identity—as a mode of patriarchy by other means. This negative image was mirrored in the notorious exclusion of transwomen from the Michigan Womyn's Music Festival.[24] Transgendered men fared little better, being seen as abandoning the sisterhood in declarative terms while still seeking a place within an extended women's community. On the other hand, those feminists vexed by transgender feminine identities would be foolish if they were not at least slightly suspicious when the category of "woman," universally denied full social recognition within living memory and still unrecognized as equal to "man" in many regions and spheres, suddenly became an object of desire for men.

Relations between transgendered people and the gay and lesbian communities were only slightly less vexed. There is an inherent gap between people whose sexuality is directed towards their own sex but who feel comfortable inhabiting the gender into which they were born and transpeople, who feel at variance with their assigned biological identity.[25] This gap has been discursively mirrored in the relative lack of communication between gay/lesbian studies and transgender studies. But work by Susan Stryker, with connections to interdisciplinary trends in the humanities, has helped remedy this gap.[26] Moreover, by the end of the twenty-first century's first decade, the major feminist journals—*Hypatia, Signs, Women's Studies Quarterly*, and *NWSA Journal*—had featured substantial work on transgender issues. The familiar acronyms "GLBT" or "LGBT" now signify the full inclusion of bisexuals and transpeople within queer movements. The transfeminist movement, which sees transgender people as an iconic emblem of a renewed feminism, has capitalized on the acceptance of bodily change on the part of third wave feminism.[27] It might seem natural to commingle the ideas of transgender theory, cyborgian feminism, and gender performativity as part of a mega-deconstruction of gender. But this would run against the fact that transgender people are individuals with specific histories who are still often denied civil rights and basic respect in society.

In the mid-1970s, Foucault, in one of his most accessible texts, brought to light the story of the nineteenth-century intersexed person Herculine Barbin.[28] Barbin was raised as a girl but failed to develop female sexual characteristics in adolescence. She (as we will call her for convenience's sake, but, of course, her story explodes the denotative sufficiency of gender pronouns) confessed to a priest who violated the sanctity of the confessional—an act which would have fascinated Foucault given his interest in parrhesia, as discussed in Chapter 1. Even more consummately interesting to Foucault, the priest then engaged the local medical authorities in examining Herculine—for once, the usually rival discourses of religion and medicine were in cahoots. The doctor determined Herculine was anatomically male, with microscopic male sex organs hidden inside an apparently female body. Herculine lived, unhappily, as a man for the remainder of her short life, which ended by suicide. Not only was neither classification of gender appropriate for Herculine, but Herculine was, in many ways, implies Foucault, killed by an overly rigid structure of gender that insisted on maintaining a gender binary no matter how individuals, biologically and in terms of their being, confounded it. People asked of Herculine, "Who is this?" What is her true nature? What forces produced this sexual misfit? Foucault, as is his wont, shifts the focus to the systems that sought to classify Herculine. What was their true nature? What produced them? Foucault, like Herculine's priest, hears the secret confessions of the binary gender system. But to reveal its secrets to the world would take a questioning of gender itself, which would entail over-hauling a rubric on whose authority culture has relied for so long.

As demonstrated by Herculine's case, there are some individuals whose very biology is misdescribed by a reductive attempt to classify humanity into only two genders. Another excursus by French theorist Roland Barthes makes this point—his analysis of Balzac's short tale *Sarrasine* in *S/Z* (1974).[29] Sarrasine is a young man who falls in love with an opera singer, La Zambinella, who represents his image of the female ideal—that which is other from him both in terms of gender and in being perfect while he is imperfect. La Zambinella turns out to be a castrato—a male singer castrated at an early age to preserve his high voice—and thus Sarrasine finds out that, beyond his surface knowledge, he has actually fallen in love with another man, or at least with someone of indeterminate gender. Instead of just seeing the gender indeterminacy in the-matic terms, though, Barthes makes a proto-queer theory move in linking the structural plurality of the various codes or meanings in the text with the variety of gender significations within it. What Tim Dean had described as "normative psychological development requiring the eradication of both homosexual *and* aesthetic tendencies" is thoroughly countermanded.[30]

Other individuals, people without Barbin's inherent or La Zambinella's acquired anatomical traits, similarly feel themselves to be beyond normative cat-egories of gender. And they sometimes feel that this evasion of gender boundaries has more than immediate implications, that it can unbind the excessive rigidity of many categories of perception and meaning. Transgender discourses have teetered between reaffirming the binary, by speaking of people born female who "really" see themselves as male (and vice versa), to jettisoning it entirely and seeing gender as fluid and expressed in multiple variations. Some have postulated an infinite variety of gender expressions on a spectrum. Others have sought to codify the multiplicity of gender in a way that will challenge the dominance of male/female dichotomies while not leaving the issue as a swirling, undifferentiated nebulosity. This approach was inspired originally by the work of Anne Fausto-Sterling, who half-playfully proclaimed the idea of "five genders" in a 1993 article that, as she reports, "Right-wing Christians somehow connected ... to the United Nations-sponsored Fourth World Conference on Women, to be held in Beijing two years later, apparently seeing some sort of global conspiracy at work."[31] Queer dis-courses, in general, seem not to want to do totally without either a core identity or the ability to revise that identity. They want both a basic standpoint and the abil-ity to dance beyond the contours of that standpoint. But this leads to problems of just how far the category of "queer" extends.

The 2000s: The Limits of Queer Theory?

We run into the same problem here as we saw earlier with the category "*mes-tizaje*" within the Americas and in discussions of hybridity in post-colonial studies. There is the danger of overextending a laudably fluid attribute into meaninglessness. To declare all people transgendered by virtue of all people being performers of gender is as problematic as Hélène Cixous's assertion that everybody is bisexual. In both cases, the experiences of a specific group are being used as a metaphor for the situation of all.[32] To say that everyone is bisexual or transgendered is like saying everyone is Swedish. It makes what is admittedly not an exclusive or rigid category into something so unrestrictive as to be meaningless. Even if one could prove its very general truth, it would still do violence to the specificity of the people involved. Marjorie Garber, for instance, who has shown the occurrence or applicability of bisexuality in a large number of texts and who has labelled Shakespeare, not unreasonably, as bisexual, also insists that bisexual experience is of a specific timbre and is neither an overarching umbrella under which both homosexual and heterosexual can be constituted nor a compromise term that invariably fractures under the pressure of competing gay and straight discourses.[33] For Garber, bisexuality may describe *par excellence* the sexuality of all people. But there are also people called bisexuals who have their own experience. Moreover, the promotion of any state of sexuality as a site of utopian freedom ignores the violence, savagery, and brutality that have characterized expressions of human sexuality, of all varieties, through the ages, and that need not be prettified or made saccharine.

Making either "bisexual" or "transgendered" a master term would also increase the burden of a negative aspect of queer theory, which is its tendency to pansexualize, to assume that sexuality is the chief or only key to all discourse. This idea, which Foucault or Gilles Deleuze might well challenge as totalizing, has some continuity with Freud's famous proclamation that everybody is, in some way, bisexual. This seemingly liberated assertion coexisted quite easily with a Freudian discourse in which heterosexuality and presumed gender appropriateness were made normative and homosexuality and gender instability were relentlessly pathologized. An approach that saw all people and their literatures as bisexual would both steamroller over historical specificity and diminish what queer theory has done such good work in directing attention to—the idiosyncrasy in affect among people, an individuality or peculiarity that is not to be subjugated to a monolithic definition. Paradoxically, even as queer theory has unfastened gay and lesbian approaches from a fixed, sexualized identity, bisexual and transgender approaches have lagged behind precisely because of this persistent difficulty in distinguishing between the specific and the general.

One of queer theory's great successes has been its opening up of fields previously cordoned off from any sense of sexuality—friendship, for instance, or spirituality. It has shown overlaps between these states of emotion and more sexualized ones, an insight made possible by a greater willingness to face the fact of same-sex affect. Similarly, masculinity studies, which started off as an expression of gay studies but expanded to include the experiences and literary constructs of heterosexual men as well, was enabled by queer studies to the extent that feminism alone, uninfluenced by queer discourses, would never have yielded. These new spheres were exhilarating side effects of the queer. Frequently, though, no autonomy was left for these spheres. They just became satellites of the sexual, in a way that often ended up being constrictive.[34] Reading the collegial and friendly relationship between the two French priests described in Cather's *Death Comes for the Archbishop* (1927) as simply code for a practised homosexuality, for example, may well be less rich than noticing the layered irony of Cather, who most likely identified herself as lesbian, writing about the lives of two males who were genuinely called to celibacy and had a productive working relationship.

Sometimes a productive overlap between the embodied and disembodied, the interested and the disinterested, might be more genuinely renovating than a reading that denominates everything as queer. As we have discussed, after a fashion, the less categorically queer approach is more "queer" in spirit. Another hurdle queer theory has faced is its overwhelming whiteness. Jennie Livingston's 1990 documentary about African American drag queens, *Paris Is Burning*, was highly influential at the discipline's outset; and the performance group "Pomo Afro Homos," which emerged in the early 1990s, was perhaps the first popular phenomenon to propagate the slang abbreviation "Pomo" for "postmodernism." Both were indicative of the ample space enabled for literary analysis by queer discourses. In most ways, of all the theories that arose from various group identities, queer theory has proven the least reductive. Queer theory has the potential to thoroughly redefine gender, and it has certainly allowed for the viability of very different styles of gender pertaining even to renditions of heterosexuality. For instance, Junot Diaz's *The Brief Wondrous Life of Oscar Wao* (2007) features a nerdy, geeky protagonist with interests that a generation before would have been deemed not only unmasculine but dangerously eccentric in cultural terms, and it adds the additional factor of the protagonist being Latino and from the Dominican Republic.[35] Multicultural geek chic is just the kind of discourse that queer theory enabled even when it was not directly adduced. It is not for nothing that "Oscar Wao" is presented as what Harold Bloom might call a misprision of "Oscar Wilde." Diaz's book is not overtly a queer novel, but it sources and samples queerness as informative and indispensable to its sense of sexual and cultural style. The reader may wonder whether much of theory is not just an attempt to cure the social conformism of the 1950s. In many respects, this is so; this is theory's importance. And to the extent that it "solved" the problems of conformism, theory, if it is obsolescent, is a victim of its own success.

Yet these problems may not have been entirely solved. Even after the general cross-cultural joy occasioned by the 2008 US election, gay and lesbian Americans felt bittersweet emotions as California, one of the nation's most ostensibly liberal states, passed a proposition forbidding gay marriage. Queerness may resemble *mestizaje* in articulation, but the acceptability of this articulation seems less comprehensive. Queer writers of colour such as James

Baldwin and Gloria Anzaldúa (both discussed in Chapter 4) as well as younger, more academic writers such as Kobena Mercer have become points of derivation for discourses that percolate across horizons of race, gender, nation, and sexuality.[36] Yet the experience of non-white and particularly non-Western gays and lesbians is too invisible in the existing body of criticism. Lorde and Anzaldúa were particularly important not just in supplementing gender and racial critiques with each other but also in showing that queer studies was not an elite, Ivy League phenomenon. Queer studies could be applied to people·in many different economic contexts and was not just a dissenting brand of what Pierre Bourdieu would call "cultural capital" to be touted by the privileged in metropolitan precincts.

Gay writers of the past often explored uncharted sexualities in correlation with other vectors of social transformation: across class boundaries in E.M. Forster's posthumously published *Maurice* and across racial and civilizational lines in the Moroccan stories of Paul Bowles. But this combination of the queer and the multicultural or socially plural is, today, curiously exotic for many.[37] The Greek-Australian novelist Christos Tsiolkas, for instance, would be much better known worldwide if this inhibition were not in place, and *will* be better known once it is not.[38] This inhibition may have to do with anxieties about Western cultural dominion as much as about sexuality. Indeed, there have been many assertions—within the Muslim world and within the Global South in various Christian denominations—that homosexuality itself is an inappropriate Western imposition in other societies, a symptom of metropolitan liberalism run amok.[39] This perspective threatens to cast queer subjects in the unaccustomed role of neo-imperialists. It also shows that, for many, queer approaches are still contested because the acceptability of non-heteronormative forms of sexuality is still contested. And theory, as such, has been an important part of this contest. Queer theory is different from feminist and anti-racist academic discourses, which were academic versions of political movements that already existed outside the university. Queer studies was coextensive with the social movement and, in many ways, crucially furthered it. The possibility that queer experience can speak through literature is one of the most significant legacies of theory. Queer theory was proof that literary theory as a whole was not simply a set of irrelevant abstractions that proliferated in the ivory tower but was powerless in the "real world." The impact of queer theory was unmistakably real and, equally unmistakably, expanded the possibilities of figuration in literature.

NOTES

1   Wayne Koestenbaum, *Double Talk: The Erotics of Male Literary Collaboration* (New York: Routledge, 1989).

2   For James, see Wendy Olivia Graham, *Henry James's Thwarted Love* (Palo Alto: Stanford University Press, 1990) as well as Colm Tóibín's novel *The Master* (New York: Scribner, 2004); for Cather, see Sharon O'Brien, *Willa Cather: The Emerging Voice* (New York: Oxford University Press, 1987); for Walter Pater, see Richard Dellamora, *Masculine Desire: The Sexual Politics of Victorian Aestheticism* (Chapel Hill: University of North Carolina Press, 1990); for Dickinson, see H. Jordan Landry,

"Animal/Insectual/Lesbian Sex: Dickinson's Queer Version of the Birds and the Bees," *The Emily Dickinson Journal* 9.2 (2000): 42–54 and, more controversially, Camille Paglia, *Sexual Personae* (New Haven: Yale University Press, 1990). Much more work has been done in a queer vein on all of these authors.

3   Joseph Pequigney, *Such Is My Love: A Study of Shakespeare's Sonnets* (Chicago: University of Chicago Press, 1985). Much earlier, G. Wilson Knight's work on Shakespeare had tacitly seen the playwright and poet as bisexual or even pansexual.

4   One of the latest and most theoretically savvy restatements of the traditionalist position can be seen in Joel Fineman, *Shakespeare's Perjured Eye: The Invention of Poetic Subjectivity in the Sonnets* (Berkeley: University of California Press 1985). Fineman sees the rhetoric of homosexuality as serving only to extol heterosexual desire, although his attitude towards this is as much elegiac as affirmative.

5   Richard E. Goodkin, *Around Proust* (Princeton: Princeton University Press, 1991) and Elisabeth Ladenson, *Proust's Lesbianism* (Ithaca: Cornell University Press, 1999) are good examples of sexuality-centred analysis in Proust studies.

6   On Wilde, see Gary Schmidgall, *The Stranger Wilde: Interpreting Oscar* (New York: Penguin, 1995); for the original trial, see, *The Three Trials of Oscar Wilde*, by Oscar Wilde; H. Montgomery Hyde; Alfred Taylor; John Sholto Douglas Queensberry, Marquess of; and the Central Criminal Court of Great Britain (New York: University Books, 1956).

7   John Boswell, *Christianity, Social Tolerance, and Homosexuality* (Chicago: University of Chicago Press, 1980).

8   Valerie Rohy, "Ahistorical," *GLQ: A Journal of Lesbian and Gay Studies* 12.1 (2006): 61–83. Lee C. Edelman eviscerates the complementary exaltation of the "future," the other side of the coin to the fetishization of the "past," which Rohy scrutinizes, in *No Future: Queer Theory and the Death Drive* (Durham: Duke University Press, 2003).

9   Eve Kosofsky Sedgwick, *Between Men: English Literature and Male Homosocial Desire* (New York: Columbia University Press, 1986).

10   Leslie A. Fiedler, *Love and Death in the American Novel* (New York: Criterion Books, 1960). The undeniable difference between what Fiedler was doing and what "queer theory" later became might be a fruitful topic of discussion.

11   On Milton's *Lycidas*, see Bruce Boehrer, "*Lycidas*: Pastoral Elegy as Same-Sex Epithalamium," *PMLA* 117.2 (2002): 222–36. On Shelley's *Adonais*, see Gregory Woods, *A History of Gay Literature: The Male Tradition* (New Haven: Yale University Press, 1998): 116. On Tennyson's *In Memoriam*, see Jeff Nunokawa, "*In Memoriam* and the Extinction of the Homosexual," *ELH* 58 (1991): 427–38 and Christopher Craft, "'Descend, and Touch, and Enter': Tennyson's Strange Manner of Address," *Genders* 1 (1988): 83–101.

12   Jane Rule, *Lesbian Images* (New York: Doubleday, 1975).

13   See Lillian Faderman, *Surpassing the Love of Men: Romantic Friendship and Love Between Women from the Renaissance to the Present* (New York: Morrow, 1981) and Bonnie Zimmerman, *The Safe Sea of Women: Lesbian Fiction, 1969–1989* (Boston: Beacon Press, 1990).

14   Adrienne Rich, *The Fact of a Doorframe: Poems Selected and New, 1950–1984* (New York: Norton, 1984).

15   See Ronald Bayer, Daniel M. Fox, and David P. Willis, *AIDS: The Public Context of an Epidemic* (New York: Cambridge University Press, 1986). The *Bowers v. Hardwick* decision was, in effect, overturned by the Supreme Court in 2003 in *Lawrence v. Texas*, although the question of full rights for gays and lesbians was still a contested one through the early 2000s.

16   Rick Perlstein, "What Gay Studies Taught the Court," *The Washington Post* 13 July 2003: B03. Perlstein's article, in turn, was one of the few mainstream journalistic pieces to grasp the potential importance of theory to a revived American Left.

17   See Judith Butler, *Gender Trouble: Feminism and the Subversion of Identity* (New York: Routledge, 1990).

18   J.L. Austin, *How To Do Things with Words*, 2nd ed. (Cambridge, MA: Harvard University Press, 1975). See Chapter 2 for more discussion of Austin and Derrida.

19   Noam Chomsky, *Aspects of Syntax* (Cambridge, MA: MIT Press, 1965) 4.

20   See Ann Cvetkovich, *An Archive of Feelings: Trauma, Sexuality, and Lesbian Public Cultures* (Durham: Duke University Press, 2004) 48. Heather Love, *Feeling Backward: Loss and the Politics of Queer History* (Cambridge, MA: Harvard University Press, 2007) further explores the often disturbing and

contradictory feelings associated with ideas of queer affect, as well as their complicated relationship to historicity and temporality.

21 See Andrew Bergman, *Gaiety Transfigured: Gay Self-Representation in American Fiction* (Madison: University of Wisconsin Press, 1991).

22 Judith Halberstam, *Female Masculinity* (Durham: Duke University Press, 1998).

23 See Craig Offman, "A Class Apart: Transgender Students at Smith College," *The Financial Times* 16 April 2005, 1 January 2009 <http://www.ft.com/cms/s/0/99065352-ae13-11d9-9c30-00000e2511c8. html>.

24 See Janice G. Raymond, *The Transsexual Empire: The Making of a She-Male* (Boston: Beacon Press, 1979) and Bernice L. Hausman, *Changing Sex: Transsexualism, Technology, and the Idea of Gender* (Durham: Duke University Press, 1995). On the debate concerning the Michigan Womyn's Music Festival, see the judicious assessment that is, unsurprisingly, given by Judith Halberstam, *In A Queer Time and Place: Transgender Bodies, Subcultural Lives* (New York: New York University Press, 2005) 180.

25 On the relation between gender identity and embodiment, see Deborah Rudacille, *The Riddle of Gender, Science, Activism, and Transgender Rights* (New York: Anchor, 2006).

26 See Susan Stryker and Stephen Whittle, *The Transgender Studies Reader* (London: Routledge, 2006).

27 See Nicholas Birns, "The Earth's Revenge: Nature, Transfeminism, and Diaspora in Larissa Lai's *Salt Fish Girl*," *China Fictions/English Language: Literary Essays in Diaspora, Memory, Story*, ed. A. Robert Lee (Amsterdam: Rodopi, 2008) 161–80 for an overview of debates about transfeminism as a term. For a positive perspective on the pertinence of the term in subaltern cultures, see Amy Lind, "Interrogating 'Queerness' in Theory and Politics: Reflections from Ecuador," *Latin American Studies Association Forum* 39.4 (2008): 30–33; Lind states that "(f)or the transfeminist current, 'trans' implies a break not only with the traditional gender/sex system but with other forms of normativities based on race, ethnicity, class, and geographical location." This is a promising sign considering, as stated, that the biggest lacuna in the queer studies movement has been a convergence with the concerns of the Global South (and, it might be said, vice versa).

28 Michel Foucault, introduction, *Herculine Barbin dite Alexina B.* (Paris: Gallimard, 1978).

29 Roland Barthes, *S/Z*, trans. Richard Miller (1974; New York: Farrar, Straus, and Giroux, 1991).

30 Tim Dean, *Beyond Sexuality* (Chicago: University of Chicago Press, 2000) 276.

31 See Anne Fausto-Sterling, *Sexing the Body: Gender Politics and the Construction of Sexuality* (New York: Basic Books, 2000). The determinacy of Fausto-Sterling's five gender approach may not be compelling in immediate terms—why is five genders inherently more plural, rather than just more numerous, than two? But, as with biological explanations of homosexuality or transgenderism that might at first seem to reaffirm the idea of innate or essential human traits, an idea often questioned or rejected by theory, the five-gender idea does provide the grounded categorization of identity that has proven a prerequisite for rights and recognition in modern Western society.

32 Hélène Cixous, "The Newly Born Woman," *Literary Theory: An Anthology*, ed. Julie Rivkin and Michael Ryan (New York: Blackwell, 2004) 347–65.

33 Marjorie B. Garber, *Vice Versa: Bisexuality and the Eroticism of Everyday Life* (New York: Simon and Schuster, 1996).

34 Kathryn Bond Stockton's *God Between Their Lips: Desire Between Women in Irigaray, Bronte, and Eliot* (Palo Alto: Stanford University Press, 1994) avoids this reductiveness and is an outstanding example of the renovative nature of the queer-spirituality connection, but other iterations of this connection do not avoid reductiveness as nimbly. Another book that takes its interpretive ground from queer theory but generalizes outward rather than exercising a procrustean constraint is Jonathan Goldberg, *The Seeds of Things* (New York: Fordham University Press, 2009). That Stockton is discussing spirituality and Goldberg materiality shows the wide range of discourses queer models can encompass.

35 Junot Diaz, *The Brief Wondrous Life of Oscar Wao* (New York: Riverhead, 2007).

36 Kobena Mercer, "Dark and Lovely Too: Black Gay Men in Independent Film," *Queer Looks: Perspectives on Lesbian and Gay Film and Video*, ed. Martha Gever, John Greyson, and Pratibha Parmar (Routledge: London, 1993).

37 Alicia Arrizón, *Queering* Mestizaje: *Transculturation and Performance* (Ann Arbor: University of Michigan Press, 2006) is a positive sign in this regard, although the presence of the inevitable

keywords "transculturation" and "performance" in the title suggests two discourses brought into apposition rather than a genuine coalescence of the two.

38 Christos Tsiolkas, *Dead Europe* (Sydney: Vintage, 2004). Tsiolkas's work interrogates conventional ideas of national and sexual spaces; yet, so far, he seems only fully hearkened to within an Australia whose national solidity his work, paradoxically, explodes.

39 See Philip Jenkins, *New Faces of Christianity: Believing the Bible in the Global South* (New York: Oxford University Press, 2006), which observes the convergence of African and Asian identity and the affirmation of heterosexuality as a norm. On the other hand, Ann Pellegrini and Janet Jakobsen, *Love the Sin: Sexual Regulation and the Limits of Religious Tolerance* (New York: New York University Press, 2003) sees even the secularism of the West as a "Christian secularism" that inherently privileges heterosexuality. Both Jenkins and Pellegrini and Jakobsen, though, argue for a vision of the relationship between religion and sexuality that departs from a unitary, progressive secularism.

CHAPTER SEVEN

Taking Account of Deconstruction
THEORY IN THE TWENTY-FIRST CENTURY

The Fate of Historicism

This final chapter will look at why and how theory lost its hegemony in literary studies, what movements both within and outside the academy attempted to replace it, and whether there is still a need for theory in the twenty-first century. Is theory, notwithstanding the history chronicled in the previous chapters, still important for people when Derrida and Foucault are now names of the past?

The age of theory most likely began to end with the Paul de Man scandal, which seemed to tarnish all of theory, even modes very different from deconstruction, with being irresponsible and deluded. The scandal also brought theory to the awareness of journalists as well as lay readers of general-interest newspapers and magazines, people who had not previously known or cared that theory existed. There was considerable pressure from the public and media sphere for the intellectual world to move beyond theory, to somehow repair the breach that theory had allegedly opened between academe and the general public. This pressure was fortified by the sense that theory had reached a state of malaise in academia, that the theory boom had been replaced by what Herman Rapaport called "the theory mess."[1] After a while, slogans and terminologies and approaches that were once novel seemed stale. *Différance* or supplementarity or *episteme* caused a thrill of excitement in the seminar room at one point, but, with the passage of time, they elicited the groan reserved for the expected and, often, the all too mechanically applied method. Also, many graduate students trained in theory felt freer to pursue less encumbered approaches once they became professors themselves and had their own classrooms in which to teach and their own departments in which to practise. They faced a growing publishing market for accessible works of literary criticism—fortified both by a sense that people were more interested in reading about literature than had been thought (partially because of all the excitement generated by controversies over theory) as well as by the sense that the cultural polity needed reinvigoration after the subtleties of theory had held their sway. As Michael Warner pointed out, though, the idea of the public often entailed a certain uniformity, and theory did have the potential to operate as a "counterpublic" that could speak with a dissident voice against a simpler consensus.[2] Yet many in the 1990s, even in the academy, began to see theory as a negative sort of counterpublic, as a circular discourse that was beginning to feel suffocating. Even people who had risen in the profession as a result of theory, who had done well by it, saw that it was time for a change. They did not want to become stuck in an endless deconstructive rut.

There had been a time in the 1980s when theory seemed on the verge of spilling into popular culture. The British rock group Scritti Politti entitled a song "Jacques Derrida." Jean Baudrillard appeared at the Palladium, a trendy New York club. The Columbia University French professor Sylvère Lotringer's pocket-sized Semiotext(e) series became an often-seen, quasi-sartorial accoutrement of the would-be chic. Yet deconstruction and its attendant theories were always too academic to be the café and cocktail-party staples that existentialism had been decades earlier. On the other side, attempts by theory to interpret popular culture were often stiff, operating with heavy cannons on phenomena they failed to come to terms with in themselves. Theoretical attitudes towards pop culture were as close to Theodor Adorno's highbrow disdain for nearly all mass entertainment as they were to Adorno's friend Walter Benjamin's reluctant yet thorough embrace of the derivative and the simulated, which Benjamin explained in his 1936 essay "The Work of Art in the Age of Mechanical Reproduction." Some theorists, such as the British critic Dick Hebdige, did analyse "subcultures," such as that of early punk rock, in a friendly if conceptualized manner. These scholars were, as sociologists of a previous generation might put it, more "-emic" than "-etic," more inside identifying than outside looking in their approach. But by the time cultural studies came fully into its own in academia, it had cast off its theoretical trappings and moved to analyse its objects of scrutiny empirically and in a matter-of-fact, case-by-case manner. The discipline of cultural studies moved from being overtheorized to being undertheorized, without theory and popular culture ever having their proper rendezvous. This led, by the 1990s, to the existence of a reading public anxious that intellectual life move on beyond theory.

Thus, many books whose titles or agendas did not explicitly mount a post-theory reassessment got their tacit impetus from a sense of theory's wane. The left-leaning British critics Terry Eagleton and Valentine Cunningham wrote books whose titles explicitly take up the "after theory" question.[3] (Previously, both had written about or from within the world of literary theory. Eagleton's guidebook to literary theory, although highly critical of theory from a Marxist point of view, had nonetheless served as a generation's introduction to the field, and Cunningham was a respected critic who had written on the British poets of the nineteenth and twentieth century.) For Eagleton, the rise of theory not only coincided with the decline of the Left politically but also was a factor in it. Whereas some might believe that critical theory in the 1980s functioned as a de facto intellectual opposition to the social doctrines of Ronald Reagan and Margaret Thatcher, and certainly supporters of those politicians interested in culture wasted no time in attacking deconstruction as subversive, Eagleton sees theory's very existence as a symptom of political despair. Eagleton takes an "ethical turn" of the sort that people who misinterpret Derrida's ethical turn want his to be—Eagleton turns towards a morally accountable, socially cohesive set of criteria. Eagleton sees theory as soullessly intellectual and out of touch with the felt realities of human life to an alienating extreme, and he seeks a new ethical and even spiritual basis founded on equality and commonality, not radical relativism. Eagleton's later work is distinctly less Leavisite and more informed by philosophical speculation and meditation than his earlier work, and his very dissent from theory paradoxically illustrates theory's broadening effects. Cunningham admires the intellectual breadth of theory but objects to its sense of play, which broadcast an aura of limitless possibility that led to a dangerous relativism. (This sense of limitless possibility could also lead to a sense of elitism, as we have seen in its incarnation as "the sublime.") As Cunningham extravagantly puts it, "Under theory the text is demonized by a clamantly Pyrronistic rhetoric of lapse, failure, lack, disablement, deficiency."[4] Cunningham does not deny theory's virtues, nor does he endorse a conservative position that would hyperbolically jettison all jargon—certainly "clamantly Pyrronistic" (loudly sceptical) would need to be explained to many undergraduates just as "trope" or "subaltern" would. Cunningham prizes a "readerly tact" that brings the text back into primacy. Many readers without Cunningham's leftist motives felt similarly. They wanted to get on with the business of reading good books and were yearning for a respite from the often-discordant polemics of the theory wars. Both Eagleton and Cunningham propose outlooks that are, at the same time, more individualistic in mien and more collective in bearing. Although these perspectives are productive as far as these critics' own intellectual trajectories are concerned, the collective answer that both seem to suggest is that critics are best advised to go their own way with as much sagacity and insight as possible. Is this enough to guide future academics?

All the waves of theory chronicled one after another in the previous chapters have long since washed over us. Even the newest strands in the grand theoretical patchwork, post-colonial and queer theory, are now well established, with sizable academic infrastructures of their own. The dolorous outcome of post-colonial critique shows that enhanced political sensitivity among literary critics does not lead to literature being an instrument of political liberation. This truth was a hard lesson that late twentieth-century theorists learned, and one of the major prompts for a new mood "after theory." What now? What happens intellectually in the wake of theory? And what theories come next in the realm of literary academia?

The most durable practice in the wake of theory was historicism. Historicist readings became popular because they anchored the text to a concrete referent while still giving a reading of the text. Historicist readings often involved reading a text thought to be non-literary, as in the case of Stephen Greenblatt's reading of the New World exploration narrative of Thomas Harriot in "Invisible Bullets," a chapter of *Shakespearean Negotiations* (1988). Greenblatt juxtaposes Harriot's *A Brief and True Report of the New Found Land of Virginia* (1588) with Shakespeare's *Henry V*, showing how both works enacted a process of "subversion and containment." In both texts, dissident elements were given space but then were ultimately contained by the continuing dominant system—Falstaff and his crew of whores and rogues in Shakespeare's play and the native peoples in the Harriot exploration text. Greenblatt did not just position the non-fiction text as background but juxtaposed it to *Henry V* to show parallel patterns and meanings. This apposition of the "fictive" and the "real" was a dramatic overthrow of the strictures of the "resolved symbolic." It epitomized just what theory, in response to the 1950s schools that had preceded it, had tried to change about literary reading.

Historicism, though, always had a vexed relation to theory. Perhaps the most prominent historicist working in American literature, Walter Benn Michaels, co-authored a manifesto entitled "Against Theory," written just as the theoretical boom was cresting.[5] (Indeed, Michaels was, in many ways, an internal critic of many theoretical platitudes, including historicist ones.) After the de Man controversy had crippled deconstruction, historicism became pretty much what advanced academics in the humanities did; to do otherwise in the 1990s was to be seen as markedly eccentric. As we saw in Chapter 2, although historicism arose as a response to deconstruction and became, at times, a refutation of it, historicist critics adopted some of deconstruction's techniques. Stephen Greenblatt analysed the contexts of Renaissance literature and their relationship to the plays of Shakespeare, as if they themselves were texts. Greenblatt's "desire to speak with the dead" privileged the past as another world that was at once the mirror of our own. Greenblatt's insistence that modern subjectivity began in the Renaissance infuriated both those who saw modern subjectivity as something exclusively modern and those who saw modern subjectivity as something that even Plato or Cicero had. But, like Bakhtin, Greenblatt did rely on a far more stage-oriented, progressive model of history than did Foucault's work, which, nevertheless, Greenblatt emulated.[6]

Greenblatt was a brilliant writer who perhaps achieved more as a stylist than any other critic considered in this book besides Barthes. But his essays were often criticized for relying too much on what Kenneth Burke had earlier called the "representative anecdote," the nugget or curio of intriguing history that, in Greenblatt's case, lent itself to parallel readings of *Henry V* but was itself isolated and anchored in the discursive frame almost as if it had been a text itself.[7] In a sense, Greenblatt made the contexts he analysed into texts themselves as much as he put the texts he analysed into contexts. Similarly, new historicism's inclination to discern capitalism in the past or to take writers and artists off the pedestal of art for art's sake and immerse them in the financial hurly-burly of their times often seemed to verge on an *endorsement* of capitalism: the art historian Svetlana Alpers, for instance, who was linked to Greenblatt through their common participation in the editing of the influential historicist journal *Representations* out of the University of California, Berkeley, wrote about Rembrandt's entrepreneurship in a way that, intentionally or not, would have made Rembrandt more than eligible to get a tax break from the Reagan administration, fitting, as it did, into that administration's concept of "enterprise zones."[8] Indeed, though James J. Paxson, in his historicist analysis of de Man, has ingeniously aligned the de Manian figure of *prosopopeia* or personified address with Reaganism, surely the new historicists' emphasis of entrepreneurialism and power was more in alignment with the ideology of this presidency.[9] (In any event, de Man died of cancer before the end of Reagan's first term.) Also, this study of past entrepreneurship helped historicists sell their ideology more successfully than either New Critics or deconstructionists had. University administrators, although recognizing that new historicism was subversive, saw it as constructively subversive, not subversively subversive. Thus, historicists were hired broadly across the profession, and, because they liked being in the classroom and communicating their ideas to students, they functioned well.

Historicism in the 1980s was highly interpretive, highly philological, and tended not to deal with actual historical events or circumstances unless these were framed in a textual or interpretive model. Indeed, the journal *Representations* was as dense as such deconstructive flagships as *Diacritics* or the more pluralistic and inclusive *Critical Inquiry*, which it more or less succeeded as the most influential journal in literary academia. At the turn of the 1990s, Alan Liu, in a series of influential articles written after he had produced a superb but conventionally new historicist book on Wordsworth, pointed out that the new historicism of the *Representations* mode relied on detail as bedrock but also helped argumentatively construct and designate this detail.[10] Jerome McGann, in *The Romantic Ideology*, pointed out that aesthetic thought often conjured false unities in divorcing art from history.[11] But, as Liu suggested, historical contexts could also be manufactured; they could be aesthetic unities with the shape of the organic past but not necessarily its underlying reality. When Carolyn Porter asked in her often-cited 1988 essay "Are We Being Historical Yet?" she did not mean to chastise the good faith of existing historicists but to point out that, when the analysis of texts had long been centred in formalist or text-oriented methods, which was especially true in the North American academy, it took more than a little recalibration to make historicism truly historical.[12] By the mid-1990s, this recalibration had begun. Historicists, for one thing, knew more history.

This increased knowledge of history among literary scholars had both advantages and disadvantages. Historicism was no longer an unsystematic shot in the dark, nor was "history" a mere code word for Marxist views of history, which considered it as a dialectical and ideology-tinged process. Now history meant empirical history—social, cultural, material, political. Ideology was still present: for example, work on the sixteenth-century poet Edmund Spenser was virtually monopolized in the 1990s and 2000s by study of his role in the English occupation of Ireland, which relied on a combination of historical and post-colonialist critiques. Still, readers of this work ended up not just appreciating the dangers of imperialism but learning a good many facts about Elizabethan-era Ireland. Historicists now knew facts and dates as well as period designations, and they knew as much about how things worked in past societies as about what ideas came out of these societies or could be applied to them. Whereas 1980s historicism would have looked unfamiliar to working academic historians, 1990s historicism would have resembled something they knew. This convergence occurred partly because even history, as a discipline, was becoming more affected by theory. Before the 1980s, history as taught in universities had not diverged far from its traditional emphases or taken a particular interest in its own methodology, despite the work of Hayden White (a historian by training) on historical writing's inherently narrative manifestations.[13] The change in historicism's own level of "being historical" also occurred, in part, because the literary historicists of the 1990s were more diligent about learning from the historians how to do research in archives and how to analyse concrete past events.

The Reaction against Theory

By the late 1990s, theoretical historicism in the sense of the early work of Greenblatt had yielded to what Caroline Levine called "historical localism," accounts of the interaction of history and literature that were satisfied with describing observable connections on the ground but not conjecturing about their ultimate significance or about the theoretical postulates of how we know the past or how the past has itself been historically known.[14] Facts were no longer lost in mazes of ideological assumption; but facts were no longer motivated or channelled by ideological interpretation. What Levine termed a more rhetorically and epistemologically aware mode of "transmission history" was often eschewed for a sense that what was to be analysed was "there." Instead of any larger rationale or premise for an historical argument, one heard that what was being studied was present in the evidence (textual or archival) being assessed. Readiness to hand became all the interpretive rationale a treatment of the past required. One wonders what Derrida would make of this reasoning? Perhaps he would have pointed to the French phrase "*il y a*," which pointed out that something was there but also privileged the act of pointing, the gestural motion of stating fact that had the potential to call as much attention to the signifier as the signified. With post-theoretical historicism, there was only the signified, no signifier, and often historicist work became a steadfast, informative, responsible, intellectually honest but frustratingly unambitious series of accountings and cataloguings.

Long before historicism, there had been politically inflected criticism, but this had largely been criticism of canonical works from a politically partisan or at least politically interested standpoint. The best-known cases of this type of criticism were from the Marxist critics or the moderate liberal public intellectuals such as George Orwell or even, in a cultural sense, F.R. Leavis. However, French classicists who leaned to the right, such as Ferdinand Brunetière in the late nineteenth century, or the American New Humanists of the 1920s were, in practice, similar as critics. As Orwell himself said, "no book is genuinely free from political bias. The opinion that art should have nothing to do with politics is itself a political attitude."[15] Historicism took a different tack, foregrounding politics itself not just as an angle of ideological vision but also as an object of methodological analysis. When, say, the writings of King James I became themselves the object of analysis and not just an adjunct to reading *Macbeth*, the critic became more knowledgeable about the king and perhaps just a shade less antagonistic to regnant institutions, even if, in intention, the critic was acting with a manifestly "progressive" agenda and in faithful step with Walter Benjamin's mission of making art political rather than aestheticizing politics. This shift changed the stance critics, who, although steeped in historicist assumptions, became more neutral and deliberate: the more they knew about the past the less easy it was to be simplistically political about it. Thus historicism was the methodology that foregrounded the political the most and manifested the most capacity for judgement about politics, but it was in its practice—especially in the 1990s and after—the least politically judgemental.

In a way, later historicism returned criticism to where it had been before the era of formalism and "the resolved symbolic." Once again, as in the 1910s and 1920s, professors of literature were researching in arcane areas and producing work that had little to do with either appreciation or analysis in the conventional sense. Now, though, instead of linguistics and internal textual issues, the focus was on book history and relations to external political history, which had been an interest of the earlier criticism but not as much as it became in the later 1990s and after. Publishing history, in particular, became a trendy area of research, and the Society for the History of Authorship, Research, and Publishing became one of the most cutting-edge associations of literary scholars. Theory still influenced research of this nature, and not only theories from historicism or reception theory. The theoretical insight of Foucault on authorship—on how the individuality of the "author" was associated with the unexpectedly brief hegemony of "man" as a concept in the modern era—was corroborated by research into the history of copyright, for instance, which originated only in the eighteenth and nineteenth centuries. Before copyright, work was routinely pirated in early print culture; currently, the onset of digital culture and its multitasking textualities have again problematized the integrity of copyright. These observations echo Foucault's metaphysical interrogation as to whether the humanist character of authorship can still stand. The impact of Derrida lingered on in the textual criticism practised by D.F. McKenzie (1931–99) and Jerome McGann, who recognized that there could never be an authoritative text of an author's work and that determining the archival history of a text entailed taking account of gaps, fissures, loopholes, and the editor's own perspective. McGann and McKenzie talked about textuality in very material terms, in drafts or iterations that could be palpably studied. Still, the idea of the multiple stages of composition and publication constituting multiple textualities would have been impossible without a Derridean sense of textual slippage and supplementarity.[16]

"Genetic criticism" coming from France, which was more author centred and less consciously theoretical in scope, also called attention to how complex the definition of a received text was. Yet there was often a windowless feeling about later historicism, a sense that only immediate problems were being addressed, without the felt need to provide a larger point. Frequently, the emphasis on publishing history had a utilitarian slant, coming closer to the tactile engagement with occasions of writing and distribution represented on campus by rhetoric and composition programs than to the cloudy, ostentatiously intellectual realms of theory. Individual historicists did not always tend this way. Greenblatt's work, for instance, became more belletristic, taking full advantage of his considerable writerly talents. It also became inferentially more politically centrist, as his sympathy with the idea of Shakespeare being a Catholic, which was subversive in the sixteenth century English context, seemed traditional and conventional in the twenty-first century American world.[17] After decades of tumultuous change, later historicism perhaps represented the need to readjust, to ensure that the reverberation of theory was, in many ways, quickly grafted into the humanities equivalent of what Thomas Kuhn called "normal science."

We discussed in the preface how New Criticism never seemed to have a succession plan, how the students of the New Critics who assumed that they would also grow up to be New Critics were caught short when, sometime around the early 1970s, they discovered that literary criticism was being done in a new way. The problem with historicism is that, even as figures such as Jameson, Greenblatt, Liu, or McGann were rebuking theory for being insufficiently historical, they were themselves doing theory or at least subjecting theory to historicization. The next generation was well acquainted with theory and willing to use it in empirical circumstances. People began to study poems and serialized novels in their original magazine-published form, no longer privileging the final book as the ultimate structure of the text. This approach led not only to an extension of already regnant modes of historicism but also to an appreciation for both book and periodical as physical products and as parts of a business concern. But very few literary critics who followed these approaches were theorists in a dedicated sense. What they were skilled at was applying theory to particular contexts and texts, in that order of priority. Original theorizing was de-emphasized and often thought supernumerary. The connection to theory, which had nurtured 1980s historicism even in antagonism, was severed. Historicists were left with an abundant practice that lacked a motivating rationale. This situation meant that what was often very interesting work in its own terms was not connected to a larger, more salient or more urgent intellectual agenda.

Yet some thinkers of ambition and wide scope remained in the historicist purview. Of these, Franco Moretti was surely the most eminent. Whereas theory had perhaps showed literary critics' envy of philosophy's ability to abstract and science's ability to make specialized jargon operationally essential, Moretti's work showed literary study aspiring to some of the concreteness of history. Facts and dates matter in history the way they have traditionally *not* mattered in literary study above the level of the encyclopaedia article, even if most historians would endorse R.G. Collingwood's twentieth-century conjecture that historical arguments are "answers to questions" and not accounts of "how it actually was," to paraphrase the nineteenth-century German historian Leopold von Ranke. In the 1970s, books such as Hayden White's *Metahistory* had posited historical argument as a series of literary tropes.[18] By the late 1990s, Moretti was seeing literature as congeries of historical and geographical patterns.[19] Moretti's *An Atlas of the European Novel* was not, in effect, so different from Colin McEvedy's atlas of the medieval European world—both featured intermittent pictorial maps and graphs accompanied by lengthy discursive arguments built around and between them.[20] Moretti, though, was far more theoretical than other mapmakers. He saw the settings of novels as representing the flow of populations and social developments and as manifesting not only demographic patterns such as industrialization and urbanization but also a linkage and dynamism almost reminiscent of Deleuze's theory of the rhizome—the underground, vegetative system that everywhere, and subversively, proliferated. Here was a wilder and more subterranean version of Foucault's Enlightenment grid. Yet, far more than a post-structuralist such as Deleuze, Moretti privileged collectible, quantifiable data.

This was a new approach in literary studies. It opposed the abstraction and subjectivity of deconstructive theory. As opposed to Derrida, who saw writing as absence, Moretti's school saw writing as a physical product and the book as an empirical and commercial object. Derrida saw writing as play whereas Moretti saw writing as work, work that was performed through physical processes and distributed by physical processes, work that was both enabled and defined by material contexts. But Moretti did not go back to New Criticism, which disdained any sort of historical reference or nailing down of the text to a determinate detail. Moretti can be seen as continuing de Man's argument against "the resolved symbolic," as trying to substitute for this concept "the unresolved literal." Yet Moretti often makes the experience of reading novels seem rather unidimensional. We are closer to the "resolved literal" than we might like.

Moretti referred to his method as "distant reading" as opposed to "close reading," which examined a text internally.[21] Distant reading studies how a text travelled institutionally, what its constituencies were, by what means it was distributed. We are close to Hans Robert Jauss's "horizon of expectations" (see Chapter 2). But Jauss's reception theory was interested in the historical context into which a book comes and which it alters, the set of particular cultural criteria shaping the way readers understand and judge a literary work, whereas Moretti attaches more importance to the institutional and tabulatable rather than to the interpretive and speculative. Indeed, compared to Moretti, Jauss seems akin to Derrida or de Man, with the horizon of expectations coming closer to a general textuality than Moretti's stress on specific reading practices will permit. This emphasis on reading habits and practices leads to some methodological issues. So much of the work of Moretti and his disciples depends on records of book purchases and library usage. But can one determine who reads a text? As anyone who has a personal library or a library card can attest, buying or borrowing a book does not always mean reading it. There is no measurable determination of which persons, in the past, actually read a book. A diary entry might come close, but even this record does not provide airtight evidence. Short of a panopticon in which external examiners can monitor reading habits, records of purchases and library withdrawals can provide important evidence as to what books were in circulation but cannot tell us that these books were actually read. To determine what writers actually read, scholars might as fruitfully use good, old-fashioned intertextuality, whether of the Bloomian or Kristevan or Derridean sort.

Perhaps the true record of someone having read a book is how it shows up, bidden or unbidden, in another text. And this observation leads us to sense a greater absence in Moretti's work: it provides no perspective on how what is put before us is postulated, on how we come into a position to be able to analyse data in the way Moretti does. An answer to this question may well involve giving a sense, if not an exclusive definition, of why we read books in the first place. Foucault and Derrida both supply such rationales, albeit dark and sceptical ones; but they are rationales. Surely they do not exhaust the stock of available rationales; there must be others, but historicism has tended not to pursue this search. Moretti's methods shed another light on how reading is performed; but it's not an authoritative one. And the fate of historicism in the wake of successive waves of theory was to dominate literary study but to fail to elucidate an overarching rationale for why, as opposed to how, literary study should be performed. Thomas Pfau has suggested that this problem is endemic to the contemporary academic profession, whose pursuit of variegated knowledge enables "the reconceptualization of knowledge as a commodity to be produced and exchanged" in an uninflected, information-based paradigm.[22] This is just the sort of uninflected process that New Critical readings so often ended up capitulating to and that historicism, along with the rest of theory, sought to escape. Yet historicism, by the 1990s, had become so institutionalized, so plural, and so willing simply to stand on its own claims that its ability to achieve the goals it had set was held sharply in check.

States of Exception: Religion and Politics "After Theory"

Though the predominance of historicism and empiricism often made theory seem a formation frozen in place in the early 1990s, a trickle of new or newly influential theorists continued to emerge. One of the most prominent of these was Giorgio Agamben. Agamben, a long-time professor at the University of Verona, was well known within Italy as a wide-ranging scholar who was particularly interested in poetry; his research extended from the medieval lyric to the contemporary work of poets such as Giorgio Caproni. It was well after his Italian emergence that Agamben became famous in other countries as a theorist.[23] In the 1990s, Agamben, Slavoj Žižek, and Alain Badiou became theory stars.[24] Agamben shone with a similar magnitude in that celebrity arena as had Derrida, Foucault, and Jean Baudrillard.[25] But by the time Agamben, Žižek, and Badiou had arrived on the scene, theory was no longer a tight formation—it had broken up. There were no more schools of theory; critics were operating on their own rather than predicating their analyses of writers and ideas under the rubric of European eminencies' dogmas. So Agamben, Žižek, and Badiou became theorists without "theory."

Agamben's stress on the "interstitial" (in between) and "potentiality" fit in well with Derridean ideas of *différance*. His idea of "bare life"—life that is merely biological with none of the perquisites of advanced existence or civilization—was often used to discuss the disparity between the perceived winners and losers of globalization within the Hardt-Negri paradigm of the late 1990s and early 2000s (see Chapter 5). Agamben's profile, though, increased considerably after September 11, 2001. His heightened fame was primarily due to his association with the phrase "state of exception," which was originally coined by the German political thinker Carl Schmitt (1888–1985). Schmitt, who, like Heidegger, had been excessively close to the Nazis without himself being a doctrinal Nazi in the strict sense, used the phrase "state of exception" positively. For Schmitt, sovereignty itself meant the power to decide when a state of emergency existed and to declare a state of exception in which normal restraints "no longer limit the sovereign state's actions." Schmitt believed in traditional authority, but he did not use the vocabulary of "legitimacy" in the way that a traditionally clerical or royalist thinker might have. He believed that the state operated more through force and might than through institutional legitimacy, although he was prepared to use the rhetoric of legitimacy to make force and might effectual. Agamben associated Schmitt's state of exception with the Roman idea of the *homo sacer*, "the life that cannot be sacrificed and yet may be killed."[26] (Agamben, like Vico before him, was crucially influenced by Roman political "state of exception"

history and Roman law.[27]) Like the *pharmakos* (scapegoat) in Derrida's work, the *homo sacer* was outside the laws of society, at once despised and privileged by its codes. But this privilege is only rhetorical; the *homo sacer* is privileged only as "the other," as the object of taunts and castigating rhetoric. The real life— what Agamben terms the "bare life"—of the *homo sacer* is one of being out- cast and persecuted, bereft of any protection from the laws of the state, which, with respect to the *homo sacer* are in a state of exception from the beginning. Agamben's theories can help us understand both how the rejection of characters or ideologies within literary texts and the rejection of certain works, authors, or cultures within literary history are done by whim and from power. They also point to the problem that seemingly universal standards are not universal as long as one single individual is harmed or not adequately recognized by them.

In his own life, Agamben made a practical example of his objection to sov- ereign powers excluding, harming, or not adequately recognizing those deemed to be "the other" when he refused to enter the United States (and gave up tre- mendously remunerative lecture fees) after the newly erected Department of Homeland Security required fingerprinting of all foreign nationals. In refusing to be treated as a specimen of bare life, Agamben was seen as reaffirming the dignity of the individual against the laws of the state. In many ways, this ges- ture was Foucauldian, but, in Foucault's universe, the threat was from modern bureaucracies that tended to cast themselves as helping people and that were sup- ported by ostensibly left-wing ideologies. Agamben's analysis was directed largely against institutions favoured by parties of the Right that claimed to be protect- ing people's security. Of course, there can be positive states of exception as well. Forgiveness, in its Derridean articulation, would certainly be one of them. But the term "state of exception" became associated, after 2001, with the suspension of ongoing legality, which was evinced both in terrorism and in the overly punitive or paranoid attempts to stop terrorism. Agamben became the point person for theory as a stance in opposition to an antiterrorist state of exception.

Theory continued in its critique of normative (or extra-normative) social institutions. But, in the changed environment of the twenty-first century, theory's critique of foundations could be potentially co-opted by an establishment no longer necessarily moored to logocentric postulates. The name of the terrorist group that attacked the United States in 2001, al-Qaeda, means "the base" or "the foundation" in Arabic. Pertinently, one of deconstruction's other names was "anti-foundationalism"; (strictly speaking, this term was applied by Richard Rorty to his own pragmatic critique of the Western philosophical tradition).[28] In the twenty-first century, even conservatives came to realize that there are some contexts in which sceptical critique is preferable to adherence to a base or a foundation. The Schmitt-Agamben discourse of "the state of exception" demonstrates the salutary potential of scepticism, yet it also showed radicals in academia the importance of the norms of legality that they had previously spurned. Similarly, Bruno Latour noted in 2004 that the political Right was adopting the slogans of relativism and arbitrariness and the tone of elasticity with respect to the rendering of reality that had long been deemed characteristic of postmodernism and that conservatives defending faith and order had once denounced regularly.[29]

Two other thinkers who became, in many ways, spokesmen for the Left in an age of perceived terror and fear were Alain Badiou and Slavoj Žižek. Badiou took Marx seriously, as did Žižek and Agamben; but this left them as something like giant, mountainous islands, monumental yet at a standstill, looming over a sea of untheoretical historicists and anti-theoretical literary journalists.[30] Europe was apparently still able to produce theory stars (the search for a US-born theory star was somewhat like the search for a US-born star soccer player). But the United States no longer had an active network of "theory" to accommodate these stars. So there were few Žižekian and Badiouvian analyses of literary texts the way that, twenty years before, there had been Derridean and Foucauldian ones. Tim Dean, in an early citation of Žižek, asked somewhat tentatively if he could be "permitted a Žižekian moment," a phrase that exactly captures the sense in which, though everyone in the humanities knew Žižek's work, it did not produce readings the way the work of his predecessor theory stars had.[31] Astra Taylor made a film about Žižek, which consciously followed in the footsteps of Ziering Kofman's Derrida film. But it was a portrait of an extraordinary individual not a guide to a body of thought. Part of this different reception was simply due to theory's waning. A contributing factor, however, was that, as described above, the twenty-first century saw a rapid series of traumatic political events and drastic changes in previously firm theoretical and polemical positions.

The ideological topsy-turviness of this era led to reconsideration of some other assumptions, such as the idea that deconstruction's critique of the Platonic absolute, the logocentric, necessarily coincided with a critique of organized religion as such, especially of Christianity. Was Christianity washed under with the logocentric in the wake of the Derridean wave? Or could the very force of this wave, its seismic turbulence, dislodge religious energies from under the previously rock-hard fastness of secular, rational, post-Enlightenment modernity? In literary criticism, "religion" has often meant the politics of religion rather than personal experience of or reflection on the ontological reality of divinity. The giant questions were these. Has Christianity disappeared from history? Has secularism triumphed over it? Charles Taylor, a social scientist who early on had favoured interpretive and empathetic models over rationalist and analytic ones, aligned what had previously been a conceptual critique with a view of history when he exposed the fallacious nature of claims that modernity was "a secular age."[32] Both the claim to have totally dispensed with religion and the claim that modernity constituted a self-sufficient epoch were, Taylor shows, spurious, although Hans Blumenberg's arguments make the second point much more difficult to prove.

Agamben's articulation of abnormal circumstances seizing the mantle of the contemporary touched on the deconstructive articulation of the sublime; also, because of the connection between sovereignty and the sacred outlined in *Homo Sacer*, it raised the issue of the religious. We have discussed Derrida's exploration of the spirituality of postmodernity without sliding into advocacy of "the return of religion." But many others, including those explicitly influenced by Derrida such as Jean-Luc Marion called for just this. One might ask why religion needed to return in terms of literary theory. Yes, in broader accounts of modernity and the sociology thereof, "secularization theories" have proliferated, theories that saw religion as a back number bound to yield, for good or ill, to sceptical, intellectual enlightenment. But within literary criticism itself, religion certainly had a role in the "resolved symbolic" era, despite the New Critical preference for keeping it out of explicit analysis. T.S. Eliot, the privileged contemporary poet of that era, converted to a High Anglican form of Christianity in mid career, as had another poet highly esteemed at the time, W.H. Auden, though Eliot's and Auden's personal modes of articulating Anglican Christianity could not have been more different. As we have seen, when that era read historically, it read in a Christian manner, as did D.W. Robertson, Jr. and Rosemond Tuve, whose approaches, in their watered-down high-school versions, became an endless, mechanical hunting for "Christ figures" that had a "symbolic" resonance in texts. The consensus in favour of the virtual equivalence of a literary and a Christian reading was such that, when William Empson began to object in his later work to this celebration of what he called a torturing God (because God had made His son suffer on the cross), many who had formerly lionized him called his objections the shrill ravings of an ingenious critic who had gone off the rails.[33] This general affirmation of a somewhat inert version of Christianity was part of the conformist atmosphere of the 1950s, a rarefied manifestation of the same energies that saw the phrase "under God" inserted into the US Pledge of Allegiance at that same time.

But the 1960s and 1970s saw their own forms of spirituality, and a counter-synthesis based on an optimistic occultism could well have emerged with, say, the criticism of Northrop Frye or that of other thinkers influenced by the analytic psychology of C.G. Jung as a basis. It did not, and the various cults of the 1970s did not impact deconstruction at all; the same people did not participate in both, though deconstruction, of course, had its own cultic characteristics. In the 1980s, as we have discussed, the work of Mikhail Bakhtin was often read with an awareness of both the Russian thinker's Orthodox Christian belief and the incarnational elements in the carnivalesque. Serious deconstructive theology, based on Derrida's work, began to be done by critics such as the American scholars John Caputo and Douglas Atkins and the Australian poet-theologian Kevin Hart. All of these linked deconstruction to a God beyond representation, who was adamantly transgressive with regard to the material world, in a manner cognate with Derridean theories of language and instability.[34] Mark

C. Taylor put deconstruction on the side of a radicalized and de-ontologized Christian belief, seeing rips and tears in the fabric of meaning as instancing the sacred.[35] In a very distinctive and individual way, Frank Kermode wrote on the mysteries, spiritual and narrative, of the New Testament in *The Genesis of Secrecy* (1979), whereas Robert Alter brought new approaches to biblical narrative by looking at the Hebrew Bible in a stylistic rather than a merely contextual way, though at the cost of severing previously discerned links between Israelite literature and that of the other countries of the ancient Near East in a way that could potentially be seen as exclusivist and ethnocentric.[36] Kermode and Alter later collaborated on an authoritative and often-consulted compendium of biblical narrative study. There is no question that the 1980s saw drastically increased biblical knowledge in literary criticism.

So, if religion disappeared from theory to the extent that it warranted a return, it only went away for twenty years, from roughly the mid-1960s to the mid-1980s. Why then did the laborious attempt to "resuscitate" religion as a force in literary studies continue long into the twenty-first century? Fairly obviously, it has to do with political trends external to academia rather than developments internal to it. In the 1960s, religion was part of the establishment. In the 1980s and after, religion was linked to the political Right. In this period, the Right saw itself as a kind of counter-insurgency (even when it wielded power), a seismic upsetter of the apple cart of complacent, secular liberalism. This is why religion migrated from a state of normativity to a state of exception—and why its discussion in literary theory carried with it an air not only of the apocalypse but also of the urgency of political force.

Ironically, although many right-wing opponents of theory saw theory attempting to deconstruct religion, to tear down transcendental signifieds, many theories invoked religion to deconstruct articulations of modernity that presumed the absence of religion. While Hans Blumenberg tried to defend modernity, skilfully refuting in his *The Legitimacy of the Modern Age* (1966) the common intellectual saw that modern ideologies were "displaced versions" of Christianity,[37] Marcel Gauchet saw Christianity itself as subversive, as "the religion at the end of religion" whose critique of earlier, more literal faiths was itself the beginning of modernity. René Girard, who wrote seminal criticism of the novel in *Deceit, Desire, and the Novel* (1965), saw nearly all narrative as motivated by a sacrificial logic that ejected the scapegoat in order to affirm society (much in the way discussed by Derrida in "Plato's Pharmacy"). Girard, whose book was perhaps second only to Wayne Booth's *Rhetoric of Fiction* as an influential account of interpreting novels (and was published only a few years after it), saw Christian doctrine, with its substitutive logic of making sacrifice metaphorical, as countermanding the cruel practice of scapegoating.[38] (Girard was, in a way, consummately refuting Empson: the Christian God was the *nontorturing* God.) The "Radical Orthodox" school based at Cambridge University in England and led by John Milbank, Catherine Pickstock, and Graham Ward tried to place religious orthodoxy in the same historical-intellectual place as theory—as mounting an exposé of the arrogant self-canonization of modernity.[39] What would Leavis have thought of these Anglo-Catholic ritualists, whose work was laced with postmodern jargon, prevailing in "his" Cambridge?

Even some thinkers explicitly affiliated with the Left and with materialist criticism, such as the Americanist Bill Brown, took issue with the anti-religious stance of previous Marxist-influenced thinkers such as Fredric Jameson. (As discussed in Chapter 2, although Jameson used medieval allegorical methods as interpretive devices, he downplayed the role of religion in his criticism.) An indication of how extensively the "return of religion" rhetoric had spread in the early 2000s was a widely discussed article by Brown in the May 2005 *PMLA* entitled "The Dark Wood of Postmodernity (Space, Faith, Allegory)." That the article was published in this journal was striking: *PMLA*, the journal of the Modern Language Association of America and one of the few periodicals guaranteed to be read by nearly everyone in the profession, had been dominated by figures friendly to theory and to multiculturalism from roughly 1990 onward. Also striking was who was making the argument. Brown had come to notice some years earlier as an Americanist who specialized in "thing studies," a branch of literary scholarship that examined both material objects in literature and literature as a material object or as a mode of representing material objects. Thing studies had connections with social studies disciplines such as material culture, which examined the aesthetic and interpretive implications of functional objects from the past. But it also evoked parallels with the modernist interest in the matter of fact over the ideal, exemplified by William Carlos Williams's dictum, "No ideas but in things." If thing studies had any theoretical implications outside of its own material plane, it was towards a modernist self-sufficiency critically placed in a Marxist framework. So it was a surprise to see Brown advocating for a renewed religious dimension to reading, even as he made clear that this dimension was somehow to be directed towards a Marxist or socialist horizon.

This mixture of Marxism and religion had always been present in historicist criticism. What Norman Cohn, Michael Walzer, and Eric Hobsbawm saw as the millenarian dimensions of Marxism were often the subject of allusion. Also, in its postmodern repletion, the thought of Walter Benjamin had a decided emphasis on the "messianic," and, often, this "messianism" was invoked as the hope for tangible social redemption, even though Benjamin had warned that the arrival of the messiah was slippery and likely to be both unheralded and inconvenient. As Franz Kafka, working in a milieu similar to Benjamin's put it aphoristically, "The Messiah will come only at that moment when he is no longer needed: he will come one day after his coming, he will come not on the last day, but on the very last."[40] Similarly, Agamben sought to recast messianism as not a discrete moment but a lengthy and contradictory process; this notion goes in the other direction from Kafka's but similarly undermines any idea of a cathartic or categorical deliverance. Despite these anticlimactic and, ultimately, anti-apocalyptic warnings, Benjamin's messianism injected enough of a religious tone into postmodern criticism that figures such as Edward Said and Jonathan Culler and Christopher Norris strove to introduce a deliberately "secular" style of thought. (Said noted that he preferred Adorno to Benjamin because the former was secular while the latter was religious.) The glimpse of a "religious turn" in Derrida, however misdiagnosed, fortified this messianic drift, which, by the time of Brown's article, had become all but orthodox.

However, one of the problems here is that behind all reassertions of religion in the postmodern age was a temporal assumption. Either religion had never gone away and was now once again having its continual presence noticed, or it had come back in a way so substantive as to be almost physical, like a politician once voted out of office and now re-elected. This would make what Nietzsche and his followers termed "the death of God" only, in effect, the temporary recusal of God. Moreover, despite the invocation of the Jewish thinkers Walter Benjamin and Emmanuel Lévinas and despite attempts by critics such as Gauri Viswanathan to broaden conversations of religion to include Hinduism and other South and East Asian religions, the "religion" in the "return of religion" criticism was overwhelmingly equivalent to Christianity.[41] Even more limiting, the idea of a return of Christianity became linked to either a) the resurgence of conservative political parties or b) the need for leftist political parties to appropriate or redeem the conservative parties' rhetoric in order to themselves win power. Although these political issues were tremendously interesting in the 2000–08 period, future generations may judge that this discussion has little to do with the horizon of literature or with coming to terms with literary complexities. As we have seen, it is possible for literary discussion to be deeply political and to concern itself with long-term issues of social and cultural subordination. But excessive dovetailing with electoral, partisan politics, though inevitable in criticism—literature and politics, as the Percy Bysshe Shelley quotation in this book's preface suggests, are far more linked than conventional scenarios assume—tends to make critiques too immediate and journalistic in portent. We care about the criticism even of extremely political figures such as Matthew Arnold a century and a half after their deaths because their political views do not exhaust their literary scholarship.

However, despite this problem of its politicization, the "religious turn" was welcome because, following the feminist, multicultural, queer, and post-colonial turns, it extended what could be talked about in criticism. Even if there was as much of a difference between religious discourse in criticism and people of faith writing criticism as existed between feminist discourse in criticism and women, as such, writing criticism, surely one effect of the pluralization of discourses is to make a diverse—and different!—set of individuals comfortable in the critical arena. The circle had widened since New Criticism, which, for all the Christianity of many of its heroes and practitioners, tended to see religion and literature as separate.[42] Theory encouraged the coalescence of discourses, though it did not condone the subordination of one discourse to another in a unitary way. The lesson of theory with respect to religion was a double-sided one, as was theory's lesson with respect to queerness and national or ethnic identity. Theory sanctioned religion's articulation without granting it unitary authority. Thus, the re-emergence of religion and macropolitics was both a reaction against theory and a symptom of its success.

As in the case of post-colonialism, though, a lot of fruitful theorizing seemed in danger of leading to a practical dead end. For all its spectacular fireworks, the dialogue between literary theory and historically manifest religion seems to have produced a sterile antinomy between the death of God and the return of religion. What it lacked was a middle ground between the personal spirituality ascribed to authors and readers of texts and a collective spirituality whose sole articulation is within the context of large-scale historical movements. This body of work made little sense, in other words, of how literature mattered to people of faith or of how religious convictions animated an attunement to wholeness and beauty—or to diversity and beauty, what the nineteenth-century Roman Catholic poet Gerard Manley Hopkins called "pied beauty"—in literary expression. On another vector, the Swedish theorist H.W. Fawkner used religious thinkers' accounts of the phenomenology of non-standard human experience without being consternated by truth claims about the nature of spirituality or by an historical metanarrative that would end up endorsing one or another party of interest in social and cultural terms.

Those who are generally in favour of the return of religion find the state of exception positive. Those who point to the power of the state to prolong an emergency find it negative. The valence of a state of exception does not seem stable. It seems a roll of the dice, contingent on the political sympathies of the people involved and on how events occurring outside literature and stretching back into the deep past are interpreted. Nor does the artificiality and playfulness of literature lend itself to a sustained sense of the suspension of norms, which would be congealed into a permanent suspension of scepticism because norms are what cause us to question phenomena. Indeed, literature, in its irony and provisionality, could be seen as a guarantor against the permanence of a state of exception; this is how Frank Kermode viewed it in *The Sense of an Ending*, although he used the term "apocalypse" where post-Agambenian critics would use "state of exception."

A stumbling block here is that literature has privileged state of exceptions. Literature, with its emphasis on individuals rather than populations, has often been very undemocratic. And there may be something inherently exceptional, inherently inequitable about the act of creativity. One of the reasons people find Shakespeare such an intriguing figure is that he seems to have been an unconventional *individual*—from all evidence, for instance, he was bisexual or could not be graphed in sexually conventional terms. And he does not seem to have adhered to any particular ideology or religion, despite the attempts of various critics to define him in this way. The creative artist, then, like Derridean forgiveness, is a positive state of exception. But literary study was faced in the wake of Agamben's work with choosing between simply trying to classify states of exception on a case-by-case basis or taking a global position for or against them categorically.

Another example of "exception" in early twenty-first century literary study was the increasing interest in "counterfactual" scenarios. Counterfactual studies analyse how events could have occurred otherwise than they did, in both historical and textual scenarios, so they offer exception without the allure of authority. This approach emerged as a provocative way to combine the diversity of perspectives offered by deconstruction with the quest for a larger purpose that has so often been seen as embodied in historical meaning. Counterfactual speculation gave a material form to the reshufflings of the given that theory, in its celebration of the exhilarations of changes, had promoted on an abstract and linguistic level. Counterfactuals also operate as a way to clarify the might-have-beens of intellectual history in ways that can help us clarify how much of the books before us are the products of individual agency and how much of historical processes. In other words, counterfactuals help us estimate whether ideas, literary movements, or other events are necessary or contingent.[43] If Derrida and Foucault had never reached North America, for example, would the New Criticism still be reigning?

Beyond the Academy? Literary Journalism "After Theory"

Theory—especially deconstruction but, in reality, all theory—never had good press. This was not necessarily because the press was revolted by the ideas. Cultural phenomena highlighted by self-awareness or self-reflexivity, phenomena that were obviously influenced in some ways by deconstruction, received rave reviews from newspapers that, twenty years earlier, acted as if "the deconstructionists" were going to destroy us all. Deconstruction generated as much paranoia among the mainstream press as did any political movement of the late twentieth century, whether of the Right or the Left. This includes communism and Islamic fundamentalism, both of which received journalistic efforts to understand them seriously in their own terms and "without prejudice" more than did deconstruction.

Although Terry Eagleton and Valentine Cunningham, our two "after theory" critics, wrote frequently for high-end general-interest journals such as the *London Review of Books*, they stayed within academia and, to their credit, within Britain rather than taking high-paying jobs in the United States, which could have been theirs for the asking. They continued to teach and publish in a conventional academic mode on their side of the Atlantic. Many younger literary scholars, though, left academia altogether and became literary journalists, returning to academe only in writer-in-residence positions that sidestepped academic routine. The journal *Lingua Franca*, which operated from 1990 to 2001 under the editorship of Jeffrey Kittay and then Alexander Star, epitomized this idea of "the flight from theory." Some of this flight was due to disillusionment with theory in the 1990s. But other aspects of it were attributable to that decade's dividing and indifferent job market, which left many job candidates who had received graduate training in the latest trends adrift and bitter. Even those institutions that did hire did not necessarily want to hire theorists. First, hiring was often in the hands of older professors who had not been trained in theory and were suspicious of it. Second, hiring departments thought that theorists were out of touch with the kinds of literary study their students actually needed to do. This judgement pertains to an issue raised in Chapter 3: the elitism of theory as practised in North America, its tendency to flourish in the most selective institutions and to refuse to re-tailor itself for institutions with a different educational rationale. And theorists did tend to indoctrinate rather than to teach, and they saw the most likely candidates for indoctrination to be among the already academically "chosen." Of course, some theorists were more pedagogically inclined, such as Gerald Graff (whose once open hostility to theory moved by the latter part of his career to a wary sympathy) or Stanley Fish (a provocative figure who, for all his often incendiary and provocative rhetoric, genuinely cared about teaching and learning).[44] Still, the recalcitrance of departments in less selective colleges and universities about hiring theorists, a reluctance half driven by surliness and incuriosity, was also spurred by a legitimate sense that theory was not producing job candidates who would function well at these institutions. The kind of criticism that theory produced also seemed out of step with the smooth functioning of these institutions. So many theorists wrote around or beside or against a text; they produced far fewer of the useful, practical readings that the New Critics and their era had produced, although theory could have inspired such readings.

With the decline in theory's prestige came a concomitant rise in the prestige of a form generally sidelined by theory—literary journalism. By the late 1990s, far more intellectual energy worldwide was being invested in book reviews and overview articles for weekend supplements, newspapers, and magazines than had been true twenty years before. There were three constituencies responsible for most of this writing. One was people who had never seen themselves as academics, though they may have taught in universities. These were creative writers or familiar essayists whose perspective had only been grazed by theory in the years of their intellectual maturation. This group included people who wrote for avant-garde but not consciously academic journals, such as *Bookforum*, *The Review of Contemporary Fiction*, and *Sulfur*, and could be extended to include writers associated with literary experimentation but indifferent or even hostile to theory, such as John Barth or William Gass. There were also former theorists who decided to branch out and become "public intellectuals" and write books of more topical interest. The US philosopher Richard Rorty and the Argentine cultural theorist Beatriz Sarlo are good examples of this; interestingly, Rorty revealed a more politically activist side than had been seen earlier in his metapragmatist recasting of the methodology of philosophical investigation, whereas Sarlo departed far more visibly from leftist dogma than she had in her early years as part of the editorial team of the journal *Punto de Vista*. In other words, even though weekend-supplement or general-interest periodical journalism sometimes seemed, as a genre, tilted towards a repudiation of leftist politics or avant-garde aesthetics, Rorty's case, at the very least, proved that this repudiation was not always necessary. Rorty or Sarlo could never be mere journalists, essayists, or book reviewers. They wrote from a greater reserve of material and operated—partially due to the public's awareness of their professional stature—with a greater heft than did those who may have published alongside them in the same periodicals. But the most consequential effect of theory on literary journalism occurred in the next generation. Younger writers emerged, writers of an age to be trained by theorists and to decide they wanted to practise a less arcane, more accessible way of writing.

This tendency has already produced one figure known and respected worldwide: James Wood (1965–). Wood was British and educated at Cambridge, maturing in a culture that, unlike that of the United States, had many national newspapers and an ongoing sphere of informed non-academic literary discussion that had not been stanched by the demands of Leavisism. This situation gave him a considerable advantage, with respect to theory, as compared to Americans of his generation. Wood is the only literary critic writing today whose every review is an intellectual event. The virtue of Wood's writing can be seen in a review of Rivka Galchen's first novel, *Atmospheric Disturbances*, which appeared in *The New Yorker* of June 23, 2008.[45] (Galchen grew up in Canada, and the book's being reviewed in *The New Yorker* is an index of the problematic of the visibility of post-colonial literature in the metropolitan centres, which was discussed in Chapter 5.) Wood immediately starts off his review of Galchen's novel by mentioning the nineteenth-century German dramatist Georg Büchner and his evocation of a man having a breakdown in his story "Lenz." Dostoyevsky, Italo Svevo, Knut Hamsun are all mentioned shortly thereafter, as are Nabokov, Borges, and contemporary American novelists such as Thomas Pynchon and Richard Powers. This is a heady, cosmopolitan collection of precedents to frame Wood's intricate, discerning analysis of Galchen's story of disorientation, cognition, and passion. The critic who not only has these references at the ready but also can deploy them meaningfully in an overview of a recent novel in such a way as to make sense is surely an estimable one. That such critics do not totally lose their audience by doing so is not only estimable but also astonishing. In fact, within living memory, George Steiner and Frank Kermode are the only critics who have done literary journalism extensively who can be compared to Wood in this respect.

Nor is Wood fazed by more exotic or riskier techniques. When Galchen depicts a scientist in her novel, a man with access to arcane knowledge styled "Dr. Gal-Chen" she is playing on her last name in a way that is immediately recognized by Wood and tacitly commended: "Galchen manages to make her novel a kind of tribute to her father, an academic meteorologist who died in 1994, in his fifties." Wood can see the emotional dimensions of fictional experimentation, and he gives us insight into how novelistic feeling—Leavis's valuing of "life"— has to be subtended by thought and into how being sensitive to this feeling can lend dignity to experimentation. How William K. Wimsatt and the New Critics would have hated Wood's knowledge of Galchen's father's profession! This alone shows that Wood, however young fogeyish in mien, does not bring us back to the "resolved symbolic." The phenomenon of reviews as felicitously expressed and steeped in learning as Wood's emerges as both a rebuke and a consequence of theory. The first seems immediately apparent. Wood eschews using the jargon concomitant with theory or making much of the big names associated with it, and his aesthetic hearkens back to nineteenth-century realism. He also seems to reject many recent writers whose achievement is associated with experimentation, self-reflexivity, or forms of novelty deriving from their angle on experience. Ironically, in this rejection of stylistically modish writers, Wood is closest to "the deconstructionists" with respect to whom he is often read as being not just the definitive opposition but also the all-healing antidote.

We are back to what J. Hillis Miller said about deconstructionists being readers of canonical, privileged texts. A post-structuralist like Hélène Cixous wrote a major book on James Joyce. Indeed, the independent critics who remained on the edge of the academy throughout theory's dominance were more likely to write on experimental writers such as William Gass or William Gaddis than people teaching theory in the academy. In turn, the books written by academic but not really theoretical critics on "postmodern" writers such as these two or on figures such as the French "New Novelist" Alain Robbe-Grillet were likely to be surprisingly clunky and untheorized, more celebratory handbooks than challenging analyses. But Wood's focus on the canonical was nonetheless very different than that of the theorists. He is not reading this literature against the grain, although he does read it rigorously. Perhaps what he was perceived as having most in common with those opposed to theory was this movement back to previous ways of doing things, whether in literature or criticism.

Many literary journalists seemed to want to reject the late twentieth century. The near past is always the most vulnerable era in terms of any historical reassessment. If a sense of the past is difficult to achieve, discerning a sense of the near past is like threading a camel through the eye of a needle. Wood's frequent takedowns of writers who had been heralded in the late twentieth century seem not only acts of aesthetic inclination but also declarations of the need to re-evaluate wholesale assumptions about the writers and techniques that were thought important during this period. As we have seen in his review of Galchen, he is not opposed to postmodern techniques. But he seems to mind them most when postmodernists of a certain generation practise them. Generation X or Y writers can be postmodern, presumably because they have avoided, by the temporal circumstances of their birth, the metaphysical errors of their forebears, which Wood almost unequivocally disdains. It is this temporal position, rather than an unbending opposition to theory as such, that Wood deploys as his marker of distinction.

Wood does not follow in the path of theory. But the depth and the seriousness with which he views literature is part of theory's legacy: both as an inheritance and as a reaction. Wood is well aware of theory. Indeed, people of Wood's generation do not have to accept or practise theory in order to have learned from it. It was so much in the air during their schooling that it has infiltrated their intellects no matter what. The main point of the present book is that, though different critics will have different reactions to theory, it cannot simply be jettisoned. Too often, Wood's name is used as shorthand for bypassing theory. But the richness of Wood's criticism comes from both a desire to speak about literature in a more affective, less clinical way and an understanding that theory has raised the stakes so that this has to be done with real effort. Wood's British background initially seemed to make this possible. In the era of high theory, Britain was less inflected by theory than the United States, and its multitude of national newspapers also contained a far more intellectual strain in public book reviewing and journalism.

It is a tribute to theory that reactions as productive as this have occurred. Intellectual history is not static. The worst move those inclined towards theory could make is to emulate the "resolved symbolic" in the 1960s—to wish for nothing to change, botch the inevitable succession crisis, and be sour about younger people who want to alter how things are run. The present book's purpose is to outline theory as a part of intellectual history. It is not to assert that theory is the *only* way to perform literary reading. In this way, Wood's disinclination towards theory is as constructive as it is destructive. But there is another issue with Wood, one that goes beyond intellectual content. Wood mainly writes reviews for widely circulated periodicals. When one compares his reviews to those of the New York Intellectuals or of other "men of letters" from earlier generations, Wood's stand out. They are much more learned, demonstrate that their author has thought about literature more, and do not seem written in a scattershot or gratuitous way. But Wood is still writing book reviews, and book reviews are, as discussed previously, a limited genre. Even when Wood writes longer essays—as he is splendidly capable of doing—he writes them largely for non-academic publications, and, consequently, his writings do not have to be refereed by outside readers. Furthermore, Wood does not use footnotes or other forms of references. In the context in which he writes, this form is necessary. Yet, as Anthony Grafton has argued, there is something to be said for the footnote, however cumbersome, as a means of sifting the essential from the complementary in an argument and of showing one's place in the tradition of learning, one's indebtedness to those who have gone before.[46] The processing machine of literary academia that emerged in the late twentieth century—its editorial boards, its anonymous evaluation of manuscripts, its almost military sense of duty, its finely honed sense of critical precedent—should not be dispensed with totally in order to return to the earlier model of the book reviewer as a man speaking to men. Academia has found neutrality, a sense of the autonomy of intellectual work, which is denied someone who writes reviews for general-interest magazines typically owned by major multinational corporations. Despite the potential for hypertextuality to cyber-embody deconstructive practices, as pointed out in the 1990s by Stuart Moulthrop, much literary criticism on the Internet—blogs, wikis, webzines—though of an intellectual quality equal to what one can find in conventional channels, lacks the institutional connectedness that gives academic criticism a history and a heritage.

The book review or the familiar literary essay may, as in Wood's review of Galchen, have a keenly felt sense of literary precedent. But, without notes and without the sense of an academic community behind it that is committed to keeping a record of what is said when, Wood's own essay will be hard to keep in the chain of intellectual conversation. In an odd way, Derrida's engagement with Ernst Robert Curtius through Maurice Blanchot, as discussed in Chapter 2, evokes tradition more readily than do Wood's reviews. Derrida does not believe in a substantive transmission from the past the way a "Burkean conservative" might. But Derrida does sketch such a palpable track of the absence of that transmission as to succeed in what Curtius called "restating tradition."[47]

Also, though Wood himself was, at the time he wrote the review of Galchen, Professor of the Practice of Literary Criticism at Harvard University, he did not teach from the beginning of his reviewing career. Some of the other younger literary journalists do not teach at all. Certainly few teach full time or in the context of an academic department. As our reading of the readings of Paul de Man and Chinua Achebe in the preface demonstrates, many an intellectual avenue can be explored by reflecting on conundrums that come up in teaching. The belletristic reviewers' tendency to restrict themselves to their private studies rather than to university common rooms limits this possibility for opening. Interacting with students—making the structural connection between the texts of the canon, the methods used to read these texts, and the personal inquisitiveness of the next generation of its explicators—is the hidden asset of many scholars. This interaction has prolonged the critical career of many who are far less talented as writers than many literary journalists who generally, though not unanimously, do not choose to pursue permanent academic positions.

Wood looks more traditional than Derrida. But in not providing notes and in not embracing the institutions of academia the way Derrida (however sportively and puckishly) did, Wood does not let the reader trace the movements of his reading or situate his reading in a pedagogical context. Wood thus puts himself in more peril of not being traced by others than might seem apparent at first. A wild card here is the Internet, which not only will make Wood's reviews available but also will classify them in just the sort of discursive chain in which Derrida enfolds Curtius and Blanchot. Will Wood's lapidary screeds become part of a larger, more amorphous maw of discourse via digital culture? But the Internet is an external agency. It has no particular or endemic sense of tradition. It certainly lacks Derrida's personal touch. Of course, Wood has both a personal touch and a sense of literary history. But, even as we delight in what Wood has contributed, we should remember that Derrida, in his own métier, had those qualities as well. Wood himself acknowledges this when he praises deconstruction's insight on "how texts can internally contradict themselves and can sometimes bend back upon and betray an author's intentions."[48] Interestingly, Wood says he uses deconstruction more in the classroom than in his written work, which is in line with our discussion in the preface of the pedagogical origins of de Man's and Achebe's essays.

Another issue arises when comparing Wood and Derrida: the different operative mode of the "public intellectual" and the "theory star." Wood operates according to the traditional notion of the public intellectual, someone who may teach in a university but who is not tethered to the academic system and someone who spends considerable time addressing a non-academic audience. Comparing Wood's work to that of the New York Intellectuals, William Deresiewicz says, "To turn from Wood to any one of these writers is to breathe an incomparably richer mental atmosphere."[49] If true, this is because, in that atmosphere, being a public intellectual was very nearly the only way for the literary critic to be famous. Wood is writing in an atmosphere that not only feels the aftermath of theory intellectually but also has the role model of the theory star as well as that of the public intellectual. The newer mode of the "theory star" represented by Derrida, Foucault, Julia Kristeva, Jean Baudrillard, and Alain Badiou is different. They were tethered to an academic system but were known beyond it. The public was attracted to them not because they were explainers but, in a way, because they were mystifiers. Whereas public intellectuals brought ideas to lay people, theory stars brought lay people to ideas. They did not seek out acclaim but courted it by their very opacity. Public intellectuals were far more responsive to shifts in public opinion. This responsiveness considerably facilitates their abilities to apply ideas helpfully to current situations or dilemmas. But it also leads to a certain faddishness, a certain "weather-vane" quality. For instance, a review by Leo Bersani, written very early in his career and published in *The New York Times* on June 11, 1967, gives the general reader of 1967 a fair reflection of what that reader expected to hear—echoes of the 1960s preference for new, unmediated creative expression. Bersani was reviewing Frank Kermode's *The Sense of an Ending*, and he chided Kermode for assuming that "novelty in the arts ... is either related to something older than itself or it cannot be communicated."[50]

Later, a post-Derridean interest in language and a concomitant recognition that texts often depend on other texts—"the anxiety of influence" for Bloom, "literary history" for de Man, "the consciousness of the working of effects" for Gadamer, or "intertextuality" for Kristeva—would make the idea of an unmediated novelty less viable. But Bersani's perspective was also animated by what was going on in the world. Writing just before the "Summer Of Love," Bersani was not particularly willing in his review to acknowledge the claims of tradition, as did those writing in the more conservative decades of the late twentieth century (as, indeed, Bersani did with flair and idiosyncrasy in his later criticism). Later on, the reviewer would no doubt have found Kermode's perspective more "hip" in its, from a 1960s perspective, decidedly un-hip embrace of literary tradition. That Bersani is a well-known academic is all the more important here, as the timeliness in his review becomes more a reflection of the mode in which he was writing than of the writer as an individual. Literary journalists are responsive to their constituency of officials; and they also have to consider those officials' vulnerability to tides of opinion. Just as the legislature of the United States benefits because one body faces the voters every two years and is responsive and another faces them every six years and is thus more deliberative, literary criticism profits by having both literary journalism and a more academic approach so that both responsiveness to a climate and intellectual independence can prosper. And the charisma generated by the theory stars in the 1980s and 1990s was precisely because of their independence from the general climate, because the reader had to come to them and understand them. They were not interested in ingratiating themselves with their audience, and that was their allure.

As compared to the English department old guard, who wanted New Criticism, Leavisism, and the thought of the New York Intellectuals to stay around unaltered, forever, Wood is a different kind of anti-theorist. He is less interested in attacking or rebutting theory than in reading, in a different way, after theory. Wood might well agree with a similarly theoretically informed post-theorist, Simon Jarvis, that "literary theory cannot but be philosophical."[51] Yet to take Wood as the only voice of his generation or to accept unequivocally his tacit sidelining of theory is to consent in the by-now traditional disregard that literary journalism has had for theory. Theory offered a challenge to conventional ways of thinking that, whatever one's individual view of it, is too strong and seismic simply to be quelled. Journalism can help articulate the negotiations in which a post-theoretical age finds itself. But it cannot simply put theory back in the box.

Aestheticism "After Theory"?

As discussed, approaches such as Wood's profited from braiding a certain sense of postmodernity into non-academic criticism, as did the less consciously "retro" perspectives of cutting-edge literary journals such as *The Believer* and *n +1* (the former informed by the self-referentiality of theory and the latter by its intellectual rigour and breadth). Still, it is good that academic criticism continues in theory's wake, though not bound by the kind of cookie-cutter groupthink that often prevailed in the 1980s. Indeed, we should differentiate decisively between the questioning of theory staged by the return to literary journalism and the questioning of theory practised by academics working in academia and pursuing traditional academic pathways of research, tenure, and promotion. If there were no more academic criticism, even the finest literary journalism, by reflecting so assiduously the mores of its own time, would tend to become a contemporary version of what Caroline Levine, in speaking of the new historicism, called "historical localism." Levine's own work on "strategic formalism" (coming from that traditional incubator of new theoretical ideas, Victorian studies) provides one way in which academic work can build upon past strengths while setting new directions for the twenty-first century. Levine defines her technique as one capable of

> Apprehending forms at work *on multiple scales* that we might grasp the interconnections between cultural objects and vast patterns of domination. Form itself emerges in my own account as the mediating apparatus that allows work across scales, an apparatus that operates on the levels of both method *and* object.[52]

Form, in other words, belongs not only to what is analysed but also to the structures of analysis itself. Analysing a text in multiple narrative languages can create a formal conjunction, much like Wittgenstein's idea of "language-games." But Levine stresses form in a way that eliminates the organicism and hominess many explicators of Wittgenstein attached to his thought and emphasizes the external tectonics of formal arrangement. In Levine's theory, form can encase form as well as content, and form can be contained by another form and still be form. Most important, form is not just "aesthetic"; it can be a mode for communication across disciplines. Yet it does not become an all-inclusive totality—a representation and an ethical stance—as form was for Lukács, for instance.

Other theorists popular in the twenty-first century go even further, arguing, as did Dave Hickey, for a return to beauty, an unabashed exaltation of the aesthetic and its delights.[53] Hickey was working in the context of the visual arts, where politicization and the hegemony of theory arguably took an even harder line at their height than occurred in literature. The changes in the arts that occurred after romanticism affected the visual arts far more than they did literature. Novels and poems and plays not totally unlike those of the eighteenth century were produced in the twenty-first; William Gass had nothing on Laurence Sterne as a practitioner of self-reflexivity. But, in painting and sculpture, what Sylviane Agacinski termed classical painting's stress on "suspending time" and presenting "the essence of things" had yielded to a radically contingent experimental practice that unhinged spatial and temporal happenstance from any overall organization of them in the picture frame.[54] Just as the painters Piet Mondrian or Kasimir Malevich were far more abstract than even Joyce or Woolf ever became, art in the postmodern era was far more defined by politics and by extra-aesthetic practice than literature was. It was rare for visual-arts discourse to discuss overtly aesthetic factors, whereas Paul de Man, reviled as the evil high priest, or the Darth Vader, of theory, spoke favourably of "the linguistics of literariness."

In an art world whose critique of late capitalism tended to become consumerist, tied in with cultural preferences, and imbued with an irony whose enunciation was streamlined and chic even in self-awareness, Hickey's promotion of unashamed beauty was revelatory. It would have been less so in literary academia. In any event, Hickey included praise of postmodern glitz, which would have reminded the literary and critical reader of Fredric Jameson's similarly fervid though highly excoriating response to the same phenomenon. An unabashed return to beauty in literature most likely will never happen. Indeed (and interestingly) one could argue that it never did happen and that deconstructive and historicist revisitings of romanticism were intended to demonstrate just that. If, in literary studies, we are never likely to have aestheticism without critique, cannot critique, though, be a mode of aestheticism? Jonathan Loesberg, in an influential 2005 book, discusses this question. Loesberg, influenced though not totally governed by de Man in his earlier work, suggests that re-aestheticization is one of the rationales for all modes of postmodern criticism, even for the political work of Foucault and of Pierre Bourdieu. Loesberg terms this process "reseeing" and suggests that what might seem disturbing situations of literary texts within contexts of rhetoric and social forces are in fact attempts to look at them, to radically encounter them, in a new way. Loesberg's stance helps explain a basic point of this book. Theory, from the 1960s to the present, often shares many of the political sympathies of the traditional Left. But it is not polemical or a mode of immediate critique. It is a longer reassessment of basic outlooks, a way to enable looking freshly at texts and contexts.

If Loesberg, in a way, sees all theory as a mode of cognitive reader response, as an infinitely unsubtle undoing of the New Critical "affective fallacy," Jacques Khalip's work on Keats and anonymity helps us determine what becomes of the author in the wake of the lapse of theory. We have already seen in Wood's analysis of Galchen's novel how even traditionalist critics can accept self-referentiality if it is linked to an author function, if one feels a determinate author is staging it. What anti-theorists fear is the very effacement of the author that the theorists presumed. But what *happens* when the author is hidden not by critical fiat but by a carefully designed self-formulation? Keats, in his poems and letters, was intuitively certain he would one day be seen as a great poet. He *wanted* to be seen as that by the future. But Keats also felt a need to escape from that identity, to be anything but a poet, to be, even in death, "a sleeping infant's breath—/The gradual sand that through an hour glass runs—/A woodland rivulet."[55] Khalip analyses Keats's anonymity in a way that makes the favourite Romantic poet of the New Critics, who liked his sense of firm control in his shorter poems and his lack of windy rhetoric, self-effacing in a very different way than the "resolved symbolic" could ever envision. For Khalip, anonymity is a way to have a text with not a dead or effaced author but an absconded and self-immured one, an author who offers us a text in which authorial identity is occulted not just out of humility but out of terror at the arrogance and, to use Bakhtin's term, monologic quality that authorial identification can bring.

Khalip undeniably gives us aestheticism. But it is a very fresh aestheticism and a very demanding one, newer and more rigorous than a mere return to aesthetics. Khalip's originality shows that many other iterations of the return to aesthetics have about them, as do the returns of politics and religion, a certain element of (to use Boym's term again) "restorative nostalgia." Also, aestheticism in most early 2000s renditions tended to become either very subjective or very theoretical. If a new aesthetic theory were to flourish, one with a more positive attitude towards beauty than deconstruction could muster, would those opposed to theory like it because it was aesthetic, or would they dislike it because it was theoretical? Levine, Loesberg, and Khalip were, in many ways, canvassing the second look at aestheticism that literary journalists such as Wood tacitly urged—but they were doing so deep inside the academy and in terms inspired and occasioned by theory.[56]

Fact and Feeling: Science and Affect "After Theory"

Perhaps the one tenet agreed upon within what Loesberg characterized as theoretical ways of re-seeing is a reluctance to grant unitary authority to "fact." Indeed, proponents of these theoretical ways followed New Criticism in seeing literature as incapable of being boiled down to verifiable, empirical assertions. Yet empiricism and even the quantitative infiltrated literary studies in a major way during the twenty-first century's initial decade. Not only did historicism become more empirical and verifiable, having far more to do with fact than ideology, but also science itself began to play an important role in theoretical discourses. Despite the potential for intellectual cross-pollination created by the apposition of science and humanities departments in the bureaucracies of major research universities, science, as such, had not played a huge role in the first stage of work after theory. Some criticism around the discursive effects of the AIDS pandemic focused on the representational aspects of the biology of the disease. In addition, the work of German sociologist Niklas Luhmann, whose theory of systems combined the specialized models of classical sociology with the self-reflexiveness of postmodernism, and the work of the Chilean biologists Santiago Varela and Humberto Maturana on "autopoiesis" or self-making had implications with regard to the status of knowledge." This combination of creativity, self-awareness, and self-regulating had great potential, but the death of Luhmann and the unexpectedly early death of Varela, as well as the lack of any dedicated successors, made this potential stillborn. So perhaps did a certain affinity of autopoiesis with the self-regulating rhetoric of the neoliberal, free-market economic ideal.

But the failure of this nascent autopoiesis paradigm might also have occurred because the idea of science in theory was still heavily yoked to ideas of "the social construction of science," which used boiled-down versions of Foucault and Kuhn to argue that science was not and could never be independent of society, that its claims to objectivity and neutrality were bogus and ideologically motivated. This was not *untrue*. But it scanted the ways in which scientific techniques not only could contribute to literary criticism but also could do so precisely because of their autonomy and immersion in their own techniques. Two very different periods of Bruno Latour's work are relevant here. Latour, in his early study (with Steve Woolgar) of the nature of scientific experimentation, saw this process, in its trial-and-error method and its articulation of "the truth" through a series of individual gestures, as something very close to the idea of iterability discussed with respect to Derrida's debate with J.L. Austin.[58] These individual experimental gestures converged only asymptotically and were never synthesized. Later on, in the 2000s, Latour decisively criticized the rhetoric of "the social construction of science" and, indeed, "the social construction of *x*," finally dispelling one of the truisms that, although not originally deconstructive, had often affixed themselves to theoretical methods and made them more trivial and banal.[59] The anti-scientific relativism of theory never really developed beyond Leavis's melodramatic anti-scientism, displayed in his debate with C.P. Snow. This perspective became corny, sophomoric, and often counterproductive, as when AIDS criticism tacitly saw all medical attempts to cure or control the disease as malevolent techniques of discipline in a Foucauldian sense. The 1996 hoax staged by the scientist Alan Sokal in the pages of *Social Text*, where he published a parody of postmodern discourses of scientific relativism just to show how empty the parroting of such mantras was, caused literary people to take a second look at the anti-scientific prejudices their *de facto* much more scientized discourses continued to inherit from the "resolved symbolic."[60] And Latour's scepticism about "social construction" was the ultimate yield of this reassessment. Social construction had always been the base of cultural studies—cultural forms were analysed as being the product of social construction. Yet several questions had always haunted social constructionist ideas. How could a society construct something? And was social construction good or bad?

Was it a conspiracy of institutions, à la Foucault, or a harmonious emergence of historical development, as Marxist theories would suggest? Latour's willingness to jettison the rhetoric of social construction as constraining and authoritarian made possible the beginnings of a new convergence between science and literature, one that recognized how theory, with its systemic and abstract qualities, had actually prepared literary scholars to be more open to scientific methods.

As a result of this move beyond social construction, more flexible paradigms of literary studies in dialogue with science began to come into view. But the potential offered by this coalescence may only fully unfold in the course of the first few decades of the twenty-first century. In May 11, 2008, Jonathan Gottschall wrote the following in *The Boston Globe*:

> Literary studies should become more like the sciences. Literature professors should apply science's research methods, its theories, its statistical tools, and its insistence on hypothesis and proof. Instead of philosophical despair about the possibility of knowledge, they should embrace science's spirit of intellectual optimism. If they do, literary studies can be transformed into a discipline in which real understanding of literature and the human experience builds up along with all of the words.[61]

Gottschall was writing as much *against* theory as *for* science. He speaks of the "swaggering authority" of Roland Barthes, a far cry from the diffident, vulnerable ironist the biographical Barthes was as a person and a writer. And Gottschall's vision of science is a far cry from the postmodern science bequeathed to us by Foucault, Kuhn, Georges Canguilhem, Imre Lakatos, and even Latour, who recognizes that historically manifest discourses of science have been mystified. Gottschall leans more towards the rationalistic and not only non-postmodern but also anti-postmodern science hailed by Norman Levitt and Philip Gross in 1996. This view of science escapes the fallacies of social construction as exposed by Latour but goes too much towards the self-confident rationalism much earlier exposed by Adorno and Horkheimer. Moreover, Gottschall writes as if science were not an academic discipline or a series of such disciplines. Sciences have their disciplinary matrices and are not uncontaminated by the outside world, something testified to by the routine scandals in academia surrounding the funding of research by pharmaceutical companies that stand to benefit from certain results or, more generally, by the tendency of those "possessing" new scientific ideas and methods to promote them formally in a way that resembles corporate public relations as much as it does the unsponsored enthusiasm generated by new ideas in the humanities.

Science, for Gottschall, will take us away from theory—give us a world never ruptured by theory. Science, indeed, will affect a restoration of the old thinking similar to that desired by proponents of the Radical Orthodoxy of John

Milbank and Catherine Pickstock in relation to religion, although Gottschall thinks even less of theory. Gottschall participates in the idea of "science and literature" mainly to refute theory. Indeed, although Darwinian criticism actually has a long history going back at least to the work of Stanley Edgar Hyman of Bennington College in the 1950s, most of the Darwinian theories operative in the wake of deconstruction are designed not only to prove the usefulness of Darwin's thought to literary study but also to invalidate other paradigms. William Flesch, for instance, provides a sophisticated view of evolutionary theory in such a way as to make it useful for reading works of primary literature; there is something of Gérard Genette's delicacy and his serene applicability in Flesch's work.[62] But Flesch has also been known as a trenchant antagonist of deconstruction, from the time of the de Man controversy onward. Just because a thinker such as Darwin is useful scientifically does not mean that he is useful in a literary sense. To reverse the case, one understands why literary people have long found the thought of Ferdinand de Saussure more useful than have practising academic linguists. Still, Darwinian literary criticism is being vigorously published, as basically a "new" intellectual movement, in the twenty-first century. Marx and Freud have been repudiated as quasi-scientific gurus, Darwin far less so. Perhaps this is why Marx and Freud *should* be studied in literature departments.

Gottschall is certainly right that theory has underestimated what science can provide it. But Gottschall's particular iteration of science will not help matters. Too often, he just uses science to rebuke or jettison deconstruction or other recent modes of critique. This oversight is seen when he refers to a survey of examples from world literature in which women are referred to as beautiful six times as frequently as are men. Gottschall triumphantly adduces this disparity as meaning that "human nature" endemically sees women as more beautiful than men. Both queer theory and feminist theory, not to mention deconstruction, would unwind that assumption at a single crack, leaving us, in an interpretive sense, back at square one. The overriding point here, aside from the fact that Gottschall's assumption seems patriarchal and heterosexist, is that it is *not useful* because it cannot stand up to existing modes of critique in the humanities, to theory-based criticism that can be deployed with little effort against it.

This limitation is unfortunate because Gottschall's overall point, that science can bring something to literary criticism, is of eminent merit. As described previously, Moretti-style empirical research into book history and print culture, when in the right interpretive hands, can yield valuable information about a text and can give us more of a complete treatment than would methods that define that work only in terms of its final, canonized product. Furthermore, the scientific and quantitative can often be more effective than relativistic interpretive methods in redressing inequality. Despite the fraudulent use of metrics in former ideologies of scientific racism, a more positive relation between the quantitative and issues of race and ethnicity is possible. Often, people of subordinated racial and ethnic groups have manifested their equality through statistics. Hank Aaron, Bill Russell, and Tiger Woods could prove that they could play sports as well as or better than any of their white counterparts because their performances were measured by quantified statistics.[63] Similarly, Barack Obama and other minority politicians achieved office because, in a democracy, political success is measured by statistically quantifiable votes, and, if nearly 53 per cent of the American people want to vote for a man whose father was from Kenya, there is nothing any mouthing of pieties can do to prevent it. In literature, though, circumstances are different, and statistics are not so easily facilitative.

Aesthetic standards are seen as inherently unquantifiable, beyond measure and number. This is not wrong in that there is an inherent irrationality about literary taste. It slips between lines and between folds; has to do as much with feeling as with formula; is, in Derridean terms, supplementary. But, too often, "aesthetic" factors have been used to explain why European literary traditions are more pleasing or the writers of European descent are more worth reading than those from other backgrounds. These kinds of generalizations are ultimately in the same category as the assertion that it is human nature to consider women as being six times more beautiful than men: worthless. This residue of subjective bias makes quantifications of what people were reading and did read important, as these measurements are beyond the arbitrary judgements of literary gatekeepers, judgements that are so often right, and wrong. But, as the Gottschall example shows, quantitative methods must have some sort of philosophical methodology behind them. The interdisciplinarity of Derridean and Foucault-era theory worked not because disciplines were mechanically meshed together but because their interdisciplinary relation was philosophically articulated—thought through in an abstract, systemic way. Future theory may swerve away from Foucault and Derrida, but, as Wallace Stevens said, "it must be abstract."[64] Theory must have some sort of overall, systemic rationale. So far, connections of literature and science have not provided this abstract rationale.

Oddly, as compared to statistics in the growingly quantitative discipline of political science, quantitative analyses of literature were not associated with a motivated ideological agenda, an affective thrust, or a theory of the field. They seemed to be mutely, neutrally descriptive, to testify, once again, to what was there. This recourse to the value free may have been needed in a discipline too often inflected, a discipline that has too often elevated moralistic ideologies over coming to grips with more complicated circumstances and that has been too little aware of what Barbara Herrnstein Smith called the "contingencies of value."[65] Still, other fields had found a way to combine a recognizable human motive with statistics, but literature, rather strangely, had more trouble effecting this combination. Literary critics seemed to see statistics as ends in themselves, and critical essays ended with statistical conclusions as if, palpable and mute, the numbers could speak for themselves. This approach to statistics no doubt coincided with a certain administrative model that required all disciplines, including literature, to furnish calculable, enumerable outcomes and data. But certain discipline-specific quirks added to the mix. Oddly, in the midst of the new quantitative perspectives, an old aesthetic attitude re-emerged—one claiming that explanation, clarification, and interpretation were not needed. Susan Sontag said that "We need not a hermeneutics" (theory of interpretation) but "an erotics" of art. Sontag was wrong. We need a hermeneutics. And quantitative analysis in political science does give us this; in literary study so far it has not.

The discipline of "biosemiotics" as practised by Thomas Sebeok (1920–2001) gave some promise of supplying this hermeneutics in the way it saw semiotics—the process of signification—amid movements within the natural world. The quantum separation of human and animal sign systems—affirmed by linguists as radical in other ways as Noam Chomsky—was seen by Sebeok as underestimating the way that communication between animals and even plants involves signs and messages. Sebeok saw communication within the natural world as governed by more than behavioural models of stimulus and response. Sebeok started out as a specialist in Uralic languages (Finnish, Estonian, and Mordovian, the languages of the autonomous region in Russia where Bakhtin was exiled in mid-career). Coincidentally or not, his thought found echoes in that of the Tartu school of semiotics in Soviet-era Estonia, whose main spokesman was Jurij Lotman (1922–93). Lotman looked at accumulations of signs as "secondary modelling systems" that not only could operate as metalanguages but also could do so independently of human agency. This concept was not far from Derridean or Barthesian ideas of textuality writing authors or Foucauldian ideas of institutions producing selves. But Lotman provided a more consistent account of how this sort of reverse production happened.

Lotman was also more confident about the ability of his own system to sustain itself interpretively than were Foucault or Derrida. This confidence is shared by other "culturologists" such as Mikhail Epstein, who seek to bring literature and science together to create new metalanguages that will explain the convergence of phenomena in the two spheres without simply disciplining one in the name of another or trivializing the truth claims of one in the name of the other's subversions. Latour, appropriately, has also made a contribution here. His idea of "actor network theory," which studies cultural transactions irrespective of whether or not human actors can be said to be accountable for the origins or motivations of events, has the potential to discuss systems without (as often occurred in deconstruction) effacing agency or making these systems imperative within the real world and unable to be of practical use in explaining political and literary history. Actor network theory has great potential for bringing hermeneutic valence to the quantitative in the way that, as argued previously, has already happened in political science.

Cognitive science and theories of creativity and about the brain in general have seen great growth in precisely the years of theory's waxing in the humanities. At first, the theories of creativity produced by cognitive science seemed simplistic to literary people, as did, for instance, the categorical differentiation between the "left brain" as the locus of rationality and the "right brain" as the locus of creativity. But later models of cognitive science became sufficiently subtle so that they could be adapted to literary studies by such critics as Jane Thrailkill, Suzanne Keen, and Lisa Zunshine.[66] Cognitive criticism was able to find a way to talk about emotions in literature that went beyond just talking about them in pop-psychology terms. As well, it was able to discuss an emotion such as "sadness" without simply acting as if sadness were another synonym for a deconstructive keyword like supplementarity or difference, as had often occurred previously. But Thrailkill, an Americanist, and Zunshine, among other things an eighteenth-century specialist, wrote about the emotions they analysed "in themselves"; they did not just use them as costumes for Derridean textuality or to nullify the attested linguistic complexity of literary works. Keen's work on empathy restated the traditional humanistic virtues of the novel—its ability to make people appreciate the feelings of others, to live richer emotional lives—but embedded these virtues in scientific, rational articulations of psychological and cognitive processes.[67]

Cognitive criticism made what Northrop Frye called for at the end of *The Anatomy of Criticism* finally a possibility. Frye envisioned a convergence of literary and scientific methods in a kind of higher, subjective totality that would somehow also have predictive validity: "The difference between mathematics and literature ... will be greatly reduced when criticism achieves its proper form of the theory of the use of words."[68] After Frye wrote these words, literary critics did become more interested in language—but their interest in post-Saussurean linguistics took criticism even further away from the objective and quantitative than it had been before, and language became viewed as more and not less slippery. That deconstruction found Austin's theories of linguistic performance so much more interesting than Chomsky's, even as ideas to oppose, is another index of deconstruction's movement away from scientific, quantitative approaches in the 1970s and 1980s. But cognitive theory seemed to bring literature's sense of language more in touch with a positivistic model.

Another body of thought that did this was the work of Alain Badiou. Badiou's emergence as a belated theory star has already been discussed. Another salient aspect of his work, however, is that he took mathematics seriously and required of his comprehending reader a full understanding of set theory and of transfinite numbers, something which limited the number of literary people who actually understood him. (Despite all the lore to the contrary, understanding Derrida or Foucault was much easier.) Although Badiou was a non-believer, he wrote extensively on St. Paul, and his interest in religious horizons and in states of exception complements rather than nullifies or balances his mathematical orientation. Mathematics has been the area of human endeavour traditionally most inaccessible to the humanities; the very term "humanities" presumes that *homo sapiens*, as social animals, do not define themselves through abstract relations that do not depend on human agents in order to have meaning. Earlier French thinkers, such as Jacques Lacan, had used mathematical metaphors, such as the imaginary nature of the square root of -1 being representative of the arbitrary quality of human subjectivity. But Badiou actually seemed to be using mathematics as something valuable in itself rather than as a way to make an outrageous point, Badiou may well prove to be a theorist hard to emulate, but the example of his approach (along with that of Haraway's cyborgian feminism) should encourage others to do the difficult but necessary work of bringing literary study into serious dialogue with natural and quantitative science, a dialogue it has long had with the social sciences. Perhaps, to go back to early Italian naturalist Ulisse Aldrovandi, the content of knowledge matters less than its arrangement. Perhaps, as Levine's metaformal theory suggests, a certain reshuffling of the adjacencies between forms and schemes or simply a recognition of the ways they already, unnoticed, subtly intertwine will allow for leavening of this parched and sere relation. The Aldrovandian model of the botanic garden, in which aesthetic delight, scientific rigour, and an inevitably arbitrary mode of arrangement coincide with and complement each other may be what literary theory, going forward, will find most congenial as a possible shape.

The Need to Theorize

It is important to keep theorizing, in whatever way possible. This is so even if the theories created in the process become very different from the particular kinds of theory that were chic in the 1980s and 1990s. For one thing, only theorizing will enable the intellectual achievements of the former mode of theory to be fully remembered, to have theory fully taken into account and subject to what Toni Morrison has termed "rememory." From Jean Baudrillard's early (and half playful) injunction to "forget Foucault," theory, like Foucault's Quixote himself, has been told that it is yesterday's news. Nothing is more insulting than to say a colleague that she or he is operating on the basis of old theoretical modes. In early 2000s, one heard names like Bakhtin, Derrida, and Foucault, names big in the 1980s, being casually dismissed as no longer chic by scholars who clearly had not read much of their work. Derrida and Foucault were no longer high in the early twenty-first century, but their impact was still so strong, as the poet Robert Frost said in another context, "probably it never lost." Even if theory was a waste, even it, which is unlikely, a book about it is what Shakespeare would call a "chronicle of wasted time" or simply fictional equivalent of what Natalka Freeland has called "trash fiction dominated the intellectual history of the English-speaking world for until no movement accomplishing that, no matter how meticulous, not to count. Theory, however, was not wasted time. It was not only showed new ways to read literature, it also brought to the study of greater rigour than it had ever received within an academic setting.

Yet this sort of eulogy implies that the age of theory has come to an end. And so it has. It is not this book's business to recommend replacements; some of the more plausible it has canvassed already, discussing both their virtues and limitations. But there is one critic whose way of relating to theory seems particularly exemplary. In *Ugly Feelings* (2005), Sianne Ngai analyses a wide range of texts—from traditional and new canonical works, such as the Harlem Renaissance writer Nella Larsen's fiction, to movies and animated television shows—to reveal how they display various "ugly feelings," including, among others, envy, paranoia, animatedness (a wonderful contribution to media studies in the tradition of Philip Auslander and Friedrich Kittler), and irritation. Ngai, also a creative writer, is dedicated to academia but not defined by it: she is able to use its tools without being its creature. In this, she resembles some New Critical figures such as William Empson.

Ngai's emphasis on feeling is important. Ngai does not just talk about *différance* or supplementarity under the guise of more emotional language, as second-generation deconstructionists tended to do. Nor does she reduce them to scientific or positive formulae, although the influence of the cognitive theorist Silvan Tomkins does lend an invigorating cross-disciplinary anchorage to her work.[69] Ngai talks about ugly feelings not only in life or literature but also in literary criticism. In her afterword on "disgust," Ngai contrasts the repulsion occasioned by disgust with the attraction occasioned by desire. (Like Theresa Hak Kyung Cha, who divides her book *Dictée* into nine parts arranged around the Greek muses, Ngai sets up a structure of the seven liberal arts, inverted, which she then subverts by adding an eighth.) But Ngai contrasts desire and disgust not just to draw a distinction between the attractive and the repulsive but to point out the singularity of disgust—the way one singles oneself out by being disgusted or singles something out for disgust—and to contrast this singularity with the pluralism occasioned by desire. Ngai is speaking of "desire" in the specific theoretical sense associated, for instance, with Kristeva, a desire not just physical or sexual but representing a yearning for the unfulfilled that knows and cherishes its (to borrow Bakhtin's term) "unfinalizability." Ngai, though, is perturbed by a too-easy pluralism associated with desire. Building on the earlier work on pluralism of Ellen Rooney, Ngai worries about "an ethic of indiscriminate tolerance" associated with what theory "prefers."[70]

Despite its generally positive stance towards theory, this book throughout has been concerned with certain easy pluralities that different schools of theory hail as beneficial. For deconstruction it is *différance*; for feminism, desire; for race and ethnicity studies, *mestizaje*; for post-colonial studies, hybridity; for gender studies, a particular definition of the queer. All of these qualities are, in one way or another, virtues. Indeed, elucidation of all of these qualities was why these various schools of theory were so appealing. Literary study lacked a sense of all these qualities before theory came along. But it is all too easy for these qualities to become prescriptive slogans that merely describe a certain aspect of the status quo and no longer pertain to actual states of feeling or being or thinking. The problem was not so much, as detractors of theory claimed, that theoretical terminology was too tight and restrictive but rather that it was too loose and amorphous. Theory became, in what it promoted, a virtual feel-good human-potential movement, even as it subjected previous terminologies to withering critique. Ngai could have chosen to rebuke theoretical absolutes in the name of human feelings. Instead, she notes that theory is, despite claims of its anti-aestheticism, full of beautiful feelings, human or not, and that the ugly ones have been left at the door. Ngai does not mean to "endorse" disgust in a mockingly provocative way. But she does mean to deflate what are sometimes overly blissful accounts of what theory has brought us to. And disgust, of course, can also deflate the would-be panaceas for the disease theory is supposed to represent. We are told that literary journalism can save us by making criticism less opaque, that turning to religion or politics will rescue us from parochialism and restore a larger sense of collective purpose. Being inoculated with a therapeutic dose of disgust may well be a needed preventive move to avoid being swept away by the siren song of theory complacency or by its strangely yoked twin, theory contempt.

Most of the ugly feelings Ngai deals with are terms from ordinary language. But there is one feeling for which she coins a neologism, much as so many theorists did before her. This word is "stuplimity." Ngai defines "stuplimity" as "a synthesis of boredom and shock," a plethora of the banal that is "opposed to the transcendent feeling of the sublime."[71] Stuplimity is not too much of a good or even a bad thing; it is too much of a mediocre thing. It is not terrible but mega-tiresome. Though "stuplimity" is a new word, what Ngai describes is a state long familiar to literary scholars. What else was Pope referring to in Book 4 of *The Dunciad*?

> Nor *public* Flame, nor *private*, dares to shine;
> Nor *human* Spark is left, nor Glimpse *divine!*
> Lo! thy dread Empire, CHAOS! is restor'd;
> Light dies before thy uncreating word:

But Ngai embeds stuplimity in a certain genealogy. We have seen how, for the deconstructionists of the 1970s, the sublime represented an opening up in the curtailed cordoned-off sphere of "the resolved symbolic." In negating, reversing, and, as it were, exposing sublimity—in stripping off its veneer of novelty and grandeur and elevation—stuplimity applies a further turn of the screw. In combining "excitation and fatigue," stuplimity could also describe how the student of literary criticism might feel after sampling so many of the doctrines and contentions associated with theory.[72] Stuplimity may help counteract the hype, the arrogance, and the vitriol projected onto theory by its proponents and detractors alike. Too much difference brings on sameness. Don Quixote may have felt the force of this observation on his peregrinations. On the level plain of being, one's very distinction can soon cease being a novelty. Yet Quixote remained motivated by possibility. The winning bravado, shorn of cheery sloganeering, that Ngai exhibits shows that, after theory, realms of possibility are still open.

NOTES

1   Herman Rapaport, *The Theory Mess* (New York: Columbia University Press, 2001). For a more systematic genealogy of the rise, fall, and fate of theory, see Claire Colebrook, *New Literary Histories. New Historicism and Contemporary Criticism* (Manchester: Manchester University Press, 1997), and for a more nuanced sense of the stasis afflicting theory in the early twenty-first century, see Amanda Anderson, *The Way We Argue Now: A Study in the Cultures of Theory* (Princeton: Princeton University Press, 2006).

2   Michael Warner, "Publics and Counterpublics," *Public Culture* 14.1 (2002): 49–90.

3   Terry Eagleton, *After Theory* (New York: Basic Books, 2003); Valentine Cunningham, *Reading After Theory* (London: Blackwell, 2002).

4   Cunningham, *Reading*, 60.

5   Steven Knapp and Walter Benn Michaels, "Against Theory," *Against Theory: Literary Studies and the New Pragmatism*, ed. W.J.T. Mitchell (Chicago: University of Chicago Press, 1985) 1–30.

6   Stephen Greenblatt, *Shakespearean Negotiations: The Circulation of Social Energy in Renaissance England* (Berkeley: University of California Press, 1988).

7   Kenneth Burke, *A Grammar of Motives* (Berkeley: University of California Press, 1969).

8   Svetlana Alpers, *Rembrandt's Enterprise: The Studio and the Market* (Chicago: University of Chicago Press, 1988).

9   James J. Paxson, "Historicizing Paul de Man's master Trope Prosopopeia. Belgium's Trauma of 1940, the Nazi *Volkskörper*, and Versions of the Allegorical Body Politic" *Historicizing Theory*, ed. Peter C. Herman (Albany: SUNY Press, 2004) 69–97.

10 Alan Liu's essays were eventually collected in *Local Transcendence: Essays on Postmodern Historicism and the Database* (Chicago: University of Chicago Press, 2000).

11 Jerome J. McGann, *The Romantic Ideology: A Critical Investigation* (Chicago: University of Chicago Press, 1983).

12 Carolyn Porter, "Are We Being Historical Yet?" *South Atlantic Quarterly* 87 (1988): 743–86.

13 Hayden White, *Metahistory: The Historical Imagination in Nineteenth-Century Europe* (1973; Baltimore: Johns Hopkins University Press, 1975).

14 Caroline Levine, "Historicism at its Limits: An Antislavery Sonnet, *Bleak House*, and *The Wire*," Columbia University, New York, 8 November 2007.

15 George Orwell, "Why I Write," *An Age Like This: 1920–1940*, ed. Ian Angus and Sonia Orwell (Boston: David R. Godine, 2000) 4.

16 D.F. McKenzie, *Making Meaning: "Printers of the Mind" and Other Essays*, ed. Peter D. McDonald and Michael F. Suarez (Amherst: University of Massachusetts Press, 2002); Jerome J. McGann, *The Textual Condition* (Princeton: Princeton University Press, 1991). Also see David Greetham, *The Margins of the Text* (Ann Arbor: University of Michigan Press, 1997).

17 Stephen Greenblatt, *Hamlet in Purgatory* (Princeton: Princeton University Press, 2002). Interestingly, Harold Bloom, often seen as far more conservative than Greenblatt, was more unwilling to acknowledge Shakespeare's Catholicism.

18 White, *Metahistory*.

19 Franco Moretti, *Atlas of the European Novel, 1800–1900* (London: Verso, 1999).

20 Colin McEvedy and David Woodroffe, *The New Penguin Atlas of Medieval History* (Harmondsworth: Penguin, 1992).

21 Franco Moretti, *Graphs, Maps, Trees: Abstract Models for a Literary History* (London: Verso, 2005).

22 Thomas Pfau, "The Philosophy of Shipwreck: Gnosticism, Skepticism, and Coleridge's Catastrophic Modernity," *MLN* 121.8 (2007): 962.

23 Giorgio Agamben, *The End of the Poem*, trans. Daniel Heller-Roazen (Palo Alto: Stanford University Press, 1999).

24 David Shumway, "The Star System in Literary Studies," *PMLA* 112.1 (1997): 85–100.

25 Leland de la Durantaye, *Giorgio Agamben: A Critical Introduction* (Palo Alto: Stanford University Press, 2009).

26 Giorgio Agamben, *Homo Sacer: Sovereign Power and Bare Life*, trans. Daniel Heller-Roazen (Stanford, CA: Stanford University Press, 1995) 82.

27 Carl Schmitt, *The Leviathan in the State Theory of Thomas Hobbes: Meaning and Failure of a Political Symbol*, trans. George Schwab (Westport: Greenwood, 1996).

28 Richard Rorty, *Philosophy and the Mirror of Nature* (Princeton: Princeton University Press. 1979).

29 Bruno Latour, "Why Has Critique Run Out of Steam? From Matters of Fact to Matters of Concern," *Critical Inquiry* 30.2 (2004): 225–48.

30 Alain Badiou, *Being and Event*, trans. Oliver Feltham (New York: Continuum, 2006); Slavoj Žižek, *The Fragile Absolute, or Why is the Christian Legacy Worth Fighting For?* (London: Verso, 2001).

31 Tim Dean, "The Psychoanalysis of AIDS," *October* 63 (1993): 83–116.

32 Charles Taylor, *A Secular Age* (Cambridge, MA: Harvard University Press, 2007).

33 William Empson, *Milton's God* (1961; Cambridge: Cambridge University Press, 1981).

34 John D. Caputo, *Radical Hermeneutics: Repetition, Deconstruction, and the Hermeneutic Project* (Bloomington: Indiana University Press, 1987); George Douglas Atkins, *Reading Deconstruction / Deconstructive Reading* (Louisville: University Press of Kentucky, 1983); Kevin Hart, *The Trespass of the Sign: Deconstruction, Theology, and Philosophy*, rev. ed. (Cambridge: Cambridge University Press, 2000).

35 Mark Taylor, *Erring: A Postmodern A/Theology* (Chicago: University of Chicago Press, 1987).

36 Robert Alter, *The Art of Biblical Narrative* (New York: Basic Books, 1981); Frank Kermode *The Genesis of Secrecy: On the Interpretation of Narrative* (Cambridge, MA: Harvard University Press, 1979).

37 Hans Blumenberg, *The Legitimacy of the Modern Age*, trans. Robert M. Wallace (Cambridge, MA: MIT Press, 1983).

38 René Girard, *Deceit, Desire, and the Novel: Self and Other in Literary Studies* (Baltimore: Johns Hopkins University Press, 1965).

39 John Milbank and Simon Oliver, eds., *The Radical Orthodoxy Reader* (London: Routledge, 2009). For the concept of "political theology," see Hent de Vries and Lawrence E. Sullivan, eds., *Political Theologies: Public Religions in a Post-Secular World* (New York: Fordham University Press, 2006), and, for a particularly intricate application of "political theology" to literary studies, see Debora Kuller Shuger, *Political Theologies in Shakespeare's England: The Sacred and the State in* Measure for Measure (New York: Palgrave Macmillan, 2001).

40 Franz Kafka, "The Coming of the Messiah," *The Basic Kafka*, ed. Erich Heller (New York: Basic Books, 1975) 262.

41 Gauri Viswanathan, *Outside the Fold: Conversion, Modernity, and Belief* (Princeton: Princeton University Press, 1998).

42 Perhaps the New Critics were influenced by the example of Dr. Samuel Johnson (1709–84) in this regard.

43 See especially Ellen O'Gorman, "Alternate Empires: Tacitus's Virtual History of the Pisonian Principate," *Arethusa* 39.2 (2006): 281–301.

44 Gerald Graff, *Professing Literature: An Institutional History* (Chicago: University of Chicago Press, 1987); Stanley Eugene Fish, *Professional Correctness: Literary Studies and Political Change* (Oxford: Clarendon, 1995).

45 James Wood, "She's Not Herself: A First Novel about Marriage and Madness," *The New Yorker* 23 June 2008.

46 Anthony Grafton, *The Footnote: A Curious History* (Cambridge, MA: Harvard University Press, 1997). As this very note shows, Grafton's argument has the property of making footnotes self-referential, "supplementary" in Derridean terms.

47 E.R. Curtius, *European Literature and the Latin Middle Ages,* trans. Willard R. Trask (Princeton: Princeton University Press, 1990).

48 Benjamin Hedin, "On Tragic Thinking and Style: An Interview With James Wood," *Salmagundi* 157 (Winter 2008): 73.

49 William Deresiewicz, "How Wood Works: The Riches and Limits of James Wood," *The Nation* 19 November 2008.

50 Leo Bersani, "Reflections on a Paradigm," *New York Times Book Review* 11 June 1967, 1 November 2008.<http://www.nytimes.com/books/00/06/25/specials/kermode-ending1.html>.

51 Simon Jarvis, "Seconds Out," *TLS* 13 January 2006: 23.

52 Caroline Levine, "Scaled Up, Writ Small: A Response to Carolyn Dever and Herbert F. Tucker," *Victorian Studies* 49.1 (2006): 100–05.

53 Dave Hickey, *The Invisible Dragon: Four Essays on Beauty* (Los Angeles: Art Issues Press, 1993).

54 Sylviane Agacinski, *Time Passing: Modernity and Nostalgia*, trans. Jody Gladding (New York: Columbia University Press, 2003) 94.

55 John Keats, "After dark vapours have oppressed our plains," *Complete Poems*, ed. Jack Stillinger (Cambridge, MA: Harvard University Press, 1982) 54.

56 One might also, in this respect, mention the work of Sara Guyer on "buccality," which sought to posit the mouth as an alternative allegorical node for the "face" championed by Emmanuel Lévinas and associated with many of the aesthetic-cum-ethical approaches to literature that bordered on the recuperative. For Guyer, the anonymity and appetitiveness of the mouth guard it against any overly categorical reconstructive humanism, leaving a radical, decentred openness that is yet unconstrained by dogma. See Guyer, "Buccality," *Derrida, Deleuze, Psychoanalysis*, ed. Gabriele M. Schwab (New York: Columbia University Press, 2007) 77–104.

57 N. Luhmann, "The Autopoiesis of Social Systems," *Sociocybernetic Paradoxes*, ed. Felix Geyer and Johannes van der Zouwen (London: Sage, 1986) 172–92; Humberto Maturana and Francisco Varela, *Autopoiesis and Cognition: The Realization of the Living* (Dordrecht: Reidel, 1980).

58 Bruno Latour and Steve Woolgar, *Laboratory Life: The Construction of Scientific Facts* (Princeton: Princeton University Press, 1986).

59 Bruno Latour, "Why Has Critique Run out of Steam? From Matters of Fact to Matters of Concern," *Critical Inquiry* 30.2 (2004): 225–48.

60 Alan D. Sokal and Jean Bricmont, *Fashionable Nonsense: Postmodern Intellectuals' Abuse of Science* (New York: Picador, 1998) gives an overview of Sokal's perspective on the incident.

61 Jonathan Gottschall, "Measure for Measure," *Boston Globe* 11 May 2008, 1 January 2009 <http://www.boston.com/bostonglobe/ideas/articles/2008/05/11/measure_for_measure/>.

62 William Flesch, *Comeuppance: Costly Signaling, Altruistic Punishment, and Other Biological Components of Fiction* (Cambridge, MA: Harvard University Press, 2007).

63 One saw, in the 2000s, a turn against concepts with irrationalist or organicist components such as "lore" and "culture" in literary studies. This change was evident in Latour's association of irrationality with neoconservative revisionism; in the 2005 special issue of the journal *Symploke*, which questioned the use of the rubric of "collegiality" in academic hiring and retention, pointing out that this term can have many vague definitions and can often be used to exclude colleagues not liked for extra-academic reasons by a majority in the department; and in Clifford Siskin's call in the 2008 issue of *Profession* and in a talk given at the 2008 MLA convention in San Francisco for academics to "stop doing" cultural studies, on the premise that cultural studies was a tired-out framework as well as superseded by newer, more quantitative and calculable modes of analysis

64 Wallace Stevens, *Collected Poems of Wallace Stevens*, ed. Holly Stevens (New York: Vintage, 1990) 378.

65 Barbara Herrnstein Smith, *Contingencies of Value: Alternative Perspectives for Critical Theory* (Cambridge, MA: Harvard University Press, 1988). Herrnstein Smith attempted to sketch an ethical and procedural framework that specified a multiplicity of values, a renunciation of an absolute value that did not mean sophomoric relativism. In practical terms, many post-deconstructive treatments of science and morality lapsed into just this sort of relativism, although hers did not.

66 Jane F. Thrailkill, *Affecting Fictions: Mind, Body, and Emotion in American Literary Realism* (Cambridge, MA: Harvard University Press, 2007); Lisa Zunshine, *Strange Concepts and the Stories They Make Possible: Cognition, Culture, Narrative* (Baltimore: Johns Hopkins University Press, 2008). These critics saw investigations of states of mind and feeling in literature as unequivocally positive; Patricia Ticineto Clough, however, has raised questions about a certain proximity of the disembodiment required by this emphasis on affect and mode of cognition to the productive imperatives of

neoliberalism. See Patricia Ticineto Clough and Jean O'Malley Halley, *The Affective Turn: Theorizing the Social* (Durham: Duke University Press, 2007). Lauren Berlant has commented that "affect is the new trauma," i.e., that it has become an all-purpose critical buzzword the way trauma studies, as made prominent by the work of Cathy Caruth, was in the late 1990s. See Berlant, "Affect is the New Trauma," *the minnesota review* 71–72 (Winter-Spring 2009), 1 January 2009 <http://www.theminnesotareview.org/journal/ns7172/credos_berlant.shtml>.

67 Suzanne Keen, *Empathy and the Novel* (New York: Oxford University Press, 2007).

68 Northrop Frye, *Anatomy of Criticism* (Princeton: Princeton University Press, 1994) 364.

69 Eve Kososky Sedgwick, though, was the first to bring Tomkins's work to the awareness of the literary-theoretical community by editing a selection of his works in the mid-1990s.

70 Sianne Ngai, *Ugly Feelings* (Cambridge, MA: Harvard University Press, 2005) 345.

71 Ngai, *Ugly Feelings*, 11.

72 Ngai, *Ugly Feelings*, 36.

324 THEORY AFTER THEORY